AN ESSAY CONCERNING
HUMAN UNDERSTANDING

JOHN LOCKE

AN ESSAY
CONCERNING
HUMAN
UNDERSTANDING

Abridged and Edited
with an introduction by
A. D. Woozley
Professor of Moral Philosophy,
St Andrews University

A MERIDIAN BOOK

MERIDIAN
Published by the Penguin Group
Penguin Books USA Inc., 375 Hudson Street,
New York, New York 10014, U.S.A.
Penguin Books Ltd, 27 Wrights Lane,
London W8 5TZ, England
Penguin Books Australia Ltd, Ringwood,
Victoria, Australia
Penguin Books Canada Ltd, 10 Alcorn Avenue,
Toronto, Ontario, Canada, M4V 3B2
Penguin Books (N.Z.) Ltd, 182–190 Wairau Road,
Auckland 10, New Zealand

Penguin Books Ltd, Registered Offices:
Harmondsworth, Middlesex, England

Published by Meridian, an imprint of New American Library, a
division of Penguin Books USA Inc. Reprinted by arrangement with
Wm. Collins Sons and Co. Ltd.

First Printing/World Publishing Company, October, 1964
First Meridian Printing/New American Library, October, 1974
20 19 18 17 16 15 14 13 12 11

 REGISTERED TRADEMARK—MARCA REGISTRADA

Printed in the United States of America

CONTENTS

INTRODUCTION BY A. D. WOOZLEY   *page* 9

√ THE EPISTLE TO THE READER   55

BOOK ONE: OF INNATE NOTIONS

  I   Introduction   63
  II No innate principles in the mind   67
  III No innate practical principles   78
  IV Other considerations concerning innate princi-
       ples, both speculative and practical   83

BOOK TWO: OF IDEAS

  I   Of ideas in general, and their original   89
  II Of simple ideas   99
  III Of ideas of one sense   101
  IV Of solidity   103
  V   Of simple ideas of divers senses   106
  VI Of simple ideas of reflection   107
  VII Of simple ideas of both sensation and reflection 108
  VIII Some further considerations concerning our
       simple ideas   110
  IX Of perception   119
  X   Of retention   123
  XI Of discerning, and other operations of the mind 127
  XII Of complex ideas   132
  XIII Of simple modes: and first, of the simple
       modes of space   135
  XIV Of duration and its simple modes   144
  [xv Of duration and expansion, considered together]
  XVI Of number   153

CONTENTS

[XVII   Of infinity]
[XVIII Of other simple modes]
  XIX   Of the modes of thinking   page 156
   XX   Of modes of pleasure and pain   159
  XXI   Of power   162
 XXII   Of mixed modes   179
XXIII   Of our complex ideas of substances   185
 XXIV   Of collective ideas of substances   198
  XXV   Of relation   200
 XXVI   Of cause and effect, and other relations   203
XXVII   Of identity and diversity   206
XXVIII Of other relations   221
 XXIX   Of clear and obscure, distinct and confused
        ideas   227
  XXX   Of real and fantastical ideas   232
 XXXI   Of adequate and inadequate ideas   235
XXXII   Of true and false ideas   242
XXXIII Of the association of ideas   250

BOOK THREE: OF WORDS

    I   Of words or language in general   256
   II   Of the signification of words   259
  III   Of general terms   263
   IV   Of the names of simple ideas   273
    V   Of the names of mixed modes and relations   277
   VI   Of the names of substances   283
 [VII   Of particles]
 VIII   Of abstract and concrete terms   297
   IX   Of the imperfection of words   299
    X   Of the abuse of words   306
   XI   Of the remedies of the foregoing imperfections
        and abuses   312

BOOK FOUR: OF KNOWLEDGE AND OPINION

    I   Of knowledge in general   320
   II   Of the degrees of our knowledge   325

CONTENTS

III Of the extent of human knowledge   *page* 331
IV Of the reality of knowledge   347
V Of truth in general   354
VI Of universal propositions, their truth and certainty   358
VII Of maxims   365
VIII Of trifling propositions   373
IX Of our knowledge of existence   377
X Of our knowledge of the existence of a God   379
XI Of our knowledge of the existence of other things   387
XII Of the improvement of our knowledge   395
[XIII Some further considerations concerning our knowledge]
XIV Of judgment   402
XV Of probability   403
XVI Of the degrees of assent   407
XVII Of reason   415
XVIII Of faith and reason, and their distinct provinces   424
XIX Of enthusiasm   428
XX Of wrong assent, or error   434
XXI Of the division of the sciences   442

APPENDIX: The controversy with Stillingfleet   447

BIBLIOGRAPHY   463

CHRONOLOGICAL TABLE   465

INDEX   467

INTRODUCTION

by A. D. Woozley

I. LIFE AND INFLUENCES

The *Essay Concerning Human Understanding*, John Locke's most important book, first appeared at the end of 1689 (the date on the title page is 1690), at the same time as his two other best known works, *A Letter Concerning Toleration* and *Two Treatises of Government;* both of the latter, for political reasons, were published anonymously and were never publicly acknowledged by Locke, although the secret of their authorship was not long kept. He was then fifty seven years old, having been born at Wrington in Somerset on 29th August, 1632. Although now remembered almost entirely as a philosopher, he led a life of diverse activity, political and diplomatic, and pursued a wide range of intellectual interests, in natural science, medicine, economics, and theology. While he spent many of his early years in Oxford, where he became a Student and Senior Censor of Christ Church, he never settled to the cloistered life of a university philosopher, partly because of the attraction of public affairs and of the world of learning in London and on the continent, partly because of his contempt for the scholastic aridity of philosophy as it was then practised in Oxford. It is significant that, although the *Essay* was being used as a text book in Trinity College, Dublin within two years of its publication, as late as 1704 (the year of Locke's death) an attempt was made by a number of Heads of Houses in Oxford to prohibit college tutors from allowing their pupils to read it.

The details of Locke's busy and active life,[1] while relevant to his other principal writings, are of very little importance to

[1] For his biography, see M. Cranston: *John Locke* (Longmans, 1957), and R. I. Aaron: *John Locke* (Oxford, 2nd ed. 1955).

the *Essay*, except as a partial explanation of the many years over which its composition was spread, of the great length to which it finally extended, and of the many inconsistencies and even more numerous repetitions which it contained. Even of these a more important cause was the fact that Locke was feeling his way in what was a new approach to philosophy, and that consequently he was consistently emending and amplifying his first thoughts. He wrote three early drafts of the *Essay*, two in 1671, one in 1685, and he made many revisions for subsequent editions after its first publication. He acknowledged himself that the final product was far too long and repetitious, but excused himself from the task of reduction on the ground that he was " too lazy or too busy to make it shorter " (*Epistle to the Reader* p. 57). In preparing the second edition (1694) he did seriously consider " whether it would not be better now to pare off a great part of that which cannot but appear superfluous to an intelligent and attentive reader", but, whether unfortunately or not, was dissuaded by his friend William Molyneux; and it has been left for later editors to do it for him.

Of those who influenced Locke the first and most obvious is Descartes, whose *Discourse on Method* was published in 1637, five years after Locke's birth, followed by the *Meditations* in 1641 and the *Principles* in 1644; it is likely too that Locke was familiar with the *Regulae* which, although not published until eleven years after the *Essay*, had for long been circulating in Holland in manuscript copies. We have Locke's own acknowledgement to Descartes that he owed to him " the great obligation of my first deliverance from the unintelligible way of talking of the philosophy in use in the schools in his time ".[2] And this is borne out by ample internal evidence in the *Essay* itself, e.g., the terminology of clear and distinct ideas and perception, the account of intuitive and of demonstrative knowledge (IV ii),[3] and of the fourfold function of reason in demonstration (IV xvii 3). But although Locke claimed that

[2] *1st Letter to Stillingfleet* (Locke, *Works*, 4th ed., 1 381)
[3] All references to the *Essay* are given by the number of the Book, Chapter and, where necessary, Section.

Descartes had liberated him from scholastiċism, and although he took many opportunities of attacking the academic exercises of Oxford philosophy, e.g., his criticisms of disputation (IV vii) and his onslaught on syllogistic argument (IV xvii), it is not true of Locke, any more than it is of Descartes himself, that he entirely escaped. While he criticised the limitations of definition by *genus* and *differentia* (III iii 10), he continued with the language of substances, modes, essences and accidents, and like Descartes he accepted the necessity of the causal principle as something that could not be doubted (cf. IV x 3); it was left for Hume to question that.

But, while Locke owed much to Descartes, he was far from being a Cartesian. Book I of the *Essay* is entirely devoted to the demolition of the doctrine of innate ideas. He rejected Descartes' two cardinal principles, that thought is the essence of mind (II i), and that extension is the essence of body (II xiii). And, most important of all, he disagreed with Descartes's view that mathematics provides the ideal for all of knowledge, for he appreciated the distinction between constructing an *a priori* deductive system and the gradual attainment of empirical knowledge, as in the natural sciences, by the inductive procedures of observation and experiment; that is the general theme of Book IV. One exception, or the possibility of one exception, he was prepared to allow, following from his theory of modes : " I am bold to think that morality is capable of demonstration, as well as mathematics " (III xi 16; cf. IV iii 18-19). But, although he was pressed to write a book on ethics, and promised to think further about his ideas, he never undertook the task, possibly because he was not convinced of the soundness of his position. In a letter to Molyneux he wrote " I thought I saw that morality might be demonstratively made out; yet whether I am able to make it out is another question ".[4]

But, while his debt to Descartes was thus mainly by disagreement, he was far more positively influenced by Gassendi, the author of the fifth set of objections to Descartes's *Meditations*, and by Robert Boyle, the chemist, who was directly involved in the inception of the *Essay*. While Locke never met

4 Cranston, p. 360.

Gassendi (died 1655), nor acknowledged his influence, he was well acquainted with his works, including his objections to Descartes; and the similarity of Gassendi's views to much in the *Essay* is too great to be a coincidence, so much so that Leibniz labelled Locke as a Gassendist. That the human mind starts as a *tabula rasa* is the same as Locke's statement that it starts as " white paper void of all characters " (II i 2) or as an " empty cabinet " (I ii 15); the Epicurean doctrine that there is nothing in the mind which was not previously in the senses corresponds to one of Locke's " twin sources " of ideas; that all other ideas are formed by construction and elaboration of these is Locke's doctrine of composition and abstraction. And many other of Locke's views are to be found very similarly expressed in Gassendi : the close interaction of body and mind argued from mental defects following on some kinds of bodily injury or disease (II x 5); the suggestion that material substances might be capable of thought (IV iii 6); that non-human animals have some powers of memory (II x 10) and of reasoning (II xi 11); the impossibility of discovering the real essences of material objects (III vi 9); and the refutation of Descartes's methodological supposition that all so-called waking experiences might be a dream (IV ii 14).

The influence of Boyle was even more personal and direct. The two men were close friends, and Locke was not only intimately acquainted with Boyle's scientific work, but undertook some of it for him. They were both members of a group whose interests in and discussions of the new experimental science led to the formation of the Royal Society, of which Boyle was one of the foundation members, Locke being elected a few years later. It was at such a discussion held in London in 1670-1 that the idea of the *Essay* was born (*Epistle to the Reader* p. 56), although we have no evidence that Boyle was present at that particular meeting. Locke's acquaintance with Boyle stimulated not only his interest in natural science, but also his conviction that the empirical method of careful and accurate observation must be applied to philosophy, in contrast to the rationalist procedure of the Cartesians. Just because the two men were so well acquainted, we cannot conclude that the influence was all one way. It is more likely to have been reciprocal, and it is enough, therefore, to recognise their similarities. One of the principal doctrines of the *Essay*, the distinction between primary and secondary qualities (II viii), had been expressed, even in the same terminology, in Boyle's *The Origin of Forms and Qualities* (1666). Boyle's corpuscular physics runs throughout the *Essay*, and Locke's emphasis on the need to recognize the limitations imposed on the possible extent of human knowledge had been anticipated by him. In a minor matter, Locke's repeated and unvaried use of gold as his example, whenever writing in the *Essay* of the defining properties of a material object, may well have been connected with his touching confidence in Boyle's claim to have discovered a formula for the alchemical production of gold, a confidence of which Newton seems finally to have disabused him a few years after the *Essay* appeared.

The publication of the *Essay* provoked much criticism, violent and sometimes abusive, directed against the allegedly sceptical and anti-religious implications of its doctrines. Most of it Locke, not unreasonably, ignored, for the authors lacked either the capacity or the industry to grasp his purpose or arguments. The only man with whom he engaged in public controversy was Edward Stillingfleet, Bishop of Worcester, whom he treated sufficiently seriously to add several lengthy footnotes to the 5th edition, summarizing objections by Stillingfleet and answers by himself; further details are given in the Appendix. It is a matter for regret that Locke refused to bother himself with the comments made by his one substantial critic, Leibniz, whose observations he curtly and contemptuously dismissed as shallow and superficial : " even the largest minds have but narrow swallows ". The only excuse that can be offered for Locke's ill-judged neglect of Leibniz's criticisms, and for his refusal to correspond with him, is the persistent ill-health which dogged the last seven years of his life. He died on 28 October 1704.

2. THE PURPOSE OF THE " ESSAY "

That the *Essay* is very long, very diffuse, and not altogether
well-proportioned is hardly surprising in the light of the
circumstances of its composition. Locke was not a professional
philosopher, undistracted by other occupations; nor did he
compose the work in a comparatively short burst of inspired
concentration, as Berkeley did with his *Principles of Human
Knowledge.* Berkeley was touched off by the sudden and
dazzling discovery, as a very young man in his early twenties,
of what seemed to him a fundamental truth, and he found
himself amazed both at its simplicity and at the surprising fact
that it had occurred to nobody before. He had suddenly hit on
an error lying at the root of his previous philosophical beliefs,
which were indeed those of Locke himself, whom he had
studied as an undergraduate at Trinity College, Dublin, and he
set himself immediately to the task of exposing it, and of
working out the consequences of substituting for it the truth
which he had unexpectedly discovered : that the *esse* of an idea
is its *percipi.* With a single stroke he had cut down all that he
saw to be fundamentally mistaken in Locke, and the *Principles
of Human Knowledge* appeared as a rapidly written although
carefully considered polemic against the *Essay.* Locke, on the
other hand, was almost forty before he began seriously to think
about the problems with which he is occupied in the *Essay;*
and he started, not from the blinding discovery of an important
truth, but from a general dissatisfaction with the way things
were philosophically at the time. He wanted to find out what
was wrong, and he turned himself to what he regarded as the
comparatively humble, pedestrian, and even middle-aged task
of seeing how they could be put right. He therefore set about
the slow and patient undertaking of determining the scope and
limitations of human knowledge by a careful and, as he
thought, empirical investigation into the workings of the
human mind, at least in its cognitive activities. In consequence,
like his successors, particularly Hume, he failed to distinguish,

as we now would, between philosophical and psychological enquiry. The resulting *Essay* took him, with several preliminary drafts and frequent interruptions for political and other activity, almost twenty years to write.

Nevertheless, the *Essay* has a clear and definite plan, which Locke enunciated in the opening chapter, and to which he adhered throughout. His purpose was two-fold : " to inquire into the original, certainty, and extent of *human knowledge* " (i i 2); and to establish " the grounds and degrees of *belief, opinion* and *assent* " (ibid). The whole *Essay* was devoted to the aim of distinguishing knowledge from belief, and of determining in what fields human curiosity could hope to attain knowledge, and in what it must rest content with belief. His answers to these questions are not given until Book iv, in which he argues against the simple Cartesian distinction between *a priori* or necessary knowledge and empirical belief which covers all else. For Locke *a priori* knowledge is to be distinguished from empirical or matter of fact knowledge, empirical knowledge must be distinguished from empirical belief, and all of these must be distinguished from faith. Each of these four has its own legitimate sphere of operation, but human progress in understanding ourselves and the world in which we live can only proceed if we observe the distinctions between them. Failure to observe them breeds confusions, bigotry and obscurantism of the kind which, he thought, had plagued free enquiry and inhibited advance in natural science.

It is important to remember that that was Locke's purpose, and that all else in the *Essay* is preliminary to the findings of Book iv. For otherwise it can easily happen, and in the case of most undergraduates reading and writing essays on the work it usually does, that one loses sight of the aim in the details of the method. The whole of the first two Books, and much of the third, is taken up with discussion of the nature of the ideas which for Locke are the raw materials of knowledge, of their origin, of their relation to reality, and of their value as information about it. And it is only too easy to become so immersed in the many problems of epistemology which they raise that one neglects the main argument of Book iv; or alternatively to become so convinced of basic errors in the theory of ideas as to suppose that one can ignore the conclusions which Locke draws from it for knowledge and belief. It may be the case, as is frequently maintained, that his account of knowledge and belief, particularly the former, is inconsistent with his theory of ideas. That there is this inconsistency is arguable, at least on the generally accepted interpretation of what he thinks ideas are; but, even so, it would not follow that Book IV deserves neglect. As an independent discussion it is valuable, for its classification of kinds of knowledge and belief anticipates much that has come to be widely accepted as philosophically beyond question. If Locke is the father of modern empiricism, or at least its grandfather with Hume as his son, he is so far more because of what he had to say about certainty and probability than because of his views on the nature and origin of ideas, on primary and secondary qualities, on abstract ideas, on modes and substances, or because of his allegedly dualistic epistemology or his supposedly representative theory of sense perception. It is unfortunate that Book IV comprises not much more than a quarter, and the last quarter at that, of what is a very long and discursive work.

3. NO INNATE PRINCIPLES

To clear the ground for presenting his thesis that all knowledge springs from experience, Locke finds it necessary to dispose of the doctrines of innate ideas and of innate propositions. He mentions no authors by name, but he should not on that account be taken to be attacking men of straw. Descartes, who started by dividing ideas into the three categories innate, adventitious and factitious, found himself compelled by his mind-body dualism to conclude that all ideas were innate. As Locke said in his opening sentence of I ii, it was a widely held view " that there are in the understanding certain *innate principles,* some primary notions, κοιναὶ ἔννοιαι, characters, as it were, stamped upon the mind of man, which the soul receives in its very first being and brings into the world with it "; and he might have cited Cudworth or Lord Herbert of Cherbury, whose *De Veritate* he does refer to by name in this connection in an early draft of the *Essay*. But, although his negative purpose was thus two-fold, his actual argument is almost entirely directed against the doctrine of innate propositions. If that can be refuted, then the main incentive for proposing that some ideas are innate, as a necessary condition of any proposition being innate, would be removed. That some of our ideas are innate would not thereby be disproved, but he seems to think that it is not worth disproving, once innate propositions are disposed of : it is enough to expose the view to ridicule and challenge. Furthermore, the doctrine of innate propositions was philosophically more sinister, because on it rested the view that some principles are not to be questioned. That any principle was to be exempted from the scrutiny of reason was as abhorrent to Locke as it had been to Descartes; that way lay the darkness of obscurantism which could lead to the fining of an undergraduate at Oxford for presuming to challenge the authority of Aristotle. We should not be required to accept any proposition as true unless either its necessity was made clear to reason or it was empirically verifiable. That some propositions of religion were acceptable as matters of faith (as distinct from knowledge or rational belief) Locke was prepared to allow, but only if the authenticity of the alleged revelation was substantiated by reason, independent of the revelation; the mere claim to revelation, however sincerely made, was no certificate of truth (iv xviii 8; xix). What he would regard as rational verification that a supposedly divine revelation really was such Locke nowhere made clear.

Most of his attack on innate principles is indirect, demolishing the arguments advanced in favour of them, a method of attack which, while depriving the doctrine of supporting reasons, does not formally refute the doctrine itself; nevertheless, a theory for which no good reasons can be given, is not left in a reputable position. The most direct attack is that made by challenging the theory's presuppositions. If a proposition is to be innate, the ideas which are its component elements must be innate; but, in fact no such ideas are innate; therefore the proposition itself cannot be innate. E.g. the maxims " Whatever is, is " or " A thing cannot both be and not be ", although undoubtedly true, are highly abstract and far beyond the comprehension of a child of several years, let alone a new born infant. What possible reason could there be for supposing that the human infant knows or accepts the truth of these maxims, when the ideas involved are far beyond anything that it is then capable of?

The chief argument for innate principles, viz. that such principles command universal consent, Locke immediately counters with two objections. First, even if it were true that any principles did receive universal consent, this would not prove them innate. This would be to confuse a proposition's being necessary with its being innate. That there are propositions which are self-evidently necessary, i.e. which nobody could seriously dispute once he had clearly understood their meaning, Locke agreed to be true, the propositions of mathematics being the obvious examples. But this has no tendency to prove them innate. It is easy enough to think of propositions which nobody would deny, but which nobody could justifiably claim as innate, because the ideas involved are themselves empirical, e.g. that white is not black or that yellowness is not sweetness. In order to understand such propositions as these, it is necessary to have had appropriate sense-experience. Locke perhaps could not say that a man could not formulate or understand the proposition that white is not black until he had learned the meanings of the *words* ' white ' and ' black ', because of his claim, made later (IV V 2) to distinguish between mental propositions (which do not involve words) and verbal propositions (which, by definition, do). But he does maintain that a man could neither have the idea of white nor understand the word ' white ' unless he had seen white objects. In advance of seeing something white, he could not formulate any proposition about white. Once he has by experience learned what it is to be white, to be black, and to be different, he can see not only that it is true that white is different from black, but that it is necessarily true. This is what he means by saying of a proposition that it is self-evident. If by universal consent to a proposition is meant (what at the least it must mean) consent of all who understand the proposition, and if some propositions which are not innate command universal consent (in this limited sense), it follows that universal consent is not a sufficient condition of the proposition assented to being innate.

Secondly, he maintains that, if 'universal consent' is used in an unlimited sense, no proposition does command universal consent. Taking what he pejoratively calls "those magnified principles of demonstration 'Whatever is, is' and 'It is impossible for the same thing to be and not to be', which, of all others, I think have the most allowed title to innate", he replies " these propositions are so far from having an universal assent, that there are a great part of mankind to whom they are not so much as known " (I ii 4). It is possible to go through life without ever hearing either of them, and "children and idiots have not the least apprehension or thought of them". He will not accept the answer that we actually have them in our minds from the start, although we may not be conscious of them until later, for he rejects altogether the notion of a sub-conscious. Therefore if the notion of having something in the mind of which one is not conscious is to be defensible at all, it must be interpreted hypothetically. It must amount either to the general claim that we have a capacity for grasping the propositions, or to the more specific claim that our reason is bound to accept the propositions, once they are brought to our attention and we are able to understand them. He may once more have had in mind Descartes, who was eventually driven to making the undoubtedly false claim that all that he had ever meant by saying that an idea was innate was that we have innately either the capacity or the tendency to form it, much as gout is said to be innate in certain families. As Locke points out, neither the general claim nor the special claim, even if accepted, would give his opponents what they required. According to the general claim, to say that a principle is innate is to say that we have a capacity for knowing it. But this will not serve to distinguish a special class of propositions as innate, because of any proposition at all that we come to know it must be true that we had a capacity for knowing it. As the object of the doctrine of innate principles is to discriminate between those propositions which are innate and those which are not, this discrimination cannot be achieved by making innateness simply a capacity for knowledge. Locke does not, in fact, consider the possibility of a counter-objection that a distinction needs to be made between innate and acquired capacities, but within the strict terms of reference of the general claim he is not required to. Alternatively, if the doctrine is advanced in its more specific form, that for a principle to be innate is for it to be such that reason will accept it once it is brought to attention and understood, Locke replies that this will entail the conclusion that any proposition is innate provided that it is self-evident, with the unacceptable consequence that a proposition must be innate even though its terms are empirical, e.g. that white is different from black. If all that were meant by the theory were that some propositions are self-evident, Locke does not disagree, but would object that it is either false or misleading to use the word ‘ innate ’ of them. The suggestion that the distinction between innate and non-innate principles is that between what we *implicitly* and what we *explicitly* accept (I ii 22) he rejects as amounting to either the general or the special claims already rejected. He does not consider the possibility that a principle might be implicitly accepted in the sense that we act as if it were true, even at a time when we may be incapable of formulating the principle, or of understanding it if formulated to us; in this sense it might be argued that a human being implicitly accepts the proposition that no object can be in two places at once long before he is capable either of asserting the proposition or of understanding it.

Locke’s discussion throughout Book I shows that, while he refused to accept the doctrine of innate principles, whether speculative or practical, as the correct answer to the question which it purported to answer, he had no qualms about the propriety of the question itself. Like his opponents he accepted it as a genetic question, when and how did we come to get certain ideas, and when and how did we come to accept certain propositions. And the whole of his positive discussion in Book II is intended as the alternative answer to at least the first part of the question, what is the *origin* of our ideas. By hindsight we may criticise him, as also Hume afterwards, for confusing empiricism as a philosophical theory with empiricism as a hypothesis of psychology. Philosophically empiricism is a theory, not about the origin of concepts, but about their cashability. A man's claim to have a certain concept or to understand a certain word is to be checked, not by inquiring when or how he acquired them, but by finding out how he uses them. If he can recognize blue objects and distinguish them from others of a different colour, and if he can use the word ' blue ' correctly, this shows that he has the idea of blue It might be psychologically very surprising if he could have the idea of blue without ever having seen anything blue, but it would be philosophically unimportant, because philosophically empiricism is a theory about the conditions of significance and verifiability. Hume, in his half-hearted admission that a man *might* be able to form the idea of a shade of blue which he had never actually seen (*Treatise* I i I), and in his refusal to worry about it as an apparent exception to his theory, may have been on the trail of the distinction between philosophical and psychological empiricism, although the rest of his writing would lead us to doubt it, i.e. to doubt that he was beginning to recognize it. Certainly, as regards Locke, all the evidence indicates that he had no inkling of the distinction, although some of what he says about the nature of ideas might be held to foreshadow it.

Nevertheless Locke's attack on innate principles is interesting, partly for the distinctions which he does make, partly for those which he does not. Although he does not use the terminology of the *a priori,* which was later introduced or re-introduced by Kant, he was in fact arguing for the distinction between an *a priori* proposition and an innate proposition. The propositions which in Book I he calls self-evident are *a priori* truths, and his division of kinds of knowledge in Book IV is in fact the division into *a priori* and into empirical knowledge. Again, although he does not make the formal

distinction between analytic and synthetic, his account of nominal essences leads him, in effect, to say that 'gold is yellow'
is analytic, but that 'a quantity of gold can be increased by
admixture with a quantity of red earth' is synthetic. An
a priori truth being one, not which is known or knowable prior
to any experience at all, but the verification of which is
logically independent of experience, this is precisely what
Locke is arguing for in saying that a proposition is self-evident
while denying that it could be known prior to any experience
at all. The argument for innate principles that they are those
which are accepted as soon as understood simply confuses the
question whether a principle is *a priori* with the question
whether it is known or knowable prior to any experience at all;
and Locke did well to point this out.

But there is another distinction which Locke did not draw,
and indeed would have been inhibited by his psychologism
from drawing, that between innate ideas and *a priori* concepts.
An *a priori* concept could be characterized negatively as one
which the mind does not and could not derive from experience, positively as one which the mind contributes to
experience. Thus, Kant was later to argue that for human
experience to be of the kind that it in fact is there must be,
in addition to the empirical data provided by the senses, certain
formal or structural elements which organize the manifold of
sense into the patterns which comprise our actual experience.
We experience the sensible world as consisting of material
objects possessing qualities, and involved in causal processes.
The concepts of substance or thinghood and of cause are not
and could not be part of what is empirically received, but are
the mind's contribution to experience; they are the formal as
opposed to the material features of experience. That there
might be such *a priori* concepts Locke, on his principles, could
not have accepted, because he would have had to argue that if a
concept was not empirical it must be innate; and he would have
had to argue that, because he did not consider the possibility or
the necessity of distinguishing between the form or structure
of experience and its content. But he was, in fact, not far off
from considering it in one particular case, that of the idea

of substance. This gave him a great deal of trouble, and much of the correspondence with Stillingfleet was taken up with it. He acknowledged, indeed himself insisted, that, while our concepts of particular substances were empirical, our concept of substance itself could not be. When driven to be more positive, he hedged by saying that although the concept of substance was not reducible to empirical elements it was somehow derived from them. It never seems to have occurred to him that he was in a corresponding difficulty over the concept of quality; because concepts of particular qualities are empirical, he seems to have accepted it without question that the concept of quality is empirical also. But he should have been at least as worried about that as he was about substance. It may be conjectural, but it seems not unreasonable, to suggest that he was, in what he was trying to say about substance, fumbling towards treating it as a formal concept. Had he accepted it as one, he would have had to conclude that his dichotomy between empirical and innate ideas was not exhaustive, and that to allow that some ideas are not empirical does not require the conclusion that some are innate. His thinking about causality was so sketchy and superficial that he never saw the problem. But Hume did, and his thesis that the idea of necessary connection, which he saw to be the essential element in the notion of cause, was an impression of the imagination came as near as it could, without actually getting there, to Kant's thesis that it was a formal category of experience.

It is a striking indication of the hold which the doctrine of innate principles held at the time that it never occurred to Locke to question whether it mattered at all. In opposing the doctrine, he shared the presupposition of it, viz. that if there are any such principles they must be true, and therefore if we possessed any such principles we possessed certain innate knowledge. From the mere fact, if it were one, that we begin life with certain principles innately implanted in our minds, nothing whatever follows about their truth; there would be nothing self-contradictory about the notion of false innate principles. No doubt the idea would have been abhorrent to Locke's religious convictions, for it would be held to reflect adversely on the goodness of God to suggest that he might really be a Cartesian deceiver. But, as a philosopher, Locke should have considered it. He did think that the existence of God needed to be philosophically established, and he did think that he had succeeded in establishing it (IV x). Certainly, the *Essay,* or the early part of it, would have been very different if it had occurred to Locke that the innateness of a principle was no guarantee of its truth. But he was half-way there in his insistence on distinguishing between innate principles and necessary truths. That he went no further is an illustration of the difficulty which an innovating philosopher has in escaping entirely from the intellectual climate of his time.

4. "THE NEW WAY OF IDEAS"

In Book II Locke turns to his positive thesis, the beginning of which is that all our ideas come from experience, i.e. from sensation and reflection (introspection). "In that all our knowledge is founded, and from that it ultimately derives itself. Our observation employed either about external sensible objects, or about the internal operations of our minds perceived and reflected on by ourselves, is that which supplies our understandings with all the materials of thinking. These two are the fountains of knowledge, from whence all the ideas we have, or can naturally have, do spring" (II i 2). He is not, of course, saying that all our ideas, however complicated, abstruse or abstract, are given to us ready-made in this or that particular experience. The human mind is capable, by working on what it is given, of producing new ideas by composition, by comparison, and by abstraction; but every such idea must be reducible by analysis to elements which have been the data of sensible or introspective experience. Nor is he saying that sensible experience is the blankly passive reception of whatever the material world puts in its way; the mind is not, in sense perception, an automatic camera taking unselected snapshots of whatever happens to be in front of it. Perception is sensation determined or interpreted according to previous experience, to what has already been learned, to what the mind, through custom or prejudice, has come to accept.

It is here that in understanding Locke difficulties of interpretation begin—or rather ought to begin; for one of the difficulties in the way of understanding him is, in fact, the long and hardly ever questioned tradition that there is no difficulty in understanding him. The word ' idea ' is a keyword in his epistemology. It was a word which had long before Locke featured prominently in philosophical terminology, and it persisted long after him. And it is usually held that, although Locke never succeeded in explaining just what he meant by it (and perhaps he never seriously attempted to), and although he can be criticised for varying its use in different passages, yet there is no real trouble in making out what in general, however vaguely, he was at. Berkeley was the chief founder of the tradition, and all subsequent exegesis and criticism have followed comfortably in the direction which Berkeley set. The time has surely come to read Locke himself and to examine the credentials of the Berkeleian tradition in order to see whether they survive the scrutiny from which they have for far too long been exempted.

The essential feature of the orthodox interpretation of Locke is the reification of ideas. He is taken to have meant by ' idea ' a special kind of *thing,* distinguished from other things such as tables and chairs in that, while they are material things, it is a mental thing locked up inside the mind. And everything that Locke says about ideas and their relation to what they are ideas of is then interpreted in accordance with the presupposition of that basic model : the mind is regarded as if it were somehow the analogue of a box, into which ideas can be introduced or in which they can be produced, but from which they cannot escape. Consequently, all sense-experience, and whatever knowledge or belief may be acquired from it, is irremediably second hand. We never directly experience objects and happenings in the external world, but only our own ideas which serve as proxies for whatever goes on outside. Sense perception consists of having ideas which represent what goes on outside, some of the ideas actually resembling what they represent, others not, the first being ideas of primary qualities, the second being of secondary qualities. We can never break out of the circle of ideas, and knowledge, which Locke defines as the perception of the agreement or disagreement of our ideas, is as inescapably bound within the circle as is sense perception itself. Two consequences follow: first the general consequence that Locke was an epistemological dualist, committed on the one hand to the world of ideas to which all human experience and thought is restricted, and on the other to a quite separate mind-independent world somehow causally related to the first; and secondly the special consequence that he held a crudely representative theory of perception, according to which we can never observe anything in the mind-independent world, but find out whatever we do find out about it solely by scrutinizing the proxy-ideas which are all that we have access to.

Now, if that was Locke's view of ideas, the objections to it are so elementary and so obvious that it hardly needed a Berkeley to point them out. If sense perception simply consists of having ideas, which are alleged to be literal pictures, some accurate and others inaccurate, of inaccessible originals, there would be no justification for supposing that there were any originals at all, let alone for supposing that some of the pictures did resemble them but others did not, still less for claiming to be able to say which were the accurate pictures and which were not. On such a view there would be no explanation how it could occur to anyone that ideas were pictures of originals, and no reason whatever for his thinking so, even if he did. For the picture-original thesis to have any ground at all, there would have to be some occasion of experiencing an original, and some possibility of confronting picture with original; but of neither, on this view of Locke, could there be any possibility at all. The condition of his thesis being true would be precisely that we could have no possible ground for supposing it to be true, nor even rational explanation of one's entertaining it. It would be hard to understand why anybody should want to rate Locke as an important philosopher if his whole theory rests on errors so elementary that a first-year student in philosophy has no difficulty in spotting them. The basic criticism can be summarized in these words: "this I cannot comprehend, for how can I know that the picture of anything is like that thing, when I never see that which it represents? . . . Thus the idea of an horse, and the idea of a centaur, will, as often as they recur in my mind, be unchangeably the same; which is no more than this, the same idea will always be the same idea; but whether the one, or the other, be the true representation of anything that exists, that, upon his principles, neither our author, nor anybody else can know." That is as concise a statement of the objection to this kind of representationalism as one could wish. But, in fact, the passage quoted comes not, as one might suppose, from a commentator on Locke, but from Locke himself: it is his objection to Malebranche's theory of perception (*Examination of Malebranche,* §51). It is scarcely credible both that Locke should be able to see and to state so clearly the fundamental objection to the picture-original theory of sense-perception, and that he should have held that theory himself. If his own theory of perception were so obviously open to precisely the same objection, how could he have failed to realise it? This, at least, should shake some of our confidence in attributing to Locke the view of perception that we usually do.

Furthermore, it is striking that critics who attribute this view to Locke are hard put to it to produce passages from the text in support. Certainly he held, and rightly held, a causal theory; that (to take the instance of sight) our seeing what we do is causally dependent on the action of light from material objects on our senses, and that thereby ideas are " imprinted in our minds "; certainly he held that we receive ideas in perception; and certainly he held *some kind* of representationalism. But the question is: what kind? He does not in fact say that perceiving a table is identical with being caused by a table to have a picture of it; that is, he does not say anything about the reception or having of sensible ideas which makes them in any way resemble the sense-data which later philosophers have offered as the immediately given in sense experience.[5] Indeed

[5] An example of this interpretation of Locke proceeding from the false assumption that he meant by ' idea of sensation ' a sense-datum

it is doubtful whether Locke produced a theory of perception
at all, if by 'theory of perception' is meant anything at all
of the kind that has been meant by the sense-datum philosophers. A typical mis-statement of his view is the following,
taken from his leading modern commentator : " the mind
does not see the physical object. It sees an object which
somehow exists in the mind, and yet is not the mind itself, nor
a modification of the mind ".[6] This has Locke not merely
holding that to see a table is identical with having an idea in
the presence of and caused by the table, but also that seeing
a table is identical with *seeing* an idea of the table; and this
indeed is to attribute to Locke a category mistake of which there
is no evidence whatever that he was guilty. He talked of
seeing tables, and of having ideas of tables, but never of
seeing ideas of tables; when interpretation leads to travesty, it
is time to question the interpretation.

An additional reason for questioning the usual interpretation
of Locke on sense-perception is provided by consideration of
his account of introspection. He offers it as closely parallel to
that of sense-perception, the difference being that it gives us
knowledge of the inner world of the mind, as contrasted with
knowledge of the outer world of matter. Locke nowhere
suggests, and has not been taken to suggest, a similarly crude
representationalism here, according to which we would be only
indirectly acquainted with the operations of our minds through
the intervention of ideas representing these operations. He
always talks directly of observing " the actings of our own
minds " (IV xvii 4), " its own actions about these ideas it has "
(II vi 1) etc. Ideas of reflection are those which we get or form
from or *as a result* of reflection, and correspondingly ideas of
sensation are those which we get or form from or as a result
of sensation. Locke does have a reason, and not necessarily
a good one, for feeling some doubt about ideas of sensation
as a source of information and knowledge which he does not
feel about ideas of reflection, viz. that observation requires an

---

is provided by R. Jackson, *Locke's Version of the Doctrine of
Representative Perception* (*Mind*, 1930).
    [6] Aaron, p. 106.

observer, with the consequence that an observer may not observe things right, and that there is no guarantee that things are exactly as we observe them to be. In this sense, he thought the real essence of material objects is for ever, and in principle, unknowable, for we can never get beyond our observations. It does not seem to have occurred to him that, if this is an insurmountable obstacle to knowledge of material objects as they really are, it would similarly apply to claims to knowledge of mental operations; he just assumed that in this case the observer is privileged, because it is himself that he is observing. But this suggests a more reasonable interpretation of what Locke was at when he said that we could never know objects directly, but only through the intervention of the ideas in our minds, viz. that we can never get away from what we think an object to be. What we think it and its qualities to be can be confirmed, refuted or modified by our observations and experiments, but what at the end we say of the object and its qualities is still what we think them to be; in this sense the human mind can never escape from itself. If a God's eye view of the world is possible at all, it is possible only to God.

Now, it would be idle to pretend that there is no excuse for the accepted interpretation of Locke, and that the *Essay* is not peppered with phrases which suggest it, indeed which, given a certain view of what he meant by 'idea', entail it. "Ideas of primary qualities of bodies are resemblances of them" (II viii 15); again are "exact resemblances of something in the things themselves" (II xxx 2); "diagrams drawn on paper are copies of the ideas in the mind" (IV iii 19); when we look at a spherical object "the idea thereby imprinted in our mind is of a flat circle" (II ix 8); ideas of substances are copies (II xxi 13), and we think of them (he does not say we are right so to think) as "pictures and representations in the mind of things that do exist" (II xxi 6), etc.. Now, given that Locke means by 'idea' a mental entity of a specific kind, viz. a mental image, the rest of the accepted interpretation follows. If an idea of a primary quality is a mental image or picture (in a literal sense) of the quality, then Locke is saying that our ideas of things, or of their qualities, are reproductions

of them, correct in the case of primary qualities, incorrect in
the case of all others. But is that what he means by ' idea '?
The difficulty is that in the *Essay* he does not make it
explicitly clear what he means, not even to himself, for there
he is concerned to use the notion of ' idea ', not to talk about
it. Furthermore, and because the *Essay* was both a pioneering
and a discontinuously composed work, he arguably uses ' idea '
in more than one way. It is not difficult to find passages where
he appears to use it to signify a mental image, as when he says
that we cannot form an idea of a 1000-sided figure distinct
from the idea of a 999-sided figure (II xxix 14). But such
passages are rare, and overwhelmingly outnumbered by
passages where he means (or could reasonably be taken to
mean) something not about images but about thoughts, so that
an idea of x will be what we think x to be, or what we mean or
understand by the word ' x '. (It should be noted that for
Locke a word is simply an " articulate sound ", (III i 1) what
modern linguists call a *phone*. The notion of a word does not
already have the notion of meaning built into it. This is why
he talks ·of words as signs of ideas, and insists that while a
parrot can be taught to talk, i.e. to use words, it is incapable
of language.) The only account he gives of ' idea ' is right at
the outset, where he insists that he is using it in the most
general kind of way to mean " whatever it is which the mind
can be employed about in thinking " (I i 8). If there is little
clear about this, there is nothing tendentious either; we must
therefore approach his actual use of ' idea ' with our minds
open, not restricted by Berkeleian blinkers. It would be
salutary to consider how we use the word ' idea ' in ordinary
English idiom, without thereby committing ourselves to ideas as
private mental entities. Cf. " I have an idea that . . .",
" I have no idea what . . .", " My idea of a . . . is . . .",
" What is your idea of . . . ?" etc.

After the *Essay* had appeared and was subjected to criticism,
Locke was compelled to do what he had not done during its
composition, viz. to attempt a clearer and more explicit
statement of what an idea is. In particular he was provoked to
this by the attacks made on him and, as he thought, by the

misunderstanding shown, by the Bishop of Worcester; and Locke's answers in his letters to the bishop are revealing. He emphasises that he is not wedded to the terminology of ideas, but has used it because he could not think of a better. " My new way by ideas, or my way by ideas . . . is, I confess, a very large and doubtful expression; and may, in the full latitude, comprehend my whole *Essay*. . . . My way by ideas . . ., if it be new, it is but a new history of an old thing : for, I think it will not be doubted that men always performed the actions of thinking, reasoning, believing and knowing, just after the same manner that they do now."[7] " The new way of ideas, and the old way of speaking intelligibly, was always, and ever will be, the same thing."[8] Forming ideas is identical with understanding words.[9] Ideas are the meaning of words : " if your Lordship tell me, what you mean by these names ('matter ', 'motion ', etc.), I shall presently reply, that there, then, are the ideas that you have of them in your mind ".[10] He would have been quite prepared to talk of notions rather than ideas, if it had not been for the fact that at one point in the *Essay* (II xxii 2) he had found it necessary to use ' notion ' in a technical sense for ideas of one particular kind.[11] But if to talk in terms of notions or conceptions is less obscure or confusing than to talk in terms of ideas, he has no objection to the change being made.[12]

There is nothing here about my ideas being a collection of pictures in the private gallery of my mind, from which they can never be let out for confrontation with the world outside the gallery,[13] or with the ideas of other people. Instead, what Locke says his supposedly new way of ideas comes to has a strongly twentieth century ring about it. My idea of a horse is what I think or take a horse to be, what I mean by the word ' horse ', what I am saying of a thing when I say that it is a horse. In the case of substances and their qualities, my ideas

---

[7] *Works* (4th ed.) 1.424   [8] ib. 1.574   [9] ib. 1.529
[10] ib. 1.565   [11] ib. 1.423   [12] ib. 1.429
[13] Locke does, it must be admitted, sometimes write somewhat in this fashion, e.g. II xi 17, but even there he distinguishes between the objects of sight and our ideas of them.

are correct if I think of things as being as they actually are; my idea, say, of gold will be incorrect if gold is different from what I think it is, or from what I mean by ' gold '. In the case of modes, such as are named by ' murder ' or ' sacrilege ', the situation is different, because modes do not have the same existential reference as do our ideas of substances and qualities (II xii 4); my idea of murder or of justice, therefore, will be correct to the extent that it conforms to the ideas of others, or to their usage of words; " when a man is thought to have a false idea of justice, or gratitude, or glory, it is for no other reason, but that his agrees not with the ideas which each of these names are the signs of in other men " (II xxxii 11).

But if that was what Locke wanted to say about ideas, how did he come to write as he did throughout the *Essay,* laying himself open to the interpretation of ideas as peculiar entities in our private, and indeed our only world? And what is one to make of his using, in connection with ideas, words like ' represent ' ' resemble ' and even ' picture '? First, it must be realised that, although Locke recognized that much in the *Essay* would be objected to and even give offence, he does not seem to have thought that the terminology of ideas would cause any trouble; in his letters to Stillingfleet he frequently expresses surprise that it did. And if a philosopher uses a term which it never occurs to him will cause trouble, the term almost certainly will cause trouble; Locke would probably have been a lot more careful and guarded in his use of ' idea ' throughout the *Essay,* if he had known what he was letting himself in for. Then, he was probably, also, the victim of the unfortunate fact that ' idea ' is a noun. Noun-proneness indeed is one of the chief occupational diseases of philosophers; it is fatally easy, because so many nouns name things (' shoes ' ' ships ' ' sealing wax', even ' shadow ' and ' echo ') to treat all nouns as if they named things—that is, not necessary to believe that they do, but to write as if you believed that they did, and thus to mislead others into taking it that you do believe it. Professional philosophers now are a good deal more word-conscious than in the seventeenth century, in that they are more aware of the trouble that their choices (or, often, non-choices) of words

can lead them into. Locke's new way of ideas does not have to
be interpreted according to the model of a man shut inescapably
up in his own private picture gallery, and, in the light of his
explanations to Stillingfleet, it is fairly clear that he meant
nothing of that kind. But, in the *Essay* alone, it is easy to take
him that way : the word ' idea ' occurs so frequently that the
reader has to work hard if he is to succeed in immunising
himself against taking it to be intended as the name of some
special kind of mental thing. It is easier, too, to take ' represent ' ' resemble ' ' picture ' etc. literally than metaphori-
cally, but being easier does not make it to be, or more likely
to be, correct. There is not one and only one relation signified by
' represent '; the travelling salesman represents his company,
the Davis Cup player represents his country, the coloured
drawing pins in the police map represent the houses broken
into during the last month, the minor key is used to represent
sadness, Godot has been said to represent a variety of things;
but in none of these cases is the relation the same. For Locke
ideas represent reality, in the sense that he is claiming, whether
justifiably or not, that there can be a correspondence between
what we think about the world and the way the world is, and
that the improvement of knowledge is the increase of this
correspondence; and they also represent reality, in the sense
that we can think about things in their absence. When Locke
says that some ideas resemble the qualities they stand for, it
is only plausible to take his meaning according to the picture-
original model, if one has already taken an idea to be a special
kind of mental thing. When somebody says of a face or a view
that it is exactly like the description of it that he has just
read, we do not misunderstand him; we do not suppose that he
is making the extraordinary mistake of believing that the word
' description ' is the name of some kind of thing that could
literally and straightforwardly be similar to a face or a view.
We can nevertheless significantly and, in the right circumstances, truly say that the face is like the description of it,
meaning that it is as it was described, that it matches the
description, or that the description fits it. Locke thinks that
some ideas resemble their qualities, while others do not : we

think of a material object, say a table, as having the shape and size which it appears to have; and there we are, or may be, right. We think of the table as having a certain colour; and there, we are, and must be, wrong. Material objects do have the properties of extension, including movement, but they do not have properties of colour; our thinking that they do is a mistake which we naturally make because it is the effect of the causal properties of insensible particles in the object. The distinction between primary and secondary qualities may not be tenable, at least in the form in which Locke proposed it. But that would not mean that we could not give sense to his assertion that ideas of primary qualities do resemble these qualities, while those of secondary qualities do not : primary qualities are just as we think them to be, our visual descriptions (to use sight as an example) would fit; secondary qualities are not as we think them to be, and our visual descriptions would never fit. And if my idea of a thing is what I think or would say that the thing was, we can hardly object to Locke occasionally speaking of an idea as a picture, or claim that he is committing himself to ideas as pictures in any literal sense. It would be a very insecure foundation on which to erect the structure of dualism and representative perception which is generally supposed to be found in the *Essay*.[14] If, as must be acknowledged, we cannot ascribe any single sense to ' idea ' used consistently throughout its thousands of occurrences in the *Essay*, we should not interpret it merely by selection. Locke's use of it was clearly confused and confusing; what we have to do is to make the best and most general sense of it that we can which is consistent with his theory of knowledge as a whole; when we take into account both his use of ' idea ' in the *Essay* and his defence and explanation of that use as given in his correspondence with Stillingfleet, that does not appear impossible. Certainly he is to be criticised for laying himself open to the interpretation usually taken of him,

[14] An interesting but now almost unknown attack on the traditional view is to be found in Thomas E. Webb, *The Intellectualism of Locke* (Dublin, McGee, 1857).

but that does not absolve us from the task of enquiring whether that interpretation is.correct.[15]

5. LANGUAGE AND THOUGHT

Locke's original intention, as indicated in his statement of method (1 i 3), had been, after completing his discussion of the nature and kinds of ideas, " secondly, to show what knowledge the understanding hath by these ideas; and the certainty, evidence and extent of it ". But, in fact, instead of proceeding straight from the preliminary to the main task, he had found that many of the problems of epistemology were problems about language : " there is so close a connexion between ideas and words, and our abstract ideas and general words have so constant a relation one to another, that it is impossible to speak clearly and distinctly of our knowledge, which all consists in propositions, without considering first the nature, use and signification of language " (II xxiii 19). This forms the subject of Book III, titled " Of Words ".

In the twentieth century philosophers have become so preoccupied with language, and so imbued with the idea that philosophical study of it is either their only task or at least the task with which they must begin, in order to achieve conceptual clarity and understanding, that little of what Locke wrote would now be thought to contribute new insights. Almost all that he said on the subject would be regarded as so obviously right or so obviously wrong as to arouse no further interest. But it would be unjust to Locke not to acknowledge his pioneering work here, nor to point out that his emphasis on linguistic questions was not taken up by his more illustrious, and otherwise more original, successors Berkeley and Hume.

His initial definition of words as " articulate sounds " (III i 1) is both unduly restricted and unduly wide. It could

[15] It would be an instructive exercise in selective misinterpretation to argue that Wittgenstein was a dualist from what he says in the *Tractatus Logico*—Philosophicus about thoughts and propositions being pictures of reality.

apply only to spoken words, not to written words. A word
for him can only enter into the vocabulary of a language if
it stands for an idea or " internal conception ". But while he
is quite right to point out that it is a matter of convention
what sounds are used for what conceptions, his definition is
such that any sound at all will be a word. In fact, the question
about any sound whether it is a word is already the question
whether there is a linguistic convention for its use. It is true
of some sounds, but of no words, that they happen to have a
meaning. It is true of some words that they happen *not* to have
a meaning, e.g. proper names and nonsense words; but they are
only words by courtesy or for certain purposes, e.g. the
printer's, the telegraph clerk's, or the radio producer's.
Indeed, Locke's definition of ' word ' exactly fits the radio
producer's use, but this is clearly parasitic on the basic use, in
accordance with which, while it is contingent that a word has
the meaning which it does, it is analytic that it has a meaning.
Fortunately, Locke in practice forgets his own definition and
reverts to the basic use of ' word '. Futhermore, his formal
distinction between words and ideas leads him to a consequence
which he openly embraces, but to which he does not adhere.
According to this consequence, words are required for the
public expression and communication of thought, but not for
thought itself; hence his distinction between mental propositions and verbal propositions (IV v 2). While he is no
doubt correct in believing that there is a primitive level of
consciousness, which could be called non-verbal or pre-verbal
thinking, it is far less clear what a non-verbal proposition could
be, given that a proposition is what he takes it to be, viz.
something which can be true or false. On the other hand, he
recognizes that in fact almost all thinking is done in words
(IV v 4), which is to make words something other than merely
public signs of thought; and, although in that passage, as
frequently elsewhere, he insists that confused thought is almost
always due to confusion about words, and recommends as a
cure getting back from words to the ideas, he is not to be
taken as advocating as the ideal totally non-verbal thought.
Certainly, for him, the meaningfulness of words is explicable

only in terms of the ideas which they signify. But he is not advancing the crude view (signs of which are to be found in Hume) that for a word to have a meaning is for it to be accompanied, on every occurrence of its use, by an idea in the mind of its user. He would have been more in sympathy with Berkeley, who held that a word was used meaningfully provided that it *could* be accompanied by such an idea. But in arguing that to avoid confusion in words it was necessary to make ideas clear, Locke was not committed to such a dualism between words and ideas at all; we should remind ourselves of a passage already quoted—" the new way of ideas, and the old way of speaking intelligibly, was always, and ever will be the same thing ". That one man fails to understand another, or (what, as Locke points out, e.g. III iv 15, is not the same thing) succeeds in misunderstanding him, may be the fault of either speaker or hearer; or again, one or both may be the victims of the fact that natural languages *are* natural languages, i.e. that their terms do not have clearly prescriptive definitions, as do those in the languages of mathematics or logic, or even of natural science so far as its terms are technical. A man may express himself unclearly, because the language available to him is unsatisfactory, because he has a poor command of it, or because his thought is unclear. But making one's thought clear is itself a matter of using the language clearly. When Locke says (e.g. IV v 4) that words occur to us more readily than the ideas for which they stand, the truth he seems to be getting at is that men have a facility for speaking which far outruns their facility for thinking, and that there is a perfectly good sense in which we do not know what we think until we hear what we say. Talking is, for almost everybody, such a familiar, effortless and unreflective activity that we are constantly in our talk constructing sentences the precise meaning of which we could not, if challenged, provide, either because they do not have a precise meaning, or because we lack the skill to formulate it; in this way our thinking is confused or unclear. The challenge to make our thinking or our ideas clear is the challenge to reformulate what we have said in other words which do it more clearly, or in other words which express what

we were originally *trying* to say. His point is that much of
our talk is not totally unlike parrot talk : it is unlike it, in
that a parrot would be completely incapable, while we would
not, of reformulating what it has " said ", for the parrot can
only learn to string together words (in Locke's strict sense),
not to speak a language; or, to put it another way, our talk is
communicative, while the parrot's is not. But much of our talk
is like parrot talk, because it is a matter simply of habitual
response to stimulus, and because it would fail at the challenge
of reformulation; it is parrot talk which for the most part goes
undetected because for the most part it goes unchallenged.
The demand for clear thinking is the demand to meet the
challenge; and that the ordinary trivialities of social inter-
course make it unnecessary or a waste of time to pose the
challenge should not blind us to the fact that where the issue
is not trivial, for example in matters of politics, morality,
science or faith the challenge is one which we must be prepared
to face or be found wanting; in such matters the sloppiness,
carelessness and muddleheadedness of ordinary discourse are
inexcusable.

The first point to recognize about a language, Locke insists, is
that, apart from proper names used to designate particular
individuals, all words are " of reason and necessity " general
(III iii 1). There is no theoretical limit to the use of proper
names : we could, if we wished, provide a proper name for
every single individual, no matter what the individual was.
There is nothing to prevent us from giving a proper name, not
only to every individual man, but also to every individual
sheep or sparrow, and to every individual blade of grass. But
such an extension would not only be a waste of time and
energy, it would also exceed practical possibility, for we should
be unable either to learn or to remember all the proper names.
Therefore we, in fact, limit the use of proper names to those
individuals which we have a practical and repetitive interest in
naming. But the important point is that, however far we
extended our vocabulary of proper names, we should not have
begun to acquire or to develop a language. Communication
would be impossible, because with a vocabulary consisting only

of proper names, while individuals could be *mentioned*, nothing could be *said*. The possibility of saying anything derives from general words, and in this way all the words of any language must be general words. Into what kinds of words they are classified (e.g. nouns, adjectives, verbs, adverbs, conjunctions etc.) is a matter of the grammatical and syntactical structure of the particular language concerned. But in no language at all could a meaningful sentence be constructed which consisted entirely of proper names. (One could think of apparent exceptions to this in the case of one-word sentences. A mother might lean out of the window and call " Peter " to her small son playing in the garden. But this is, in fact, no exception, for here her use of " Peter " is not just the loud uttering of the boy's name, it is an accepted brachylogy understood by mother and son alike as meaning " Peter, come here " or " Peter, I want you ".)

The central question, therefore, to which Locke addresses himself is the question how words become general (III iii 6). Terminologically, this is an odd question, for the use of ' become ' suggests that a word starts by being non-general and then that something happens to it, after which it is general. But that is not Locke's meaning. He is asking what has to be the case for a word to be general. Even that question is not altogether clear, and it can be seen from the various answers which Locke in different places produces that he was by no means clear in his own mind just what the problem was that he was trying to resolve. What he thinks have to be reconciled are the fact that words are and must be general in their use and the fact that each word, like everything else which exists, is itself a particular. (The distinction between type-words and token-words seems never to have occurred to him. In the phrase ' red hair and red cheeks ' there are five token-words, but they are tokens of only four types, for the two ' reds ', while in one sense different words, one occurring as the first word in the phrase and the other as the fourth, are in another sense the same word. If Locke had recognized this distinction, he might have been less happy than he was about saying of words that they were particular in their existence. He failed to see that his question about the relation of universal to particular arose within words themselves, not merely between words and something else.)

His first move was to say that a word became general by being made the sign of a general idea, (III iii 6); but he recognized that this was no solution, for it merely generated the new question how an idea becomes general. And to that question he produces different answers in different passages. Nor are his answers sufficiently clearly distinguished for us to be able to say exactly how many there are. All that we can do is to indicate different lines on which his thought seems to have moved.

One account, which constantly runs throughout the *Essay* (cf. II xi 9; III iii 11; IV xi 9), and which was first stated in one of the early drafts[16], is identical with that afterwards given by Berkeley, viz. that a general idea is a particular idea taken as representative of all other similar particulars. " This is called abstraction, which is nothing else but the considering any idea barely and precisely in itself stripped of all external existence and circumstance." On this view a mental image becomes general by the mind's attending to its relevant features and ignoring others. Thus an image of a red ball could serve either as the general idea of red (when we attend to its being coloured red and ignore its shape) or as the general idea of ball (if we ignore the colour and attend only to its shape). As this view, which Locke repeatedly states and which he says (as in the passage quoted above) is what he means by ' abstraction ', is indistinguishable from Berkeley's own view, we may ask why Berkeley thought it necessary to devote the Introduction to his *Principles of Human Knowledge* to a violent attack on what he regarded as Locke's pernicious doctrine of abstract ideas. The answer is that Berkeley simply ignored this view in Locke, and concentrated on two others which he found, or thought he found, in the *Essay*. On one of them, an image becomes general, not by by the mind attending to those features in which it resembles other particulars said to be of the same sort, but by

[16] Aaron, p. 65.

possessing all possible relevant features which particulars of that sort could possess. Berkeley fastened on the notorious passage about the triangle (IV vii 9), took Locke to be saying that an image of a triangle, because it had to stand indifferently for equilateral, isosceles, and scalene triangles, had to be all of these at once, and quite rightly pointed out that it was logically impossible for an image of a triangle to be at one and the same time all those shapes, because they were mutually inconsistent. Locke's view was therefore untenable, because it required the existence of images of a kind the existence of which was logically impossible. There is some plausibility in Berkeley's interpretation, if we confine our attention to the first sentence from Locke which he quotes : "the general idea of a triangle . . . must be neither oblique nor rectangle, neither equilateral, equicrural nor scalenon; but all and none of these at once." But the immediately following sentence suggests something different : "It is something imperfect, which cannot exist; an idea wherein some parts of several different and inconsistent ideas are put together." Had Locke said that it was an idea in which inconsistent parts of different ideas are put together, Berkeley's criticism would have been justified. But that is not what Locke did say. Parts of inconsistent ideas can be put together, provided that they are not inconsistent parts. We can hardly do more than conjecture what Locke is trying to get at here. It is clear from the earlier part of the paragraph that he is talking about general ideas, not at the level at which we must use them for any experience, thought or communication at all, but at the level at which we try to talk and think *about* them : that is the point of his stressing the relative difficulty of forming them. He may, in fact, be advocating a different view of images, that they are (or may be) abstract in the sense of being indeterminate. A man *can* form a determinate image of an equilateral triangle, which therefore could not also be a determinate image of a scalene triangle; but he does not have to. More commonly an image of a triangle is indeterminate in the sense that it is neither true that it is an image of an equilateral triangle nor true that it is

not. This may not have any of the philosophical importance
which Locke attached to it, but it is a fact about images that the
laws of contradiction and excluded middle cannot always (or
even often) be applied to them. There is a perfectly good sense
in which an image of a triangle can be " all and none of
these at once "; and consequently, if there is anything to be
said at all for general ideas in terms of images, Berkeley's
misreading of this passage in Locke would not dispose of it.

The other view, on which Berkeley spent more time and
which he regarded as more seriously wrongheaded, was that
Locke thought abstract or general ideas were mental occurrences
but not images : they were somehow abstract occurrences. This
view Berkeley had to reject, in order to prepare the way for his
own view that all ideas must be particular occurrences or
images. Again, if Berkeley's interpretation is correct, his
criticism is just : not merely is there no introspective evidence
for non-particular mental occurrences, but it is inconceivable
that there could be. If Locke had said that there were two
kinds of mental occurrents that were of cognitive interest, viz.
occurrent images and occurrent concepts, he certainly would
have been open to Berkeley's attack. But did he say so? The
answer is surely No. Berkeley seems to have been misled by the
words ' abstract ', ' abstraction ' and ' abstract idea ' into
thinking that Locke maintained that there were abstract mental
occurrences which were not particular occurrences of images.
But Locke did not use the terms that way : as he explained in
the passage quoted above from Draft c ' abstraction ' was the
name not for a peculiar kind of mental entity, but for a peculiar
mental operation. Berkeley was simply attacking a man of
straw; in so far as Locke was trying to give an account of
general ideas in terms of mental occurrences, the account was
exactly the same as his own.

All such accounts as those so far mentioned suffer from two
defects, that even in their own terms they are inadequate, and
that they are totally misdirected. They are inadequate, for not
all thinking can be reduced to having images; we cannot form
images of everything that we can think and talk intelligibly
about, as Berkeley recognized in his doctrine of notions, which

he introduced precisely because not all words can be paralleled by images. And, even if they could, it would do nothing to answer the question about words or ideas being general. We do not find out what it is for a man to have a general idea of x, or what his idea is, or what he means by the word ' x ' by getting from him an introspective report about his imagery. That might be of psychological interest, but is philosophically irrelevant. The philosopher who, like Locke and Berkeley, starts by thinking that ' general idea ' must be the *name* of psychological possessions or occurrences of a peculiar sort is starting off on the wrong foot and in the wrong direction. Here again we have a case of the confusion between philosophical and psychological questions.

In fact, Locke in Book III moves towards an entirely different type of account, and almost liberates himself from psychologism. He realises that what has to be explained is how we generalize, how we come to experience things, qualities and relations as belonging to various kinds. And he realises, as already indicated, that the problem breaks out at two different levels : how we form general ideas, in the sense of having the kind of experience that we do, viz. of things belonging to classes or sorts; and how we form general ideas in the sense of being able to analyse or formulate general ideas in the first sense. Everybody must have general ideas in the first sense, only the intellectually curious have them in the second. We form the general ideas that we do on the basis of the similarities and differences which we observe, but it is we who divide things up into kinds, we do not find them divided up for us by nature : " the essences of the sorts of things, and consequently the sorting of things, is the workmanship of the understanding " (III iii 12). We notice similarities and differences but we *make* the distinction between one general idea and another by decision or convention (III vi 36). Here Locke is recognizing the vagueness or open-endedness of concepts. Where the concepts have to conform with definitions, as in mathematics, they are not open-ended; but where definitions have to conform with the concepts they are—and almost all our concepts are of this kind. Consequently, at the one level, for a

man to have a general idea of x is for him to have the ability
to recognize *x*'s and discriminate them from non-*x*'s, and to
use of the word ' *x* ' correctly. And, at the other level, it is for
him to be able to explain what the general idea of *x* at the
lower level is. This is what the doctrine of nominal essences,
introduced in Book III, comes to, where he makes it clear that
these essences *are* abstract ideas (not that we have abstract
ideas *of* these essences). "The having the essence of any
species being that which makes anything to be of that species,
and the conformity to the idea to which the name is annexed
being that which gives a right to that name, the having the
essence and the having the conformity must needs be the same
thing, since to be of any species and to have a right to the
name of that species is all one. As, for example, to be a man,
or of the species man, and to have a right to the name ' man '
is the same thing " (*ibid*.). A general idea now is not, as
on the image theory, an item of psychological furniture, but an
ability to discriminate and classify and to use words accordingly. Furthermore, in the case of words which can with any
plausibility be called names, i.e. common names, a general
idea is not just what the word stands for, it is what the word
means, so that the connection between word and idea is not
contingent in the way in which Locke originally presented it;
his claim that the new way of ideas and the old way of speaking
intelligibly are the same is explained.

6. KNOWLEDGE AND BELIEF

The final book of the *Essay*, although the most important,
stands least in need of explanation, for it raises no serious
difficulties of interpretation that have not previously occurred.
In his classification of the kinds of knowledge, and in his
distinction between knowledge and belief, Locke prepared the
way for much that has come to be accepted, and he liberated
epistemology from the rationalist strait-jacket in which Cartesianism was threatening to clamp it. Descartes had broken the
fetters of scholasticism, but in arguing that nothing could be

knowledge that could not be reduced to a system of propositions logically deduced from self-evident premisses he forged new ones of his own. That Descartes stood for freedom of human thought Locke did not doubt; but that the freedom offered was untenably restricted he could not doubt either. Locke's thesis that what is achieved by observation and experiment, by the confirmation or refutation of empirical hypotheses, is as respectable as, although different from, the abstract knowledge of a deductive system, was an acknowledgement and a justification of the new won freedom of natural science. Book IV of the *Essay* is an early blueprint of the procedures of induction, untroubled by the scepticism which Hume was soon to exercise on them.

Defining knowledge as the perception of the agreement or disagreement of ideas (IV i 1), Locke divides it into four kinds : of identity and diversity, of relation, of coexistence or necessary connexion, and of existence. The third kind gives him some trouble, partly because his discussion leads to the conclusion that no propositions belonging to it can strictly be said to be known, partly because he seems not to have made up his mind clearly what the logical form of such propositions must be. Propositions of identity and of relation are clearly hypothetical, neither asserting nor requiring the existence of anything : that red is the same as red and different from green, that the sum of the interior angles of a triangle is 180°, are propositions which neither assert the existence of red objects or triangles, nor are false if none exist. Propositions of existence are clearly categorical : that this is a book, that there is a book in the next room, that there is life on Mars do assert the existence of something, and will therefore be false if the object said to exist does not. To the third class Locke assigns all general propositions which are not logically necessary (i.e. which do not fall into either of the first two classes), instances of which would be propositions asserting natural laws e.g. that heated metals expand, that all material objects are subject to gravity, that full employment produces economic inflation, or causal propositions in general. But he does not commit himself clearly to the view either that such propositions are wholly hypothetical or that they are not : by the phrase 'necessary connexion' he seems to imply that they are, and to that extent assimilates them to his first two classes, by the word 'coexistence' he seems to imply that they are not, and to that extent assimilates them to the fourth class. In insisting on a difference between the first two classes he anticipated Kant's distinction between analytic and synthetic *a priori* propositions, and he expressly refused to assign mathematical knowledge to the first class on the ground that it was not trivial but instructive (IV viii 8) : a man coming to see that an external angle of a triangle is greater than any of its internal angles is learning something new, for that proposition does not form part of the definition of 'triangle'. Here Locke, like many philosophers, has confused the question whether a proposition is a tautology (which is a question about its logical form) with the question whether it is an obvious or trivial tautology (which is a question about the intellectual capacities and limitations of the person concerned). Logically, there is no distinction to be drawn between his first and his second kind of knowledge.

In Chapter ii Locke declares that there are three different ways of knowing, viz. intuitive, demonstrative and sensitive knowledge. Unfortunately, he calls them " degrees of knowledge ", and thereby commits himself to a not uncommon confusion, inherited from Descartes, as though of propositions which can be said to be known to be true some can be said to be more known or better known than others; this, of course, does not make sense. It rests on the confusion between knowledge, which by definition cannot be false, and a claim to knowledge, which can be either incorrect or unjustified, and which can be made with more or less assurance. His account of intuition and demonstration is exactly the same as Descartes's, and shows clear evidence of the influence of the *Regulæ* : about demonstration he in effect says both that it is as good as intuition, because it is a sequence of intuitions of the successive logically necessary implications of a deductive proof, and that it is not as good as intuition, because memory is involved and memory is not infallible. Here he is perpetuating the Cartesian fallacy that if no logically watertight guarantee can be provided (as it cannot) that an individual will not make a mistake in an argument or a mathematical calculation, the argument cannot be logically sound. This is a fallacy, because mathematical knowledge in particular, or deductive knowledge in general, is not shown to be in any degree suspect because human thinkers are fallible. In maintaining that no *general* propositions can be known to be true except those which are known by intuition or demonstration (IV ii 14), he is rebutting his original classification of kinds of proposition which can be known, for he is now saying that a proposition asserting coexistence (or matter of fact connexion) of qualities cannot be known to be true. But he does not confine intuition and demonstration to general or non-existential propositions : a man knows by intuition that he himself exists (IV ix 3), and the existence of God can be established by demonstration (IV x). Only one other kind of existential proposition can be known, viz. that asserting the existence of what is at the time of assertion sensibly perceived (IV ii 14; xi 8-9). Locke is not restricting himself here to the modest so-called incorrigible propositions of the sense-datum theorists (of the " red here now " variety), but is admitting material object propositions (e.g. " I see a candle burning "); and to anybody who professes to doubt that such a proposition can be certain he replies with the same robustness later used by Thomas Reid and G. E. Moore. Here he has not entirely emancipated himself from the extreme rationalism of Descartes, for he professes that " the notice we have by our senses of the existing of things without us [is] not altogether so certain as our intuitive knowledge, or the deductions of our reason " (IV xi 3); but he goes on "yet it is an assurance that deserves the name of 'knowledge'". He later extends the realm of sensitive knowledge to include memory (IV xi 11), and even further to include general propositions asserting the coexistence of qualities of substances, provided that they are based on (or confined to?) the evidence of previous observation and experience (IV vi 13). Once more he has changed his view on the status of general propositions which are empirically verifiable. His whole treatment of probability shows that, while he believed empirical knowledge was possible and needed to be distinguished from empirical belief, he had not thought the matter through. He was clearly heading for the view that an empirical proposition could be said to be known to be true if the evidence for it is conclusive, but at the same time could not rid himself of the view that evidence, just because it is evidence, never can be conclusive. The class of propositions of which we can have an assurance which amounts to knowledge therefore hovers uncertainly between the class of logically necessary propositions which can be known and the class of empirical propositions which have such a high degree of probability that it would be unreasonable not to accept them. It is symptomatic of Locke's uncertainty here that while in one part of the book " assurance " is admitted as knowledge, later it is named as the highest degree of probability (IV xvi 6). It is hardly surprising that he did not propound a clear and unwavering answer to the question of empirical knowledge, as he was the first of the empiricist school to address himself to the problem at all.

On the accepted interpretation of Locke's theory of ideas, his account of knowledge runs immediately into an insuperable objection. Given that knowledge is what he defines it to be, the perception of the agreement or disagreement of ideas, the only propositions that even in principle could be known would be hypothetical non-existential propositions, e.g. those of mathematics. Existential propositions not only could not in fact be verified (for that would require breaking out of the circle of ideas), but they could not even in principle be candidates for knowledge, because such propositions not only do not assert a relation between one idea and others, but are not relational propositions at all. The whole of Book IV would therefore have to be regarded as inconsistent with all that has gone before, and would fall to be examined simply as an essay on its own. On the other hand if, as has been argued, the reification of ideas is a misinterpretation, the stumbling block is removed, and Book IV can be treated as a piece with the rest of the *Essay*. If the usual interpretation is correct, Locke might be regarded as remarkably obtuse for having devoted a whole chapter (IV iv) to the "reality of knowledge" and yet having failed to detect the fatal objection to which his whole enterprise would be subject.

To believe a proposition is to accept it or to assent to it, when it is not known to be true. Not only would it be absurd to refuse assent to a proposition on the ground that it was not and could not be known to be true, but it would be, in a practical sense, disastrous. "He that, in the ordinary affairs of life, would admit of nothing but direct plain demonstration, would be sure of nothing in this world, but of perishing quickly" (IV xi 10). A belief is rational if it accords with probability, i.e. "likeliness to be true" (IV xv 3); and the problem of the reasonableness of an empirical belief is therefore the problem of clarifying the grounds and degrees of probability, to which Chapters xv-xvi are devoted. The grounds of probability are two : conformity with one's own previous experience, and the testimony of others the value of which will vary with the integrity and competence of the witnesses. The degrees of probability are three : the highest, assurance, is attained when general consent agrees with one's own experience that a factual proposition is *always* true, i.e. where the proposition is of the form ' all *x* is *y* '; the second, confidence, when general consent and one's own experience agree that a factual proposition is *usually* true, i.e. where the proposition is of the form ' most *x* is *y* '; the third, assent, where there is no independent reason why a thing should happen one way rather than another, but that it happened the one way is "vouched by the concurrent testimony of unsuspected witnesses". The difficulties arise where the testimony conflicts with experience, or where some testimony conflicts with other testimony. And the most important single factor in an inductive argument is *analogy* (IV xvi 12). Locke's insight here was taken up by Berkeley : "there is a certain analogy, constancy and uniformity in the phenomena or appearances of nature, which are a foundation for general rules" (*Siris* §252); and it has been developed in modern treatments of the problem of induction. Locke did not do more than sketch out the lines on which a theory of probability should be developed, but the lines which he did sketch were eminently sound. Finally he issued a warning, elaborated afterwards by Hume, against the mistake of supposing that believing is something which we *do,* as though we do or could *decide* whether or not to believe a given proposition; instead believing is something we find ourselves doing, or happening to us. All that we can decide or refuse to do is to inquire and search after truth : " a man can no more avoid assenting, or taking it to be true, where he perceives the greater probability, than he can avoid knowing it to be true, where he perceives the agreement or disagreement of any two ideas " (IV xx 16).

Locke may have underrated himself in describing his work in epistemology as that of " an underlabourer in clearing ground a little, and removing some of the rubbish that lies in the way to knowledge" *(Epistle to the Reader* p. 58). But it has been made easier for modern readers to accept him on his own assessment, partly because he was immediately eclipsed, in Berkeley and Hume, by two philosophers of far greater original talent, and partly because so much of what he wrote has, from Berkeley onwards, been so assiduously misinterpreted. It is to be hoped that, by the present edition's reduction of the *Essay* to more manageable proportions, readers may be encouraged to find out for themselves what he actually said, instead of depending heavily on what others say that he said.

7. THE TEXT

During Locke's lifetime the *Essay* ran through four editions, and a French translation which he himself supervised; in each edition, except the third, he made many alterations, mainly by way of addition. At the time of his death he had completed the preparation of a fifth edition, which he expressly wished to be regarded as definitive, and which appeared posthumously in 1706. Fraser's edition of the *Essay* (Oxford, 1894) incorporates many of the successive changes reached by the fourth edition, but contains so many mistakes as to be quite unreliable. The Everyman version by J. W. Yolton (Dent, 1961), while perpetuating a few of Fraser's errors, reproduces the fifth edition far more faithfully.

The text of the present abridgement adheres to that of the fifth edition, except for corrections of obvious misprints, modernisation of spelling and punctuation, and modification of Locke's use of italics. The Table of Contents is printed in full (excluding section headings), the titles of chapters which have been entirely omitted in this edition being enclosed in square brackets. No gaps appear in the text to show where sentences, passages or whole paragraphs have been deleted; Locke's numbering of sections has been retained, and the omission of a complete section is thus indicated by a discontinuity in the sequence of section numbers.

My thanks are due to Professor P. L. Heath, who worked through the whole of my original abridgement and showed me the need to make a number of changes in it; to Dr. P. H. Nidditch who helped me on several matters of scholarship; to Mr. E. R. S. Fifoot, Librarian of Edinburgh University, who placed his library's copy of the fifth edition at my disposal; and to Miss D. Robertson who, besides doing all the typing, assisted me in the correction of proofs.

AN ESSAY CONCERNING HUMAN UNDERSTANDING

THE EPISTLE TO THE READER

Reader,

I here put into thy hands what has been the diversion of some of my idle and heavy hours. If it has the good luck to prove so of any of thine, and thou hast but half so much pleasure in reading as I had in writing it, thou wilt as little think thy money, as I do my pains, ill bestowed. Mistake not this for a commendation of my work; nor conclude, because I was pleased with the doing of it, that therefore I am fondly taken with it now it is done. He that hawks at larks and sparrows has no less sport, though a much less considerable quarry, than he that flies at nobler game : and he is little acquainted with the subject of this treatise, the UNDERSTANDING, who does not know that, as it is the most elevated faculty of the soul, so it is employed with a greater and more constant delight than any of the other. Its searches after truth are a sort of hawking and hunting, wherein the very pursuit makes a great part of the pleasure. Every step the mind takes in its progress towards Knowledge makes some discovery, which is not only new, but the best too, for the time at least.

This, Reader, is the entertainment of those who let loose their own thoughts, and follow them in writing; which thou oughtest not to envy them, since they afford thee an opportunity of the like diversion, if thou wilt make use of thy own thoughts in reading. It is to them, if they are thy own, that I refer myself; but if they are taken upon trust from others, it is no great matter what they are, they not following truth, but some meaner consideration; and it is not worth while to be concerned what he says or thinks who says or thinks only as he is directed by another. If thou judgest for thyself I know thou wilt judge candidly, and then I shall not be harmed or offended, whatever be thy censure. For

though it be certain that there is nothing in this treatise
of the truth whereof I am not fully persuaded, yet I consider
myself as liable to mistakes as I can think thee, and know
that this book must stand or fall with thee, not by any
opinion I have of it, but thy own. If thou findest little in it
new or instructive to thee, thou art not to blame me for it.
It was not meant for those that had already mastered this
subject, and made a thorough acquaintance with their own
understandings; but for my own information, and the satisfaction of a few friends, who acknowledged themselves not to
have sufficiently considered it. Were it fit to trouble thee with
the history of this *Essay,* I should tell thee that five or six
friends, meeting at my chamber and discoursing on a subject
very remote from this, found themselves quickly at a stand, by
the difficulties that rose on every side. After we had awhile
puzzled ourselves, without coming any nearer a resolution of
those doubts which perplexed us, it came into my thoughts that
we took a wrong course; and that before we set ourselves upon
inquiries of that nature, it was necessary to examine our own
abilities, and see what objects our understandings were, or were
not, fitted to deal with. This I proposed to the company, who
all readily assented; and thereupon it was agreed that this
should be our first inquiry. Some hasty and undigested
thoughts, on a subject I had never before considered, which
I set down against our next meeting, gave the first entrance
into this discourse; which having been thus begun by chance,
was continued by entreaty; written by incoherent parcels;
and after long intervals of neglect, resumed again, as my
humour or occasions permitted; and at last, in a retirement
where an attendance on my health gave me leisure, it was
brought into that order thou now seest it.

This discontinued way of writing may have occasioned,
besides others, two contrary faults, viz., that too little and
too much may be said in it. If thou findest anything
wanting, I shall be glad that what I have writ gives thee
any desire that I should have gone further. If it seems too
much to thee, thou must blame the subject; for when I put
pen to paper, I thought all I should have to say on this

matter would have been contained in one sheet of paper; but the further I went the larger prospect I had; new discoveries led me still on, and so it grew insensibly to the bulk it now appears in. I will not deny but possibly it might be reduced to a narrower compass than it is, and that some parts of it might be contracted, the way it has been writ in, by catches, and many long intervals of interruption, being apt to cause some repetitions. But to confess the truth, I am now too lazy, or too busy, to make it shorter.

I am not ignorant how little I herein consult my own reputation, when I knowingly let it go with a fault, so apt to disgust the most judicious, who are always the nicest readers. But they who know sloth is apt to content itself with any excuse will pardon me if mine has prevailed on me, where I think I have a very good one. I will not therefore allege in my defence that the same notion, having different respects, may be convenient or necessary to prove or illustrate several parts of the same discourse, and that so it has happened in many parts of this; but, waiving that, I shall frankly avow that I have sometimes dwelt long upon the same argument, and expressed it different ways, with a quite different design. I pretend not to publish this *Essay* for the information of men of large thoughts and quick apprehensions; to such masters of knowledge I profess myself a scholar, and therefore warn them beforehand not to expect anything here but what, being spun out of my own coarse thoughts, is fitted to men of my own size, to whom, perhaps, it will not be unacceptable that I have taken some pains to make plain and familiar to their thoughts some truths which established prejudice, or the abstractness of the *ideas* themselves, might render difficult. Some objects had need be turned on every side; and when the notion is new, as I confess some of these are to me, or out of the ordinary road, as I suspect they will appear to others, it is not one simple view of it that will gain it admittance into every understanding, or fix it there with a clear and lasting impression. There are few, I believe, who have not observed in themselves or others that what in one way of proposing was very obscure, another way of expressing it has made very clear and intelligible, though afterward the mind found little difference in the phrases, and wondered why one failed to be understood more than the other. But everything does not hit alike upon every man's imagination. We have our understandings no less different than our palates. The truth is, those who advised me to publish it, advised me, for this reason, to publish it as it is; and, since I have been brought to let it go abroad, I desire it should be understood by whoever gives himself the pains to read it. I have so little affection to be in print, that if I were not flattered this *Essay* might be of some use to others, as I think it has been to me, I should have confined it to the view of some friends, who gave the first occasion to it. My appearing therefore in print being on purpose to be as useful as I may, I think it necessary to make what I have to say as easy and intelligible to all sorts of readers as I can. And I had much rather the speculative and quick-sighted should complain of my being in some parts tedious, than that anyone, not accustomed to abstract speculations, or prepossessed with different notions, should mistake or not comprehend my meaning.

It will possibly be censured as a great piece of vanity or insolence in me, to pretend to instruct this our knowing age; it amounting to little less, when I own that I publish this *Essay* with hopes it may be useful to others.

The commonwealth of learning is not at this time without master-builders, whose mighty designs, in advancing the sciences, will leave lasting monuments to the admiration of posterity; but everyone must not hope to be a Boyle or a Sydenham; and in an age that produces such masters as the great Huygenius and the incomparable Mr. Newton, with some other of that strain, it is ambition enough to be employed as an under-labourer in clearing ground a little, and removing some of the rubbish that lies in the way to knowledge; which certainly had been very much more advanced in the world, if the endeavours of ingenious and industrious men had not been much cumbered with the learned but frivolous use of uncouth, affected, or unintelligible terms, introduced into the sciences, and there made an art of, to that degree that philosophy, which is nothing but the true knowledge of things, was thought unfit or incapable to be brought into well-bred company and polite conversation. Vague and insignificant forms of speech, and abuse of language, have so long passed for mysteries of science; and hard and misapplied words, with little or no meaning, have, by prescription, such a right to be mistaken for deep learning and height of speculation, that it will not be easy to persuade either those who speak or those who hear them that they are but the covers of ignorance, and hindrance of true knowledge. To break in upon the sanctuary of vanity and ignorance will be, I suppose, some service to human understanding; though so few are apt to think they deceive or are deceived in the use of words, or that the language of the sect they are of has any faults in it which ought to be examined or corrected, that I hope I shall be pardoned if I have in the Third Book dwelt long on this subject, and endeavoured to make it so plain, that neither the inveterateness of the mischief, nor the prevalency of the fashion, shall be any excuse for those who will not take care about the meaning of their own words, and will not suffer the significancy of their expressions to be inquired into.

The booksellers, preparing for the Fourth Edition of my *Essay*, gave me notice of it, that I might, if I had leisure, make any additions or alterations I should think fit. Whereupon I thought it convenient to advertise the reader that, besides several corrections I had made here and there, there was one alteration which it was necessary to mention, because it ran through the whole book, and is of consequence to be rightly understood. What I thereupon said was this:—

Clear and distinct ideas are terms which, though familiar and frequent in men's mouths, I have reason to think everyone who uses does not perfectly understand. And possibly it is but here and there one who gives himself the trouble to consider them so far as to know what he himself or others precisely mean by them. I have therefore in most places chose to put *determinate* or *determined,* instead of *clear* and *distinct,* as more likely to direct men's thoughts to my meaning in this matter. By those denominations I mean some object in the mind, and consequently *determined,* i.e. such as it is there seen and perceived to be. This, I think, may fitly be called a *determinate* or *determined* idea, when such as it is at any time objectively in the mind, and so *determined* there, it is annexed, and without variation *determined,* to a name or articulate sound, which is to be steadily the sign of that very same object of the mind, or *determinate* idea.

To explain this a little more particularly. By *determinate,* when applied to a simple idea, I mean that simple appearance which the mind has in its view, or perceives in itself, when that idea is said to be in it; by *determined,* when applied to a *complex idea,* I mean such an one as consists of a determinate number of certain simple or less complex ideas, joined in such a proportion and situation as the mind has before its view, and sees in itself, when that idea is present in it, or should be present in it, when a man gives a name to it. I say *should* be, because it is not everyone, nor perhaps anyone, who is so careful of his language as to use no word till he views in his mind the precise *determined* idea which he resolves to make it the sign of. The want of this is the cause of no small obscurity and confusion in men's thoughts and discourses.

I know there are not words enough in any language to answer all the variety of ideas that enter into men's discourses and reasonings. But this hinders not but that when anyone uses any term, he may have in his mind a *determined* idea, which he makes it the sign of, and to which he should keep it steadily annexed during that present discourse. Where he does not, or cannot do this, he in vain pretends to *clear* or *distinct* ideas : it is plain his are not so; and therefore there can be expected nothing but obscurity and confusion, where such terms are made use of which have not such a precise determination.

Upon this ground I have thought *determined* ideas a way

of speaking less liable to mistake, than *clear* and *distinct*; and where men have got such *determined* ideas of all that they reason, inquire, or argue about, they will find a great part of their doubts and disputes at an end; the greatest part of the questions and controversies that perplex mankind depending on the doubtful and uncertain use of words, or (which is the same) *indetermined* ideas, which they are made to stand for. I have made choice of these terms to signify, (1) some immediate object of the mind, which it perceives and has before it, distinct from the sound it uses as a sign of it; (2) that this idea, thus *determined,* i.e. which the mind has in itself and knows and sees there, be *determined* without any change to that name, and that name *determined* to that precise idea. If men had such *determined* ideas in their inquiries and discourses, they would both discern how far their own inquiries and discourses went, and avoid the greatest part of the disputes and wranglings they have with others.

BOOK ONE

OF INNATE NOTIONS

CHAPTER I

INTRODUCTION

1. *An Inquiry into the Understanding pleasant and useful.* Since it is the *understanding* that sets man above the rest of sensible beings, and gives him all the advantage and dominion which he has over them, it is certainly a subject, even for its nobleness, worth our labour to inquire into. The understanding, like the eye, whilst it makes us see and perceive all other things, takes no notice of itself; and it requires art and pains to set it at a distance and make it its own object. But whatever be the difficulties that lie in the way of this inquiry, whatever it be that keeps us so much in the dark to ourselves, sure I am that all the light we can let in upon our own minds, all the acquaintance we can make with our own understandings, will not only be very pleasant, but bring us great advantage, in directing our thoughts in the search of other things.

2. *Design.* This, therefore, being my *purpose*—to inquire into the original, certainty, and extent of *human knowledge, together with the grounds and degrees of belief, opinion, and assent*—I shall not at present meddle with the physical consideration of the mind; or trouble myself to examine wherein its essence consists; or by what motions of our spirits or alterations of our bodies we come to have any *sensation* by our organs, or any *ideas* in our understandings; and whether those ideas do in their formation, any or all of them, depend on matter or no. These are speculations which, however curious and entertaining, I shall decline, as lying out

of my way in the design I am now upon. It shall suffice to my present purpose to consider the discerning faculties of a man, as they are employed about the objects which they have to do with. And I shall imagine I have not wholly misemployed myself in the thoughts I shall have on this occasion, if, in this historical, plain method, I can give any account of the ways whereby our understandings come to attain those notions of things we have, and can set down any measures of the certainty of our knowledge, or the grounds of those persuasions which are to be found amongst men, so various, different, and wholly contradictory; and yet asserted somewhere or other with such assurance and confidence that he that shall take a view of the opinions of mankind, observe their opposition, and at the same time consider the fondness and devotion wherewith they are embraced, the resolution and eagerness wherewith they are maintained, may perhaps have reason to suspect that either there is no such thing as truth at all, or that mankind hath no sufficient means to attain a certain knowledge of it.

3. *Method.* It is therefore worth while to search out the *bounds* between opinion and knowledge, and examine by what measures, in things whereof we have no certain knowledge, we ought to regulate our assent and moderate our persuasions. In order whereunto I shall pursue this following method :—

First, I shall inquire into the *original* of those *ideas,* notions, or whatever else you please to call them, which a man observes, and is conscious to himself he has in his mind; and the ways whereby the understanding comes to be furnished with them.

Secondly, I shall endeavour to show what *knowledge* the understanding hath by those *ideas;* and the certainty, evidence, and extent of it.

Thirdly, I shall make some inquiry into the nature and grounds of *faith* or *opinion* : whereby I mean that assent which we give to any proposition as true, of whose truth yet we have no certain knowledge. And here we shall have occasion to examine the reasons and degrees of *assent.*

4. *Useful to know the Extent of our Comprehension.* If by this inquiry into the nature of the understanding, I

can discover the powers thereof, how far they reach, to what things they are in any degree proportionate, and where they fail us, I suppose it may be of use to prevail with the busy mind of man to be more cautious in meddling with things exceeding its comprehension; to stop when it is at the utmost extent of its tether; and to sit down in a quiet ignorance of those things which, upon examination, are found to be beyond the reach of our capacities. We should not then perhaps be so forward, out of an affectation of an universal knowledge, to raise questions, and perplex ourselves and others with disputes about things to which our understandings are not suited, and of which we cannot frame in our minds any clear or distinct perceptions, or whereof (as it has perhaps too often happened) we have not any notions at all. If we can find out how far the understanding can extend its view, how far it has faculties to attain certainty, and in what cases it can only judge and guess, we may learn to content ourselves with what is attainable by us in this state.

(6.) *Knowledge of our Capacity a Cure of Scepticism and Idleness.* When we know our own strength, we shall the better know what to undertake with hopes of success; and when we have well surveyed the *powers* of our own minds, and made some estimate what we may expect from them, we shall not be inclined either to sit still, and not set our thoughts on work at all, in despair of knowing anything, nor, on the other side, question everything, and disclaim all knowledge, because some things are not to be understood. It is of great use to the sailor to know the length of his line, though he cannot with it fathom all the depths of the ocean. It is well he knows that it is long enough to reach the bottom at such places as are necessary to direct his voyage, and caution him against running upon shoals that may ruin him. Our business here is not to know all things, but those which concern our conduct. If we can find out those measures, whereby a rational creature, put in that state which man is in in this world, may and ought to govern his opinions, and actions depending thereon, we need not to be troubled that some other things escape our knowledge.

7. *Occasion of this Essay.* This was that which gave the first rise to this *Essay* concerning the understanding. For I thought that the first step towards satisfying several inquiries the mind of man was very apt to run into was to take a survey of our own understandings, examine our own powers, and see to what things they were adapted. Till that was done, I suspected we began at the wrong end, and in vain sought for satisfaction in a quiet and sure possession of truths that most concerned us, whilst we let loose our thoughts into the vast ocean of Being, as if all that boundless extent were the natural and undoubted possession of our understandings, wherein there was nothing exempt from its decisions, or that escaped its comprehension. Thus, men extending their inquiries beyond their capacities, and letting their thoughts wander into those depths where they can find no sure footing, it is no wonder that they raise questions and multiply disputes, which, never coming to any clear resolution, are proper only to continue and increase their doubts, and to confirm them at last in perfect scepticism. Whereas, were the capacities of our understandings well considered, the extent of our knowledge once discovered, and the horizon found which sets the bounds between the enlightened and dark parts of things, between what is and what is not comprehensible by us, men would perhaps with less scruple acquiesce in the avowed ignorance of the one, and employ their thoughts and discourse with more advantage and satisfaction in the other.

8. *What Idea stands for.* Thus much I thought necessary to say concerning the occasion of this Inquiry into human understanding. But, before I proceed on to what I have thought on this subject, I must here in the entrance beg pardon of my read for the frequent use of the word '*idea*' which he will find in the following treatise. It being that term which, I think, serves best to stand for whatsoever is the *object* of the understanding when a man thinks, I have used it to express whatever is meant by *phantasm, notion, species,* or *whatever it is which the mind can be employed about in thinking*; and I could not avoid frequently using it.

I presume it will be easily granted me that there are such

ideas in men's minds : everyone is conscious of them in himself; and men's words and actions will satisfy him that they are in others.

Our first inquiry then shall be how they come into the mind.

CHAPTER II

NO INNATE PRINCIPLES IN THE MIND

1. *The way shown how we come by any Knowledge, sufficient to prove it not innate.* It is an established opinion amongst some men that there are in the understanding certain *innate principles,* some primary notions, κοιναì ἔννοιαι, characters, as it were stamped upon the mind of man, which the soul receives in its very first being, and brings into the world with it. It would be sufficient to convince unprejudiced readers of the falseness of this supposition, if I should only show (as I hope I shall in the following parts of this Discourse) how men, barely by the use of their natural faculties, may attain to all the knowledge they have, without the help of any innate impressions, and may arrive at certainty, without any such original notions or principles.

2. *General Assent the great Argument.* There is nothing more commonly taken for granted than that there are certain *principles,* both *speculative* and *practical* (for they speak of both), universally agreed upon by all mankind : which therefore, they argue, must needs be constant impressions which the souls of men receive in their first beings, and which they bring into the world with them, as necessarily and really as they do any of their inherent faculties.

3. *Universal Consent proves nothing innate.* This argument, drawn from universal consent, has this misfortune in it, that, if it were true in matter of fact that there were certain truths wherein all mankind agreed, it would not prove them

innate, if there can be any other way shown how men may come to that universal agreement in the things they do consent in, which I presume may be done.

4. *"What is, is," and " It is impossible for the same Thing to be and not to be" not universally assented to.* But, which is worse, this argument of universal consent, which is made use of to prove innate principles, seems to me a demonstration that there are none such, because there are none to which all mankind give an universal assent. I shall begin with the speculative, and instance in those magnified principles of demonstration, " Whatsoever is, is," and " It is impossible for the same thing to be and not to be," which, of all others, I think have the most allowed title to innate. These have so settled a reputation of maxims universally received that it will no doubt be thought strange if anyone should seem to question it. But yet I take liberty to say that these propositions are so far from having an universal assent, that there are a great part of mankind to whom they are not so much as known.

5. *Not on the Mind naturally imprinted, because not known to Children, Idiots, &c.* For, first, it is evident, that all children and idiots have not the least apprehension or thought of them. And the want of that is enough to destroy that universal assent which must needs be the necessary concomitant of all innate truths; it seeming to me near a contradiction to say, that there are truths imprinted on the soul, which it perceives or understands not : imprinting, if it signify anything, being nothing else but the making certain truths to be perceived. For to imprint anything on the mind without the mind's perceiving it seems to me hardly intelligible. If therefore children and idiots have souls, have minds, with those impressions upon them, they must unavoidably perceive them, and necessarily know and assent to these truths; which since they do not, it is evident that there are no such impressions. For if they are not notions naturally imprinted, how can they be innate? And if they are notions imprinted, how can they be unknown? To say a notion is imprinted on the mind, and yet at the same time to say that the mind is ignorant of it and never yet took notice of it, is to make this

impression nothing. No proposition can be said to be in the mind which it never yet knew, which it was never yet conscious of. For if any one may, then, by the same reason, all propositions that are true, and the mind is capable ever of assenting to, may be said to be in the mind, and to be imprinted; since, if any one can be said to be in the mind, which it never yet knew, it must be only because it is capable of knowing it; and so the mind is of all truths it ever shall know. Nay, thus truths may be imprinted on the mind which it never did, nor ever shall know; for a man may live long, and die at last in ignorance of many truths which his mind was capable of knowing, and that with certainty. So that if the capacity of knowing be the natural impression contended for, all the truths a man ever comes to know will, by this account, be every one of them innate; and this great point will amount to no more, but only to a very improper way of speaking; which, whilst it pretends to assert the contrary, says nothing different from those who deny innate principles. For nobody, I think, ever denied that the mind was capable of knowing several truths. The capacity, they say, is innate, the knowledge acquired. But then to what end such contest for certain innate maxims? If truths can be imprinted on the understanding without being perceived, I can see no difference there can be between any truths the mind is capable of knowing in respect of their original : they must all be innate or all adventitious; in vain shall a man go about to distinguish them.

6. *That men know them when they come to the Use of Reason answered.* To avoid this, it is usually answered that all men know and assent to them, *when they come to the use of reason*; and this is enough to prove them innate.

7. This answer must signify one of these two things : either that as soon as men come to the use of reason these supposed native inscriptions come to be known and observed by them; or else, that the use and exercise of men's reasons assists them in the discovery of these principles, and certainly makes them known to them.

8. *If Reason discovered them, that would not prove them*

innate. If they mean that by the use of reason men may discover these principles, and that this is sufficient to prove them innate, their way of arguing will stand thus, viz. that whatever truths reason can certainly discover to us, and make us firmly assent to, those are all naturally imprinted on the mind; since that universal assent, which is made the mark of them, amounts to no more but this,—that by the use of reason we are capable to come to a certain knowledge of and assent to them; and, by this means, there will be no difference between the maxims of the mathematicians and theorems they deduce from them : all must be equally allowed innate, they being all discoveries made by the use of reason, and truths that a rational creature may certainly come to know, if he apply his thoughts rightly that way.

9. *It is false that Reason discovers them.* But how can these men think the use of reason necessary to discover principles that are supposed innate, when reason (if we may believe them) is nothing else but the faculty of deducing unknown truths from principles or propositions that are already known? That certainly can never be thought innate which we have need of reason to discover, unless, as I have said, we will have all the certain truths that reason ever teaches us to be innate. We may as well think the use of reason necessary to make our eyes discover visible objects, as that there should be need of reason, or the exercise thereof, to make the understanding see what is originally engraven in it, and cannot be in the understanding before it be perceived by it. So that to make reason discover those truths thus imprinted, is to say that the use of reason discovers to a man what he knew before; and if men have those innate impressed truths originally, and before the use of reason, and yet are always ignorant of them till they come to the use of reason, it is in effect to say, that men know and know them not at the same time.

10. It will here perhaps be said that mathematical demonstrations, and other truths that are not innate, are not assented to as soon as proposed, wherein they are distinguished from these maxims and other innate truths. I shall have occasion

to speak of assent upon the first proposing more particularly by and by.[1] I shall here only, and that very readily, allow that these maxims and mathematical demonstrations are in this different : that the one has need of reason, using of proofs, to make them out and to gain our assent; but the other, as soon as understood, are, without any the least reasoning, embraced and assented to.

11. Those who will take the pains to reflect with a little attention on the operations of the understanding will find that this ready assent of the mind to some truths depends not either on native inscription or the use of reason, but on a faculty of the mind quite distinct from both of them, as we shall see hereafter.[2] Reason, therefore, having nothing to do in procuring our assent to these maxims, if by saying that " men know and assent to them, when they come to the use of reason " be meant that the use of reason assists us in the knowledge of these maxims, it is utterly false; and, were it true, would prove them not to be innate.

12. *The coming to the Use of Reason not the time we come to know these Maxims.* If by knowing and assenting to them " when we come to the use of reason " be meant that this is the time when they come to be taken notice of by the mind; and that, as soon as children come to the use of reason, they come also to know and assent to these maxims; this also is false and frivolous. First, it is false, because it is evident these maxims are not in the mind so early as the use of reason; and therefore the coming to the use of reason is falsely assigned as the time of their discovery. How many instances of the use of reason may we observe in children, a long time before they have any knowledge of this maxim, " That it is impossible for the same thing to be and not to be "? And a great part of illiterate people and savages pass many years, even of their rational age, without ever thinking on this and the like general propositions. I grant, men come not to the knowledge of these general and more abstract truths, which are thought innate, till they come to the use of reason; and I

[1] §§ 17-21.
[2] IV ii l; vii 19; xvii 14.

add, nor then neither. Which is so, because, till after they come to the use of reason, those general abstract ideas are not framed in the mind, about which those general maxims are, which are mistaken for innate principles, but are indeed discoveries made and verities introduced and brought into the mind by the same way, and discovered by the same steps, as . several other propositions, which nobody was ever so extravagant as to suppose innate.

14. *If coming to the Use of Reason were the time of their discovery, it would not prove them innate.* But, secondly, were it true that the precise time of their being known and assented to were when men come to the use of reason, neither would that prove them innate. This way of arguing is so frivolous as the supposition of itself is false. For, by what kind of logic will it appear that any notion is originally by nature imprinted in the mind in its first constitution, because it comes first to be observed and assented to when a faculty of the mind, which has quite a distinct province, begins to exert itself?

15. *The Steps by which the Mind attains several Truths.* The senses at first let in *particular* ideas, and furnish the yet empty cabinet, and, the mind by degrees growing familiar with some of them, they are lodged in the memory, and names got to them. Afterwards, the mind proceeding further abstracts them, and by degrees learns the use of general names. In this manner the mind comes to be furnished with ideas and language, the materials about which to exercise its discursive faculty. And the use of reason becomes daily more visible, as these materials that give it employment increase. But, though the having of general ideas and the use of general words and reason usually grow together, yet I see not how this any way proves them innate. The knowledge of some truths,·I confess, is very early in the mind; but in a way that shows them not to be innate. For, if we will observe, we shall find it still to be about ideas, not innate, but acquired; it being about those first which are imprinted by external things, with which infants have earliest to do, which make the most frequent impressions on their senses. In ideas thus got the mind

discovers that some agree and others differ, probably as soon as it has any use of memory, as soon as it is able to retain and receive distinct ideas. But whether it be then or no, this is certain, it does so long before it has the use of words, or comes to that which we commonly call " the use of reason ". For a child knows as certainly before it can speak the difference between the ideas of sweet and bitter (i.e. that sweet is not bitter), as it knows afterwards (when it comes to speak) that wormwood and sugarplums are not the same thing.

16. A child knows not that three and four are equal to seven, till he comes to be able to count to seven, and has got the name and idea of equality; and then, upon explaining those words, he presently assents to, or rather perceives the truth of, that proposition. But neither does he then readily assent because it is an innate truth, nor was his assent wanting till then because he wanted the use of reason; but the truth of it appears to him as soon as he has settled in his mind the clear and distinct ideas that these names stand for. And then he knows the truth of that proposition upon the same grounds and by the same means, that he knew before that a rod and cherry are not the same thing; and upon the same grounds also that he may come to know afterwards " That it is impossible for the same thing to be and not to be ". So that the later it is before anyone comes to have those general ideas about which those maxims are, or to know the signification of those general terms that stand for them, or to put together in his mind the ideas they stand for, the later also will it be before he comes to assent to those maxims;—whose terms, with the ideas they stand for, being no more innate than those of a cat or a weasel, he must stay till time and observation have acquainted him with them; and then he will be in a capacity to know the truth of these maxims, upon the first occasion that shall make him put together those ideas in his mind, and observe whether they agree or disagree, according as is expressed in those propositions.

17. *Assenting as soon as proposed and understood, proves them not innate.* This evasion therefore of general assent when men come to the use of reason, failing as it does, and

leaving no difference between those supposed innate and other truths that are afterwards acquired and learnt, men have endeavoured to secure an universal assent to those they call maxims, by saying they are generally assented to as soon as proposed, and the terms they are proposed in understood; seeing all men, even children, as soon as they hear and understand the terms, assent to these propositions, they think it is sufficient to prove them innate.

18. *If such an Assent be a mark of innate, then " that One and Two are equal to three, that Sweetness is not Bitterness" and a thousand the like, must be innate.* In answer to this I demand whether ready assent given to a proposition, upon first hearing and understanding the terms, be a certain mark of an innate principle? If it be not, such a general assent is in vain urged as a proof of them; if it be said that it is a mark of innate, they must then allow all such propositions to be innate which are generally assented to as soon as heard, whereby they will find themselves plentifully stored with innate principles. For upon the same ground, viz. of assent at first hearing and understanding the terms, that men would have those maxims pass for innate, they must also admit several propositions about numbers to be innate. Even natural philosophy, and all the other sciences, afford propositions which are sure to meet with assent as soon as they are understood. That " two bodies cannot be in the same place " is a truth that nobody any more sticks at than at this maxim, that " it is impossible for the same thing to be and not to be," that " white is not black," that " a square is not a circle," that "yellowness is not sweetness ". But, since no proposition can be innate unless the *ideas* about which it is be innate, this will be to suppose all our ideas of colours, sounds, tastes, figure, &c., innate, than which there cannot be anything more opposite to reason and experience. Universal and ready assent upon hearing and understanding the terms is, I grant, a mark of self-evidence; but self-evidence, depending not on innate impressions but on something else, belongs to several propositions which nobody was yet so extravagant as to pretend to be innate.

19. *Such less general Propositions known before these uni-*

versal Maxims. Nor let it be said that those more particular self-evident propositions, which are assented to at first hearing, as that " one and two are equal to three," that " green is not red," &c., are received as the consequences of those more universal propositions which are looked on as innate principles, since anyone, who will but take the pains to observe what passes in the understanding, will certainly find that these, and the like less general propositions, are certainly known and firmly assented to by those who are utterly ignorant of those more general maxims; and so, being earlier in the mind than those (as they are called) first principles, cannot owe to them the assent wherewith they are received at first hearing.

21. *These Maxims not being known sometimes till proposed, proves them not innate.* Men grow first acquainted with many of these self-evident truths upon their being proposed; but it is clear that whosoever does so finds in himself that he then begins to know a proposition, which he knew not before, and which from thenceforth he never questions, not because it was innate, but because the consideration of the nature of the things contained in those words would not suffer him to think otherwise, how, or whensoever he is brought to reflect on them.

22. *Implicitly known before proposing, signifies that the Mind is capable of understanding them, or else signifies nothing.* If it be said the understanding hath an *implicit* knowledge of these principles, but not an *explicit,* before this first hearing (as they must who will say that they are in the understanding before they are known), it will be hard to conceive what is meant by a principle imprinted on the understanding implicitly, unless it be this,—that the mind is capable of understanding and assenting firmly to such propositions. And thus all mathematical demonstrations, as well as first principles, must be received as native impressions on the mind.

23. *The Argument of assenting on first hearing, is upon a false supposition of no precedent teaching.* There is, I fear, this further weakness in the foregoing argument, that men are supposed not to be taught nor to learn anything *de novo,*

when, in truth, they are taught, and do learn something they were ignorant of before. For, first, it is evident that they have learned the terms, and their signification, neither of which was born with them. But this is not all the acquired knowledge in the case : the ideas themselves, about which the proposition is, are not born with them, no more than their names, but got afterwards. For, though a child quickly assent to this proposition, "that an apple is not fire," when by familiar acquaintance he has got the ideas of those two different things distinctly imprinted on his mind, and has learnt that the names ' apple ' and ' fire ' stand for them, yet it will be some years after, perhaps, before the same child will assent to this proposition, "that it is impossible for the same thing to be and not to be " ; because that, though perhaps the words are as easy to be learnt, yet the signification of them being more large, comprehensive, and abstract than of the names annexed to those sensible things the child hath to do with, it is longer before he learns their precise meaning, and it requires more time plainly to form in his mind those general ideas they stand for.

25. *These Maxims not the first known.*   But that I may not be accused to argue from the thoughts of infants, which are unknown to us, and to conclude from what passes in their understandings before they express it, I say next that these two general propositions are not the truths that first possess the minds of children, nor are antecedent to all acquired and adventitious notions; which, if they were innate, they must needs be. Whether we can determine it or no, it matters not, there is certainly a time when children begin to think, and their words and actions do assure us that they do so. When therefore they are capable of thought, of knowledge, of assent, can it rationally be supposed they can be ignorant of those notions that nature has imprinted, were there any such? The child certainly knows that the nurse that feeds it is neither the cat it plays with, nor the blackamoor it is afraid of, that the wormseed or mustard it refuses is not the apple or sugar it cries for; this it is certainly and undoubtedly assured of; but will anyone say, it is by virtue of this principle, "That it is

impossible for the same thing to be and not to be," that it so firmly assents to these and other parts of its knowledge?

26. *And so not innate.* Though therefore there be several general propositions that meet with constant and ready assent, as soon as proposed to men grown up, who have attained the use of more general and abstract ideas, and names standing for them, yet, they not being to be found in those of tender years, who nevertheless know other things, they cannot pretend to universal assent of intelligent persons, and so by no means can be supposed innate; it being impossible that any truth which is innate (if there were any such) should be unknown, at least to anyone who knows anything else. Since, if they are innate truths, they must be innate thoughts, there being nothing a truth in the mind that it has never thought on. Whereby it is evident, if there be any innate truths, they must necessarily be the first of any thought on, the first that appear there.

27. *Not innate, because they appear least, where what is innate shows itself clearest.* There is this further argument in it against their being innate : that these characters, if they were native and original impressions, should appear fairest and clearest in those persons in whom yet we find no footsteps of them; and it is, in my opinion, a strong presumption that they are not innate, since they are least known to those in whom, if they were innate, they must needs exert themselves with most force and vigour. For children, idiots, savages, and illiterate people, being of all others the least corrupted by custom, or borrowed opinions; learning and education having not cast their native thoughts into new moulds, nor by superinducing foreign and studied doctrines, confounded those fair characters nature had written there; one might reasonably imagine that in *their* minds these innate notions should lie open fairly to everyone's view, as it is certain the thoughts of children do. But he that from a child untaught, or a wild inhabitant of the woods, will expect these abstract maxims and reputed principles of science, will, I fear, find himself mistaken. Such kind of general propositions are seldom mentioned in the huts of Indians; much less are they to be found in the thoughts of children, or any impressions of them on the minds of naturals.

They are the language and business of the schools and academies of learned nations, accustomed to that sort of conversation or learning, where disputes are frequent; these maxims being suited to artificial argumentation and useful for conviction, but not much conducing to the discovery of truth or advancement of knowledge. But of their small use for the improvement of knowledge I shall have occasion to speak more at large, IV vii.

CHAPTER III

NO INNATE PRACTICAL PRINCIPLES

1. *No moral Principles so clear and so generally received as the forementioned speculative Maxims.*   If those speculative Maxims, whereof we discoursed in the foregoing chapter, have not an actual universal assent from all mankind, as we there proved, it is much more visible concerning *practical principles,* that they come short of an universal reception; and I think it will be hard to instance any one moral rule which can pretend to so general and ready an assent as " What is, is ", or to be so manifest a truth as this, that " It is impossible for the same thing to be and not to be ". Whereby it is evident that they are further removed from a title to be innate; and the doubt of their being native impressions on the mind is stronger against these moral principles than the other. Not that it brings their truth at all in question. They are equally true, though not equally evident.

2. *Faith and Justice not owned as Principles by all Men.* Whether there be any such moral principles wherein all men do agree, I appeal to any who have been but moderately conversant in the history of mankind, and looked abroad beyond the smoke of their own chimneys. Where is that practical truth that is universally received, without doubt or question, as it must be if innate? *Justice,* and keeping

of contracts, is that which most men seem to agree in. This is a principle which is thought to extend itself to the dens of thieves, and the confederacies of the greatest villains; and they who have gone furthest towards the putting off of humanity itself keep faith and rules of justice one with another. I grant that outlaws themselves do this one amongst another; but it is without receiving these as the innate laws of nature. They practise them as rules of convenience within their own communities; but it is impossible to conceive that he embraces justice as a practical principle, who acts fairly with his fellow-highwaymen, and at the same time plunders or kills the next honest man he meets with. Justice and truth are the common ties of society; and therefore even outlaws and robbers, who break with all the world besides, must keep faith and rules of equity amongst themselves, or else they cannot hold together. But will anyone say, that those that live by fraud and rapine have innate principles of truth and justice which they allow and assent to?

4. *Moral rules need a Proof,* ergo *not innate.* Another reason that makes me doubt of any innate practical principles is that I think *there cannot any one moral rule be proposed whereof a man may not justly demand a reason*: which would be perfectly ridiculous and absurd if they were innate, or so much as self-evident, which every innate principle must needs be, and not need any proof to ascertain its truth, nor want any reason to gain it approbation. He would be thought void of common sense who asked on the one side, or on the other side went to give a reason why " it is impossible for the same thing to be and not to be ". It carries its own light and evidence with it, and needs no other proof; he that understands the terms assents to it for its own sake or else nothing will ever be able to prevail with him to do it. But should that most unshaken rule of morality and foundation of all social virtue, " That one should do as he would be done unto," be proposed to one who never heard it before, but yet is of capacity to understand its meaning, might he not without any absurdity ask a reason why?

6. *Virtue generally approved, not because innate, but because*

profitable. Hence naturally flows the great variety of opinions concerning moral rules which are to be found amongst men, according to the different sorts of happiness they have a prospect of, or propose to themselves; which could not be if practical principles were innate, and imprinted in our minds immediately by the hand of God. I grant the existence of God is so many ways manifest, and the obedience we owe him so congruous to the light of reason, that a great part of mankind give testimony to the law of nature; but yet I think it must be allowed that several moral rules may receive from mankind a very general approbation, without either knowing or admitting the true ground of morality; which can only be the will and law of a God, who sees men in the dark, has in his hand rewards and punishments, and power enough to call to account the proudest offender.

7. *Men's Actions convince us, that the Rule of Virtue is not their internal Principle.* If we will not in civility allow too much sincerity to the professions of most men, but think their actions to be the interpreters of their thoughts, we shall find that they have no such internal veneration for these rules, nor so full a persuasion of their certainty and obligation.

10. *Men have contrary practical Principles.* He that will carefully peruse the history of mankind, and look abroad into the several tribes of men, and with indifferency survey their actions, will be able to satisfy himself that there is scarce that principle of morality to be named, or rule of virtue to be thought on (those only excepted that are absolutely necessary to hold society together, which commonly too are neglected betwixt distinct societies), which is not, somewhere or other, slighted and condemned by the general fashion of whole societies of men, governed by practical opinions and rules of living quite opposite to others.

11. *Whole Nations reject several Moral Rules.* Here perhaps it will be objected that it is no argument that the rule is not known because it is broken. I grant the objection good where men, though they transgress, yet disown not the law, where fear of shame, censure, or punishment carries the mark of some awe it has upon them. But it is impossible

to conceive that a whole nation of men should all publicly reject and renounce what every one of them certainly and infallibly knew to be a law; for so they must who have it naturally imprinted on their minds.

12. The breaking of a rule, say you, is no argument that it is unknown. I grant it : but the generally allowed breach of it anywhere, I say, is a proof that it is not innate. For example, let us take any of these rules, which, being the most obvious deductions of human reason, and conformable to the natural inclination of the greatest part of men, fewest people have had the impudence to deny or inconsideration to doubt of. When, therefore, you say that this is an innate rule, what do you mean? Either that it is an innate principle which upon all occasions excites and directs the actions of all men, or else, that it is a truth which all men have imprinted on their minds, and which therefore they know and assent to. But in neither of these senses is it innate.

13. From what has been said I think we may safely conclude that whatever practical rule is in any place generally and with allowance broken, cannot be supposed innate.

14. *Those who maintain innate practical Principles tell us not what they are.* The difference there is amongst men in their practical principles is so evident that I think I need say no more to evince that it will be impossible to find any innate moral rules by this mark of general assent; and it is enough to make one suspect that the supposition of such innate principles is but an opinion taken up at pleasure, since those who talk so confidently of them are so sparing to tell us *which they are.*

20. *Objection, Innate Principles may be corrupted, answered.* Nor will it be of much moment here to offer that very ready but not very material answer, viz. that the innate principles of morality may, by education, and custom, and the general opinion of those amongst whom we converse, be darkened, and at last quite worn out of the minds of men. Which assertion of theirs, if true, quite takes away the argument of universal consent by which this opinion of innate principles is endeavoured to be proved; unless those men will think it reasonable that their private persuasions, or that of

their party, should pass for universal consent, a thing not infrequently done, when men, presuming themselves to be the only masters of right reason, cast by the votes and opinions of the rest of mankind as not worthy the reckoning. And then their argument stands thus : " The principles which all mankind allow for true are innate; those that men of right reason admit are the principles allowed by all mankind; we, and those of our mind, are men of reason; therefore, we agreeing, our principles are innate"; which is a very pretty way of arguing, and a short cut to infallibility.

21. *Contrary Principles in the World.* I easily grant that there are great numbers of opinions which, by men of different countries, educations, and tempers, are received and embraced as first and unquestionable principles; many whereof, both for their absurdity as well as opposition one to another, it is impossible should be true. But yet all those propositions, how remote soever from reason, are so sacred somewhere or other that men even of good understanding in other matters will sooner part with their lives, and whatever is dearest to them, than suffer themselves to doubt, or others to question, the truth of them.

22. *How men commonly come by their Principles.* This, however strange it may seem, is that which every day's experience confirms; and will not, perhaps, appear so wonderful, if we consider the ways and steps by which it is brought about, and how really it may come to pass, that doctrines that have been derived from no better original than the superstition of a nurse, or the authority of an old woman, may, by length of time and consent of neighbours, grow up to the dignity of *principles* in religion or morality.

24. There is scarce anyone so floating and superficial in his understanding, who hath not some reverenced propositions, which are to him the principles on which he bottoms his reasonings, and by which he judgeth of truth and falsehood, right and wrong; which some, wanting skill and leisure, and others the inclination, and some being taught that they ought not to examine, there are few to be found who are not exposed

by their ignorance, laziness, education, or precipitancy, to *take them upon trust.*

27. *Principles must be examined.*   By this progress, how many there are who arrive at principles which they believe innate may be easily observed in the variety of opposite principles held and contended for by all sorts and degrees of men. And he that shall deny this to be the method wherein most men proceed to the assurance they have of the truth and evidence of their principles will perhaps find it a hard matter any other way to account for the contrary tenets, which are firmly believed, confidently asserted, and which great numbers are ready at any time to seal with their blood. From what has been said, I think it past doubt that there are no practical principles wherein all men agree, and therefore none innate.

CHAPTER IV

OTHER CONSIDERATIONS
CONCERNING INNATE PRINCIPLES,
BOTH SPECULATIVE AND PRACTICAL

1. *Principles not innate, unless their Ideas be innate.*   Had those who would persuade us that there are innate principles not taken them together in gross, but considered separately the parts out of which those propositions are made, they would not, perhaps, have been so forward to believe they were innate. Since, if the *ideas* which made up those truths were not, it was impossible that the *propositions* made up of them should be innate, or our knowledge of them be born with us. For, if the ideas be not innate, there was a time when the mind was without those principles; and then they will not be innate, but be derived from some other original. For, where the ideas themselves are not, there can be no knowledge, no assent, no mental or verbal propositions about them.

2. *Ideas, especially those belonging to Principles, not born with Children.*   If we will attentively consider new-born

children, we shall have little reason to think that they bring many ideas into the world with them. For, bating perhaps some faint ideas of hunger, and thirst; and warmth, and some pains, which they may have felt in the womb, there is not the least appearance of any settled ideas at all in them, especially of *ideas answering the terms which make up those universal propositions that are esteemed innate principles.* One may perceive how, by degrees, afterwards, ideas come into their minds, and that they get no more, nor no other, than what experience, and the observation of things that come in their way, furnish them with; which might be enough to satisfy us that they are not original characters stamped on the mind.

8. *Idea of God not innate.* If any idea can be imagined innate, the idea of *God* may, of all others, for many reasons, be thought so, since it is hard to conceive how there should be innate moral principles, without an innate idea of a Deity. Without a notion of a law-maker it is impossible to have a notion of a law and an obligation to observe it. Besides the atheists taken notice of amongst the ancients, and left branded upon the records of history, hath not navigation discovered, in these latter ages, whole nations amongst whom there was to be found no notion of a God, no religion? These are instances of nations where uncultivated nature has been left to itself without the help of letters and discipline, and the improvements of arts and sciences. But there are others to be found who have enjoyed these in a very great measure, who yet, for want of a due application of their thoughts this way, want the idea and knowledge of God.

9. But had all mankind everywhere a notion of a God (whereof yet history tells us the contrary), it would not from thence follow that the idea of him was innate. For, though no nation were to be found without a name and some few dark notions of him, yet that would not prove them to be natural impressions on the mind, no more than the names of fire, or the sun, heat, or number, do prove the ideas they stand for to be innate, because the names of those things, and the ideas of them, are so universally received and known amongst mankind. For, men being furnished with words by

the common language of their own countries can scarce avoid having some kind of ideas of those things whose names those they converse with have occasion frequently to mention to them.

13. *Ideas of God various in different men.* I grant that, if there were any ideas to be found imprinted on the minds of men, we have reason to expect it should be the notion of his Maker, as a mark God set on his own workmanship, to mind man of his dependence and duty, and that herein should appear the first instances of human knowledge. But how late is it before any such notion is discoverable in children? And when we find it there, how much more does it resemble the opinion and notion of the teacher than represent the true God? He that shall observe in children the progress whereby their minds attain the knowledge they have, will think that the objects they do first and most familiarly converse with are those that make the first impressions on their understandings, nor will he find the least footsteps of any other. It is easy to take notice how their thoughts enlarge themselves only as they come to be acquainted with a greater variety of sensible objects, to retain the ideas of them in their memories, and to get the skill to compound and enlarge them, and several ways put them together. How, by these means, they come to frame in their minds an idea men have of a Deity, I shall hereafter show.[1]

14. Can it be thought that the ideas men have of God are the characters and marks of himself, engraven in their minds by his own finger, when we see that, in the same country, under one and the same name, men have far different, nay often contrary, and inconsistent ideas and conceptions of him? Their agreeing in a name, or sound, will scarce prove an innate notion of him.

19. *Idea of Substance not innate.* I confess there is another idea which would be of general use for mankind to have, as it is of general talk as if they had it; and that is the idea of *substance,* which we neither have nor can have by sensation or reflection. If nature took care to provide us any ideas, we

[1] II xxiii 33; IV x

might well expect it should be such as by our own faculties we cannot procure to ourselves; but we see, on the contrary, that since, by those ways whereby other ideas are brought into our minds, this is not, we have no such *clear idea* at all; and therefore signify nothing by the word ' substance ' but only an uncertain supposition of we know not what, i.e. of something whereof we have no particular distinct positive idea, which we take to be the *substratum,* or support, of those ideas we do know.

21. *No innate ideas in the Memory.* To which let me add : if there be any innate ideas, any ideas in the mind which the mind does not actually think on, they must be lodged in the memory, and from thence must be brought into view by remembrance, i.e. must be known, when they are remembered, to have been perceptions in the mind before, unless remembrance can be without remembrance. For, to remember is to perceive anything with memory, or with a consciousness that it was known or perceived before. Without this, whatever idea comes into the mind is new, and not remembered; this consciousness of its having been in the mind before being that which distinguishes remembering from all other ways of thinking. Whatever idea was never perceived by the mind was never in the mind. Whatever idea is in the mind is either an actual perception or else, having been an actual perception, is so in the mind that by the memory it can be made an actual perception again. Whenever there is the actual perception of an idea without memory, the idea appears perfectly new and unknown before to the understanding. Whenever the memory brings any idea into actual view, it is with a consciousness that it had been there before, and was not wholly a stranger to the mind. Whether this be not so I appeal to everyone's observation. And then I desire an instance of an idea, pretended to be innate, which (before any impression of it by ways hereafter to be mentioned) anyone could revive and remember, as an idea he had formerly known, without which consciousness of a former perception there is no remembrance; and whatever idea comes into the mind without that consciousness is not remembered, or comes not out of the memory,

nor can be said to be in the mind before that appearance. For what is not either actually in view or in the memory is in the mind no way at all, and is all one as if it had never been there.

25. *Whence the Opinion of innate Principles.*   When men have found some general propositions that could not be doubted of as soon as understood, it was, I know, a short and easy way to conclude them innate. This being once received, it eased the lazy from the pains of search, and stopped the inquiry of the doubtful concerning all that was once styled innate. And it was of no small advantage to those who affected to be masters and teachers, to make this the principle of principles,—*that principles must not be questioned.* For, having once established this tenet, that there are innate principles, it put their followers upon a necessity of receiving some doctrines as such; which was to take them off from the use of their own reason and judgment, and put them upon believing and taking them upon trust without further examination; in which posture of blind credulity they might be more easily governed by, and made useful to some sort of men, who had the skill and office to principle and guide them. Nor is it a small power it gives one man over another, to have the authority to be the dictator of principles, and teacher of unquestionable truths, and to make a man swallow that for an innate principle which may serve to his purpose who teacheth them. Whereas had they examined the ways whereby men came to the knowledge of many universal truths, they would have found them to result in the minds of men from the being of things themselves, when duly considered; and that they were discovered by the application of those faculties that were fitted by nature to receive and judge of them, when duly employed about them.

26. *Conclusion.*   To show how the understanding proceeds herein is the design of the following Discourse; which I shall proceed to when I have first premised, that hitherto, to clear my way to those foundations which I conceive are the only true ones whereon to establish those notions we can have of our own knowledge, it hath been necessary for me to give an

account of the reasons I had to doubt of innate principles. And since the arguments which are against them do, some of them, rise from common received opinions, I have been forced to take several things for granted; which is hardly avoidable to anyone, whose task it is to show the falsehood or improbability of any tenet; it happening in controversial discourses as it does in assaulting of towns, where, if the ground be but firm whereon the batteries are erected, there is no further inquiry of whom it is borrowed, nor whom it belongs to, so it affords but a fit rise for the present purpose. But in the future part of this Discourse, designing to raise an edifice uniform and consistent with itself, as far as my own experience and observation will assist me, I hope to erect it on such a basis that I shall not need to shore it up with props and buttresses, leaning on borrowed or begged foundations; or at least, if mine prove a castle in the air, I will endeavour it shall be all of a piece and hang together.

BOOK TWO

OF IDEAS

CHAPTER I

OF IDEAS IN GENERAL, AND
THEIR ORIGINAL

1. *Idea is the Object of Thinking.* Every man being conscious to himself that he thinks, and that which his mind is applied about whilst thinking being the *ideas* that are there, it is past doubt that men have in their minds several ideas, such as are those expressed by the words 'whiteness', 'hardness', 'sweetness', 'thinking', 'motion', 'man', 'elephant', 'army', 'drunkenness', and others: it is in the first place then to be inquired, How he come by them?

I know it is a received doctrine that men have native ideas, and original characters stamped upon their minds in their very first being. This opinion I have at large examined already; and, I suppose what I have said in the foregoing Book will be much more easily admitted, when I have shown whence the understanding may get all the ideas it has, and by what ways and degrees they may come into the mind; for which I shall appeal to everyone's own observation and experience.

2. *All Ideas come from Sensation or Reflection.* Let us then suppose the mind to be, as we say, white paper, void of all characters, without any ideas; how comes it to be furnished? Whence comes it by that vast store which the busy and boundless fancy of man has painted on it with an almost endless variety? Whence has it all the materials of reason and knowledge? To this I answer, in one word, from *experience.* In that all our knowledge is founded, and from that it ultimately derives itself. Our observation employed either

89

about external sensible objects, or about the internal operations of our minds perceived and reflected on by ourselves, is that which supplies our understandings with all the materials of thinking. These two are the fountains of knowledge, from whence all the ideas we have, or can naturally have, do spring.

3. *The Objects of Sensation one Source of Ideas.* First, our senses, conversant about particular sensible objects, do convey into the mind several distinct perceptions of things, according to those various ways wherein those objects do affect them. And thus we come by those *ideas* we have of *yellow, white, heat, cold, soft, hard, bitter, sweet,* and all those which we call sensible qualities; which when I say the senses convey into the mind, I mean, they from external objects convey into the mind what produces there those perceptions. This great source of most of the ideas we have, depending wholly upon our senses, and derived by them to the understanding, I call SENSATION.

4. *The Operations of our Minds, the other Source of them.* Secondly, the other fountain from which experience furnisheth the understanding with ideas is the perception of the operations of our own mind within us, as it is employed about the ideas it has got; which operations, when the soul comes to reflect on and consider, do furnish the understanding with another set of ideas, which could not be had from things without. And such are *perception, thinking, doubting, believing, reasoning, knowing, willing,* and all the different actings of our own minds; which we being conscious of, and observing in ourselves, do from these receive into our understandings as distinct ideas as we do from bodies affecting our senses. This source of ideas every man has wholly in himself; and though it be not sense, as having nothing to do with external objects, yet it is very like it, and might properly enough be called internal sense. But as I call the other sensation, so I call this REFLECTION, the ideas it affords being such only as the mind gets by reflecting on its own operations within itself. By 'reflection' then, in the following part of this discourse, I would be understood to mean that notice which the mind takes of its own operations, and the manner of them, by reason whereof there come to be ideas of these operations in the understanding. These two, I

say, viz. external material things, as the objects of SENSATION, and the operations of our own minds within, as the objects of REFLECTION, are to me the only originals from whence all our ideas take their beginnings. The term 'operations' here I use in a large sense, as comprehending not barely the actions of the mind about its ideas, but some sort of passions arising sometimes from them, such as is the satisfaction or uneasiness arising from any thought.

⑤ *All our Ideas are of the one or the other of these.* The understanding seems to me not to have the least glimmering of any ideas which it doth not receive from one of these two. *External objects* furnish the mind with the ideas of sensible qualities, which are all those different perceptions they produce in us; and *the mind* furnishes the understanding with ideas of its own operations.

These, when we have taken a full survey of them, and their several modes, combinations, and relations, we shall find to contain all our whole stock of ideas; and that we have nothing in our minds which did not come in one of these two ways. Let anyone examine his own thoughts, and thoroughly search into his understanding; and then let him tell me whether all the original ideas he has there are any other than of the objects of his senses, or of the operations of his mind, considered as objects of his reflection. And how great a mass of knowledge soever he imagines to be lodged there, he will, upon taking a strict view, see that he has not any idea in his mind but what one of these two have imprinted, though perhaps, with infinite variety compounded and enlarged by the understanding, as we shall see hereafter.[1]

⑥ *Observable in Children.* He that attentively considers the state of a child at his first coming into the world will have little reason to think him stored with plenty of ideas, that are to be the matter of his future knowledge. It is by degrees he comes to be furnished with them. And though the ideas of obvious and familiar qualities imprint themselves before the memory begins to keep a register of time and order, yet it is often so late before some unusual qualities come in the way,

[1] II. xii-xxviii.

that there are few men that cannot recollect the beginning of their acquaintance with them. And if it were worth while, no doubt a child might be so ordered as to have but a very few, even of the ordinary ideas, till he were grown up to a man. But all that are born into the world, being surrounded with bodies that perpetually and diversely affect them, variety of ideas, whether care be taken about it or no, are imprinted on the minds of children. Light and colours are busy at hand everywhere, when the eye is but open; sounds and some tangible qualities fail not to solicit their proper senses, and force an entrance to the mind; but yet, I think, it will be granted easily that, if a child were kept in a place where he never saw any other but black and white till he were a man, he would have no more ideas of scarlet or green, than he that from his childhood never tasted an oyster, or a pine-apple, has of those particular relishes.

7. *Men are differently furnished with these, according to the different Objects they converse with.* Men then come to be furnished with fewer or more simple ideas from without, according as the objects they converse with afford greater or less variety; and from the operations of their minds within, according as they more or less reflect on them. For, though he that contemplates the operations of his mind cannot but have plain and clear ideas of them; yet, unless he turn his thoughts that way, and considers them *attentively,* he will no more have clear and distinct ideas of all the operations of his mind, and all that may be observed therein, than he will have all the particular ideas of any landscape, or of the parts and motions of a clock, who will not turn his eyes to it, and with attention heed all the parts of it.

8. *Ideas of Reflection later, because they need Attention.* And hence we see the reason why it is pretty late before most children get ideas of the operations of their own minds; and some have not any very clear or perfect ideas of the greatest part of them all their lives. Because, though they pass there continually, yet, like floating visions, they make not deep impressions enough to leave in the mind clear, distinct, lasting ideas, till the understanding turns inward

upon itself, reflects on its own operations, and makes them the object of its own contemplation. The first years are usually employed and diverted in looking abroad. Men's business in them is to acquaint themselves with what is to be found without; and so growing up in a constant attention to outward sensations, seldom make any considerable reflection on what passes within them, till they come to be of riper years; and some scarce ever at all.

9. *The soul begins to have Ideas when it begins to perceive.* To ask at what time a man has first any ideas is to ask when he begins to perceive; having ideas and perception being the same thing. I know it is an opinion that the soul always thinks, and that it has the actual perception of ideas in itself constantly, as long as it exists; and that actual thinking is as inseparable from the soul as actual extension is from the body; which if true, to inquire after the beginning of a man's ideas is the same as to inquire after the beginning of his soul. For, by this account, soul and its ideas, as body and its extension, will begin to exist both at the same time.

10. *The Soul thinks not always; for this wants Proofs.* But whether the soul be supposed to exist antecedent to, or coeval with, or some time after the first rudiments of organization, or the beginnings of life in the body, I leave to be disputed by those who have better thought of that matter. I confess myself to have one of those dull souls, that doth not perceive itself always to contemplate ideas; nor can conceive it any more necessary for the soul always to think, than for the body always to move; the perception of ideas being (as I conceive) to the soul, what motion is to the body, not its essence, but one of its operations. And therefore, though thinking be supposed never so much the proper action of the soul, yet it is not necessary to suppose that it should be always thinking, always in action. That, perhaps, is the privilege of the infinite Author and Preserver of things, *who never slumbers nor sleeps*; but is not competent to any finite being, at least not to the soul of man. We know certainly, by experience, that we sometimes think; and thence draw this infallible consequence, that there is something in us that has a

power to think. But whether that substance perpetually thinks or no, we can be no further assured than experience informs us. For, to say that actual thinking is essential to the soul, and inseparable from it, is to beg what is in question, and not to prove it by reason; which is necessary to be done, if it be not a self-evident proposition. But whether this, " That the soul always thinks ", be a self-evident proposition, that everybody assents to at first hearing, I appeal to mankind. It is doubted whether I thought all last night or no. The question being about a matter of fact, it is begging it to bring, as a proof for it, an hypothesis, which is the very thing in dispute; which way of proving amounts to this, that I must necessarily think all last night, because another supposes I always think, though I myself cannot perceive that I always do so. I do not say there is no soul in a man, because he is not sensible of it in his sleep; but I do say he cannot think at any time, waking or sleeping, without being sensible of it. Our being sensible of it is not necessary to anything but to our thoughts; and to them it is, and to them it will always be necessary, till we can think without being conscious of it.

11. *It is not always conscious of it.* I grant that the soul, in a waking man, is never without thought, because it is the condition of being awake. But whether sleeping without dreaming be not an affection of the whole man, mind as well as body, may be worth a waking man's consideration; it being hard to conceive that anything should think and not be conscious of it. If the soul doth think in a sleeping man without being conscious of it, I ask whether during such thinking it has any pleasure or pain, or be capable of happiness or misery? I am sure the man is not, no more than the bed or earth he lies on. For to be happy or miserable without being conscious of it seems to me utterly inconsistent and impossible.

13. *Impossible to convince those that sleep without dreaming that they think.* Thus, methinks, every drowsy nod shakes their doctrine, who teach that the soul is always thinking. Those, at least, who do at any time sleep without dreaming can never be convinced that their thoughts are sometimes for four hours busy without their knowing of it; and

if they are taken in the very act, waked in the middle of that
sleeping contemplation, can give no manner of account of it.

14. *That Men dream without remembering it, in vain
urged.* It will perhaps be said that the soul thinks even
in the soundest sleep, but the *memory* retains it not. That
the soul in a sleeping man should be this moment busy a-
thinking, and the next moment in a waking man not remember
nor be able to recollect one jot of all those thoughts, is very
hard to be conceived, and would need some better proof than
bare assertion to make it be believed. For who can without any
more ado, but being barely told so, imagine that the greatest
part of men do, during all their lives, for several hours every
day, think of something, which if they were asked, even in the
middle of these thoughts, they could remember nothing at all
of?

16. *On this Hypothesis, the Soul must have Ideas not
derived from Sensation or Reflection, of which there is no
appearance.* It is true, we have sometimes instances of
perception whilst we are asleep, and retain the memory of those
thoughts; but how extravagant and incoherent for the most part
they are, how little conformable to the perfection and order of
a rational being, those who are acquainted with dreams need
not be told. This I would willingly be satisfied in : whether
the soul, when it thinks thus apart, and as it were separate
from the body, acts less rationally than when conjointly with
it, or no. If its separate thoughts be less rational, then these
men must say that the soul owes the perfection of rational
thinking to the body; if it does not, it is a wonder that our
dreams should be, for the most part, so frivolous and irrational,
and that the soul should retain none of its more rational
soliloquies and meditations.

17. *If I think when I know it not, nobody else can know it.*
Those who so confidently tell us that the soul always actually
thinks, I would they would also tell us what those ideas
are that are in the soul of a child before or just at the union
with the body, before it hath received any by sensation.
The dreams of sleeping men are, as I take it, all made up of
the waking man's ideas, though for the most part oddly put

together. It is strange, if the soul has ideas of its own that it derived not from sensation or reflection (as it must have, if it thought before it received any impressions from the body), that it should never, in its private thinking (so private, that the man himself perceives it not), retain any of them the very moment it wakes out of them, and then make the man glad with new discoveries.

18. *How knows anyone that the Soul always thinks? For if it be not a self-evident Proposition, it needs proof.* I would be glad also to learn from these men who so confidently pronounce that the human soul, or, which is all one, that a man always thinks, how they come to know it; nay, how they come to know that they themselves think, when they themselves do not perceive it. This, I am afraid, is to be sure without proofs, and to know without perceiving.

19. *That a Man should be busy in thinking, and yet not retain it the next moment, very improbable.* To suppose the soul to think, and the man not to perceive it, is to make two persons in one man. And if one considers well these men's way of speaking, one should be led into a suspicion that they do so. For they who tell us that the *soul* always thinks, do never, that I remember, say that a *man* always thinks. Can the soul think, and not the man? Or a man think, and not be conscious of it? This, perhaps, would be suspected of jargon in others. They who talk thus may, with as much reason, if it be necessary to their hypothesis, say that a man is always hungry, but that he does not always feel it; whereas hunger consists in that very sensation, as thinking consists in being conscious that one thinks. If they say that a man is always conscious to himself of thinking. I ask how they know it. Consciousness is the perception of what passes in a man's own mind. Can another man perceive that I am conscious of anything, when I perceive it not myself? They must needs have a penetrating sight who can certainly see that I think, when I cannot perceive it myself, and when I declare that I do not; and yet can see that dogs or elephants do not think, when they give all the demonstration of it imaginable, except only telling us that they do so.

20) *No Ideas but from Sensation, Reflection, evident, if we observe Children.* I see no reason, therefore, to believe that the soul thinks before the senses have furnished it with ideas to think on; and, as those are increased and retained, so it comes, by exercise, to improve its faculty of thinking in the several parts of it; as well as, afterwards, by compounding those ideas, and reflecting on its own operations, it increases its stock, as well as facility in remembering, imagining, reasoning, and other modes of thinking.

22) Follow a child from its birth, and observe the alterations that time makes, and you shall find, as the mind by the senses comes more and more to be furnished with ideas, it comes to be more and more awake; thinks more, the more it has matter to think on. After some time it begins to know the objects which, being most familiar with it, have made lasting impressions. Thus it comes by degrees to know the persons it daily converses with, and distinguish them from strangers; which are instances and effects of its coming to retain and distinguish the ideas the senses convey to it. And so we may observe how the mind by degrees improves in these; and advances to the exercise of those other faculties of enlarging, compounding, and abstracting its ideas, and of reasoning about them, and reflecting upon all these; of which I shall have occasion to speak more hereafter.

23) If it shall be demanded then, when a man begins to have any ideas, I think the true answer is when he first has any sensation. For, since there appear not to be any ideas in the mind before the senses have conveyed any in, I conceive that ideas in the understanding are coeval with *sensation; which is such an impression or motion made in some part of the body, as produces some perception in the understanding.* It is about these impressions made on our senses by outward objects that the mind seems first to employ itself in such operations as we call perception, remembering, consideration, reasoning, &c.

24. *The Original of all our Knowledge.* In time the mind comes to reflect on its own operations about the ideas got by sensation, and thereby stores itself with a new set of ideas,

which I call ideas of reflection. These are the impressions that are made on our senses by outward objects that are extrinsical to the mind; and its own operations, proceeding from powers intrinsical and proper to itself, which, when reflected on by itself, become also objects of its contemplation, are, as I have said, the original of all knowledge. Thus the first capacity of human intellect is that the mind is fitted to receive the impressions made on it, either through the senses by outward objects, or by its own operations when it reflects on them. This is the first step a man makes towards the discovery of anything, and the groundwork whereon to build all those notions which ever he shall have naturally in this world. All those sublime thoughts which tower above the clouds, and reach as high as heaven itself, take their rise and footing here; in all that great extent wherein the mind wanders, in those remote speculations it may seem to be elevated with, it stirs not one jot beyond those *ideas* which *sense* or *reflection* have offered for its contemplation.

25. *In the Reception of simple Ideas, the Understanding is for the most part passive*. In this part the understanding is merely passive; and whether or no it will have these beginnings, and as it were materials of knowledge, is not in its own power. For the objects of our senses do, many of them, obtrude their particular ideas upon our minds whether we will or no; and the operations of our minds will not let us be without, at least, some obscure notions of them. No man can be wholly ignorant of what he does when he thinks. These simple ideas, when offered to the mind, the understanding can no more refuse to have, nor alter when they are imprinted, nor blot them out and make new ones itself, than a mirror can refuse, alter, or obliterate the images or ideas which the objects set before it do therein produce. As the bodies that surround us do diversely affect our organs, the mind is forced to receive the impressions; and cannot avoid the perception of those ideas that are annexed to them.

CHAPTER II

OF SIMPLE IDEAS

(1) *Uncompounded Appearances.* The better to understand the nature, manner, and extent of our knowledge, one thing is carefully to be observed concerning the ideas we have; and that is, that some of them are *simple* and some *complex.*

Though the qualities that affect our senses are, in the things themselves, so united and blended that there is no separation, no distance between them, yet it is plain, the ideas they produce in the mind enter by the senses simple and unmixed. For, though the sight and touch often take in from the same object, at the same time, different ideas, as a man sees at once motion and colour, the hand feels softness and warmth in the same piece of wax; yet the simple ideas thus united in the same subject are as perfectly distinct as those that come in by different senses. The coldness and hardness which a man feels in a piece of ice being as distinct ideas in the mind as the smell and whiteness of a lily, or as the taste of sugar, and smell of a rose. And there is nothing can be plainer to a man than the clear and distinct perception he has of those simple ideas; which, being each in itself uncompounded, contains in it nothing but *one uniform appearance, or conception in the mind,* and is not distinguishable into different ideas.

(2) *The mind can neither make nor destroy them.* These simple ideas, the materials of all our knowledge, are suggested and furnished to the mind only by those two ways above mentioned, viz. sensation and reflection. When the understanding is once stored with these simple ideas, it has the power to repeat, compare, and unite them, even to an almost infinite variety, and so can make at pleasure new complex ideas. But it is not in the power of the most exalted wit, or enlarged understanding, by any quickness or variety of thought, to

invent or *frame* one new simple idea in the mind, not taken in by the ways before mentioned : nor can any force of the understanding *destroy* those that are there. I would have anyone try to fancy any taste which had never affected his palate, or frame the idea of a scent he had never smelt : and when he can do this, I will also conclude that a blind man hath ideas of colours, and a deaf man true distinct notions of sounds.

③ This is the reason why I think it is not possible for anyone to imagine any other qualities in bodies, howsoever constituted, whereby they can be taken notice of, besides sounds, tastes, smells, visible and tangible qualities. And had mankind been made with but four senses, the qualities then which are the objects of the fifth sense had been as far from our notice, imagination, and conception, as now any belonging to a sixth, seventh, or eighth sense can possibly be; which, whether yet some other creatures, in some other parts of this vast and stupendous universe, may not have, will be a great presumption to deny. He that will not set himself proudly at the top of all things, but will consider the immensity of this fabric, and the great variety that is to be found in this little and inconsiderable part of it which he has to do with, may be apt to think that in other mansions of it there may be other and different intelligent beings, of whose faculties he has as little knowledge or apprehension as a worm shut up in one drawer of a cabinet hath of the senses or understanding of a man, such variety and excellency being suitable to the wisdom and power of the Maker. I have here followed the common opinion of man's having but five senses, though, perhaps, there may be justly counted more; but either supposition serves equally to my present purpose.

CHAPTER III

OF IDEAS OF ONE SENSE

1. *Division of simple Ideas.* The better to conceive the ideas we receive from sensation, it may not be amiss for us to consider them, in reference to the different ways whereby they make their approaches to our minds, and make themselves perceivable by us.

First, then, There are some which come into our minds *by one sense only.*

Secondly, There are others that convey themselves into the mind *by more senses than one.*

Thirdly, Others that are had from *reflection only.*

Fourthly, There are some that make themselves way, and are suggested to the mind *by all the ways of sensation and reflection.*

We shall consider them apart under these several heads.

First, there are some ideas which have admittance only through one sense, which is peculiarly adapted to receive them. Thus light and colours, as white, red, yellow, blue, with their several degrees or shades and mixtures, as green, scarlet, purple, sea-green, and the rest, come in only by the eyes. All kinds of noises, sounds, and tones only by the ears. The several tastes and smells by the nose and palate. And if these organs, or the nerves which are the conduits to convey them from without to their audience in the brain, the mind's presence-room (as I may so call it), are any of them so disordered as not to perform their functions, they have no postern to be admitted by, no other way to bring themselves into view, and be perceived by the understanding.

The most considerable of those belonging to the touch are heat and cold, and solidity; all the rest, consisting almost wholly in the sensible configuration, as smooth and rough;

or else, more or less firm adhesion of the parts, as hard and soft, tough and brittle, are obvious enough.

2. I think it will be needless to enumerate all the particular simple ideas belonging to each sense. Nor indeed is it possible if we would, there being a great many more of them belonging to most of the senses than we have names for. The variety of smells, which are as many almost, if not more, than species of bodies in the world, do most of them want names. '*Sweet*' *and* '*stinking*' commonly serve our turn for these ideas, which in effect is little more than to call them pleasing or displeasing, though the smell of a rose and violet, both sweet, are certainly very distinct ideas. Nor are the different tastes, that by our palates we receive ideas of, much better provided with names. 'Sweet', 'bitter', 'sour', 'harsh', and 'salt' are almost all the epithets we have to denominate that numberless variety of relishes, which are to be found distinct, not only in almost every sort of creatures, but in the different parts of the same plant, fruit, or animal. The same may be said of colours and sounds. I shall, therefore, in the account of simple ideas I am here giving, content myself to set down only such as are most material to our present purpose, or are in themselves less apt to be taken notice of, though they are very frequently the ingredients of our complex ideas; amongst which, I think, I may well account solidity, which therefore I shall treat of in the next chapter.

CHAPTER IV

OF SOLIDITY

(1.) *We receive this Idea from Touch*. The idea of *solidity* we receive by our touch; and it arises from the resistance which we find in body to the entrance of any other body into the place it possesses, till it has left it. There is no idea which we receive more constantly from sensation than solidity. Whether we move or rest, in what posture soever we are, we always feel something under us that supports us, and hinders our farther sinking downwards; and the bodies which we daily handle make us perceive that, whilst they remain between them, they do, by an insurmountable force, hinder the approach of the parts of our hands that press them. That which thus hinders the approach of two bodies, when they are moved one towards another, I call solidity. I will not dispute whether this acceptation of the word 'solid' be nearer to its original signification than that which mathematicians use it in. It suffices that I think the common notion of solidity will allow, if not justify, this use of it; but if any one think it better to call it *impenetrability,* he has my consent. This, of all other, seems the idea most intimately connected with, and essential to body, so as nowhere else to be found or imagined, but only in matter. And though our senses take no notice of it but in masses of matter, of a bulk sufficient to cause a sensation in us, yet the mind, having once got this idea from such grosser sensible bodies, traces it farther, and considers it, as well as figure, in the minutest particle of matter that can exist, and finds it inseparably inherent in body, wherever or however modified.

(2.) *Solidity fills Space*. This is the idea which belongs to body, whereby we conceive it to fill space. The idea of which filling of space is that, where we imagine any space taken up by a solid substance, we conceive it so to possess it, that it excludes all other solid substances; and will for ever hinder any two other bodies, that move towards one another in a straight line, from coming to touch one another, unless it removes from between them in a line not parallel to that which they move in. This idea of it the bodies which we ordinarily handle sufficiently furnish us with.

(3.) *Distinct from Space.* This resistance, whereby it keeps other bodies out of the space which it possesses, is so great, that no force, how great soever, can surmount it. All the bodies in the world, pressing a drop of water on all sides, will never be able to overcome the resistance which it will make, as soft as it is, to their approaching one another, till it be removed out of their way; whereby our idea of solidity is distinguished both from pure space, which is capable neither of resistance nor motion, and from the ordinary idea of hardness. For a man may conceive two bodies at a distance, so as they may approach one another, without touching or displacing any solid thing, till their superficies come to meet; whereby, I think, we have the clear idea of space without solidity. For (not to go so far as annihilation of any particular body) I ask whether a man cannot have the idea of the motion of one single body alone, without any other succeeding immediately into its place? I think it is evident he can, the idea of motion in one body no more including the idea of motion in another, than the idea of a square figure in one body includes the idea of a square figure in another. I do not ask, whether bodies do so *exist* that the motion of one body cannot really be without the motion of another. To determine this either way is to beg the question for or against a *vacuum*. But my question is whether one cannot have the *idea* of one body moved, whilst others are at rest? And I think this no one will deny. If so, then the place it deserted gives us the idea of pure space without solidity; whereinto another body may enter, without either resistance or protrusion of anything.

(4.) *From Hardness.* Solidity is hereby also differenced from hardness, in that solidity consists in repletion, and so an utter exclusion of other bodies out of the space it possesses; but hardness in a firm cohesion of the parts of matter, making up masses of a sensible bulk, so that the whole does not easily change its figure. And indeed, 'hard' and 'soft' are names that we give to things only in relation to the constitutions of our own bodies : that being generally called hard by us which will put us to pain sooner than change figure by the pressure of any part of our bodies; and that, on the contrary, soft which changes the situation of its parts upon an easy and unpainful touch.

But this difficulty of changing the situation of the sensible parts amongst themselves, or of the figure of the whole, gives no more solidity to the hardest body in the world than to the softest; nor is an adamant one jot more solid than water. For, though the two flat sides of two pieces of marble will more easily approach each other, between which there is nothing but water or air, than if there be a diamond between them; yet it is not that the parts of the diamond are more solid than those of water, or resist more, but because the parts of water, being more easily separable from each other, they will, by a side motion, be more easily removed, and give way to the approach of the two pieces of marble. But if they could be kept from making place by that side motion, they would eternally hinder the approach of these two pieces of marble, as much as the diamond; and it would be as impossible by any force to surmount their resistance, as to surmount the resistance of the parts of a diamond. The softest body in the world will as invincibly resist the coming together of any two other bodies, if it be not put out of the way, but remain between them, as the hardest that can be found or imagined. He that shall fill a yielding soft body well with air or water will quickly find its resistance. And he that thinks that nothing but bodies that are hard can keep his hands from approaching one another, may be pleased to make a trial, with the air inclosed in a football.

(5.) *On Solidity depends Impulse, Resistance and Protrusion.*

By this idea of solidity is the extension of body distinguished from the extension of space, the extension of body being nothing but the cohesion or continuity of solid, separable, movable parts; and the extension of space the continuity of unsolid, inseparable, and immovable parts. Upon the solidity of bodies also depend their mutual impulse, resistance, and protrusion. Of pure space then, and solidity, there are several (amongst which I confess myself one) who persuade themselves they have clear and distinct ideas; and that they can think on space, without anything in it that resists or is protruded by body. This is the idea of pure space, which they think they have as clear as any idea they can have of the extension of body.

CHAPTER V

OF SIMPLE IDEAS OF DIVERS SENSES

The ideas we get by more than one sense are of *space* or *extension, figure, rest* and *motion*. For these make perceivable impressions, both on the eyes and touch; and we can receive and convey into our minds the ideas of the extension, figure, motion, and rest of bodies, both by seeing and feeling. But having occasion to speak more at large of these in another place,[1] I here only enumerate them.

---

[1] II xiii; xiv

CHAPTER VI

OF SIMPLE IDEAS OF REFLECTION

1. *Are the Operations of Mind about its other Ideas.* The mind receiving the ideas mentioned in the foregoing chapters from without, when it turns its view inward upon itself, and observes its own actions about those ideas it has, takes from thence other ideas, which are as capable to be the objects of its contemplation as any of those it received from foreign things.

2. *The Idea of Perception, and Idea of Willing, we have from Reflection.* The two great and principal actions of the mind, which are most frequently considered, and which are so frequent that everyone that pleases may take notice of them in himself, are these two :—

Perception, or *Thinking*; and

Volition, or *Willing*.

The power of thinking is called the *understanding*, and the power of volition is called the *will*; and these two powers or abilities in the mind are denominated faculties. Of some of the *modes* of these simple ideas of reflection, such as are *remembrance, discerning, reasoning, judging, knowledge, faith,* &c., I shall have occasion to speak hereafter.[1]

CHAPTER VII

OF SIMPLE IDEAS OF BOTH
SENSATION AND REFLECTION

1. *Pleasure and Pain.* There be other simple ideas which convey themselves into the mind by all the ways of sensation and reflection, viz. *pleasure* or *delight,* and its opposite, *pain,* or *uneasiness; power; existence; unity.*

2. Delight or uneasiness, one or other of them, join themselves to almost all our ideas both of sensation and reflection; and there is scarce any affection of our senses from without, any retired thought of our mind within, which is not able to produce in us pleasure or pain. By ' *pleasure* ' and ' *pain* ' I would be understood to signify whatsoever delights or molests us, whether it arises from the thoughts of our minds, or anything operating on our bodies. For, whether we call it satisfaction, delight, pleasure, happiness, &c., on the one side, or uneasiness, trouble, pain, torment, anguish, misery, &c., on the other, they are still but different degrees of the same thing, and belong to the ideas of pleasure and pain, delight or uneasiness, which are the names I shall most commonly use for those two sorts of ideas.

7. *Existence* and *Unity* are two other ideas that are suggested to the understanding by every object without, and every idea within. When ideas are in our minds, we consider them as being actually there, as well as we consider things to be actually without us; which is, that they exist, or have *existence.* And whatever we can consider as one thing, whether a real being or idea, suggests to the understanding the idea of unity.

8. *Power* also is another of those simple ideas which we receive from sensation and reflection. For, observing in ourselves that we can at pleasure move several parts of our bodies which were at rest, the effects, also, that natural bodies

are able to produce in one another, occurring every moment to our senses, we both these ways get the idea of power.

9. *Succession.* Besides these there is another idea, which, though suggested by our senses, yet is more constantly offered us by what passes in our minds; and that is the idea of *succession.* For if we look immediately into ourselves, and reflect on what is observable there, we shall find our ideas always, whilst we are awake, or have any thought, passing in train, one going and another coming, without intermission.

10. *Simple Ideas the Materials of all our Knowledge.* These, if they are not all, are at least (as I think) the most considerable of those simple ideas which the mind has, and out of which is made all its other knowledge; all which it receives only by the two forementioned ways of sensation and reflection.

Nor let anyone think these too narrow bounds for the capacious mind of man to expatiate in, which takes its flight farther than the stars, and cannot be confined by the limits of the world; that extends its thoughts often even beyond the utmost expansion of matter, and makes excursions into that incomprehensible inane. I grant all this, but desire anyone to assign any *simple idea* which is not received from one of those inlets before mentioned, or any *complex idea* not made out of those simple ones. Nor will it be so strange to think these few simple ideas sufficient to employ the quickest thought, or largest capacity, and to furnish the materials of all that various knowledge, and more various fancies and opinions of all mankind, if we consider how many words may be made out of the various composition of twenty-four letters; or if, going one step farther, we will but reflect on the variety of combinations may be made with barely one of the above-mentioned ideas, viz. number, whose stock is inexhaustible and truly infinite : and what a large and immense field doth extension alone afford the mathematicians!

CHAPTER VIII

SOME FURTHER CONSIDERATIONS CONCERNING OUR SIMPLE IDEAS

① *Positive Ideas from privative causes.* Concerning the simple ideas of sensation, it is to be considered that whatsoever is so constituted in nature as to be able, by affecting our senses, to cause any perception in the mind, doth thereby produce in the understanding a simple idea; which, whatever be the external cause of it, when it comes to be taken notice of by our discerning faculty, it is by the mind looked on and considered there to be a real positive idea in the understanding, as much as any other whatsoever; though, perhaps, the cause of it be but a privation in the subject.

② Thus the ideas of heat and cold, light and darkness, white and black, motion and rest, are equally clear and positive ideas in the mind, though, perhaps, some of the causes which produce them are barely privations, in those subjects from whence our senses derive those ideas. These the understanding, in its view of them, considers all as distinct positive ideas, without taking notice of the causes that produce them; which is an inquiry not belonging to the idea, as it is in the understanding, but to the nature of the things existing without us. These are two very different things, and carefully to be distinguished, it being one thing to perceive and know the idea of white or black, and quite another to examine what kind of particles they must be, and how ranged in the superficies, to make any object appear white or black.

③ A painter or dyer who never inquired into their causes hath the ideas of white and black, and other colours, as clearly, perfectly, and distinctly in his understanding, and perhaps more distinctly, than the philosopher who hath busied himself in considering their natures, and thinks he knows how far either of them is, in its cause, positive or privative; and the idea of black is no less positive in his mind than that of white, however the cause of that colour in the external object may be only a privation.

(5) I appeal to everyone's own experience whether the shadow of a man, though it consists of nothing but the absence of light (and the more the absence of light is, the more discernible is the shadow) does not, when a man looks on it, cause as clear and positive idea in his mind as a man himself, though covered over with clear sunshine? And the picture of a shadow is a positive thing. Indeed, we have negative names, which stand not directly for positive ideas, but for their absence, such as *insipid, silence, nihil*, &c.; which words denote positive ideas, v.g. *taste, sound, being*, with a signification of their absence.

(6) And thus one may truly be said to see darkness. For, supposing a hole perfectly dark, from whence no light is reflected, it is certain one may see the figure of it, or it may be painted; or whether the ink I write with makes any other idea is a question. The privative causes I have here assigned of positive ideas are according to the common opinion; but, in truth, it will be hard to determine whether there be really any ideas from a privative cause, till it be determined whether rest be any more a privation than motion.

(7) *Ideas in the Mind, Qualities in Bodies.* To discover the nature of our ideas the better, and to discourse of them intelligibly, it will be convenient to distinguish them *as they are ideas or perceptions in our minds;* and *as they are modifications of matter in the bodies that cause such perceptions in us;* that so we may not think (as perhaps usually is done) that they are exactly the images and resemblances of something inherent in the subject, most of those of sensation being in the mind no more the likeness of something existing without us, than the names that stand for them are the likeness of our ideas, which yet upon hearing they are apt to excite in us.

(8) Whatsoever the mind perceives in itself, or is the immediate object of perception, thought, or understanding, that

I call *idea;* and the power to produce any idea in our mind I call *quality* of the subject wherein that power is. Thus a snowball having the power to produce in us the ideas of white, cold, and round, the powers to produce those ideas in us, as they are in the snowball, I call qualities; and as they are sensations or perceptions in our understandings, I call them ideas; which ideas, if I speak of sometimes as in the things themselves, I would be understood to mean those qualities in the objects which produce them in us.

9. *Primary Qualities.* Qualities thus considered in bodies are,

First, such as are utterly inseparable from the body, in what estate soever it be; and such as in all the alterations and changes it suffers, all the force can be used upon it, it constantly keeps; and such as sense constantly finds in every particle of matter which has bulk enough to be perceived; and the mind finds inseparable from every particle of matter, though less than to make itself singly be perceived by our senses : v.g. take a grain of wheat, divide it into two parts : each part has still solidity, extension, figure, and mobility; divide it again, and it retains still the same qualities; and so divide it on, till the parts become insensible; they must retain still each of them all those qualities. For division (which is all that a mill, or pestle, or any other body, does upon another, in reducing it to insensible parts) can never take away either solidity, extension, figure, or mobility from any body, but only makes two or more distinct separate masses of matter, of that which was but one before; all which distinct masses, reckoned as so many distinct bodies, after division, make a certain number. These I call *original* or *primary qualities* of body, which I think we may observe to produce simple ideas in us, viz. solidity, extension, figure, motion or rest, and number.

10. Secondly, such qualities which in truth are nothing in the objects themselves but powers to produce various sensations in us by their primary qualities, i.e. by the bulk, figure, texture, and motion of their insensible parts, as colours, sounds, tastes, &c. These I call *secondary qualities.* To these might be added a *third* sort, which are allowed to

be barely powers, though they are as much real qualities in the subject as those which I, to comply with the common way of speaking, call qualities, but for distinction, secondary qualities. For the power in fire to produce a new colour, or consistency, in wax or clay, by its primary qualities, is as much a quality in fire, as the power it has to produce in me a new idea or sensation of warmth or burning, which I felt not before, by the same primary qualities, viz. the bulk, texture, and motion of its insensible parts.

11. *How Primary qualities produce Ideas.* The next thing to be considered is, how bodies produce ideas in us; and that is manifestly by impulse, the only way which we can conceive bodies operate in.

12. If then external objects be not united to our minds when they produce ideas therein, and yet we perceive these *original* qualities in such of them as singly fall under our senses, it is evident that some motion must be thence continued by our nerves, or animal spirits, by some parts of our bodies, to the brains or the seat of sensation, there to produce in our minds the particular ideas we have of them. And since the extension, figure, number, and motion of bodies of an observable bigness, may be perceived at a distance by the sight, it is evident some singly imperceptible bodies must come from them to the eyes, and thereby convey to the brain some motion; which produces these ideas which we have of them in us.

13. *How secondary.* After the same manner that the ideas of these original qualities are produced in us, we may conceive that the ideas of *secondary* qualities are also produced, viz. by the operation of insensible particles on our senses. For, it being manifest that there are bodies and good store of bodies, each whereof are so small, that we cannot by any of our senses discover either their bulk, figure, or motion, as is evident in the particles of the air and water, and other extremely smaller than those, perhaps as much smaller than the particles of air or water, as the particles of air or water are smaller than peas or hail-stones; let us suppose at present that the different motions and figures, bulk and number, of such particles, affecting the

several organs of our senses, produce in us those different sensations which we have from the colours and smells of bodies : v.g. that a violet, by the impulse of such insensible particles of matter, of peculiar figures and bulks, and in different degrees and modifications of their motions, causes the ideas of the blue colour and sweet scent of that flower to be produced in our minds. It being no more impossible to conceive that God should annex such ideas to such motions, with which they have no similitude, than that he should annex the idea of pain to the motion of a piece of steel dividing our flesh, with which that idea hath no resemblance.

14. What I have said concerning colours and smells may be understood also of tastes and sounds, and other the like sensible qualities; which, whatever reality we by mistake attribute to them, are in truth nothing in the objects themselves but powers to produce various sensations in us; and, depend on those primary qualities, viz. bulk, figure, texture, and motion of parts as I have said.

15. *Ideas of primary Qualities are Resemblances; of secondary, not.* From whence I think it easy to draw this observation, that the ideas of primary qualities of bodies are resemblances of them, and their patterns do really exist in the bodies themselves, but the ideas produced in us by these secondary qualities have no resemblance of them at all. There is nothing like our ideas existing in the bodies themselves. They are, in the bodies we denominate from them, only a power to produce those sensations in us; and what is sweet, blue, or warm in idea is but the certain bulk, figure, and motion of the insensible parts, in the bodies themselves, which we call so.

16. Flame is denominated hot and light; snow, white and cold; and manna, white and sweet, from the ideas they produce in us. Which qualities are commonly thought to be the same in those bodies that those ideas are in us, the one the perfect resemblance of the other, as they are in a mirror, and it would by most men be judged very extravagant if one should say otherwise. And yet he that will consider that the same fire that, at one distance produces in us the

sensation of warmth, does, at a nearer approach, produce in us the far different sensation of pain, ought to bethink himself what reason he has to say that his idea of warmth, which was produced in him by the fire, is *actually in the fire;* and his idea of pain, which the same fire produced in him the same way, is *not* in the fire. Why is whiteness and coldness in snow, and pain not, when it produces the one and the other idea in us; and can do neither, but by the bulk, figure, number, and motion of its solid parts?

⑰ The particular bulk, number, figure, and motion of the part of fire or snow are really in them, whether anyone's senses perceive them or no, and therefore they may be called *real* qualities, because they really exist in those bodies. But light, heat, whiteness, or coldness, are no more really in them than sickness or pain is in manna. Take away the sensation of them; let not the eyes see light or colours, nor the ears hear sounds; let the palate not taste, nor the nose smell, and all colours, tastes, odours, and sounds, as they are such particular ideas, vanish and cease, and are reduced to their causes, i.e. bulk, figure, and motion of parts.

⑱ A piece of manna of a sensible bulk is able to produce in us the idea of a round or square figure; and by being removed from one place to another, the idea of motion. This idea of motion represents it as it really is in the manna moving; a circle or square are the same, whether in idea or existence, in the mind or in the manna. And this, both motion and figure, are really in the manna, whether we take notice of them or no; this everybody is ready to agree to. Besides, manna, by the bulk, figure, texture, and motion of its parts, has a power to produce the sensations of sickness, and sometimes of acute pains or gripings in us. That these ideas of sickness and pain are not in the manna, but effects of its operations on us, and are nowhere when we feel them not: this also everyone readily agrees to. And yet men are hardly to be brought to think that sweetness and whiteness are not really in manna, which are but the effects of the operations of manna, by the motion, size, and figure of its particles, on the eyes and palate, as the pain and sickness caused by manna are confessedly nothing but the effects of its operations on the stomach and guts, by the size, motion, and figure of its insensible parts, (for by nothing else can a body operate, as has been proved); as if it could not operate on the eyes and palate, and thereby produce in the mind particular distinct ideas, which in itself it has not, as well as we allow it can operate on the guts and stomach, and thereby produce distinct ideas, which in itself it has not. These ideas, being all effects of the operations of manna on several parts of our bodies, by the size, figure, number, and motion of its parts; why those produced by the eyes and palate should rather be thought to be really in the manna, than those produced by the stomach and guts; or why the pain and sickness, ideas that are the effects of manna, should be thought to be nowhere when they are not felt; and yet the sweetness and whiteness, effects of the same manna on other parts of the body, by ways equally as unknown, should be thought to exist in the manna, when they are not seen nor tasted, would need some reason to explain.

⑲ *Ideas of primary qualities are resemblances, of secondary not.* Let us consider the red and white colours in porphyry. Hinder light but from striking on it, and its colours vanish; it no longer produces any such ideas in us; upon the return of light it produces these appearances on us again. Can anyone think any real alterations are made in the porphyry by the presence or absence of light, and that those ideas of whiteness and redness are really in porphyry in the light, when it is plain *it has no colour in the dark*? It has, indeed, such a configuration of particles, both night and day, as are apt, by the rays of light rebounding from some parts of that hard stone, to produce in us the idea of redness, and from others the idea of whiteness; but whiteness or redness are not in it at any time, but such a texture that hath the power to produce such a sensation in us.

⑳ Pound an almond, and the clear white colour will be altered into a dirty one, and the sweet taste into an oily one. What real alteration can the beating of the pestle make in any body, but an alteration of the texture of it?

(21) Ideas being thus distinguished and understood, we may be able to give an account how the same water, at the same time, may produce the idea of cold by one hand and of heat by the other, whereas it is impossible that the same water, if those ideas were really in it, should at the same time be both hot and cold. For, if the sensation of heat and cold be nothing but the increase or diminution of the motion of the minute parts of our bodies, caused by the corpuscles of any other body, it is easy to be understood that, if that motion be greater in one hand than in the other, if a body be applied to the two hands, which has in its minute particles a greater motion than in those of one of the hands, and a less than in those of the other, it will increase the motion of the one hand and lessen it in the other, and so cause the different sensations of heat and cold that depend thereon.

(23) *Three Sorts of Qualities in Bodies.* The qualities, then, that are in bodies, rightly considered, are of three sorts :—

First, The bulk, figure, number, situation, and motion or rest of their solid parts. Those are in them, whether we perceive them or no; and when they are of that size that we can discover them, we have by these an idea of the thing as it is in itself, as is plain in artificial things. These I call *primary qualities.*

Secondly, The power that is in any body, by reason of its insensible primary qualities, to operate after a peculiar manner on any of our senses, and thereby produce in *us* the different ideas of several colours, sounds, smells, tastes, &c. These are usually called *sensible qualities.*

Thirdly, The power that is in any body, by reason of the particular constitution of its primary qualities, to make such a change in the bulk, figure, texture, and motion of *another body,* as to make it operate on our senses differently from what it did before. Thus the sun has a power to make wax white, and fire to make lead fluid. These are usually called *powers.*

The first of these, as has been said, I think may be properly called real, original, or primary qualities, because they are in the things themselves, whether they are perceived or no;

and upon their different modifications it is that the secondary qualities depend.

The other two are only powers to act differently upon other things, which powers result from the different modifications of those primary qualities.

24. *The first are Resemblances; the second thought Resemblances, but are not; the third neither are, nor are thought so.* But, though these two latter sorts of qualities are powers barely, and nothing but powers, relating to several other bodies, and resulting from the different modifications of the original qualities, yet they are generally otherwise thought of. For the second sort, viz. the powers to produce several ideas in us by our senses, are looked upon as real qualities in the things thus affecting us; but the third sort are called and esteemed barely powers. V.g. the idea of heat or light, which we receive by our eyes, or touch, from the sun, are commonly thought real qualities existing in the sun, and something more than mere powers in it. But when we consider the sun in reference to wax, which it melts or blanches, we look upon the whiteness and softness produced in the wax, not as qualities in the sun, but effects produced by powers in it. Whereas, if rightly considered, these qualities of light and warmth, which are perceptions in me when I am warmed or enlightened by the sun, are no otherwise in the sun, than the changes made in the wax, when it is blanched or melted, are in the sun. They are all of them equally powers in the sun, depending on its primary qualities.

25. The reason why the one are ordinarily taken for real qualities, and the other only for bare powers, seems to be because the ideas we have of distinct colours, sounds, &c., containing nothing at all in them of bulk, figure, or motion, we are not apt to think them the effects of these primary qualities; which appear not, to our senses, to operate in their production, and with which they have not any apparent congruity or conceivable connexion. Hence it is that we are so forward to imagine that those ideas are the resemblances of something really existing in the objects themselves, since sensation discovers nothing of bulk, figure, or motion of

parts in their production; nor can reason show how bodies, by their bulk, figure, and motion, should produce in the mind the ideas of blue or yellow, &c. But, in the other case, in the operations of bodies changing the qualities one of another, we plainly discover that the quality produced hath commonly no resemblance with anything in the thing producing it; wherefore we look on it as a bare effect of power.

CHAPTER IX

OF PERCEPTION

1. *It is the first simple Idea of Reflection. Perception,* as it is the first faculty of the mind exercised about our ideas, so it is the first and simplest idea we have from reflection, and is by some called thinking in general. Though *thinking,* in the propriety of the English tongue, signifies that sort of operation in the mind about its ideas wherein the mind is active, where it, with some degree of voluntary attention, considers anything. For in bare naked perception the mind is, for the most part, only passive; and what it perceives, it cannot avoid perceiving.

2. *Perception is only when the Mind receives the Impression.* What perception is everyone will know better by reflecting on what he does himself, when he sees, hears, feels, &c., or thinks, than by any discourse of mine. Whoever reflects on what passes in his own mind cannot miss it. And if he does not reflect, all the words in the world cannot make him have any notion of it.

3. This is certain, that whatever alterations are made in the body, if they reach not the mind, whatever impressions are made on the outward parts, if they are not taken notice of within, there is no perception. Fire may burn our bodies with no other effect than it does a billet, unless the motion be continued to the brain, and there the sense of heat, or idea of pain, be produced in the mind; wherein consists actual perception.

4. How often may a man observe in himself that whilst his mind is intently employed in the contemplation of some objects, and curiously surveying some ideas that are there, it takes no notice of impressions of sounding bodies made upon the organ of hearing, with the same alteration that uses to be for the producing the idea of sound? A sufficient impulse there may be on the organ, but, it not reaching the observation of the mind, there follows no perception; and though the motion that uses to produce the idea of sound be made in the ear, yet no sound is heard. Want of sensation, in this case, is not through any defect in the organ, or that the man's ears are less affected than at other times when he does hear; but that which uses to produce the idea, though conveyed in by the usual organ, not being taken notice of in the understanding, and so imprinting no idea on the mind, there follows no sensation. So that wherever there is sense or perception, there some idea is actually produced, and present in the understanding.

5. *Children, though they have Ideas in the Womb, have none innate.* Therefore I doubt not but children, by the exercise of their senses about objects that affect them in the womb, receive some few ideas before they are born, as the unavoidable effects, either of the bodies that environ them, or else of those wants or diseases they suffer; amongst which (if one may conjecture concerning things not very capable of examination) I think the ideas of hunger and warmth are two; which probably are some of the first that children have, and which they scarce ever part with again.

6. But though it be reasonable to imagine that children receive some ideas before they come into the world, yet these simple ideas are far from those *innate principles* which some contend for, and we, above, have rejected. These here mentioned, being the effects of sensation, are only from some affections of the body, which happen to them there, and so depend on something exterior to the mind, no otherwise differing in their manner of production from other ideas derived from sense, but only in the precedency of time. Whereas those innate principles are supposed to be quite of

another nature, not coming into the mind by any accidental alterations in, or operations on the body, but, as it were, original characters impressed upon it, in the very first moment of its being and constitution.

8 *Ideas of Sensation often changed by the Judgment*. We are further to consider concerning perception, that the ideas we receive by sensation are often, in grown people, altered by the judgment, without our taking notice of it. When we set before our eyes a round globe of any uniform colour, v.g. gold, alabaster, or jet, it is certain that the idea thereby imprinted in our mind is of a flat circle, variously shadowed, with several degrees of light and brightness coming to our eyes. But we having, by use, been accustomed to perceive what kind of appearance convex bodies are wont to make in us, what alterations are made in the reflections of light by the difference of the sensible figures of bodies, the judgment presently, by an habitual custom, alters the appearances into their causes. So that from that which truly is variety of shadow or colour, collecting the figure, it makes it pass for a mark of figure, and frames to itself the perception of a convex figure and an uniform colour, when the idea we receive from thence is only a plane variously coloured, as is evident in painting. To which purpose I shall here insert a problem of that very ingenious and studious promoter of real knowledge, the learned and worthy Mr. Molineux, which he was pleased to send me in a letter some months since; and it is this: " Suppose a man *born* blind, and now adult, and taught by his *touch* to distinguish between a cube and a sphere of the same metal, and nighly of the same bigness, so as to tell, when he felt one and the other, which is the cube, which the sphere. Suppose then the cube and sphere placed on a table, and the blind man to be made to see: *quære,* whether *by his sight, before he touched them,* he could now distinguish and tell which is the globe, which the cube?" To which the acute and judicious proposer answers, " Not. For, though he has obtained the experience of how a globe, how a cube affects his touch, yet he has not yet obtained the experience that what affects his touch so or so must affect his sight so or so; or

that a protuberant angle in the cube, that pressed his hand unequally, shall appear to his eye as it does in the cube." I agree with this thinking gentleman, whom I am proud to call my friend, in his answer to this problem; and am of opinion that the blind man, at first sight, would not be able with certainty to say which was the globe, which the cube, whilst he only saw them, though he could unerringly name them by his touch, and certainly distinguish them by the difference of their figures felt.

11. *Perception puts the difference between Animals and Inferior Beings.* This faculty of perception seems to me to be that which puts the distinction betwixt the animal kingdom and the inferior parts of nature. For, however vegetables have, many of them, some degrees of motion, and upon the different application of other bodies to them do very briskly alter their figures and motions, and so have obtained the name of sensitive plants, from a motion which has some resemblance to that which in animals follows upon sensation; yet I suppose it is all bare mechanism, and no otherwise produced than the turning of a wild oat-beard by the insinuation of the particles of moisture, or the shortening of a rope by the affusion of water. All which is done without any sensation in the subject, or the having or receiving any ideas.

12. Perception, I believe, is, in some degree, in all sorts of animals, though in some possibly the avenues provided by nature for the reception of sensations are so few, and the perception they are received with so obscure and dull, that it comes extremely short of the quickness and variety of sensation which is in other animals; but yet it is sufficient for, and wisely adapted to, the state and condition of that sort of animals who are thus made.

15. *Perception the Inlet of the Knowledge.* Perception then being the first step and degree towards knowledge, and the inlet of all the materials of it, the fewer senses any man, as well as any other creature, hath, and the fewer and duller the impressions are that are made by them, and the duller the faculties are that are employed about them, the more remote are they from that knowledge which is to be found in some

men. But this being in great variety of degrees (as may be perceived amongst men) cannot certainly be discovered in the several species of animals, much less in their particular individuals. It suffices me only to have remarked here that perception is the first operation of all our intellectual faculties, and the inlet of all knowledge into our minds. And I am apt too to imagine that it is perception, in the lowest degree of it, which puts the boundaries between animals and the inferior ranks of creatures. But this I mention only as my conjecture by the by, it being indifferent to the matter in hand which way the learned shall determine of it.

CHAPTER X

OF RETENTION

1. *Contemplation.* The next faculty of the mind, whereby it makes a further progress towards knowledge, is that which I call *retention,* or the keeping of those simple ideas which from sensation or reflection it hath received. This is done two ways. First, by keeping the idea which is brought into it for some time actually in view, which is called *contemplation.*

2. *Memory.* The other way of retention is the power to revive again in our minds those ideas which, after imprinting, have disappeared, or have been, as it were, laid aside out of sight. And thus we do, when we conceive heat or light, yellow or sweet, the object being removed. This is *memory,* which is as it were the storehouse of our ideas. For, the narrow mind of man not being capable of having many ideas under view and consideration at once, it was necessary to have a repository, to lay up those ideas which, at another time, it might have use of. But, our ideas being nothing but actual perceptions in the mind, which cease to be anything when there is no perception of them, this laying up of our ideas in the repository of the memory signifies no more but this, that the mind has a power in many cases to revive

perceptions which it has once had, with this additional perception annexed to them, that *it has had them before*. And in this sense it is that our ideas are said to be in our memories, when indeed they are actually nowhere; but only there is an ability in the mind when it will to revive them again, and as it were paint them anew on itself, though some with more, some with less difficulty, some more lively, and others more obscurely.

3. *Attention, Repetition, Pleasure and Pain, fix Ideas.* Attention and repetition help much to the fixing any ideas in the memory. But those which naturally at first make the deepest and most lasting impression are those which are accompanied with pleasure or pain. The great business of the senses being to make us take notice of what hurts or advantages the body, it is wisely ordered by nature, as has been shown, that pain should accompany the reception of several ideas; which, supplying the place of consideration and reasoning in children, and acting quicker than consideration in grown men, makes both the young and old avoid painful objects with that haste which is necessary for their preservation; and in both settles in the memory a caution for the future.

5. Many of those ideas which were produced in the minds of children, in the beginning of their sensation (some of which perhaps, as of some pleasures and pains, were before they were born, and others in their infancy), if in the future course of their lives they are not repeated again, are quite lost, without the least glimpse remaining of them. This may be observed in those who by some mischance have lost their sight when they were very young, in whom the ideas of colours having been but slightly taken notice of, and ceasing to be repeated, do quite wear out; so that some years after, there is no more notion nor memory of colours left in their minds than in those of people born blind. The memory in some men, it is true, is very tenacious, even to a miracle. But yet there seems to be a constant decay of all our ideas, even of those which are struck deepest, and in minds the most retentive, so that if they be not sometimes renewed, by repeated exercise of the senses, or reflection on those kinds

of objects which at first occasioned them, the print wears out, and at last there remains nothing to be seen. How much the constitution of our bodies and the make of our animal spirits are concerned in this, and whether the temper of the brain makes this difference, that in some it retains the characters drawn on it like marble, in others like freestone, and in others little better than sand, I shall not here inquire; though it may seem probable that the constitution of the body does sometimes influence the memory, since we oftentimes find a disease quite strip the mind of all its ideas, and the flames of a fever in a few days calcine all those images to dust and confusion, which seemed to be as lasting as if graved in marble.

7. *In Remembering, the Mind is often active.* This further is to be observed, concerning ideas lodged in the memory, and upon occasion revived by the mind, that they are not only (as the word *revive* imports) none of them new ones, but also that the mind takes notice of them as of a former impression, and renews its acquaintance with them, as with ideas it had known before. So that though ideas formerly imprinted are not all constantly in view, yet in remembrance they are constantly known to be such as have been formerly imprinted, i.e. in view, and taken notice of before by the understanding.

8. *Two defects in the Memory, Oblivion and Slowness.* Memory, in an intellectual creature, is necessary in the next degree to perception. It is of so great moment that, where it is wanting, all the rest of our faculties are in a great measure useless. And we in our thoughts, reasonings, and knowledge, could not proceed beyond present objects, were it not for the assistance of our memories; wherein there may be two defects :

First, That it loses the idea quite, and so far it produces perfect ignorance. For, since we can know nothing further than we have the idea of it, when that is gone, we are in perfect ignorance.

Secondly, That it moves slowly, and retrieves not the ideas that it has, and are laid up in store, quick enough to serve the mind upon occasions. This, if it be to a great degree, is stupidity; and he who, through this default in his memory, has not the ideas that are really preserved there, ready at hand when need and occasion calls for them, were almost as good be without them quite, since they serve him to little purpose.

10. *Brutes have Memory.* This faculty of laying up and retaining the ideas that are brought into the mind several other animals seem to have to a great degree, as well as man. For, to pass by other instances, birds learning of tunes, and the endeavours one may observe in them to hit the notes right, put it past doubt with me that they have perception, and retain ideas in their memories, and use them for patterns. For it seems to me impossible that they should endeavour to conform their voices to notes (as it is plain they do) of which they had no ideas. For, though I should grant sound may mechanically cause a certain motion of the animal spirits in the brains of those birds, whilst the tune is actually playing, and that motion may be continued on to the muscles of the wings, and so the bird mechanically be driven away by certain noises, because this may tend to the bird's preservation; yet that can never be supposed a reason why it should cause mechanically—either whilst the tune is playing, much less after it has ceased—such a motion in the organs in the bird's voice as should conform it to the notes of a foreign sound, which imitation can be of no use to the bird's preservation. But, which is more, it cannot with any appearance of reason be supposed (much less proved) that birds, without sense and memory, can approach their notes nearer and nearer by degrees to a tune played yesterday; which if they have no idea of in their memory, is now nowhere, nor can be a pattern for them to imitate, or which any repeated essays can bring them nearer to. Since there is no reason why the sound of a pipe should leave traces in their brains, which, not at first, but by their after-endeavours, should produce the like sounds; and why the sounds they make themselves should not make traces which they should follow, as well as those of the pipe, is impossible to conceive.

CHAPTER XI

OF DISCERNING, AND OTHER
OPERATIONS OF THE MIND

1. *No Knowledge without it.* Another faculty we may take notice of in our minds is that of *discerning* and *distinguishing* between the several ideas it has. It is not enough to have a confused perception of something in general. Unless the mind had a distinct perception of different objects and their qualities, it would be capable of very little knowledge, though the bodies that affect us were as busy about us as they are now, and the mind were continually employed in thinking. On this faculty of distinguishing one thing from another depends the evidence and certainty of several, even very general, propositions, which have passed for innate truths; because men, overlooking the true cause why those propositions find universal assent, impute it wholly to native uniform impressions; whereas it in truth depends upon this clear discerning faculty of the mind, whereby it perceives two ideas to be the same, or different.

3. *Clearness alone hinders Confusion.* To the well distinguishing our ideas it chiefly contributes they be *clear* and *determinate.* And when they are so, it will not breed any confusion or mistake about them, though the senses should (as sometimes they do) convey them from the same object differently on different occasions, and so seem to err. For, though a man in a fever should from sugar have a bitter taste, which at another time would produce a sweet one, yet the idea of bitter in that man's mind would be as clear and distinct from the idea of sweet as if he had tasted only gall.

4. *Comparing.* The COMPARING them one with another, in respect of extent, degrees, time, place, or any other circumstances, is another operation of the mind about its ideas, and is

that upon which depends all that large tribe of ideas comprehended under *relation*; which, of how vast an extent it is, I shall have occasion to consider hereafter.[1]

5. *Brutes compare, but imperfectly.* How far brutes partake in this faculty is not easy to determine. I imagine they have it not in any great degree; for, though they probably have several ideas distinct enough, yet it seems to me to be the prerogative of human understanding, when it has sufficiently distinguished any ideas, so as to perceive them to be perfectly different, and so consequently two, to cast about and consider in what circumstances they are capable to be compared. And therefore, I think, beasts compare not their ideas further than some sensible circumstances annexed to the objects themselves. The other power of comparing, which may be observed in men, belonging to general ideas, and useful only to abstract reasonings, we may probably conjecture beasts have not.

6. *Compounding.* The next operation we may observe in the mind about its ideas is COMPOSITION, whereby it puts together several of those simple ones it has received from sensation and reflection, and combines them into complex ones. Under this of composition may be reckoned also that of ENLARGING, wherein, though the composition does not so much appear as in more complex ones, yet it is nevertheless a putting several ideas together, though of the same kind. Thus, by adding several units together, we make the idea of a dozen; and putting together the repeated ideas of several perches, we frame that of furlong.

7. *Brutes compound but little.* In this also, I suppose, brutes come far short of men. For, though they take in, and retain together, several combinations of simple ideas, as possibly the shape, smell, and voice of his master make up the complex idea a dog has of him, or rather are so many distinct marks whereby he knows him; yet I do not think they do of themselves ever compound them, and make complex ideas.

8. *Naming.* When children have, by repeated sensations, got ideas fixed in their memories, they begin by degrees to

[1] II xxv-xxviii

learn the use of signs. And when they have got the skill to apply the organs of speech to the framing of articulate sounds, they begin to make use of words, to signify their ideas to others. These verbal signs they sometimes borrow from others, and sometimes make themselves, as one may observe among the new and unusual names children often give to things in their first use of language.

9. *Abstraction.* The use of words then being to stand as outward marks of our internal ideas, and those ideas being taken from particular things, if every particular idea that we take in should have a distinct name, names must be endless. To prevent this, the mind makes the particular ideas received from particular objects to become general; which is done by considering them as they are in the mind such appearances, separate from all other existences, and the circumstances of real existence, as time, place, or any other concomitant ideas. This is called ABSTRACTION, whereby ideas taken from particular beings become general representatives of all of the same kind; and their names general names, applicable to whatever exists conformable to such abstract ideas. Such precise, naked appearances in the mind, without considering how, whence, or with what others they came there, the understanding lays up (with names commonly annexed to them) as the standards to rank real existences into sorts, as they agree with these patterns, and to denominate them accordingly. Thus the same colour being observed to-day in chalk or snow, which the mind yesterday received from milk, it considers that appearance alone, makes it a representative of all of that kind; and having given it the name *whiteness,* it by that sound signifies the same quality wheresoever to be imagined or met with; and thus universals, whether ideas or terms, are made.

10. *Brutes abstract not.* If it may be doubted whether beasts compound and enlarge their ideas that way to any degree, this, I think, I may be positive in, that the power of abstracting is not at all in them, and that the having of general ideas is that which puts a perfect distinction betwixt man and

brutes, and is an excellency which the faculties of brutes do by no means attain to. For it is evident we observe no footsteps in them of making use of general signs for universal ideas; from which we have reason to imagine that they have not the faculty of abstracting, or making general ideas, since they have no use of words, or any other general signs.

11. Nor can it be imputed to their want of fit organs to frame articulate sounds, that they have no use or knowledge of general words, since many of them, we find, can fashion such sounds, and pronounce words distinctly enough, but never with any such application. And, on the other side, men who, through some defect in the organs, want words, yet fail not to express their universal ideas by signs, which serve them instead of general words, a faculty which we see beasts come short in. And, therefore, I think, we may suppose that it is in this that the species of brutes are discriminated from man; and it is that proper difference wherein they are wholly separated, and which at last widens to so vast a distance. For if they have any ideas at all, and are not bare machines (as some would have them), we cannot deny them to have some reason. It seems as evident to me that they do some of them in certain instances reason, as that they have sense; but it is only in particular ideas, just as they received them from their senses. They are the best of them tied up within those narrow bounds, and have not (as I think) the faculty to enlarge them by any kind of abstraction.

14. *Method.* These, I think, are the first faculties and operations of the mind, which it makes use of in understanding; and though they are exercised about all its ideas in general, yet the instances I have hitherto given have been chiefly in simple ideas. And I have subjoined the explication of these faculties of the mind to that of simple ideas, before I come to what I have to say concerning complex ones, for these following reasons:

First, because several of these faculties being exercised at first principally about simple ideas, we might, by following nature in its ordinary method, trace and discover them, in their rise, progress, and gradual improvements.

Secondly, because observing the faculties of the mind, how they operate about simple ideas—which are usually, in most men's minds, much more clear, precise, and distinct than complex ones—we may the better examine and learn how the mind abstracts, denominates, compares, and exercises its other operations about those which are complex, wherein we are much more liable to mistake.

Thirdly, because these very operations of the mind about ideas received from sensation are themselves, when reflected on, another set of ideas, derived from that other source of our knowledge, which I call reflection; and therefore fit to be considered in this place after the simple ideas of sensation. Of compounding, comparing, abstracting, &c., I have but just spoken, having occasion to treat of them more at large in other places.[1]

17. *Dark Room.* I pretend not to teach, but to inquire; and therefore cannot but confess here again that external and internal sensation are the only passages that I can find of knowledge to the understanding. These alone, as far as I can discover, are the windows by which light is let into this *dark room*. For, methinks, the understanding is not much unlike a closet wholly shut from light, with only some little opening left, to let in external visible resemblances, or ideas of things without; would the pictures coming into such a dark room but stay there, and lie so orderly as to be found upon occasion, it would very much resemble the understanding of a man, in reference to all objects of sight, and the ideas of them.

[1] II xiii-xxviii; III iii

CHAPTER XII

OF COMPLEX IDEAS

1. *Made by the Mind out of simple ones.* We have hitherto considered those ideas in the reception whereof the mind is only passive, which are those simple ones received from sensation and reflection before mentioned, whereof the mind cannot make one to itself, nor have any idea which does not wholly consist of them. But as the mind is wholly passive in the reception of all its simple ideas, so it exerts several acts of its own, whereby out of its simple ideas, as the materials and foundations of the rest, the others are framed. The acts of the mind, wherein it exerts its power over its simple ideas, are chiefly these three : (1) Combining several simple ideas into one compound one; and thus all *complex ideas* are made. (2) The second is bringing two ideas, whether simple or complex, together, and setting them by one another, so as to take a view of them at once, without uniting them into one; by which way it gets all its *ideas of relations.* (3) The third is separating them from all other ideas that accompany them in their real existence; this is called *abstraction* : and thus all its *general ideas* are made. This shows man's power, and its way of operation, to be much what the same in the material and intellectual world. For the materials in both being such as he has no power over, either to make or destroy, all that man can do is either to unite them together, or to set them by one another, or wholly separate them. I shall here begin with the first of these in the consideration of complex ideas, and come to the other two in their due places. As simple ideas are observed to exist in several combinations united together, so the mind has a power to consider several of them united together as one idea, and that not only as they are united in external objects, but as itself has joined them. Ideas thus made up of several

simple ones put together, I call *complex*;—such as are beauty, gratitude, a man, an army, the universe; which, though complicated of various simple ideas, or complex ideas made up of simple ones, yet are, when the mind pleases, considered each by itself, as one entire thing, and signified by one name.

2. *Made voluntarily.* In this faculty of repeating and joining together its ideas the mind has great power in varying and multiplying the objects of its thoughts, infinitely beyond what sensation or reflection furnished it with; but all this still confined to those simple ideas which it received from those two sources, and which are the ultimate materials of all its compositions. But when it has once got these simple ideas, it is not confined barely to observation, and what offers itself from without; it can, by its own power, put together those ideas it has, and make new complex ones, which it never received so united.

3. *Are either Modes, Substances, or Relations. Complex ideas,* however compounded and decompounded, though their number be infinite, and the variety endless, wherewith they fill and entertain the thoughts of men, yet I think they may be all reduced under these three heads :

  1. *Modes.*
  2. *Substances.*
  3. *Relations.*

4. *Modes.* First, *Modes* I call such complex ideas which, however compounded, contain not in them the supposition of subsisting by themselves, but are considered as dependences on, or affections of substances; such are the ideas signified by the words *triangle, gratitude, murder,* &c. And if in this I use the word *mode* in somewhat a different sense from its ordinary signification, I beg pardon; it being unavoidable in discourses differing from the ordinary received notions either to make new words, or to use old words in somewhat a new signification; the latter whereof, in our present case, is perhaps the more tolerable of the two.

5. *Simple and mixed Modes.* Of these *modes* there are two sorts which deserve distinct consideration : First, there are some which are only variations, or different combinations, of

the same simple idea, without the mixture of any other, as a dozen, or score; which are nothing but the ideas of so many distinct units added together, and these I call *simple modes* as being contained within the bounds of one simple idea. Secondly, there are others compounded of simple ideas of several kinds, put together to make one complex one: v.g. beauty, consisting of a certain composition of colour and figure, causing delight in the beholder; theft, which being the concealed change of the possession of anything, without the consent of the proprietor, contains, as is visible, a combination of several ideas of several kinds; and these I call *mixed modes*.

6. *Substances, single or collective.* Secondly, the ideas of *substances* are such combinations of simple ideas as are taken to represent distinct particular things subsisting by themselves; in which the supposed or confused idea of substance, such as it is, is always the first and chief. Thus if to substance be joined the simple idea of a certain dull whitish colour, with certain degrees of weight, hardness, ductility, and fusibility, we have the idea of lead; and a combination of the ideas of a certain sort of figure, with the powers of motion, thought and reasoning, joined to substance, make the ordinary idea of a man. Now of substances also, there are two sorts of ideas: one of *single* substances, as they exist separately, as of a man or a sheep; the other of several of those put together, as an army of men, or flock of sheep—which *collective* ideas of several substances thus put together are as much each of them one single idea as that of a man or an unit.

7. *Relation.* Thirdly, the last sort of complex ideas is that we call *relation,* which consists in the consideration and comparing one idea with another. Of these several kinds we shall treat in their order.

CHAPTER XIII

OF SIMPLE MODES: AND FIRST, OF THE SIMPLE MODES OF SPACE

1. *Simple Modes.* Though in the foregoing part I have often mentioned simple ideas, which are truly the materials of all our knowledge; yet having treated of them there, rather in the way that they come into the mind, than as distinguished from others more compounded, it will not be perhaps amiss to take a view of some of them again under this consideration, and examine those different modifications of the same idea, which the mind either finds in things existing, or is able to make within itself without the help of any extrinsical object, or any foreign suggestion.

Those modifications of any *one* simple idea (which, as has been said, I call *simple modes*) are as perfectly different and distinct ideas in the mind as those of the greatest distance or contrariety. For the idea of two is as distinct from that of one, as blueness from heat, or either of them from any number; and yet it is made up only of that simple idea of an unit repeated; and repetitions of this kind joined together make those distinct simple modes, of a dozen, a gross, a million.

2. *Idea of Space.* I shall begin with the simple idea of *space.* I have showed above, chap. 4, that we get the idea of space, both by our sight and touch.

3. *Space and Extension.* This space, considered barely in length between any two beings, without considering anything else between them, is called *distance* : if considered in length, breadth, and thickness, I think it may be called *capacity.* The term *extension* is usually applied to it in what manner soever considered.

4. *Immensity.* Each different distance is a different modifi-

cation of space; and each idea of any different distance, or space, is a *simple mode* of this idea. Men, for the use and by the custom of measuring, settle in their minds the ideas of certain stated lengths, such as are an inch, foot, yard, fathom, mile, diameter of the earth, &c., which are so many distinct ideas made up only of space. When any such stated lengths or measures of space are made familiar to men's thoughts, they can, in their minds, repeat them as often as they will, without mixing or joining to them the idea of body, or anything else; and frame to themselves the ideas of long, square, or cubic feet, yards or fathoms, here amongst the bodies of the universe, or else beyond the utmost bounds of all bodies; and, by adding these still one to another, enlarge their idea of space as much as they please. This power of repeating or doubling any idea we have of any distance, and adding it to the former as often as we will, without being ever able to come to any stop or stint, let us enlarge it as much as we will, is that which gives us the idea of *immensity*.

5. *Figure*. There is another modification of this idea, which is nothing but the relation which the parts of the termination of extension, or circumscribed space, have amongst themselves. This the touch discovers in sensible bodies, whose extremities come within our reach; and the eye takes both from bodies and colours, whose boundaries are within its view : where, observing how the extremities terminate, either in straight lines which meet at discernible angles, or in crooked lines wherein no angles can be perceived; by considering these as they relate to one another, in all parts of the extremities of any body or space, it has that idea we call *figure,* which affords to the mind infinite variety.

7. *Place*. Another idea coming under this head, and belonging to this tribe, is that we call *place.* As in simple space, we consider the relation of distance between any two bodies or points; so in our idea of place, we consider the relation of distance betwixt anything and any two or more points, which are considered as keeping the same distance one with another, and so considered as at rest.

8. Thus, a company of chess-men, standing on the same

squares of the chess-board where we left them, we say they are all in the *same* place, or unmoved, though perhaps the chess-board hath been in the meantime carried out of one room into another; because we compared them only to the parts of the chess-board, which keep the same distance one with another. The chess-board, we also say, is in the same place it was, if it remain in the same part of the cabin, though perhaps the ship which it is in sails all the while. And the ship is said to be in the same place, supposing it kept the same distance with the parts of the neighbouring land; though perhaps the earth hath turned round, and so both chess-men, and board, and ship, have every one changed place, in respect of remoter bodies, which have kept the same distance one with another.

9. But this modification of distance we call place, being made by men for their common use, that by it they might be able to design the particular position of things, where they had occasion for such designation; men consider and determine of this place by reference to those adjacent things which best served to their present purpose, without considering other things which, to another purpose, would better determine the place of the same thing. Thus in the chess-board, the use of the designation of the place of each chess-man being determined only within that chequered piece of wood, it would cross that purpose to measure it by anything else; but when these very chess-men are put up in a bag, if anyone should ask where the black king is, it would be proper to determine the place by the parts of the room it was in, and not by the chess-board; there being another use of designing the place it is now in than when in play it was on the chess-board, and so must be determined by other bodies.

10. *Place.* That our idea of place is nothing else but such a relative position of anything as I have before mentioned I think is plain, and will be easily admitted, when we consider that we can have no idea of the place of the universe, though we can of all the parts of it; because beyond that we have not the idea of any fixed, distinct, particular beings, in reference to which we can imagine it to have any relation of distance; but all beyond it is one uniform space or expansion,

wherein the mind finds no variety, no marks. For to say that the world is somewhere, means no more than that it does exist; this, though a phrase borrowed from place, signifying only its existence, not location.

11. *Extension and Body not the same.*   There are some that would persuade us that body and extension are the same thing. If they mean by *body* and *extension* the same that other people do, viz. by *body* something that is solid and extended, whose parts are separable and movable different ways; and by *extension* only the space that lies between the extremities of those solid coherent parts, and which is possessed by them, they confound very different ideas one with another; for I appeal to every man's own thoughts, whether the idea of space be not as distinct from that of solidity, as it is from the idea of scarlet colour? It is true, solidity cannot exist without extension, neither can scarlet colour exist without extension, but this hinders not, but that they are distinct ideas. And if it be a reason to prove that spirit is different from body, because thinking includes not the idea of extension in it, the same reason will be as valid, I suppose, to prove that space is not body, because it includes not the idea of solidity in it; *space* and *solidity* being as distinct ideas as *thinking* and *extension,* and as wholly separable in the mind one from another. Body then and extension, it is evident, are two distinct ideas. For,

12. First, extension includes no solidity, nor resistance to the motion of body, as body does.

13. Secondly, the parts of pure space are inseparable one from the other, so that the continuity cannot be separated, neither really nor mentally. For I demand of anyone to remove any part of it from another, with which it is continued, even so much as in thought. To divide and separate actually is, as I think, by removing the parts one from another, to make two superficies, where before there was a continuity; and to divide mentally is to make in the mind two superficies, where before there was a continuity, and consider them as removed one from the other; which can only

be done in things considered by the mind as capable of being separated, and by separation, of acquiring new distinct superficies, which they then have not, but are capable of. But neither of these ways of separation, whether real or mental, is, as I think, compatible to pure space.

14. Thirdly, the parts of pure space are immovable, which follows from their inseparability, motion being nothing but change of distance between any two things; but this cannot be between parts that are inseparable, which, therefore, must needs be at perpetual rest one amongst another.

Thus the determined idea of simple space distinguishes it plainly and sufficiently from body, since its parts are inseparable, immovable, and without resistance to the motion of body.

16. *Division of Beings into Bodies and Spirits proves not Space and Body the same.* Those who contend that space and body are the same bring this dilemma : either this space is something or nothing; if nothing be between two bodies, they must necessarily touch; if it be allowed to be something, they ask, Whether it be body or spirit? To which I answer by another question, Who told them that there was, or could be, nothing but solid beings, which could not think, and thinking beings that were not extended?—which is all they mean by the terms *body* and *spirit*.

17. *Substance, which we know not, no Proof against Space without Body.* If it be demanded (as usually it is) whether this space, void of body, be *substance* or *accident*, I shall readily answer I know not; nor shall be ashamed to own my ignorance, till they that ask show me a clear distinct idea of substance.

18. I endeavour as much as I can to deliver myself from those fallacies which we are apt to put upon ourselves, by taking words for things. It helps not our ignorance to feign a knowledge where we have none, by making a noise with sounds, without clear and distinct significations. Names made at pleasure neither alter the nature of things, nor make us understand them, but as they are signs of and stand for determined ideas. And I desire those who lay so much

stress on the sound of these two syllables, *substance,* to consider whether applying it, as they do, to the infinite, incomprehensible God, to finite spirit, and to body, it be in the same
sense; and whether it stands for the same idea, when each of
those three so different beings are called substances. If so,
whether it will not thence follow that God, spirits, and body,
agreeing in the same common nature of substance, differ not
any otherwise than in a bare different modification of that
substance; as a tree and a pebble, being in the same sense
body, and agreeing in the common nature of body, differ only
in a bare modification of that common matter, which will be
a very harsh doctrine. If they say that they apply it to God,
finite spirit, and matter, in three different significations and
that it stands for one idea when God is said to be a substance,
for another when the soul is called substance, and for a third
when a body is called so; if the name substance stands for
three several distinct ideas, they would do well to make known
those distinct ideas, or at least to give three distinct names
to them, to prevent in so important a notion the confusion
and errors that will naturally follow from the promiscuous use
of so doubtful a term; which is so far from being suspected to
have three distinct, that in ordinary use it has scarce one
clear distinct signification. And if they can thus make three
distinct ideas of substance, what hinders why another may
not make a fourth?

19. *Substance and accidents of little use in Philosophy.*
They who first ran into the notion of *accidents,* as a sort
of real beings that needed something to inhere in, were forced
to find out the word *substance* to support them. Had the
poor Indian philosopher (who imagined that the earth also
wanted something to bear it up) but thought of this word
" substance ", he needed not to have been at the trouble to find
an elephant to support it, and a tortoise to support his
elephant; the word " substance " would have done it effectually.
And he that inquired might have taken it for as good an
answer from an Indian philosopher that substance, without
knowing what it is, is that which supports the earth, as we

take it for a sufficient answer and good doctrine from our European philosophers that substance, without knowing what it is, is that which supports accidents. So that of substance we have no idea of what it is, but only a confused, obscure one of what it does.

21. *A Vacuum beyond the utmost Bounds of Body.* But to return to our idea of space. If body be not supposed infinite (which I think no one will affirm), I would ask whether, if God placed a man at the extremity of corporeal beings, he could not stretch his hand beyond his body? If he could, then he would put his arm where there was before space without body; and if there he spread his fingers, there would still be space between them without body. If he could not stretch out his hand, it must be because of some external hindrance; and then I ask whether that which hinders his hand from moving outwards be substance or accident, something or nothing? And when they have resolved that, they will be able to resolve themselves what that is, which is or may be between two bodies at a distance, that is not body, and has no solidity. In the meantime, the argument is at least as good, that, where nothing hinders (as beyond the utmost bounds of all bodies), a body put into motion may move on, as where there is nothing between, there two bodies must necessarily touch. For pure space between is sufficient to take away the necessity of mutual contact; but bare space in the way is not sufficient to stop motion. The truth is, these men must either own that they think body infinite, though they are loth to speak it out, or else affirm that space is not body.

22. *The Power of Annihilation proves a Vacuum.* Further, those who assert the impossibility of space existing without matter must not only make body infinite, but must also deny a power in God to annihilate any part of matter. No one, I suppose, will deny that God can put an end to all motion that is in matter, and fix all the bodies of the universe in a perfect quiet and rest, and continue them so long as he pleases. Whoever then will allow that God can, during such a

general rest, annihilate either this book or the body of him that reads it, must necessarily admit the possibility of a vacuum. For, it is evident that the space that was filled by the parts of the annihilated body will still remain, and be a space without body. And those who dispute for or against a vacuum do thereby confess they have distinct ideas of vacuum and plenum, i.e. that they have an idea of extension void of solidity, though they deny its existence; or else they dispute about nothing at all. For they who so much alter the signification of words, as to call extension body, and consequently make the whole essence of body to be nothing but pure extension without solidity, must talk absurdly whenever they speak of *vacuum;* since it is impossible for extension to be without extension.

23. *Motion proves a Vacuum.* But not to go so far as beyond the utmost bounds of body in the universe, nor appeal to God's omnipotency to find a vacuum, the motion of bodies that are in our view and neighbourhood seems to me plainly to evince it. For I desire anyone so to divide a solid body, of any dimension he pleases, as to make it possible for the solid parts to move up and down freely every way within the bounds of that superficies, if there be not left in it a void space as big as the least part into which he has divided the said solid body. And let this void space be as little as it will, it destroys the hypothesis of plenitude.

24. *The Ideas of Space and Body distinct.* But the question being here whether the idea of space or extension be the same with the idea of body, it is not necessary to prove the real existence of a vacuum, but the idea of it; which it is plain men have when they inquire and dispute whether there be a vacuum or no. For, if they had not the idea of space without body, they could not make a question about its existence; and, if their idea of body did not include in it something more than the bare idea of space, they could have no doubt about the plenitude of the world; and it would be as absurd to demand whether there were space without body, as whether there were space without space, or body without body, since these were but different names of the same idea.

25. *Extension being inseparable from Body, proves it not the same.* It is true, the idea of extension joins itself so inseparably with all visible, and most tangible qualities, that it suffers us to see no one, or feel very few external objects, without taking in impressions of extension too. This readiness of extension to make itself be taken notice of so constantly with other ideas has been the occasion, I guess, that some have made the whole essence of body to consist in extension; which is not much to be wondered at, since some have had their minds, by their eyes and touch (the busiest of all our senses), so filled with the idea of extension, and, as it were, wholly possessed with it, that they allowed no existence to anything that had not extension. I shall not now argue with those men, I shall desire them to consider that, had they reflected on their ideas of tastes and smells as much as on those of sight and touch; nay, had they examined their ideas of hunger and thirst, and several other pains, they would have found that they included in them no idea of extension at all, which is but an affection of body, as well as the rest, discoverable by our senses, which are scarce acute enough to look into the pure essences of things.

27. *Ideas of Space and Solidity distinct.* To conclude: whatever men shall think concerning the existence of a vacuum, this is plain to me: that we have as clear an idea of space distinct from solidity, as we have of solidity distinct from motion, or motion from space. We have not any two more distinct ideas, and we can as easily conceive space without solidity, as we can conceive body or space without motion, though it be never so certain that neither body nor motion can exist without space.

CHAPTER XIV

OF DURATION AND ITS SIMPLE MODES

1. *Duration is fleeting Extension.* There is another sort of distance, or length, the idea whereof we get not from the permanent parts of space, but from the fleeting and perpetually perishing parts of succession. This we call *duration*; the simple modes whereof are any different lengths of it whereof we have distinct ideas, as *hours, days, years,* &c., *time* and *eternity.*

2. *Its Idea from Reflection on the Train of our Ideas.* The answer of a great man, to one who asked what time was, *Si non rogas intelligo* (which amounts to this; The more I set myself to think of it, the less I understand it), might perhaps persuade one that time, which reveals all other things, is itself not to be discovered. Duration, time, and eternity, are, not without reason, thought to have something very abstruse in their nature. But however remote these may seem from our comprehension, yet if we trace them right to their originals, I doubt not but one of those sources of all our knowledge, viz. sensation and reflection, will be able to furnish us with these ideas, as clear and distinct as many others which are thought much less obscure; and we shall find that the idea of eternity itself is derived from the same common original with the rest of our ideas.

3. To understand *time* and *eternity* aright, we ought with attention to consider what idea it is we have of *duration,* and how we came by it. It is evident to anyone who will but observe what passes in his own mind that there is a train of ideas which constantly succeed one another in his understanding, as long as he is awake. Reflection on these appearances of several ideas one after another in our minds, is that which furnishes us with the idea of *succession*; and the

distance between any parts of that succession, or between the appearance of any two ideas in our minds, is that we call *duration*. For whilst we are thinking, or whilst we receive successively several ideas in our minds, we know that we do exist; and so we call the existence, or the continuation of the existence of ourselves, or anything else, commensurate to the succession of any ideas in our minds, the duration of ourselves, or any such other thing co-existing with our thinking.

4. *Its idea from reflection on the train of our Ideas.* That we have our notion of succession and duration from this original, viz. from reflection on the train of ideas, which we find to appear one after another in our own minds, seems plain to me, in that we have no perception of duration but by considering the train of ideas that take their turns in our understandings. When that succession of ideas ceases, our perception of duration ceases with it; which everyone clearly experiments in himself, whilst he sleeps soundly, whether an hour or a day, a month or a year; of which duration of things, whilst he sleeps or thinks not, he has no perception at all, but it is quite lost to him; and the moment wherein he leaves off to think, till the moment he begins to think again, seems to him to have no distance. And so I doubt not but it would be to a waking man, if it were possible for him to keep only one idea in his mind, without variation and the succession of others. And we see that one who fixes his thoughts very intently on one thing, so as to take but little notice of the succession of ideas that pass in his mind, whilst he is taken up with that earnest contemplation, lets slip out of his account a good part of that duration, and thinks that time shorter than it is. But if sleep commonly unites the distant parts of duration, it is because during that time we have no succession of ideas in our minds. For, if a man, during his sleep, dreams, and variety of ideas make themselves perceptible in his mind one after another, he hath then, during such a dreaming, a sense of duration, and of the length of it. By which it is to me very clear that men derive their ideas of duration from their reflection on the train of the ideas they observe to succeed one another in their own under-

standings; without which observation they can have no notion of duration, whatever may happen in the world.

5. *The Idea of Duration applicable to Things whilst we sleep.* Indeed a man having, from reflecting on the succession and number of his own thoughts, got the notion or idea of duration, he can apply that notion to things which exist while he does not think, as he that has got the idea of extension from bodies by his sight or touch, can apply it to distances, where no body is seen or felt. And therefore, though a man has no perception of the length of duration which passed whilst he slept or thought not, yet, having observed the revolution of days and nights, and found the length of their duration to be in appearance regular and constant, he can, upon the supposition that that revolution has proceeded after the same manner whilst he was asleep or thought not, as it used to do at other times, he can, I say, imagine and make allowance for the length of duration whilst he slept.

6. *The Idea of Succession not from Motion.* Thus by reflecting on the appearing of various ideas one after another in our understandings we get the notion of succession; which, if anyone should think we did rather get from our observation of motion by our senses, he will perhaps be of my mind when he considers that even motion produces in his mind an idea of succession no otherwise than as it produces there a continued train of distinguishable ideas. For a man looking upon a body really moving perceives yet no motion at all unless that motion produces a constant train of successive ideas: v.g. a man becalmed at sea, out of sight of land, in a fair day may look on the sun, or sea, or ship, a whole hour together, and perceive no motion at all in either, though it be certain that two, and perhaps all of them, have moved during that time a great way. But as soon as he perceives either of them to have changed distance with some other body, as soon as this motion produces any new idea in him, then he perceives that there has been motion. But wherever a man is, with all things at rest about him, without perceiving any motion at all, if during this hour of quiet he has been thinking, he will perceive the

various ideas of his own thoughts in his own mind appearing one after another, and thereby observe and find succession where he could observe no motion.

7. And this, I think, is the reason why motions very slow, though they are constant, are not perceived by us; because in their remove from one sensible part towards another their change of distance is so slow that it causes no new ideas in us, but a good while one after another. And so not causing a constant train of new ideas to follow one another immediately in our minds, we have no perception of motion; which consisting in a constant succession, we cannot perceive that succession without a constant succession of varying ideas arising from it.

8. On the contrary, things that move so swift as not to affect the senses distinctly with several distinguishable distances of their motion, and so cause not any train of ideas in the mind, are not also perceived to move. For anything that moves round about in a circle, in less time than our ideas are wont to succeed one another in our minds, is not perceived to move, but seems to be a perfect entire circle of that matter or colour, and not a part of a circle in motion.

10. Let a cannon-bullet pass through a room, and in its way take with it any limb or fleshy parts of a man, it is as clear as any demonstration can be that it must strike successively the two sides of the room; it is also evident, that it must touch one part of the flesh first, and another after, and so in succession; and yet, I believe, nobody who ever felt the pain of such a shot, or heard the blow against the two distant walls, could perceive any succession either in the pain or sound of so swift a stroke. Such a part of duration as this, wherein we perceive no succession, is that which we may call an *instant*, and is that which takes up the time of only one idea in our minds, without the succession of another, wherein, therefore, we perceive no succession at all.

12. *This Train, the Measure of other Successions.* So that to me it seems that the constant and regular succession of *ideas* in a waking man is, as it were, the measure and standard of all other successions. Whereof, if any one either exceeds the

pace of our ideas, as where two sounds or pains, &c., take up in their succession the duration of but one idea; or else where any motion or succession is so slow, as that it keeps not pace with the ideas in our minds, or the quickness in which they take their turns, as when any one or more ideas in their ordinary course come into our mind, between those which are offered to the sight by the different perceptible distances of a body in motion, or between sounds or smells following one another, there also the sense of a constant continued succession is lost, and we perceive it not, but with certain gaps of rest between.

16. *Ideas, however made, include no Sense of Motion.* It is not then *motion,* but the constant train of ideas in our minds whilst we are waking, that furnishes us with the idea of duration, whereof motion no other wise gives us any perception than as it causes in our minds a constant succession of ideas, as I have before showed; and we have as clear an idea of succession and duration by the train of other ideas succeeding one another in our minds, without the idea of any motion, as by the train of ideas caused by the uninterrupted sensible change of distance between two bodies, which we have from motion; and therefore we should as well have the idea of duration were there no sense of motion at all.

17. *Time is Duration set out by Measures.* Having thus got the idea of duration, the next thing natural for the mind to do is to get some *measure* of this common duration, whereby it might judge of its different lengths, and consider the distinct order wherein several things exist, without which a great part of our knowledge would be confused, and a great part of history be rendered very useless. This consideration of duration, as set out by certain periods, and marked by certain measures or epochs, is that, I think, which most properly we call *time.*

18. *A good Measure of Time must divide its whole Duration into equal Periods.* In the measuring of extension there is nothing more required but the application of the standard or measure we make use of to the thing of whose extension we

would be informed. But in the measuring of duration this cannot be done, because no two different parts of succession can be put together to measure one another. And nothing being a measure of duration but duration, as nothing is of extension but extension, we cannot keep by us any standing, unvarying measure of duration, which consists in a constant fleeting succession, as we can of certain lengths of extension, as inches, feet, yards, &c., marked out in permanent parcels of matter. Nothing then could serve well for a convenient measure of time but what has divided the whole length of its duration into apparently equal portions by constantly repeated periods.

19. *The Revolutions of the Sun and Moon, the properest Measures of Time.* The diurnal and annual revolutions of the sun, as having been, from the beginning of nature, constant, regular, and universally observable by all mankind, and supposed equal to one another, have been with reason made use of for the measure of duration. But the distinction of days and years having depended on the motion of the sun, it has brought this mistake with it, that it has been thought that motion and duration were the measure one of another. For men, in the measuring of the length of time, having been accustomed to the ideas of minutes, hours, days, months, years, &c., which they found themselves upon any mention of time or duration presently to think on, all which portions of time were measured out by the motion of those heavenly bodies, they were apt to confound time and motion, or at least to think that they had a necessary connexion one with another. Whereas any constant periodical appearance, or alteration of ideas, in seemingly equidistant spaces of duration, if constant and universally observable, would have as well distinguished the intervals of time as those that have been made use of. For, supposing the sun, which some have taken to be a fire, had been lighted up at the same distance of time that it now every day comes about to the same meridian, and then gone out again about twelve hours after, and that in the space of an annual revolution it had sensibly increased

in brightness and heat, and so decreased again, would not such regular appearances serve to measure out the distances of duration to all that could observe it, as well without as with motion? For if the appearances were constant, universally observable, and in equidistant periods, they would serve mankind for measure of time as well were the motion away.

20. *But not by their Motion, but periodical Appearances.* For the freezing of water, or the blowing of a plant, returning at equidistant periods in all parts of the earth, would as well serve men to reckon their years by, as the motions of the sun; and in effect we see that some people in America counted their years by the coming of certain birds amongst them at their certain seasons, and leaving them at others.. And if the sun moved from the creation to the flood constantly in the equator, and so equally dispersed its light and heat to all the habitable parts of the earth, in days all of the same length, without its annual variations to the tropics, as a late ingenious author supposes, I do not think it very easy to imagine that (notwithstanding the motion of the sun) men should in the antediluvian world, from the beginning, count by years, or measure their time by periods that had no sensible marks very obvious to distinguish them by.

21. *No two Parts of Duration can be certainly known to be equal.* We must, therefore, carefully distinguish betwixt duration itself and the measures we make use of to judge of its length. Duration, in itself, is to be considered as going on in one constant, equal, uniform course; but none of the measures of it which we make use of can be known to do so, nor can we be assured that their assigned parts or periods are equal in duration one to another, for two successive lengths of duration, however measured, can never be demonstrated to be equal. The motion of the sun, which the world used so long and so confidently for an exact measure of duration, has, as I said, been found in its several parts unequal. And though men have, of late, made use of a pendulum, as a more steady and regular motion than that of the sun, or (to speak more truly) of the earth, yet if anyone should be asked how he certainly knows that the two successive swings

of a pendulum are equal, it would be very hard to satisfy him that they are infallibly so; since we cannot be sure that the cause ·of that motion, which is unknown to us, shall always operate equally; and we are sure that the medium in which the pendulum moves is not constantly the same; either of which varying may alter the equality of such periods, and thereby destroy the certainty and exactness of the measure by motion, as well as any other periods of other appearances; the notion of duration still remaining clear, though our measures of it cannot (any of them) be demonstrated to be exact. Since then no two portions of succession can be brought together, it is impossible ever certainly to know their equality. All that we can do for a measure of time is to take such as have continual successive appearances at seemingly equidistant periods, of which seeming equality we have no other measure, but such as the train of our own ideas have lodged in our memories, with the concurrence of other probable reasons, to persuade us of their equality.

24. *Our Measure of Time applicable to Duration before Time.* The mind, having once got such a measure of time as the annual revolution of the sun, can apply that measure to duration wherein that measure itself did not exist, and with which, in the reality of its being, it had nothing to do. The idea of duration equal to an annual revolution of the sun is as easily applicable in our thoughts to duration, where no sun nor motion was, as the idea of a foot or yard, taken from bodies here, can be applied in our thoughts to distances beyond the confines of the world, where are no bodies at all.

27. *Eternity.* By the same means, therefore, and from the same original that we come to have the idea of time, we have also that idea which we call Eternity; viz. having got the idea of succession and duration by reflecting on the train of our own ideas, caused in us either by the natural appearances of those ideas coming constantly of themselves into our waking thoughts, or else caused by external objects successively affecting our senses; and having from the revolutions of the sun got the ideas of certain lengths of duration, we can in our thoughts add such lengths of duration to one another,

as often as we please, and apply them, so added, to durations past or to come. And this we can continue to do on, without bounds or limits, and proceed *in infinitum,* and apply thus the length of the annual motion of the sun to duration, supposed before the sun's or any other motion had its being; which is no more difficult or absurd, than to apply the notion I have of the moving of a shadow one hour to-day upon the sun-dial to the duration of something last night, v.g. the burning of a candle, which is now absolutely separate from all actual motion; it is no more than to think that, had the sun shone then on the dial, and moved after the same rate it doth now, the shadow on the dial would have passed from one hour-line to another whilst that flame of the candle lasted.

31. And thus I think it is plain that from these two fountains of all knowledge before mentioned, viz. reflection and sensation, we get the ideas of duration, and the measures of it.

For, First, by observing what passes in our minds, how our ideas there in train constantly some vanish and others begin to appear, we come by the idea of *succession.*

Secondly, by observing a distance in the parts of this succession, we get the idea of *duration.*

Thirdly, by sensation observing certain appearances, at certain regular and seeming equidistant periods, we get the ideas of certain *lengths* or *measures of duration,* as minutes, hours, days, years, &c.

Fourthly, by being able to repeat those measures of time, or ideas of stated length of duration in our minds, as often as we will, we can come to *imagine duration, where nothing does really endure or exist*; and thus we imagine to-morrow, next year, or seven years hence.

Fifthly, by being able to repeat any such idea of any length of time, as of a minute, a year, or an age, as often as we will in our own thoughts, and adding them one to another, without ever coming to the end of such addition, any nearer than we can to the end of number, to which we can always add, we come by the idea of *eternity,* as the future eternal duration of our souls, as well as the eternity of that infinite Being which must necessarily have always existed.

Sixthly, by considering any part of infinite duration, as set out by periodical measures, we come by the idea of what we call *time* in general.

[CHAPTER XV]

[OF DURATION AND EXPANSION, CONSIDERED TOGETHER]

CHAPTER XVI

OF NUMBER

1. *Number the simplest and most universal Idea.* Amongst all the ideas we have, as there is none suggested to the mind by more ways, so there is none more simple, than that of *unity,* or one; it has no shadow of variety or composition in it; every object our senses are employed about, every idea in our understandings, every thought of our minds, brings this idea along with it. And therefore it is the most intimate to our thoughts, as well as it is, in its agreement to all other things, the most universal idea we have. For number applies itself to men, angels, actions, thoughts, everything that either doth exist, or can be imagined.

2. *Its Modes made by Addition.* By repeating this idea in our minds, and adding the repetitions together, we come by the *complex* ideas of the *modes* of it. Thus, by adding one to one, we have the complex idea of a couple; by putting twelve units together, we have the complex idea of a dozen; and of a score, or a million, or any other number.

3. *Each Mode distinct.* The *simple modes* of *number* are of all other the most distinct; every the least variation, which is

an unit, making each combination as clearly different from that which approacheth nearest to it, as the most remote; two being as distinct from one, as two hundred; and the idea of two as distinct from the idea of three, as the magnitude of the whole earth is from that of a mite. This is not so in other simple modes, in which it is not so easy, nor perhaps possible for us to distinguish betwixt two approaching ideas, which yet are really different. For who will undertake to find a difference between the white of this paper and that of the next degree to it, or can form distinct ideas of every the least excess in extension?

4. *Therefore Demonstrations in Numbers the most precise.* The clearness and distinctness of each mode of number from all others, even those that approach nearest, makes me apt to think that demonstrations in numbers, if they are not more evident and exact than in extension, yet they are more general in their use, and more determinate in their application. Because the ideas of numbers are more precise and distinguishable than in extension, where every equality and excess are not so easy to be observed or measured, because our thoughts cannot in space arrive at any determined smallness beyond which it cannot go, as an unit; and therefore the quantity or proportion of any the least excess cannot be discovered.

5. *Names necessary to Numbers.* By the repeating, as has been said, the idea of an unit, and joining it to another unit, we make thereof one collective idea, marked by the name ' two'. And whosoever can do this, and proceed on, still adding one more to the last collective idea which he had of any number, and give a name to it, may count, or have ideas, for several collections of units, distinguished one from another, as far as he hath a series of names for following numbers, and a memory to retain that series, with their several names. For, the several simple modes of numbers being in our minds but so many combinations of units, which have no variety, nor are capable of any other difference but more or less, names or marks for each distinct combination seem more necessary than in any other sort of ideas. For, without such names or marks, we can hardly well make use of numbers in reckon-

ing, especially where the combination is made up of any great multitude of units; which put together, without a name or mark to distinguish that precise collection, will hardly be kept from being a heap in confusion.

6. This I think to be the reason why some Americans[1] I have spoken with (who were otherwise of quick and rational parts enough), could not, as we do, by any means count to 1000, nor had any distinct idea of that number, though they could reckon very well to 20. Because their language being scanty, and accommodated only to the few necessaries of a needy, simple life, unacquainted either with trade or mathematics, had no words in it to stand for 1000; so that when they were discoursed with of those greater numbers, they would show the hairs of their head, to express a great multitude, which they could not number; which inability, I suppose, proceeded from their want of names.

7. *Why Children number not earlier.* For he that will count twenty, or have any idea of that number, must know that nineteen went before, with the distinct name or sign of every one of them, as they stand marked in their order; for wherever this fails a gap is made, the chain breaks, and the progress in numbering can go no further. So that to reckon right, it is required: (1) that the mind distinguish carefully two ideas, which are different one from another only by the addition or subtraction of one unit; (2) that it retain in memory the names or marks of the several combinations, from an unit to that number, and that not confusedly, and at random, but in that exact order that the numbers follow one another. In either of which, if it trips, the whole business of numbering will be disturbed, and there will remain only the confused idea of multitude, but the ideas necessary to distinct numeration will not be attained to.

8. *Number measures all Measurables.* This further is observable in number that it is that which the mind makes use of in measuring all things that by us are measurable, which principally are *expansion* and *duration*; and our idea of infinity, even when applied to those, seems to be nothing but

[1] American Indians.

the infinity of number. For what else are our ideas of eternity and immensity, but the repeated additions of certain ideas of imagined parts of duration and expansion, with the infinity of number; in which we can come to no end of addition? For such an inexhaustible stock number (of all other our ideas) most clearly furnishes us with, as is obvious to everyone. For let a man collect into one sum as great a number as he pleases, this multitude, how great soever, lessens not one jot the power of adding to it, or brings him any nearer the end of the inexhaustible stock of number, where still there remains as much to be added, as if none were taken out. And this *endless addition* or *addibility* (if anyone like the word better) of numbers, so apparent to the mind, is that, I think, which gives us the clearest and most distinct idea of infinity.

[CHAPTER XVII]

[OF INFINITY]

[CHAPTER XVIII]

[OF OTHER SIMPLE MODES]

CHAPTER XIX

OF THE MODES OF THINKING

1. *Sensation, Remembrance, Contemplation,* &c. When the mind turns its view inwards upon itself, and contemplates its own actions, *thinking* is the first that occurs. In it the mind observes a great variety of modifications, and from thence receives distinct ideas. Thus the perception which actually

accompanies, and is annexed to, any impression on the body made by an external object, being distinct from all other modifications of thinking, furnishes the mind with a distinct idea, which we call *sensation*; which is, as it were, the actual entrance of any idea into the understanding by the senses. The same idea, when it again recurs without the operation of the like object on the external sensory, is *remembrance*; if it be sought after by the mind, and with pain and endeavour found, and brought again in view, it is *recollection*: if it be held there long under attentive consideration, it is *contemplation*; when ideas float in our mind, without any reflection or regard of the understanding, it is that which the French call *rêverie*; our language has scarce a name for it; when the ideas that offer themselves (for, as I have observed in another place, whilst we are awake, there will always be a train of ideas succeeding one another in our minds) are taken notice of, and, as it were, registered in the memory, it is *attention*; when the mind with great earnestness, and of choice, fixes its view on any idea, considers it on all sides, and will not be called off by the ordinary solicitation of other ideas, it is that we call *intention* or *study*. Sleep, without dreaming, is rest from all these; and *dreaming* itself is the having of ideas (whilst the outward senses are stopped, so that they receive not outward objects with their usual quickness) in the mind, not suggested by any external objects, or known occasion, nor under any choice or conduct of the understanding at all: and whether that which we call *ecstasy* be not dreaming with the eyes open I leave to be examined.

2. These are some few instances of those various modes of thinking which the mind may observe in itself, and so have as distinct ideas of as it hath of white and red, a square or a circle. I do not pretend to enumerate them all, nor to treat at large of this set of ideas, which are got from reflection; that would be to make a volume. It suffices to my present purpose to have shown here, by some few examples, of what sort these ideas are, and how the mind comes by them, especially since I shall have occasion hereafter to treat more

at large of *reasoning, judging, volition,* and *knowledge,* which are some of the most considerable operations of the mind, and modes of thinking.[1]

3. *The various Attention of the Mind in thinking.* But perhaps it may not be an unpardonable digression, nor wholly impertinent to our present design, if we reflect here upon the different state of the mind in thinking, which those instances of attention, reverie, and dreaming, &c., before mentioned, naturally enough suggest. That there are ideas, some or other, always present in the mind of a waking man, everyone's experience convinces him, though the mind employs itself about them with several degrees of attention. Sometimes the mind fixes itself with so much earnestness on the contemplation of some objects that it turns their ideas on all sides, remarks their relations and circumstances, and views every part so nicely and with such intention that it shuts out all other thoughts, and takes no notice of the ordinary impressions made then on the senses, which at another season would produce very sensible perceptions. At other times it barely observes the train of ideas that succeed in the understanding, without directing and pursuing any of them; and at other times it lets them pass almost quite unregarded, as faint shadows that make no impression.

4. *Hence it is probable that Thinking is the Action, not Essence of the Soul.* This difference of intention, and remission of the mind in thinking, with a great variety of degrees between earnest study and very near minding nothing at all, everyone, I think, has experimented in himself. Trace it a little further, and you find the mind in sleep retired as it were from the senses, and out of the reach of those motions made on the organs of sense, which at other times produce very vivid and sensible ideas. I need not, for this, instance in those who sleep out whole stormy nights, without hearing the thunder, or seeing the lightning, or feeling the shaking of the house, which are sensible enough to those who are waking. But in this retirement of the mind from the senses it often retains a yet more loose and incoherent manner of thinking which we

[1] Volition, II, xxi; reasoning, judging, knowledge, IV.

call dreaming. And, last of all, sound sleep closes the scene quite, and puts an end to all appearances. This I think almost everyone has experience of in himself, and his own observation without difficulty leads him thus far. That which I would further conclude from hence is that since the mind can sensibly put on, at several times, several degrees of thinking, and be sometimes, even in a waking man, so remiss, as to have thoughts dim and obscure to that degree that they are very little removed from none at all; and at last, in the dark retirements of sound sleep, loses the sight perfectly of all ideas whatsoever; since, I say, this is evidently so in matter of fact and constant experience, I ask whether it be not probable that thinking is the action and not the essence of the soul? Since the operations of agents will easily admit of intention and remission, but the essences of things are not conceived capable of any such variation. But this by the by.

CHAPTER **XX**

OF MODES OF PLEASURE AND PAIN

1. *Pleasure and Pain, simple Ideas.* Amongst the simple ideas which we receive both from sensation and reflection *pain* and *pleasure* are two very considerable ones. For, as in the body there is sensation barely in itself, or accompanied with pain or pleasure, so the thought or perception of the mind is simply so, or else accompanied also with pleasure or pain, delight or trouble, call it how you please. These, like other simple ideas, cannot be described, nor their names defined; the way of knowing them is, as of the simple ideas of the senses, only by experience. For, to define them by the presence of good or evil is no otherwise to make them known to us than by making us reflect on what we feel in ourselves, upon the several and various operations of good and evil upon our minds, as they are differently applied to or considered by us.

2. *Good and Evil, what.* Things then are good or evil only

in reference to pleasure or pain. That we call *good* which is apt to cause or increase pleasure, or diminish pain in us, or else to procure or preserve us the possession of any other good or absence of any evil. And, on the contrary, we name that *evil* which is apt to produce or increase any pain, or diminish any pleasure in us, or else to procure us any evil, or deprive us of any good. By *pleasure* and *pain* I must be understood to mean of body or mind, as they are commonly distinguished, though in truth they be only different constitutions of the mind, sometimes occasioned by disorder in the body, sometimes by thoughts of the mind.

3. *Our passions moved by Good and Evil.* Pleasure and pain and that which causes them, good and evil, are the hinges on which our passions turn. And if we reflect on ourselves, and observe how these, under various considerations, operate in us; what modifications or tempers of mind, what internal sensations (if I may so call them) they produce in us we may thence form to ourselves the ideas of our passions.

4. *Love.* Thus anyone reflecting upon the thought he has of the delight which any present or absent thing is apt to produce in him has the idea we call *love*.

5. *Hatred.* On the contrary, the thought of the pain which anything present or absent is apt to produce in us is what we call *hatred*.

6. *Desire.* The uneasiness a man finds in himself upon the absence of anything whose present enjoyment carries the idea of delight with it is that we call *desire*; which is greater or less, as that uneasiness is more or less vehement.

7. *Joy.* *Joy* is a delight of the mind from the consideration of the present or assured approaching possession of a good; and we are then possessed of any good, when we have it so in our power that we can use it when we please.

8. *Sorrow.* *Sorrow* is uneasiness in the mind, upon the thought of a good lost, which might have been enjoyed longer, or the sense of a present evil.

9. *Hope.* *Hope* is that pleasure in the mind which everyone finds in himself, upon the thought of a profitable future enjoyment of a thing which is apt to delight him.

10. *Fear.* *Fear* is an uneasiness of the mind upon the thought of future evil likely to befall us.

11. *Despair.* *Despair* is the thought of the unattainableness of any good, which works differently in men's minds, sometimes producing uneasiness or pain, sometimes rest and indolency.

12. *Anger.* *Anger* is uneasiness or discomposure of the mind upon the receipt of any injury, with a present purpose of revenge.

13. *Envy.* *Envy* is an uneasiness of mind, caused by the consideration of a good we desire obtained by one we think should not have had it before us.

14. *What Passions all Men have.* These two last, *envy* and *anger,* not being caused by pain and pleasure simply in themselves, but having in them some mixed considerations of ourselves and others, are not therefore to be found in all men, because those other parts, of valuing their merits, or intending revenge, is wanting in them. But all the rest, terminating purely in pain and pleasure, are, I think, to be found in all men.

16. It is further to be considered that, in reference to the passions, the removal or lessening of a pain is considered, and operates as a pleasure; and the loss or diminishing of a pleasure as a pain.

17. *Shame.* The passions too have most of them, in most persons, operations on the body, and cause various changes in it, which not being always sensible, do not make a necessary part of the idea of each passion. For *shame,* which is an uneasiness of the mind upon the thought of having done something which is indecent, or will lessen the valued esteem which others have for us, has not always blushing accompanying it.

CHAPTER XXI

OF POWER

① *This Idea how got.* The mind being every day informed by the senses of the alteration of those simple ideas it observes in things without; and taking notice how one comes to an end, and ceases to be, and another begins to exist which was not before; reflecting also on what passes within itself, and observing a constant change of its ideas, sometimes by the impression of outward objects on the senses, and sometimes by the determination of its own choice; and concluding from what it has so constantly observed to have been, that the like changes will for the future be made in the same things, by like agents, and by the like ways, considers in one thing the possibility of having any of its simple ideas changed, and in another the possibility of making that change; and so comes by that idea which we call *power.* Thus we say, fire has a power to melt gold, i.e. to destroy the consistency of its insensible parts, and consequently its hardness, and make it fluid, and gold has a power to be melted; that the sun has a power to blanch wax, and wax a power to be blanched by the sun, whereby the yellowness is destroyed, and whiteness made to exist in its room. In which, and the like cases, the power we consider is in reference to the change of perceivable ideas. For we cannot observe any alteration to be made in, or operation upon anything, but by the observable change of its sensible ideas, nor conceive any alteration to be made, but by conceiving a change of some of its ideas.

②. *Power, active and passive.* Power thus considered is two-fold, viz. as able to make, or able to receive any change. The one may be called *active,* and the other *passive* power. Whether matter be not wholly destitute of active power, as its author, God, is truly above all passive power, and whether the intermediate state of created spirits be not that

alone which is capable of both active and passive power, may
be worth consideration. I shall not now enter into that inquiry,
my present business being not to search into the original of
power, but how we come by the idea of it. But since active
powers make so great a part of our complex ideas of natural
substances (as we shall see hereafter[1]), and I mention them as
such, according to common apprehension; yet they being not,
perhaps, so truly active powers as our hasty thoughts are apt
to represent them, I judge it not amiss, by this intimation, to
direct our minds to the consideration of God and spirits, for
the clearest idea of active power.

(3.) *Power includes Relation.* I confess power includes in it
some kind of *relation* (a relation to action or change), as
indeed which of our ideas, of what kind soever, when
attentively considered, does not? For, our ideas of extension,
duration, and number, do they not all contain in them a secret
relation of the parts? Figure and motion have something
relative in them much more visibly. And sensible qualities,
as colours and smells, &c., what are they but the powers of
different bodies, in relation to our perception, &c.? And, if
considered in the things themselves, do they not depend on the
bulk, figure, texture, and motion of the parts? All which
include some kind of relation in them. Our idea therefore of
power, I think, may well have a place amongst other simple
ideas, and be considered as one of them; being one of those
that make a principal ingredient in our complex ideas of
substances, as we shall hereafter have occasion to observe.[2]

(4.) *The clearest Idea of active Power had from Spirit.* We
are abundantly furnished with the idea of passive power
by almost all sorts of sensible things. In most of them we
cannot avoid observing their sensible qualities, nay, their very
substances, to be in a continual flux. And therefore with reason
we look on them as liable still to the same change. Nor have
we of active power (which is the more proper signification of
the word ' power ') fewer instances. Since, whatever change
is observed, the mind must collect a power somewhere able

[1] II viii 23-25; xxiii 7-11

[2] II xxiii 7

to make that change, as well as a possibility in the thing itself to receive it. But yet, if we will consider it attentively, bodies, by our senses, do not afford us so clear and distinct an idea of active power as we have from reflection on the operations of our minds. For all power relating to action, and there being but two sorts of action whereof we have any idea, viz. *thinking* and *motion,* let us consider whence we have the clearest ideas of the powers which produce these actions. (1) Of thinking, body affords us no idea at all; it is only from reflection that we have that. (2) Neither have we from body any idea of the beginning of motion. A body at rest affords us no idea of any active power to move, and when it is set in motion itself, that motion is rather a passion than an action in it. For, when the ball obeys the stroke of a billiard-stick, it is not any action of the ball, but bare passion. Also when by impulse it sets another ball in motion that lay in its way, it only communicates the motion it had received from another, and loses in itself so much as the other received : which gives us but a very obscure idea of an active power of moving in body, whilst we observe it only to *transfer,* but not *produce* any motion. The idea of the beginning of motion we have only from reflection on what passes in ourselves, where we find by experience that, barely by willing it, barely by a thought of the mind, we can move the parts of our bodies, which were before at rest. So that it seems to me we have, from the observation of the operation of bodies by our senses, but a very imperfect obscure idea of active power, since they afford us not any idea in themselves of the power to begin any action, either motion or thought. But, if from the impulse bodies are observed to make one upon another anyone thinks he has a clear idea of power, it serves as well to my purpose, sensation being one of those ways whereby the mind comes by its ideas; only I thought it worth while to consider here, by the way, whether the mind doth not receive its idea of active power clearer from reflection on its own operations, than it doth from any external sensation.

5. *Will and Understanding two Powers.* This, at least, I think evident, that we find in ourselves a power to begin or

forbear, continue or end several actions of our minds, and motions of our bodies, barely by a thought or preference of the mind ordering, or as it were commanding, the doing or not doing such or such a particular action. This power which the mind has thus to order the consideration of any idea, or the forbearing to consider it, or to prefer the motion of any part of the body to its rest, and *vice versa,* in any particular instance, is that which we call the *will.* The actual exercise of that power, by directing any particular action, or its forbearance, is that which we call *volition* or *willing.* The forbearance of that action, consequent to such order or command of the mind, is called *voluntary.* And whatsoever action is performed without such a thought of the mind is called *involuntary.* The power of perception is that which we call the *understanding.* Perception, which we make the act of the understanding, is of three sorts: 1. The perception of ideas in our minds. 2. The perception of the signification of signs. 3. The perception of the connexion or repugnancy, agreement or disagreement, that there is between any of our ideas. All these are attributed to the understanding, or perceptive power, though it be the two latter only that use allows us to say we understand.

(6.) *Faculties.* These powers of the mind, viz. of perceiving, and of preferring, are usually called by another name. And the ordinary way of speaking is that the understanding and will are two *faculties* of the mind: a word proper enough, if it be used, as all words should be, so as not to breed any confusion in men's thoughts, by being supposed (as I suspect it has been) to stand for some real beings in the soul that performed those actions of understanding and volition. For when we say the will is the commanding and superior faculty of the soul; that it is or is not free; that it determines the inferior faculties; that it follows the dictates of the understanding, &c.; though these and the like expressions, by those that carefully attend to their own ideas, and conduct their thoughts more by the evidence of things than the sound of words, may be understood in a clear and distinct sense, yet I suspect, I say, that this way of speaking of *faculties* has misled many into a confused notion of so many distinct agents in us, which had their several provinces and authorities, and did command, obey, and perform several actions, as so many distinct beings; which has been no small occasion of wrangling, obscurity, and uncertainty, in questions relating to them.

(7.) *Whence the Ideas of Liberty and Necessity*. Everyone, I think, finds in himself a power to begin or forbear, continue or put an end to several actions in himself. From the consideration of the extent of this power of the mind over the actions of the man, which everyone finds in himself, arise the *ideas* of *liberty* and *necessity*.

(8.) *Liberty, what*. All the actions that we have any idea of reducing themselves, as has been said, to these two, viz. thinking and motion, so far as a man has power to think or not to think, to move or not to move, according to the preference or direction of his own mind, so far is a man *free*. Wherever any performance or forbearance are not equally in a man's power, wherever doing or not doing will not equally follow upon the preference of his mind directing it, there he is not free, though perhaps the action may be voluntary. So that the idea of *liberty* is the idea of a power in any agent to do or forbear any particular action, according to the determination or thought of the mind, whereby either of them is preferred to the other; where either of them is not in the power of the agent to be produced by him according to his volition, there he is not at liberty; that agent is under *necessity*. So that liberty cannot be where there is no thought, no volition, no will; but there may be thought, there may be will, there may be volition, where there is no liberty. A little consideration of an obvious instance or two may make this clear.

(10.) *Belongs not to Volition*. Suppose a man be carried, whilst fast asleep, into a room where is a person he longs to see and speak with, and be there locked fast in, beyond his power to get out; he awakes, and is glad to find himself in so desirable company, which he stays willingly in, i.e. prefers his stay to going away. I ask, is not this stay voluntary? I think nobody will doubt it; and yet, being locked fast in, it is evident he is not at liberty not to stay, he has not freedom to be gone. So that liberty is not an idea belonging to volition, or preferring;

but to the person having the power of doing, or forbearing to do, according as the mind shall choose or direct. Our idea of liberty reaches as far as that power, and no farther. For wherever restraint comes to check that power, or compulsion takes away that indifferency of ability on either side to act, or to forbear acting, there liberty, and our notion of it, presently ceases.

(11) *Voluntary opposed to Involuntary, not to Necessary.* We have instances enough, and often more than enough, in our own bodies. A man's heart beats, and the blood circulates, which it is not in his power by any thought or volition to stop; and therefore in respect of these motions, where rest depends not on his choice, nor would follow the determination of his mind, if it should prefer it, he is not a free agent. Convulsive motions agitate his legs, so that though he wills it ever so much, he cannot by any power of his mind stop their motion, (as in that odd disease called *chorea Sancti Viti*), but he is perpetually dancing; he is not at liberty in this action, but under as much necessity of moving, as a stone that falls, or a tennis-ball struck with a racket. On the other side, a palsy or the stocks hinder his legs from obeying the determination of his mind, if it would thereby transfer his body to another place. In all these there is want of freedom; though the sitting still, even of a paralytic, whilst he prefers it to a removal, is truly voluntary. Voluntary, then, is not opposed to necessary, but to involuntary. For a man may prefer what he can do, to what he cannot do; the state he is in, to its absence or change; though necessity has made it in itself unalterable.

(12.) *Liberty, what.* As it is in the motions of the body, so it is in the thoughts of our minds : where any one is such that we have power to take it up, or lay it by, according to the preference of the mind, there we are at liberty. A waking man, being under the necessity of having some ideas constantly in his mind, is not at liberty to think or not to think, no more than he is at liberty, whether his body shall touch any other or no; but whether he will remove his contemplation from one idea to another is many times in his choice, and then he is, in

respect of his ideas, as much at liberty as he is in respect of
bodies he rests on; he can at pleasure remove himself from one
to another. But yet some ideas to the mind, like some motions
to the body, are such as in certain circumstances it cannot avoid,
nor obtain their absence by the utmost effort it can use.
A man on the rack is not at liberty to lay by the idea of pain,
and divert himself with other contemplations; and sometimes
a boisterous passion hurries our thoughts, as a hurricane does
our bodies, without leaving us the liberty of thinking on other
things, which we would rather choose. But as soon as the mind
regains the power to stop or continue, begin or forbear, any
of these motions of the body without, or thoughts within,
according as it thinks fit to prefer either to the other, we then
consider the man as a free agent again.

(14) *Liberty belongs not to the Will.* If this be so (as I
imagine it is), I leave it to be considered whether it may not
help to put an end to that long agitated, and, I think,
unreasonable, because unintelligible question, viz. *Whether
man's will be free or no?* For if I mistake not, it follows from
what I have said, that the question itself is altogether
improper; and it is as insignificant to ask whether man's *will*
be free, as to ask whether his sleep be swift, or his virtue
square; liberty being as little applicable to the will, as swiftness
of motion is to sleep, or squareness to virtue. Everyone would
laugh at the absurdity of such a question as either of these:
because it is obvious that the modifications of motion belong
not to sleep, nor the difference of figure to virtue; and when
anyone well considers it, I think he will as plainly perceive
that liberty, which is but a power, belongs only to *agents,* and
cannot be an attribute or modification of the will, which is also
but a power.

(6) *Powers belong to Agents.* It is plain then that the will is
nothing but one power or ability, and freedom another power
or ability so that to ask whether the will has freedom, is to ask
whether one power has another power, one ability another
ability; a question at first sight too grossly absurd to make a
dispute, or need an answer.

(7) However, the name 'faculty' which men have given to

this power called the will, and whereby they have been led into a way of talking of the will as acting, may, by an appropriation that disguises its true sense, serve a little to palliate the absurdity; yet the ' will ' in truth signifies nothing but a power or ability to prefer or choose : and when the will, under the name of a faculty, is considered as it is, barely as an ability to do something, the absurdity in saying it is free, or not free, will easily discover itself. For, if it be reasonable to suppose and talk of faculties as distinct beings that can act (as we do, when we say the will orders, and the will is free), it is fit that we should make a speaking faculty, and a walking faculty, and a dancing faculty, by which those actions are produced, which are but several modes of motion; as well as we make the will and understanding to be faculties, by which the actions of choosing and perceiving are produced, which are but several modes of thinking. And we may as properly say that it is the singing faculty sings, and the dancing faculty dances, as that the will chooses, or that the understanding conceives; or, as is usual, that the will directs the understanding, or the understanding obeys or obeys not the will; it being altogether as proper and intelligible to say that the power of speaking directs the power of singing, or the power of singing obeys or disobeys the power of speaking.

20. *Liberty belongs not to the Will.* The attributing to faculties that which belonged not to them has given occasion to this way of talking; but the introducing into discourses concerning the mind, with the name of faculties, a notion of their operating, has, I suppose, as little advanced our knowledge in that part of ourselves, as the great use and mention of the like invention of faculties in the operations of the body has helped us in the knowledge of physic.

21. *But to the Agent, or Man.* To return, then, to the inquiry about liberty, I think the question is not proper, *whether the will be free,* but *whether a man be free.* Thus, I think,

(1) That so far as anyone can, by the direction or choice of his mind, preferring the existence of any action to the non-existence of that action, and *vice versa,* make it to exist or not

exist, so far he is free. For if I can, by a thought directing the motion of my finger, make it move when it was at rest, or *vice versa,* it is evident that in respect of that I am free; and if I can, by a like thought of my mind, preferring one to the other, produce either words or silence, I am at liberty to speak or hold my peace; and as far as this power reaches, of acting or not acting, by the determination of his own thought preferring either, so far is a man free. For how can we think anyone freer than to have the power to do what he will? And so far as anyone can, by preferring any action to its not being, or rest to any action, produce that action or rest, so far can he do what he will. For such a preferring of action to its absence is the willing of it; and we can scarce tell how to imagine any being freer than to be able to do what he wills. So that in respect of actions within the reach of such a power in him a man seems as free as it is possible for freedom to ma'e him.

23. (2). That willing, or volition, being an action, and freedom consisting in a power of acting or not acting, a man in respect of willing or the act of volition, when any action in his power is once proposed to his thoughts, as presently to be done, cannot be free. The reason whereof is very manifest. For, it being unavoidable that the action depending on his will should exist or not exist, and its existence or not existence following perfectly the determination and preference of his will, he cannot avoid willing the existence or non-existence of that action, it is absolutely necessary that he will the one or the other, i.e. prefer the one to the other, since one of them must necessarily follow; and that which does follow follows by the choice and determination of his mind, that is, by his willing it; for if he did not will it, it would not be.

24. This, then, is evident, *That in all proposals of present action a man is not at liberty to will, or not to will, because he cannot forbear willing;* liberty consisting in a power to act or to forbear acting, and in that only. For a man that sits still is said yet to be at liberty, because he can walk if he wills it. But if a man sitting still has not a power to remove himself, he

is not at liberty; so likewise a man falling down a precipice, though in motion, is not at liberty, because he cannot stop that motion if he would. This being so, it is plain that a man that is walking, to whom it is proposed to give off walking, is not at liberty whether he will determine himself to walk, or give off walking or no : he must necessarily prefer one or the other of them, walking or not walking. And so it is in regard of all other actions in our power so proposed, which are the far greater number.

(25) *The Will determined by something without it.* Since then it is plain that in most cases a man is not at liberty whether he will will or no, the next thing demanded is *whether a man be at liberty to will which of the two he pleases, motion or rest?* This question carries the absurdity of it so manifestly in itself that one might thereby sufficiently be convinced that liberty concerns not the will. For to ask whether a man be at liberty to will either motion or rest, speaking or silence, which he pleases, is to ask whether a man can will what he wills, or be pleased with what he is pleased with. A question which, I think, needs no answer; and they who can make a question of it must suppose one will to determine the acts of another, and another to determine that, and so on *in infinitum*.

(26) To avoid these and the like absurdities, nothing can be of greater use than to establish in our minds determined ideas of the things under consideration.

(27) *Freedom.* First, then, it is carefully to be remembered that freedom consists in the dependence of the existence, or not existence of any action, upon our volition of it, and not in the dependence of any action, or its contrary, on our *pre-ference.* He that is a close prisoner in a room twenty foot square, being at the north side of his chamber, is at liberty to walk twenty feet southward, because he can walk or not walk it; but is not, at the same time, at liberty to do the contrary, i.e. to walk twenty feet northward.

In this, then, consists freedom, viz. in our being able to act or not to act, according as we shall choose or will.

(30) *Will and Desire must not be confounded.* Though I have above endeavoured to express the act of volition by

'choosing', 'preferring', and the like terms, that signify desire as well as volition, for want of other words to mark that act of the mind whose proper name is 'willing' or 'volition'; yet, it being a very simple act, whosoever desires to understand what it is will better find it by reflecting on his own mind, and observing what it does when it wills, than by any variety of articulate sounds whatsoever. This caution of being careful not to be misled by expressions that do not enough keep up the difference between the will and several acts of the mind that are quite distinct from it I think the more necessary, because I find the will often confounded with several of the affections, especially desire, and one put for the other. This, I imagine, has been no small occasion of obscurity and mistake in this matter, and therefore is, as much as may be, to be avoided. For he that shall turn his thoughts inwards upon what passes in his mind when he wills, shall see that the will or power of volition is conversant about nothing but that particular determination of the mind, whereby, barely by a thought, the mind endeavours to give rise, continuation, or stop, to any action which it takes to be in its power. This, well considered, plainly shows that the will is perfectly distinguished from desire; which, in the very same action, may have a quite contrary tendency from that which our will sets us upon. A man, whom I cannot deny, may oblige me to use persuasions to another, which, at the same time I am speaking, I may wish may not prevail on him. In this case, it is plain the will and desire run counter. I will the action; that tends one way, whilst my desire tends another, and that the direct contrary. Whence it is evident that desiring and willing are two distinct acts of the mind; and consequently, that the will, which is but the power of volition, is much more distinct from desire.

(31) *Uneasiness determines the Will.* To return, then, to the inquiry, what is it that determines the will in regard to our actions? And that, upon second thoughts, I am apt to imagine is not, as is generally supposed, the greater good in view; but some (and for the most part the most pressing) *uneasiness* a man is at present under. This is that which successively

determines the will, and sets us upon those actions we perform. This uneasiness we may call, as it is, *desire*; which is an uneasiness of the mind for want of some absent good.

35. *The greatest positive Good determines not the Will, but Uneasiness.* It seems so established and settled a maxim, by the general consent of all mankind, that good, the greater good, determines the will, that I do not at all wonder that, when I first published my thoughts on this subject, I took it for granted; and I imagine that, by a great many, I shall be thought more excusable for having then done so, than that now I have ventured to recede from so received an opinion. But yet, upon a stricter inquiry, I am forced to conclude that *good,* the *greater good,* though apprehended and acknowledged to be so, does not determine the will, until our desire, raised proportionably to it, makes us uneasy in the want of it. Convince a man never so much that plenty has its advantages over poverty, make him see and own that the handsome conveniences of life are better than nasty penury; yet, as long as he is content with the latter, and finds no uneasiness in it, he moves not, his will never is determined to any action that shall bring him out of it.

38. *Because all who allow the Joys of Heaven possible, pursue them not.* Were the will determined by the views of good, as it appears in contemplation greater or less to the understanding, which is the state of all absent good, and that which, in the received opinion, the will is supposed to move to, and to be moved by, I do not see how it could ever get loose from the infinite eternal joys of heaven, once proposed and considered as possible.

39. *But any great Uneasiness is never neglected.* But that it is not so, is visible in experience, the infinitely greatest confessed good being often neglected, to satisfy the successive uneasiness of our desires pursuing trifles.

41. *All desire Happiness.* If it be further asked, what it is moves desire? I answer, happiness, and that alone. ' Happiness ' and ' misery ' are the names of two extremes, the utmost bounds whereof we know not; it is what " eye hath not seen, ear hath not heard, nor hath it entered into the heart of man

to conceive." But of some degrees of both we have very lively impressions, made by several instances of delight and joy on the one side, and torment and sorrow on the other; which, for shortness' sake, I shall comprehend under the names of 'pleasure' and 'pain', there being pleasure and pain of the mind as well as the body : "With him is fulness of joy, and pleasure for evermore." Or, to speak truly, they are all of the mind; though some have their rise in the mind from thought, others in the body from certain modifications of motion.

42. *Happiness, what.* Now, because pleasure and pain are produced in us by the operation of certain objects, either on our minds or our bodies, and in different degrees; therefore, what has an aptness to produce pleasure in us is that we call *good,* and what is apt to produce pain in us we call *evil,* for no other reason but for its aptness to produce pleasure and pain in us, wherein consists our happiness and misery.

43. *What Good is desired, what not?* Though this be that which is called good and evil, and all good be the proper object of desire in general, yet all good, even seen and confessed to be so, does not necessarily move every particular man's desire; but only that part, or so much of it as is considered and taken to make a necessary part of his happiness. All other good, however great in reality or appearance, excites not a man's desires who looks not on it to make a part of that happiness wherewith he, in his present thoughts, can satisfy himself. Happiness, under this view, everyone constantly pursues, and desires what makes any part of it; other things, acknowledged to be good, he can look upon without desire, pass by, and be content without.

44. *Why the greatest Good is not always desired.* This, I think, anyone may observe in himself and others, that the greater visible good does not always raise men's desires in proportion to the greatness it appears, and is acknowledged, to have; though every little trouble moves us, and sets us on work to get rid of it. The reason whereof is evident from the nature of our happiness and misery itself. All present pain, whatever it be, makes a part of our present misery; but all absent good does not at any time make a necessary part of our

present happiness, nor the absence of it make a part of our misery.

47. *The Power to suspend the Prosecution of any Desire makes way for Consideration.* There being in us a great many uneasinesses, always soliciting and ready to determine the will, it is natural, as I have said, that the greatest and most pressing should determine the will to the next action; and so it does for the most part, but not always. For, the mind having in most cases, as is evident in experience, a power to suspend the execution and satisfaction of any of its desires, and so all, one after another, is at liberty to consider the objects of them, examine them on all sides, and weigh them with others. In this lies the liberty man has; and from the not using of it right comes all that variety of mistakes, errors, and faults which we run into in the conduct of our lives, and our endeavours after happiness, whilst we precipitate the deter-mination of our wills, and engage too soon, before due examination. To prevent this, we have a power to suspend the prosecution of this or that desire, as everyone daily may experiment in himself. This seems to me the source of all liberty; in this seems to consist that which is (as I think improperly) called *free-will.* For, during this suspension of any desire, before the will be determined to action, and the action (which follows that determination) done, we have opportunity to examine, view, and judge of the good or evil of what we are going to do; and when, upon due examination, we have judged, we have done our duty, all that we can, or ought to do, in pursuit of our happiness; and it is not a fault, but a perfection of our nature, to desire, will, and act according to the last result of a fair examination.

52. *The Reason of it.* This is the hinge on which turns the *liberty* of intellectual beings, in their constant endeavours after, and a steady prosecution of, true felicity, that they *can suspend* this prosecution in particular cases, till they have looked before them, and informed themselves whether that particular thing which is then proposed or desired lie in the way to their main end, and make a real part of that which is their greatest good. For the inclination and tendency of their

nature to happiness is an obligation and motive to them, to take care not to mistake or miss it; and so necessarily puts them upon caution, deliberation, and wariness, in the direction of their particular actions, which are the means to obtain it. Whatever necessity determines to the pursuit of real bliss, the same necessity, with the same force, establishes suspense, deliberation, and scrutiny of each successive desire, whether the satisfaction of it does not interfere with our true happiness, and mislead us from it. This, as seems to me, is the great privilege of finite intellectual beings; and I desire it may be well considered whether the great inlet and exercise of all the liberty men have, are capable of, or can be useful to them, and that whereon depends the turn of their actions, does not lie in this.

64. *How Men come to pursue different Courses.* From what has been said, it is easy to give an account how it comes to pass that, though all men desire happiness, yet their wills carry them so contrarily, and consequently some of them to what is evil. And to this I say that the various and contrary choices that men make in the world do not argue that they do not all pursue good, but that the same thing is not good to every man alike. This variety of pursuits shows that everyone does not place his happiness in the same thing, or choose the same way to it. Were all the concerns of man terminated in this life, why one followed study and knowledge, and another hawking and hunting, why one chose luxury and debauchery, and another sobriety and riches, would not be because every one of these did not aim at his own happiness, but because their happiness was placed in different things. And therefore it was a right answer of the physician to his patient that had sore eyes : if you have more pleasure in the taste of wine than in the use of your sight, wine is good for you; but if the pleasure of seeing be greater to you than that of drinking, wine is naught.

72. Before I close this chapter, it may perhaps be to our purpose, and help to give us clearer conceptions about *power,* if we make our thoughts take a little more exact survey of *action.* I have said above that we have ideas but of two

sorts of action, viz. motion and thinking. These, in truth, though called and counted actions, yet, if nearly considered, will not be found to be always perfectly so. For, if I mistake not, there are instances of both kinds, which, upon due consideration, will be found rather passions than actions; and consequently so far the effects barely of *passive powers* in those subjects, which yet on their account are thought agents. For, in these instances, the substance that hath motion or thought receives the impression, whereby it is put into that action, purely from without, and so acts merely by the capacity it has to receive such an impression from some external agent; and such a power is not properly an active power, but a mere passive capacity in the subject. Sometimes the substance or agent puts itself into action by its own power, and this is properly *active power*. Whatsoever modification a substance has, whereby it produces any effect, that is called action, v.g. a solid substance, by motion, operates on or alters the sensible ideas of another substance, and therefore this modification of motion we call action. But yet this motion in that solid substance is, when rightly considered, but a passion, if it received it only from some external agent. So that the active power of motion is in no substance which cannot begin motion in itself or in another substance when at rest. So likewise in thinking, a power to receive ideas or thoughts from the operation of any external substance is called a power of thinking, but this is but a passive power, or capacity. But to be able to bring into view ideas out of sight at one's own choice, and to compare which of them one thinks fit, this is an active power. This reflection may be of some use to preserve us from mistakes about powers and actions, which grammar, and the common frame of languages, may be apt to lead us into. Since what is signified by verbs that grammarians call active, does not always signify action : v.g. this proposition. ' I *see* the moon, or a star ', or ' I *feel* the heat of the sun ' though expressed by a verb active, does not signify any action in me, whereby I operate on those substances, but the reception of the ideas of light, roundness, and heat, wherein I am not active, but barely passive, and cannot, in that position of my eyes or body, avoid receiving them. But when I turn my eyes another way, or remove my body out of the sunbeams, I am properly active; because of my own choice, by a power within myself, I put myself into that motion. Such an action is the product of active power.

(73) And thus I have, in a short draught, given a view of *our original ideas,* from whence all the rest are derived, and of which they are made up; which, if I would consider as a philosopher, and examine on what causes they depend, and of what they are made, I believe they all might be reduced to these very few primary and original ones, viz.

> *Extension,*
> *Solidity,*
> *Mobility,* or the power of being moved;

which by our senses we receive from body;

> *Perceptivity,* or the power of perception, or thinking;
> *Motivity,* or the power of moving:

which by reflection we receive from *our minds.*

I crave leave to make use of these two new words, to avoid the danger of being mistaken in the use of those which are equivocal.

To which if we add

> *Existence,*
> *Duration,*
> *Number,*

which belong both to the one and the other, we have, perhaps, all the original ideas on which the rest depend. For by these, I imagine, might be explained the nature of colours, sounds, tastes, smells, and all other ideas we have, if we had but faculties acute enough to perceive the severally modified extensions and motions of these minute bodies, which produce those several sensations in us. But my present purpose being only to inquire into the knowledge the mind has of things, by those ideas and appearances which God has fitted it to receive from them, and how the mind comes by that knowledge, rather than into their causes or manner of production, I shall not, contrary to the design of this *Essay,* set myself to inquire philosophically into the peculiar constitution of bodies, and the configuration of parts, whereby they have the power to produce in us the ideas of their sensible qualities. I shall not enter any further into that disquisition, it sufficing to my purpose to observe, that gold or saffron has a power to produce in us the idea of yellow, and snow or milk the idea of white, which we can only have by our sight; without examining the texture of the parts of those bodies, or the particular figures or motion of the particles which rebound from them, to cause in us that particular sensation; though, when we go beyond the bare ideas in our minds, and would inquire into their causes, we cannot conceive anything else to be in any sensible object, whereby it produces different ideas in us, but the different bulk, figure, number, texture, and motion of its insensible parts.

CHAPTER XXII

OF MIXED MODES

1. *Mixed Modes, what.* Having treated of *simple modes* in the foregoing chapters, and given several instances of some of the most considerable of them, to show what they are, and how we come by them, we are now in the next place to consider those we call *mixed modes;* such are the complex ideas we mark by the names *obligation, drunkenness,* a *lie,* &c.; which consisting of several combinations of simple ideas of different kinds, I have called *mixed modes,* to distinguish them from the more simple modes, which consist only of simple ideas of the same kind. These mixed modes, being also such combinations of simple ideas as are not looked upon to be characteristical marks of any real beings that have a steady existence, but scattered and independent ideas put together by the mind, are thereby distinguished from the complex ideas of substances.

2. *Made by the Mind.* That the mind, in respect of its simple ideas, is wholly passive, and receives them all from the existence and operations of things, such as sensation or

reflection offers them, without being able to make any one idea, experience shows us. But if we attentively consider these ideas I call mixed modes we are now speaking of, we shall find their original quite different. The mind often exercises an *active* power in making these several combinations. For, it being once furnished with simple ideas, it can put them together in several compositions, and so make variety of complex ideas, without examining whether they exist so together in nature. And hence I think it is that these ideas are called *notions,* as if they had their original, and constant existence, more in the thoughts of men, than in the reality of things; and to form such ideas, it sufficed that the mind put the parts of them together, and that they were consistent in the understanding, without considering whether they had any real being; though I do not deny but several of them might be taken from observation, and the existence of several simple ideas so combined, as they are put together in the understanding. For the man who first framed the idea of *hypocrisy* might have either taken it at first from the observation of one who made show of good qualities which he had not, or else have framed that idea in his mind without having any such pattern to fashion it by.

3. *Sometimes got by the Explication of their Names.* Indeed, now that languages are made, and abound with words standing for such combinations, an usual way of *getting* these complex ideas is by the explication of those terms that stand for them. For, consisting of a company of simple ideas combined, they may, by words standing for those simple ideas, be represented to the mind of one who understands those words, though that complex combination of simple ideas were never offered to his mind by the real existence of things. Thus a man may come to have the idea of *sacrilege* or *murder* by enumerating to him the simple ideas which these words stand for, without ever seeing either of them committed.

4. *The Name ties the Parts of mixed Modes into one Idea.* Every mixed mode consisting of many distinct simple ideas,

it seems reasonable to inquire whence it has its unity, and how such a precise multitude comes to make but one idea, since that combination does not always exist together in nature. To which I answer, it is plain it has its unity from an act of the mind, combining those several simple ideas together, and considering them as one complex one, consisting of those parts; and the mark of this union, or that which is looked on generally to complete it, is one *name* given to that combination. For it is by their names that men commonly regulate their account of their distinct species of mixed modes, seldom allowing or considering any number of simple ideas to make one complex one, but such collections as there be names for. Thus, though the killing of an old man be as fit in nature to be united into one complex idea, as the killing of a man's father, yet, there being no name standing precisely for the one, as there is the name of " parricide " to mark the other, it is not taken for a particular complex idea, nor a distinct species of actions from that of killing a young man, or any other man.

5. *The Cause of making mixed Modes.* If we should inquire a little further, to see what it is that occasions men to make several combinations of simple ideas into distinct, and, as it were, settled modes, and neglect others, which in the nature of things themselves, have as much an aptness to be combined and make distinct ideas, we shall find the reason of it to be the end of language; which being to mark, or communicate men's thoughts to one another with all the dispatch that may be, they usually make such collections of ideas into complex modes, and affix names to them, as they have frequent use of in their way of living and conversation, leaving others, which they have but seldom an occasion to mention, loose and without names that tie them together; they rather choosing to enumerate (when they have need) such ideas as make them up by the particular names that stand for them, than to trouble their memories by multiplying of complex ideas with names to them, which they shall seldom or never have any occasion to make use of.

6. *Why Words in one Language have none answering in another.*   This shows us how it comes to pass that there are in every language many particular words which cannot be rendered by any one single word of another. For the several fashions, customs, and manners of one nation, making several combinations of ideas familiar and necessary in one, which another people have had never any occasion to make, or perhaps so much as take notice of, names come of course to be annexed to them, to avoid long periphrases in things of daily conversation; and so they become so many distinct complex ideas in their minds. Thus ὀστρακισμός amongst the Greeks, and *proscriptio* amongst the Romans, were words which other languages had no names that exactly answered, because they stood for complex ideas which were not in the minds of the men of other nations. Where there was no such custom, there was no notion of any such actions; no use of such combinations of ideas as were united, and, as it were, tied together, by those terms; and therefore in other countries there were no names for them.

7. *And Languages change.*   Hence also we may see the reason why languages constantly change, take up new and lay by old terms. Because change of customs and opinions bringing with it new combinations of ideas, which it is necessary frequently to think on and talk about, new names, to avoid long descriptions, are annexed to them; and so they become new species of complex modes. What a number of different ideas are by this means wrapped up in one short sound, and how much of our time and breath is thereby saved, anyone will see, who will but take the pains to enumerate all the ideas that either 'reprieve' or 'appeal' stand for; and instead of either of those names, use a periphrasis, to make anyone understand their meaning.

9. *How we get the Ideas of mixed Modes.*   There are therefore three ways whereby we get the complex ideas of mixed modes: (1) By experience and *observation* of things themselves; thus, by seeing two men wrestle or fence, we get the idea of wrestling or fencing. (2) By *invention*, or voluntary putting together of several simple ideas in our own

minds; so he that first invented printing or etching, had an idea of it in his mind before it ever existed. (3) Which is the most usual way, by *explaining the names* of actions we never saw, or notions we cannot see; and by enumerating, and thereby, as it were, setting before our imaginations all those ideas which go to the making them up, and are the constituent parts of them. All our complex ideas are ultimately resolvable into simple ideas, of which they are compounded and originally made up, though perhaps their immediate ingredients, as I may so say, are also complex ideas. Thus, the mixed mode which the word 'lie' stands for is made of these simple ideas: (1) Articulate sounds. (2) Certain ideas in the mind of the speaker. (3) Those words the signs of those ideas. (4) Those signs put together, by affirmation or negation, otherwise than the ideas they stand for are in the mind of the speaker. I think I need not go any further in the analysis of that complex idea we call a lie; what I have said is enough to show that it is made up of simple ideas.

10. *Motion, Thinking, and Power have been most modified.* It is worth our observing which of all our simple ideas have been most modified, and had most mixed modes made out of them, with names given to them. And those have been these three: *thinking* and *motion* (which are the two ideas which comprehend in them all action), and *power,* from whence these actions are conceived to flow. These simple ideas, I say, of thinking, motion, and power, have been those which have been most modified; and out of whose modifications have been made most complex modes, with names to them. For action being the great business of mankind, and the whole matter about which all laws are conversant, it is no wonder that the several modes of thinking and motion should be taken notice of, the ideas of them observed, and laid up in the memory, and have names assigned to them; without which laws could be but ill made, or vice and disorders repressed.

To conclude: let us examine any modes of action, v.g. *consideration* and *assent,* which are actions of the mind; *running* and *speaking,* which are actions of the body; *revenge* and *murder,* which are actions of both together, and we shall find them but so many collections of simple ideas, which, together, make up the complex ones signified by those names.

11. *Several Words seeming to signify Action, signify but the Effect. Power* being the source from whence all action proceeds, the substances wherein these powers are, when they exert this power into act, are called *causes,* and the substances which thereupon are produced, or the simple ideas which are introduced into any subject by the exerting of that power, are called *effects.* The *efficacy* whereby the new substance or idea is produced is called, in the subject exerting that power, *action*; but in the subject wherein any simple idea is changed or produced it is called *passion*; which efficacy, however various, and the effects almost infinite, yet we can, I think, conceive it, in intellectual agents, to be nothing else but modes of thinking and willing; in corporeal agents, nothing else but modifications of motion. And therefore many words which seem to express some action, signify nothing of the action or *modus operandi* at all, but barely the effect, with some circumstances of the subject wrought on, or cause operating: v.g. 'creation', 'annihilation' contain in them no idea of the action or manner whereby they are produced, but barely of the cause, and the thing done. And when a countryman says the cold freezes water, though the word 'freezing' seems to import some action, yet truly it signifies nothing but the effect, viz. that water that was before fluid is become hard and consistent, without containing any idea of the action whereby it is done.

12. *Mixed Modes made also of other Ideas.* I think I shall not need to remark here that, though power and action make the greatest part of mixed modes, marked by names, and familiar in the minds and mouths of men, yet other simple ideas, and their several combinations, are not excluded; much less, I think, will it be necessary for me to enumerate all the mixed modes which have been settled, with names to them. That would be to make a dictionary of the greatest part of the words made use of in divinity, ethics, law, and politics, and several other sciences. All that is requisite to my present

design is to show what sort of ideas those are which I call mixed modes; how the mind comes by them; and that they are compositions made up of simple ideas got from sensation and reflection; which I suppose I have done.

CHAPTER XXIII

OF OUR COMPLEX IDEAS OF SUBSTANCES

1. *Ideas of Substances, how made.* The mind being, as I have declared, furnished with a great number of the simple ideas, conveyed in by the senses as they are found in exterior things, or by reflection on its own operations, takes notice also that a certain number of these simple ideas go constantly together; which, being presumed to belong to one thing, and words being suited to common apprehensions, and made use of for quick dispatch, are called, so united in one subject, by one name; which, by inadvertency, we are apt afterward to talk of and consider as one simple idea, which indeed is a complication of many ideas together; because, as I have said, not imagining how these simple ideas can subsist by themselves, we accustom ourselves to suppose some *substratum* wherein they do subsist, and from which they do result, which therefore we call *substance.*

2. *Our Idea of Substance in general.* So that if anyone will examine himself concerning his notion of pure substance in general, he will find he has no other idea of it at all, but only a supposition of he knows not what *support* of such qualities which are capable of producing simple ideas in us, which qualities are commonly called accidents. If anyone should be asked what is the subject wherein colour or weight inheres, he would have nothing to say, but the solid extended parts; and if he were demanded what is it that that solidity and extension adhere in, he would not be in a much better case than the Indian before mentioned who, saying that the world

was supported by a great elephant, was asked what the elephant rested on; to which his answer was : a great tortoise; but being again pressed to know what gave support to the broad-backed tortoise, replied : *something, he knew not what.* And thus here, as in all other cases where we use words without having clear and distinct ideas, we talk like children; who, being questioned what such a thing is, which they know not, readily give this satisfactory answer that it is *something*; which in truth signifies no more, when so used, either by children or men, but that they know not what, and that the thing they pretend to know, and talk of, is what they have no distinct idea of at all, and so are perfectly ignorant of it, and in the dark. The idea then we have, to which we give the general name ' substance ', being nothing but the supposed, but unknown, support of those qualities we find existing, which we imagine cannot subsist *sine re substante,* without something to support them, we call that support *substantia*; which, according to the true import of the word, is, in plain English, standing under or upholding.

(3) *Of the Sorts of Substances.* An obscure and relative idea of *substance in general* being thus made we come to have the ideas of *particular sorts of substances,* by collecting such combinations of simple ideas as are, by experience and observation of men's senses, taken notice of to exist together, and are therefore supposed to flow from the particular internal constitution, or unknown *essence* of that substance. Thus we come to have the ideas of a man, horse, gold, water, &c.; of which substances, whether anyone has any other clear idea, further than of certain simple ideas co-existing together, I appeal to everyone's own experience. It is the ordinary qualities observable in iron, or a diamond, put together, that make the true complex idea of those substances, which a smith or a jeweller commonly knows better than a philosopher; who, whatever *substantial forms* he may talk of, has no other idea of those substances than what is framed by a collection of those simple ideas which are to be found in them; only we must take notice that our complex ideas of substances, besides all these simple ideas they are made up of, have always the

confused idea of something to which they belong, and in which they subsist; and therefore when we speak of any sort of substance, we say it is a thing having such or such qualities : as body is a thing that is extended, figured, and capable of motion; a spirit, a thing capable of thinking; and so hardness, friability, and power to draw iron, we say, are qualities to be found in a loadstone. These, and the like fashions of speaking, intimate that the substance is supposed always *something besides* the extension, figure, solidity, motion, thinking, or other observable ideas, though we know not what it is.

(5) *As Clear an Idea of Spirit as Body.* The same thing happens concerning the operations of the mind, viz. thinking, reasoning, fearing, &c., which we concluding not to subsist of themselves, nor apprehending how they can belong to body, or be produced by it, we are apt to think these the actions of some other substance, which we call *spirit*; whereby yet it is evident that, having no other idea or notion of matter but something wherein those many sensible qualities which affect our senses do subsist, by supposing a substance wherein thinking, knowing, doubting, and a power of moving, &c., do subsist, we have as clear a notion of the substance of spirit, as we have of body; the one being supposed to be (without knowing what it is) the *substratum* to those simple ideas we have from without; and the other supposed (with a like ignorance of what it is) to be the *substratum* to those operations we experiment in ourselves within. It is plain then that the idea of *corporeal substance* in matter is as remote from our conceptions and apprehensions as that of *spiritual substance*, or spirit; and therefore, from our not having any notion of the substance of spirit we can no more conclude its non-existence, than we can, for the same reason, deny the existence of body; it being as rational to affirm there is no body, because we have no clear and distinct idea of the substance of matter, as to say there is no spirit, because we have no clear and distinct idea of the substance of a spirit.

(6) *Of the Sorts of Substances.* Whatever therefore be the secret and abstract nature of substance in general, all the ideas

we have of particular distinct sorts of substances are nothing but several combinations of simple ideas, co-existing in such, though unknown, cause of their union, as makes the whole subsist of itself. It is by such combinations of simple ideas, and nothing else, that we represent particular sorts of substances to ourselves; such are the ideas we have of their several species in our minds; and such only do we, by their specific names, signify to others, v.g. 'man', 'horse', 'sun', 'water', 'iron': upon hearing which words everyone who understands the language frames in his mind a combination of those several simple ideas which he has usually observed, or fancied to exist together under that denomination; all which he supposes to rest in and be, as it were, adherent to that unknown common subject, which inheres not in anything else.

7. *Powers a great part of our complex Ideas of Substances.* For he has the perfectest idea of any of the particular sorts of substances, who has gathered, and put together, most of those simple ideas which do exist in it; among which are to be reckoned its active powers, and passive capacities, which, though not simple ideas, yet in this respect, for brevity's sake, may conveniently enough be reckoned amongst them. Thus, the power of drawing iron is one of the ideas of the complex one of that substance we call a loadstone; and a power to be so drawn is a part of the complex one we call iron; which powers pass for inherent qualities in those subjects. Because every substance being as apt by the powers we observe in it, to change some sensible qualities in other subjects, as it is to produce in us those simple ideas which we receive immediately from it, does, by those new sensible qualities introduced into other subjects, discover to us those powers which do thereby mediately affect our senses, as regularly as its sensible qualities do it immediately: v.g. we immediately by our senses perceive in fire its heat and colour; which are, if rightly considered, nothing but powers in it to produce those ideas in us. We also by our senses perceive the colour and brittleness of charcoal, whereby we come by the knowledge of another power in fire, which it has to

change the colour and consistency of wood. By the former fire immediately, by the latter it mediately discovers to us these several powers; which therefore we look upon to be a part of the qualities of fire, and so make them a part of the complex idea of it.

8. *And why.* Nor are we to wonder that powers make a great part of our complex ideas of substances, since their secondary qualities are those which in most of them serve principally to distinguish substances one from another, and commonly make a considerable part of the complex idea of the several sorts of them. For, our senses failing us in the discovery of the bulk, texture, and figure of the minute parts of bodies, on which their real constitutions and differences depend, we are fain to make use of their secondary qualities as the characteristical notes and marks whereby to frame ideas of them in our minds, and distinguish them one from another; all which secondary qualities, as has been shown[1], are nothing but bare powers. For the colour and taste of opium are, as well as its soporific or anodyne virtues, mere powers, depending on its primary qualities, whereby it is fitted to produce different operations on different parts of our bodies.

9. *Three sorts of Ideas make our complex ones of Substances.* The ideas that make our complex ones of corporeal substances are of these three sorts. First, the ideas of the primary qualities of things, which are discovered by our senses, and are in them even when we perceive them not: such are the bulk, figure, number, situation, and motion of the parts of bodies; which are really in them, whether we take notice of them or no. Secondly, the sensible secondary qualities, which, depending on these, are nothing but the powers those substances have to produce several ideas in us by our senses; which ideas are not in the things themselves, otherwise than as anything is in its cause. Thirdly, the aptness we consider in any substance to give or receive such alterations of primary qualities, as that the substance so altered should produce in us different ideas from what it did before; these are called active and passive powers; all

[1] II viii 10, 13-14.

which powers, as far as we have any notice or notion of them, terminate only in sensible simple ideas. For whatever alteration a loadstone has the power to make in the minute particles of iron, we should have no notion of any power it had at all to operate on iron, did not its sensible motion discover it; and I doubt not but there are a thousand changes, that bodies we daily handle have a power to cause in one another, which we never suspect, because they never appear in sensible effects.

10. *Powers make a great Part of our complex Ideas of Substances.* Powers therefore justly make a great part of our complex ideas of substances. He that will examine his complex idea of gold will find several of its ideas that make it up to be only powers: as the power of being melted, but of not spending itself in the fire, of being dissolved in *aqua regia,* are ideas as necessary to make up our complex idea of gold, as its colour and weight; which, if duly considered, are also nothing but different powers. For, to speak truly, yellowness is not actually in gold, but is a power in gold to produce that idea in us by our eyes, when placed in a due light; and the heat, which we cannot leave out of our idea of the sun, is no more really in the sun, than the white colour it introduces into wax. These are both equally powers in the sun, operating, by the motion and figure of its insensible parts, so on a man, as to make him have the idea of heat; and so on wax, as to make it capable to produce in a man the idea of white.

11. *The now secondary Qualities of Bodies would disappear, if we could discover the primary ones of their minute Parts.* Had we senses acute enough to discern the minute particles of bodies, and the real constitution on which their sensible qualities depend, I doubt not but they would produce quite different ideas in us; and that which is now the yellow colour of gold would then disappear, and instead of it we should see an admirable texture of parts, of a certain size and figure. This miscroscopes plainly discover to us; for what to our naked eyes produces a certain colour, is, by thus augmenting the acuteness of our senses, discovered to be quite a different thing; and the thus altering, as it were, the proportion of the

bulk of the minute parts of a coloured object to our usual
sight produces different ideas from what it did before. Thus,
sand or pounded glass, which is opaque, and white to the
naked eye, is pellucid in a microscope; and a hair seen in this
way loses its former colour, and is, in a great measure, pellucid,
with a mixture of some bright sparkling colours, such as
appear from the refraction of diamonds, and other pellucid
bodies. Blood, to the naked eye, appears all red; but by a good
microscope, wherein its lesser parts appear, shows only some
few globules of red, swimming in a pellucid liquor, and
how these red globules would appear, if glasses could be found
that yet could magnify them a thousand or ten thousand times
more, is uncertain.

(12) *Our Faculties of Discovery suited to our State.* The
infinite wise Contriver of us, and all things about us, hath
fitted our senses, faculties, and organs, to the conveniences
of life, and the business we have to do here. We are able,
by our senses, to know and distinguish things; and to examine
them so far as to apply them to our uses, and several ways to
accommodate the exigences of this life. But it appears not that
God intended we should have a perfect, clear, and adequate
knowledge of them; that perhaps is not in the comprehension
of any finite being. Were our senses altered, and made much
quicker and acuter, the appearance and outward scheme of
things would have quite another face to us; and, I am apt to
think, would be inconsistent with our being, or at least well-
being, in this part of the universe which we inhabit. If that
most instructive of our senses, seeing, were in any man a thous-
and or a hundred thousand times more acute than it is now by
the best microscope, things several millions of times less than
the smallest object of his sight now would then be visible to his
naked eyes, and so he would come nearer the discovery of the
texture and motion of the minute parts of corporeal things, and
in many of them probably get ideas of their internal constitutions; but then he would be in a quite different world from
other people: nothing would appear the same to him and
others; the visible ideas of everything would be different.
So that I doubt whether he and the rest of men could discourse

concerning the objects of sight, or have any communication about colours, their appearances being so wholly different. And perhaps such a quickness and tenderness of sight could not endure bright sunshine, or so much as open daylight, nor take in but a very small part of any object at once, and that too only at a very near distance. And if by the help of such *microscopical eyes* (if I may so call them) a man could penetrate further than ordinary into the secret composition and radical texture of bodies, he would not make any great advantage by the change, if such an acute sight would not serve to conduct him to the market and exchange; if he could not see things he was to avoid at a convenient distance; nor distinguish things he had to do with by those sensible qualities others do.

15. *Idea of spiritual Substances, as clear as of bodily Substances*. Besides the complex ideas we have of material sensible substances, of which I have last spoken, by the simple ideas we have taken from those operations of our own minds, which we experiment daily in ourselves, as thinking, understanding, willing, knowing, and power of beginning motion, &c., co-existing in some substance, we are able to frame the *complex idea of an immaterial spirit*. And thus, by putting together the ideas of thinking, perceiving, liberty, and power of moving themselves and other things, we have as clear a perception and notion of immaterial substances as we have of material. For putting together the ideas of thinking and willing, or the power of moving or quieting corporeal motion, joined to substance, of which we have no distinct idea, we have the idea of an immaterial spirit; and by putting together the ideas of coherent solid parts, and a power of being moved, joined with substance, of which likewise we have no positive idea, we have the idea of matter. The one is as clear and distinct an idea as the other: the idea of thinking, and moving a body, being as clear and distinct ideas as the ideas of extension, solidity, and being moved. For our idea of substance is equally obscure, or none at all, in both; it is but a supposed I know not what, to support those ideas we call accidents. It is for want of reflection that we are apt to think that our senses show us nothing but material things.

Every act of sensation, when duly considered, gives us an equal view of both parts of nature, the corporeal and spiritual. For whilst I know, by seeing or hearing, &c., that there is some corporeal being without me, the object of that sensation, I do more certainly know that there is some spiritual being within me that sees and hears. This, I must be convinced, cannot be the action of bare insensible matter; nor ever could be, without an immaterial thinking being.

17. *The Cohesion of solid parts and Impulse, the Primary Ideas of Body.* The primary ideas we have *peculiar to body,* as contradistinguished to spirit, are the *cohesion of solid, and consequently separable, parts,* and a *power of communicating motion by impulse.* These, I think, are the original ideas proper and peculiar to body; for figure is but the consequence of finite extension.

18. *Thinking and Motivity the primary Ideas of Spirit.* The ideas we have belonging and *peculiar to spirit* are *thinking,* and *will,* or *a power of putting body into motion by thought, and, which is consequent to it, liberty.* For, as body cannot but communicate its motion by impulse to another body, which it meets with at rest, so the mind can put bodies into motion, or forbear to do so, as it pleases. The ideas of *existence, duration, and mobility* are common to them both.

19. *Spirits capable of Motion.* There is no reason why it should be thought strange that I make mobility belong to spirit; for having no other idea of motion but change of distance with other beings that are considered as at rest, and finding that spirits, as well as bodies, cannot operate but where they are, and that spirits do operate at several times in several places, I cannot but attribute change of place to all finite spirits (for of the Infinite Spirit I speak not here). For my soul, being a real being as well as my body, is certainly as capable of changing distance with any other body, or being, as body itself; and so is capable of motion.

20. Everyone finds in himself that his soul can think, will, and operate on his body in the place where that is, but cannot operate on a body, or in a place, an hundred miles distant from it. Nobody can imagine that his soul can think

or move a body at Oxford, whilst he is at London; and cannot but know, that, being united to his body, it constantly changes place all the whole journey between Oxford and London, as the coach or horse does that carries him, and I think may be said to be truly all that while in motion; or if that will not be allowed to afford us a clear idea enough of its motion, its being separated from the body in death, I think, will; for to consider it as going out of the body, or leaving it, and yet to have no idea of its motion, seems to me impossible.

22. *Idea of Soul and of Body compared.*   Let us compare, then, our complex idea of an immaterial spirit with our complex idea of body, and see whether there be any more obscurity in one than in the other and in which most. Our idea of *body,* as I think, is *an extended solid substance, capable of communicating motion by impulse:* and our idea of *our soul, as an immaterial spirit,* is of *a substance that thinks, and has a power of exciting motion in body, by will, or thought.* These, I think, are our complex ideas of soul and body, as contra-distinguished; and now let us examine which has most obscurity in it, and difficulty to be apprehended.

23. *Cohesion of solid Parts in Body as hard to be conceived as thinking in a Soul.*   If anyone say he knows not what it is thinks in him, he means he knows not what the substance is of that thinking thing; no more, say I, knows he what the substance is of that solid thing. Further, if he says he knows not how he thinks, I answer, neither knows he how he is extended, how the solid parts of body are united, or cohere together to make extension.

25. I allow it is usual for most people to wonder how anyone should find a difficulty in what they think they every day observe. Do we not see (will they be ready to say) the parts of bodies stick firmly together? Is there anything more common? And what doubt can there be made of it? And the like, I say, concerning thinking and voluntary motion. Do we not every moment experiment it in ourselves, and therefore can it be doubted? The matter of fact is clear,

I confess; but when we would a little nearer look into it, and consider how it is done, there I think we are at a loss, both in the one and the other; and can as little understand how the parts of body cohere, as how we ourselves perceive or move. I would have anyone intelligibly explain to me how the parts of gold, or brass (that but now in fusion were as loose from one another as the particles of water, or the sands of an hour-glass), come in a few moments to be so united, and adhere so strongly one to another, that the utmost force of men's arms cannot separate them? A considering man will, I suppose, be here at a loss to satisfy his own, or another man's understanding.

28. *Communication of Motion by Impulse, or by Thought, equally intelligible.* Another idea we have of body is *the power of communication of motion by impulse*; and of our souls *the power of exciting of motion by thought.* These ideas, the one of body, the other of our minds, every day's experience clearly furnishes us with; but if here again we inquire how this is done, we are equally in the dark. For, in the communication of motion by impulse, wherein as much motion is lost to one body as is got to the other, which is the ordinariest case, we can have no other conception but of the passing of motion out of one body into another; which, I think, is as obscure and inconceivable as how our minds move or stop our bodies by thought, which we every moment find they do. The increase of motion by impulse, which is observed or believed sometimes to happen, is yet harder to be understood. We have by daily experience clear evidence of motion produced both by impulse and by thought; but the manner how, hardly comes within our comprehension : we are equally at a loss in both. So that, however we consider motion, and its communication, either from body or spirit, the idea which belongs to spirit is at least as clear as that that belongs to body. And if we consider the active power of moving, or, as I may call it, *motivity,* it is much clearer in spirit than body; since two bodies, placed by one another at rest, will never afford us the idea of a power in the one to move the other, but by a

borrowed motion, whereas the mind every day affords us ideas of an active power of moving of bodies; and therefore it is worth our consideration whether active power be not the proper attribute of spirits, and passive power of matter. Hence may be conjectured that created spirits are not totally separate from matter, because they are both active and passive. Pure spirit, viz. God, is only active; pure matter is only passive; those beings that are both active and passive we may judge to partake of both.

30) *Ideas of Body and Spirit compared.* So that, in short, the idea we have of spirit, compared with the idea we have of body, stands thus : the substance of spirit is unknown to us, and so is the substance of body equally unknown to us. Two primary qualities or properties of body, viz. solid coherent parts and impulse, we have distinct clear ideas of; so likewise we know, and have distinct clear ideas, of two primary qualities or properties of spirit, viz. thinking, and a power of action, i.e. a power of beginning or stopping several thoughts or motions. We have also the ideas of several qualities inherent in bodies, and have the clear distinct ideas of them; which qualities are but the various modifications of the extension of cohering solid parts, and their motion. We have likewise the ideas of the several modes of thinking viz. believing, doubting, intending, fearing, hoping; all which are but the several modes of thinking. We have also the ideas of willing, and moving the body consequent to it, and with the body itself too; for, as has been shown, spirit is capable of motion.

32. *We know nothing of things beyond our simple Ideas.* We have as much reason to be satisfied with our notion of immaterial spirit as with our notion of body, and the existence of the one as well as the other. For, it being no more a contradiction that thinking should exist separate and independent from solidity, than it is a contradiction that solidity should exist separate and independent from thinking, they being both but simple ideas, independent one from another, and having as clear and distinct ideas in us of thinking as of solidity, I know not why we may not as well allow a thinking thing without solidity, i.e. immaterial, to exist, as a solid thing without

thinking, i.e. matter, to exist; especially since it is no harder to conceive how thinking should exist without matter, than how matter should think. For whensoever we would proceed beyond these simple ideas we have from sensation and reflection, and dive further into the nature of things, we fall presently into darkness and obscurity, perplexedness and difficulties, and can discover nothing further but our own blindness and ignorance. But whichever of these complex ideas be clearest, that of body, or immaterial spirit, this is evident, that the simple ideas that make them up are no other than what we have received from sensation or reflection; and so is it of all our other ideas of substances, even of God himself.

33. *Idea of God.* For if we examine the idea we have of the incomprehensible Supreme Being, we shall find that we come by it the same way; and that the complex ideas we have both of God and separate spirits are made up of the simple ideas we receive from reflection: v.g. having, from what we experiment in ourselves, got the ideas of existence and duration, of knowledge and power, of pleasure and happiness, and of several other qualities and powers, which it is better to have than to be without; when we would frame an idea the most suitable we can to the Supreme Being, we enlarge every one of these with our idea of infinity, and so putting them together, make our complex idea of God. For that the mind has such a power of enlarging some of its ideas, received from sensation and reflection, has been already shown.[1]

37. *Recapitulation.* And thus we have seen what kind of ideas we have of substances of all kinds, wherein they consist, and how we come by them. From whence, I think, it is very evident,

First, that all our ideas of the several sorts of substances are nothing but collections of simple ideas, with a supposition of *something* to which they belong, and in which they subsist; though of this supposed something we have no clear distinct idea at all.

Secondly, that all the simple ideas, that thus united in one

[1] II xvii

common *substratum* make up our complex ideas of several *sorts* of substances, are no other but such as we have received from sensation or reflection. So that even in those which we think we are most intimately acquainted with, and come nearest the comprehension of our most enlarged conceptions, we cannot reach beyond those simple ideas. And even in those which seem most remote from all we have to do with, and do infinitely surpass anything we can perceive in ourselves by reflection, or discover by sensation in other things, we can attain to nothing but those simple ideas, which we originally received from sensation or reflection; as is evident in the complex ideas we have of angels, and particularly of God himself.

Thirdly, that most of the simple ideas that make up our complex ideas of substances, when truly considered, are only *powers,* however we are apt to take them for positive qualities; v.g. the greatest part of the ideas that make our complex idea of gold are yellowness, great weight, ductility, fusibility, and solubility in *aqua regia,* &c., all united together in an unknown *substratum*; all which ideas are nothing else but so many relations to other substances, and are not really in the gold, considered barely in itself, though they depend on those real and primary qualities of its internal constitution, whereby it has a fitness differently to operate, and be operated on by several other substances.

CHAPTER XXIV

OF COLLECTIVE IDEAS OF SUBSTANCES

1. *One Idea.* Besides these complex ideas of several *single* substances, as of man, horse, gold, violet, apple, &c., the mind hath also complex *collective* ideas of substances; which I so call, because such ideas are made up of many particular substances considered together, as united into one idea, and

which so joined are looked on as one : v.g. the idea of such a collection of men as make an *army,* though consisting of a great number of distinct substances, is as much one idea as the idea of a man; and the great collective idea of all bodies whatsoever, signified by the name ' world ', is as much one idea as the idea of any the least particle of matter in it; it sufficing to the unity of any idea, that it be considered as one representation or picture, though made up of never so many particulars.

2. *Made by the Power of composing in the Mind.* Nor is it harder to conceive how an army of ten thousand men should make one idea than how a man should make one idea; it being as easy to the mind to unite into one the idea of a great number of men, and consider it as one, as it is to unite into one particular all the distinct ideas that make up the composition of a man, and consider them all together as one.

3. *All Artificial Things are collective Ideas.* Amongst such kind of collective ideas are to be counted most part of artificial things, at least such of them as are made up of distinct substances; and, in truth, if we consider all these collective ideas aright, as *army, constellation, universe,* as they are united into so many single ideas, they are but the artificial draughts of the mind, bringing things very remote, and independent on one another, into one view, the better to contemplate and discourse of them, united into one conception, and signified by one name. For there are no things so remote, nor so contrary, which the mind cannot, by this art of composition, bring into one idea, as is visible in that signified by the name *universe.*

CHAPTER XXV

OF RELATION

1. *Relation, what.* Besides the ideas, whether simple or complex, that the mind has of things as they are in themselves, there are others it gets from their comparison one with another. The understanding, in the consideration of anything, is not confined to that precise object; it can carry any idea as it were beyond itself, or at least look beyond it, to see how it stands in conformity to any other. When the mind so considers one thing that it does as it were bring it to, and set it by another, and carry its view from one to the other, this is, as the words import, *relation* and *respect*; and the denominations given to positive things, intimating that respect, and serving as marks to lead the thoughts beyond the subject itself denominated to something distinct from it, are what we call *relatives*; and the things so brought together, *related*. Thus, when the mind considers Caius as such a positive being, it takes nothing into that idea but what really exists in Caius; v.g. when I consider him as a man, I have nothing in my mind but the complex idea of the species, man. So likewise, when I say Caius is a white man, I have nothing but the bare consideration of a man who hath that white colour. But when I give Caius the name 'husband', I intimate some other person; and when I give him the name 'whiter', I intimate some other thing; in both cases my thought is led to something beyond Caius, and there are two things brought into consideration. And since any idea, whether simple or complex, may be the occasion why the mind thus brings two things together, and as it were takes a view of them at once, though still considered as distinct, therefore any of our ideas may be the foundation of relation.

2. *Relations without correlative Terms, not easily perceived.* These and the like relations, expressed by relative terms

that have others answering them, with a reciprocal intimation, as *father* and *son, bigger* and *less, cause* and *effect,* are very obvious to everyone, and everybody at first sight perceives the relation. But where languages have failed to give correlative names, there the relation is not always so easily taken notice of. ' Concubine ' is, no doubt, a relative name, as well as ' wife '; but in languages where this and the like words have not a correlative term, there people are not so apt to take them to be so, as wanting that evident mark of relation which is between correlatives, which seem to explain one another, and not to be able to exist but together. Hence it is that many of those names which, duly considered, do include evident relations, have been called *external denominations.*

3. *Some seemingly absolute Terms contain Relations.* Another sort of relative terms there is, which are not looked on to be either relative, or so much as external denominations; which yet, under the form and appearance of signifying something absolute in the subject, do conceal a tacit, though less observable, relation. Such are the seemingly positive terms of ' old ', ' great ', ' imperfect ', &c., whereof I shall have occasion to speak more at large in the following chapters.

7. *All Things capable of Relation.* Concerning relation in general, these things may be considered :

First, that there is no one thing, whether simple idea, substance, mode, or relation, or name of either of them, which is not capable of almost an infinite number of considerations in reference to other things; and therefore this makes no small part of men's thoughts and words : v.g. one single man may at once be concerned in, and sustain all these following relations, and many more, viz. father, brother, son, grandfather, grandson, father-in-law, son-in-law, husband, friend, enemy, subject, general, judge, patron, client, professor, European, Englishman, islander, servant, master, possessor, captain, superior, inferior, bigger, less, older, younger, contemporary, like, unlike, &c., to an almost infinite number; he being capable of as many relations as there can be occasions of comparing him to other things, in any manner of agreement, disagreement, or respect whatsoever. For, as I said, relation is a way of comparing or considering two things together, and giving one or both of them some appellation from that comparison, and sometimes giving even the relation itself a name.

8 *The Ideas of Relations clearer often than of the Subjects related.* Secondly, this further may be considered concerning relation that, though it be not contained in the real existence of things, but something extraneous and superinduced, yet the ideas which relative words stand for are often clearer and more distinct than of those substances to which they do belong. The notion we have of a father or brother is a great deal clearer and more distinct than that we have of a man; or, if you will, *paternity* is a thing whereof it is easier to have a clear idea than of humanity; and I can much easier conceive what a friend is than what God; because the knowledge of one action, or one simple idea, is oftentimes sufficient to give me the notion of a relation, but to the knowing of any substantial being an accurate collection of sundry ideas is necessary. A man, if he compares two things together, can hardly be supposed not to know what it is wherein he compares them; so that when he compares any things together, he cannot but have a very clear idea of that relation. *The ideas, then, of relations are capable at least of being more perfect and distinct in our minds than those of substances.* Thus, having the notion that one laid the egg out of which the other was hatched, I have a clear idea of the relation of *dam* and *chick* between the two cassowaries in St. James's Park, though perhaps I have but a very obscure and imperfect idea of those birds themselves.

9. *Relations all terminate in simple Ideas.* Thirdly, though there be a great number of considerations wherein things may be compared one with another, and so a multitude of relations, yet they all terminate in, and are concerned about, those simple ideas, either of sensation or reflection, which I think to be the whole materials of all our knowledge.

10. *Terms leading the Mind beyond the Subject denominated, are Relative.* Fourthly, that relation being the considering of one thing with another which is extrinsical to it,

it is evident that all words that necessarily lead the mind to any other ideas than are supposed really to exist in that thing to which the word is applied are relative words : v.g. a 'man', 'black' 'merry', 'thoughful', 'thirsty', 'angry', 'extended'; these and the like are all absolute, because they neither signify nor intimate anything but what does or is supposed really to exist in the man thus denominated; but 'father', 'brother', 'king', 'husband', 'blacker', 'merrier', &c., are words which, together with the thing they denominate, imply also something else separate and exterior to the existence of that thing.

11. *Conclusion.* Having laid down these premises concerning relation in general, I shall now proceed to show, in some instances, how all the ideas we have of relation are made up, as the others are, only of simple ideas; and that they all, how refined or remote from sense soever they seem, terminate at last in simple ideas. I shall begin with the most comprehensive relation, wherein all things that do, or can exist, are concerned, and that is the relation of *cause* and *effect*; the idea whereof, how derived from the two fountains of all our knowledge, sensation and reflection, I shall in the next place consider.

CHAPTER XXVI

OF CAUSE AND EFFECT, AND OTHER RELATIONS

1. *Whence their Ideas got.* In the notice that our senses take of the constant vicissitude of things we cannot but observe that several particular, both qualities and substances, begin to exist, and that they receive this their existence from the due application and operation of some other being. From this observation we get our ideas of *cause* and *effect*. That which produces any simple or complex *idea* we denote by the general name, *cause,* and that which is produced, *effect.* Thus, finding

that in that substance which we call wax, fluidity, which is a simple idea that was not in it before, is constantly produced by the application of a certain degree of heat we call the simple idea of heat, in relation to fluidity in wax, the cause of it, and fluidity the effect.

2. *Creation, Generation, making Alteration.* Having thus, from what our senses are able to discover in the operations of bodies on one another, got the notion of cause and effect, viz. that a cause is that which makes any other thing, either simple idea, substance, or mode, begin to be; and an effect is that which had its beginning from some other thing; the mind finds no great difficulty to distinguish the several originals of things into two sorts:

First, when the thing is wholly made new, so that no part thereof did ever exist before; as when a new particle of matter doth begin to exist *in rerum natura,* which had before no being, and this we call *creation.*

Secondly, when a thing is made up of particles which did all of them before exist; but that very thing, so constituted of pre-existing particles, which, considered all together, make up such a collection of simple ideas, had not any existence before, as this man, this egg, rose, or cherry, &c. And this, when referred to a substance, produced in the ordinary course of nature by an internal principle, but set on work by, and received from, some external agent, or cause, and working by insensible ways which we perceive not, we call *generation.* When the cause is extrinsical, and the effect produced by a sensible separation, or juxtaposition of discernible parts, we call it *making;* and such are all artificial things. When any simple idea is produced, which was not in that subject before, we call it *alteration.* Thus a man is generated, a picture made; and either of them altered, when any new sensible quality or simple idea is produced in either of them, which was not there before; and the things thus made to exist, which were not there before, are effects; and those things which operated to the existence, causes. In which, and all other cases, we may observe that the notion of cause and effect has its rise from ideas received by sensation or reflection;

and that this relation, how comprehensive soever, terminates at last in them. For to have the idea of cause and effect it suffices to consider any simple idea or substance, as beginning to exist, by the operation of some other, without knowing the manner of that operation.

3. *Relations of Time.* Time and place are also the foundations of very large relations, and all finite beings at least are concerned in them. But, having already shown in another place[1] how we get those ideas, it may suffice here to intimate that most of the denominations of things received from time are only relations. Thus, when anyone says that Queen Elizabeth lived sixty-nine, and reigned forty-five years, these words import only the relation of that duration to some other, and mean no more but this, that the duration of her existence was equal to sixty-nine, and the duration of her government to forty-five annual revolutions of the sun; and so are all words, answering, *How long?*

4. There are yet, besides those, other words of time, that ordinarily are thought to stand for positive ideas, which yet will, when considered, be found to be relative; such as are 'young', 'old', &c., which include and intimate the relation anything has to a certain length of duration whereof we have the idea in our minds. Thus, having settled in our thoughts the idea of the ordinary duration of a man to be seventy years, when we say a man is young we mean that his age is yet but a small part of that which usually men attain to; and when we denominate him old we mean that his duration is run out almost to the end of that which men do not usually exceed. But the sun and stars, though they have outlasted several generations of men, we call not old, because we do not know what period God hath set to that sort of beings. This term belonging properly to those things which we can observe in the ordinary course of things, by a natural decay, to come to an end in a certain period of time; and so have in our minds, as it were, a standard to which we can compare the several parts of their duration; and, by the relation they bear thereunto, call them young or old; which we cannot, therefore,

[1] II xiii, xiv

do to a ruby or a diamond, things whose usual periods we know not.

5. *Relations of Place and Extension.* The relation also that things have to one another in their places and distances is very obvious to observe; as above, below, a mile distant from Charing-Cross, in England, and in London. But as in duration, so in extension and bulk there are some ideas that are relative which we signify by names that are thought positive; as *great* and *little* are truly relations. For here also having, by observation, settled in our minds the ideas of the bigness of several species of things from those we have been most accustomed to, we make them as it were the standards, whereby to denominate the bulk of others.

6. *Absolute terms often stand for Relations.* So likewise *weak* and *strong* are but relative denominations of power, compared to some ideas we have at that time of greater or less power.

CHAPTER XXVII

OF IDENTITY AND DIVERSITY

1. *Wherein Identity consists.* Another occasion the mind often takes of comparing is the very being of things, when, considering anything as existing at any determined time and place, we compare it with itself existing at another time, and thereon form the ideas of *identity* and *diversity*. When we see anything to be in any place in any instant of time, we are sure (be it what it will) that it is that very thing, and not another which at that same time exists in another place, how like and undistinguishable soever it may be in all other respects; and in this consists *identity*, when the ideas it is attributed to vary not at all from what they were that moment wherein we consider their former existence, and to which we compare the present. For we never finding, nor conceiving it possible, that two things of the same kind should exist in the same place at

the same time, we rightly conclude that whatever exists anywhere at any time excludes all of the same kind, and is there itself alone. When therefore we demand whether anything be the same or no, it refers always to something that existed such a time in such a place, which it was certain, at that instant, was the same with itself, and no other. From whence it follows that one thing cannot have two beginnings of existence, nor two things one beginning; it being impossible for two things of the same kind to be or exist in the same instant, in the very same place; or one and the same thing in different places. That, therefore, that had one beginning, is the same thing; and that which had a different beginning in time and place from that, is not the same, but diverse. That which has made the difficulty about this relation has been the little care and attention used in having precise notions of the things to which it is attributed.

(2) *Identity of Substances.* We have the ideas but of three sorts of substances: (1) God. (2) Finite intelligences. (3) Bodies. First, God is without beginning, eternal, unalterable, and everywhere, and therefore concerning his identity there can be no doubt. Secondly, finite spirits having had each its determinate time and place of beginning to exist, the relation to that time and place will always determine to each of them its identity, as long as it exists. Thirdly, the same will hold of every particle of matter, to which no addition or subtraction of matter being made, it is the same. For, though these three sorts of substances, as we term them, do not exclude one another out of the same place, yet we cannot conceive but that they must necessarily each of them exclude any of the same kind out of the same place; or else the notions and names of identity and diversity would be in vain, and there could be no such distinctions of substances, or anything else one from another. *Identity of Modes.* All other things being but modes or relations ultimately terminated in substances, the identity and diversity of each particular existence of them too will be by the same way determined; only as to things whose existence is in succession, such as are the actions of finite beings, v.g. *motion* and *thought,* both which consist in a

continued train of succession, concerning their diversity there can be no question; because, each perishing the moment it begins, they cannot exist in different times, or in different places, as permanent beings can at different times exist in distant places; and therefore no motion or thought, considered as at different times, can be the same, each part thereof having a different beginning of existence.

(3.) *Principium Individuationis.* From what has been said, it is easy to discover what is so much inquired after, the *principium individuationis*; and that, it is plain, is existence itself; which determines a being of any sort to a particular time and place, incommunicable to two beings of the same kind. This, though it seems easier to conceive in simple substances or modes, yet, when reflected on, is not more difficult in compounded ones, if care be taken to what it is applied: v.g. let us suppose an atom, i.e. a continued body under one immutable superficies, existing in a determined time and place; it is evident that, considered in any instant of its existence, it is in that instant the same with itself. For, being at that instant what it is, and nothing else, it is the same, and so must continue as long as its existence is continued; for so long it will be the same, and no other. In like manner, if two or more atoms be joined together into the same mass, every one of those atoms will be the same, by the foregoing rule; and whilst they exist united together, the mass, consisting of the same atoms, must be the same mass, or the same body, let the parts be never so differently jumbled. But if one of these atoms be taken away, or one new one added, it is no longer the same mass or the same body. In the state of living creatures, their identity depends not on a mass of the same particles, but on something else. For in them the variation of great parcels of matter alters not the identity: an oak growing from a plant to a great tree, and then lopped, is still the same oak; and a colt grown up to a horse, sometimes fat, sometimes lean, is all the while the same horse: though, in both these cases, there may be a manifest change of the parts, so that truly they are not either of them the same masses of matter, though they be truly one of them the same oak, and the other the same horse. The reason whereof is that in these two cases— a mass of matter and a living body—identity is not applied to the same thing.

4. *Identity of Vegetables.* We must therefore consider wherein an oak differs from a mass of matter, and that seems to me to be in this, that the one is only the cohesion of particles of matter any how united, the other such a disposition of them as constitutes the parts of an oak, and such an organization of those parts as is fit to receive and distribute nourishment, so as to continue and frame the wood, bark, and leaves, &c., of an oak, in which consists the vegetable life. That being then one plant which has such an organization of parts in one coherent body, partaking of one common life, it continues to be the same plant as long as it partakes of the same life, though that life be communicated to new particles of matter vitally united to the living plant, in a like continued organization conformable to that sort of plants. For this organization, being at any one instant in any one collection of matter, is in that particular concrete distinguished from all other, and is that individual life; which existing constantly from that moment both forwards and backwards, in the same continuity of insensibly succeeding parts united to the living body of the plant, it has that identity which makes the same plant, and all the parts of it, parts of the same plant, during all the time that they exist united in that continued organization, which is fit to convey that common life to all the parts so united.

5. *Identity of Animals.* The case is not so much different in *brutes* but that anyone may hence see what makes an animal and continues it the same. Something we have like this in machines, and may serve to illustrate it. For example, what is a watch? It is plain it is nothing but a fit organization or construction of parts to a certain end, which, when a sufficient force is added to it, it is capable to attain. If we would suppose this machine one continued body, all whose organized parts were repaired, increased, or diminished by a constant addition or separation of insensible parts, with one common life, we should have something very much like the body of an animal; with this difference, that in an animal the fitness of the

organization, and the motion wherein life consists, begin together, the motion coming from within; but in machines the force, coming sensibly from without, is often away when the organ is in order, and well fitted to receive it.

6. *Identity of Man.* This also shows wherein the identity of the same *man* consists : viz. in nothing but a participation of the same continued life, by constantly fleeting particles of matter, in succession vitally united to the same organized body. He that shall place the identity of man in anything else, but, like that of other animals, in one fitly organized body, taken in any one instant, and from thence continued, under one organization of life, in several successively fleeting particles of matter united to it, will find it hard to make an embryo, one of years, mad and sober, the same man, by any supposition, that will not make it possible for Seth, Ismael, Socrates, Pilate, St. Austin, and Cæsar Borgia to be the same man. For if the identity of *soul alone* makes the same *man,* and there be nothing in the nature of matter why the same individual spirit may not be united to different bodies, it will be possible that those men, living in distant ages, and of different tempers, may have been the same man; which way of speaking must be from a very strange use of the word *man,* applied to an idea out of which body and shape are excluded. And that way of speaking would agree yet worse with the notions of those philosophers who allow of transmigration, and are of opinion that the souls of men may, for their miscarriages, be detruded into the bodies of beasts, as fit habitations, with organs suited to the satisfaction of their brutal inclinations. But yet I think nobody, could he be sure that the soul of Heliogabalus were in one of his hogs, would yet say that hog were a *man* or *Heliogabalus.*

7. *Identity suited to the Idea.* It is not therefore unity of substance that comprehends all sorts of identity, or will determine it in every case; but to conceive and judge of it aright, we must consider what idea the word it is applied to stands for; it being one thing to be the same *substance,* another the same *man,* and a third the same *person,* if *person, man,* and *substance* are three names standing for three different ideas;

for such as is the idea belonging to that name, such must be the identity; which, if it had been a little more carefully attended to, would possibly have prevented a great deal of that confusion which often occurs about this matter, with no small seeming difficulties, especially concerning *personal* identity, which therefore we shall in the next place a little consider.

8 *Same man.* An animal is a living organized body; and consequently the same animal, as we have observed, is the same continued *life* communicated to different particles of matter, as they happen successively to be united to that organized living body. And whatever is talked of other definitions, ingenuous observation puts it past doubt that the idea in our minds, of which the sound ' man ' in our mouths is the sign, is nothing else but of an animal of such a certain form. Since I think I may be confident that, whoever should see a creature of his own shape or make, though it had no more reason all its life than a cat or a parrot, would call him still a man; or whoever should hear a cat or a parrot discourse, reason, and philosophize, would call or think it nothing but a cat or a parrot; and say the one was a dull irrational man, and the other a very intelligent rational parrot. For I presume it is not the idea of a thinking or rational being alone that makes the idea of a man in most people's sense, but of a body, so and so shaped, joined to it; and if that be the idea of a man, the same successive body not shifted all at once must, as well as the same immaterial spirit, go to the making of the same man.

9 *Personal Identity.* This being premised, to find wherein personal identity consists, we must consider what *person* stands for; which, I think, is a thinking intelligent being, that has reason and reflection, and can consider itself as itself, the same thinking thing, in different times and places; which it does only by that consciousness which is inseparable from thinking, and, as it seems to me, essential to it; it being impossible for anyone to perceive without perceiving that he does perceive. When we see, hear, smell, taste, feel, meditate, or will anything, we know that we do so. Thus it is always as to our present sensations and perceptions; and by this everyone is to himself that which he calls *self*; it not being considered,

in this case, whether the same self be continued in the same or divers substances. For, since consciousness always accompanies thinking, and it is that that makes everyone to be what he calls self, and thereby distinguishes himself from all other thinking things, in this alone consists personal identity, i.e. the sameness of a rational being; and as far as this consciousness can be extended backwards to any past action or thought, so far reaches the identity of that person; it is the same self now it was then; and it is by the same self with this present one that now reflects on it, that that action was done.

10. *Consciousness makes personal Identity.* But it is further inquired whether it be the same identical substance. This few would think they had reason to doubt of, if these perceptions, with their consciousness, always remained present in the mind, whereby the same thinking thing would be always consciously present, and, as would be thought, evidently the same to itself. But that which seems to make the difficulty is this, that this consciousness being interrupted always by forgetfulness, there being no moment of our lives wherein we have the whole train of all our past actions before our eyes in one view, but even the best memories losing the sight of one part whilst they are viewing another; and we sometimes, and that the greatest part of our lives, not reflecting on our past selves, being intent on our present thoughts, and in sound sleep having no thoughts at all, or at least none with that consciousness which remarks our waking thoughts; I say, in all these cases, our consciousness being interrupted, and we losing the sight of our past selves, doubts are raised whether we are the same thinking thing, i.e. the same substance or no. Which, however reasonable or unreasonable, concerns not *personal* identity at all. The question being what makes the same person; and not whether it be the same identical substance, which always thinks in the same person, which, in this case, matters not at all; different substances, by the same consciousness (where they do partake in it) being united into one person, as well as different bodies by the same life are united into one animal, whose identity is preserved in that change of substances by the unity of one continued life. For, it being the same

consciousness that makes a man be himself to himself, personal identity depends on that only, whether it be annexed only to one individual substance, or can be continued in a succession of several substances. For as far as any intelligent being *can* repeat the idea of any past action with the same consciousness it had of it at first, and with the same consciousness it has of any present action, so far it is the same personal self. For it is by the consciousness it has of its present thoughts and actions, that it is *self to itself* now, and so will be the same self, as far as the same consciousness can extend to actions past or to come; and would be by distance of time, or change of substance, no more two persons, than a man be two men by wearing other clothes today than he did yesterday, with a long or a short sleep between; the same consciousness uniting those distant actions into the same person, whatever substances contributed to their production.

(11) *Personal Identity in Change of Substances.* That this is so, we have some kind of evidence in our very bodies, all whose particles, whilst vitally united to this same thinking conscious self, so that *we feel* when they are touched, and are affected by, and conscious of good or harm that happens to them, are a part of ourselves, i.e. of our thinking conscious self. Thus, the limbs of his body are to everyone a part of himself; he sympathizes and is concerned for them. Cut off a hand, and thereby separate it from that consciousness he had of its heat, cold, and other affections, and it is then no longer a part of that which is himself, any more than the remotest part of matter. Thus, we see the substance whereof personal self consisted at one time may be varied at another, without the change of personal identity; there being no question about the same person, though the limbs which but now were a part of it be cut off.

(12) *Whether in the Change of thinking Substances.* But the question is whether, if the same substance which thinks be changed, it can be the same person; or, remaining the same, it can be different persons?

And to this I answer: first, this can be no question at all to those who place thought in a purely material animal constitution, void of an immaterial substance. For, whether their supposition be true or no, it is plain they conceive personal identity preserved in something else than identity of substance, as animal identity is preserved in identity of life, and not of substance. And therefore those who place thinking in an immaterial substance only, before they can come to deal with these men, must show why personal identity cannot be preserved in the change of immaterial substances, or variety of particular immaterial substances, as well as animal identity is preserved in the change of material substances, or variety of particular bodies; unless they will say, it is one immaterial spirit that makes the same life in brutes, as it is one immaterial spirit that makes the same person in men; which the Cartesians at least will not admit, for fear of making brutes thinking things too.

13. But next, as to the first part of the question, whether, if the same thinking substance (supposing immaterial substances only to think) be changed, it can be the same person, I answer, that cannot be resolved but by those who know what kind of substances they are that do think; and whether the consciousness of past actions can be transferred from one thinking substance to another. I grant, were the same consciousness the same individual action, it could not; but, it being a present representation of a past action, why it may not be possible that that may be represented to the mind to have been which really never was, will remain to be shown. And therefore how far the consciousness of past actions is annexed to any individual agent, so that another cannot possibly have it, will be hard for us to determine, till we know what kind of action it is that cannot be done without a reflex act of perception accompanying it, and how performed by thinking substances, who cannot think without being conscious of it. But that which we call the same consciousness, not being the same individual act, why one intellectual substance may not have represented to it, as done by itself, what *it* never did, and was perhaps done by some other agent—why, I say, such a representation may not possibly be without reality of matter of fact, as well as several representations in dreams are, which yet

whilst dreaming we take for true, will be difficult to conclude from the nature of things.

14. As to the second part of the question, whether, the same immaterial substance remaining, there may be two distinct persons; which question seems to me to be built on this, whether the same immaterial being, being conscious of the actions of its past duration, may be wholly stripped of all the consciousness of its past existence, and lose it beyond the power of ever retrieving again, and so as it were beginning a new account from a new period, have a consciousness that cannot reach beyond this new state. All those who hold pre-existence are evidently of this mind, since they allow the soul to have no remaining consciousness of what it did in that pre-existent state, either wholly separate from body, or informing any other body; and, if they should not, it is plain experience would be against them. So that personal identity, reaching no further than consciousness reaches, a pre-existent spirit, not having continued so many ages in a state of silence, must needs make different persons. Let anyone reflect upon himself, and conclude that he has in himself an immaterial spirit, which is that which thinks in him, and, in the constant change of his body keeps him the same : and is that which he calls himself; let him also suppose it to be the same soul that was in Nestor or Thersites at the siege of Troy (for souls being, as far as we know anything of them, in their nature indifferent to any parcel of matter, the supposition has no apparent absurdity in it), which it may have been, as well as it is now the soul of any other man; but he now having no consciousness of any of the actions either of Nestor or Thersites, does or can he conceive himself the same person with either of them? Can he be concerned in either of their actions? attribute them to himself, or think them his own, more than the actions of any other man that ever existed? So that this consciousness, not reaching to any of the actions of either of those men, he is no more one *self* with either of them than if the soul or immaterial spirit that now informs him had been created, and began to exist, when it began to inform his present body; though it were never so true that the

same *spirit* that informed Nestor's or Thersites's body were numerically the same that now informs his. But let him once find himself conscious of any of the actions of Nestor, he then finds himself the same person with Nestor.

15. And thus may we be able, without any difficulty, to conceive the same person at the resurrection, though in a body not exactly in make or parts the same which he had here, the same consciousness going along with the soul that inhabits it. But yet the soul alone, in the change of bodies, would scarce to anyone but to him that makes the soul the man, be enough to make the same man. For should the soul of a prince, carrying with it the consciousness of the prince's past life, enter and inform the body of a cobbler, as soon as deserted by his own soul, everyone sees he would be the same *person* with the prince, accountable only for the prince's actions; but who would say it was the same *man?* The body too goes to the making the man, and would, I guess, to everybody determine the man in this case, wherein the soul, with all its princely thoughts about it, would not make another man; but he would be the same cobbler to everyone besides himself. I know that, in the ordinary way of speaking, 'the same person' and 'the same man' stand for one and the same thing. And indeed everyone will always have a liberty to speak as he pleases, and to apply what articulate sounds to what ideas he thinks fit, and change them as often as he pleases. But yet, when we will inquire what makes the same *spirit, man,* or *person,* we must fix the ideas of spirit, man, or person in our minds; and having resolved with ourselves what we mean by them, it will not be hard to determine, in either of them, or the like, when it is the same, and when not.

18. *Object of Reward and Punishment.* In this personal identity is founded all the right and justice of reward and punishment; happiness and misery being that for which everyone is concerned for *himself,* and not mattering what becomes of any substance, not joined to, or affected with that consciousness.

19. To punish Socrates waking for what sleeping Socrates thought, and waking Socrates was never conscious of, would be

no more of right than to punish one twin for what his brother-twin did, whereof he knew nothing, because their outsides were so like, that they could not be distinguished; for such twins have been seen.

(20) But yet possibly it will still be objected, suppose I wholly lose the memory of some parts of my life, beyond a possibility of retrieving them, so that perhaps I shall never be conscious of them again; yet am I not the same person that did those actions, had those thoughts that I once was conscious of, though I have now forgot them? To which I answer that we must here take notice what the word *I* is applied to; which, in this case, is the man only. And the same man being presumed to be the same person, *I* is easily here supposed to stand also for the same person. But if it be possible for the same man to have distinct incommunicable consciousness at different times, it is past doubt the same man would at different times make different persons; which, we see, is the sense of mankind in the solemnest declaration of their opinions, human laws not punishing the mad man for the sober man's actions, nor the sober man for what the mad man did; thereby making them two persons, which is somewhat explained by our way of speaking in English when we say such an one is *not himself*, or is *beside himself*; in which phrases it is insinuated, as if those who now, or at least first used them, thought that self was changed; the self-same person was no longer in that man.

(22) But is not a man drunk and sober the same person? Why else is he punished for the fact he commits when drunk, though he be never afterwards conscious of it? Just as much the same person as a man that walks, and does other things in his sleep, is the same person, and is answerable for any mischief he shall do in it. Human laws punish both, with a justice suitable to their way of knowledge, because, in these cases, they cannot distinguish certainly what is real, what counterfeit; and so the ignorance in drunkenness or sleep is not admitted as a plea. For, though punishment be annexed to personality, and personality to consciousness, and the drunkard perhaps be not conscious of what he did, yet human judicatures justly punish him, because the fact is proved against him, but

want of consciousness cannot be proved for him. But in the Great Day, wherein the secrets of all hearts shall be laid open, it may be reasonable to think, no one shall be made to answer for what he knows nothing of, but shall receive his doom, his conscience accusing or excusing him.

23. *Consciousness alone makes Self.* Nothing but consciousness can unite remote existences into the same person; the identity of substance will not do it, for whatever substance there is, however framed, without consciousness there is no person; and a carcass may be a person, as well as any sort of substance be so, without consciousness.

Could we suppose two distinct incommunicable consciousnesses acting the same body, the one constantly by day, the other by night; and, on the other side, the same consciousness acting by intervals two distinct bodies: I ask, in the first case, whether the day- and the night-man would not be two as distinct persons as Socrates and Plato? And whether, in the second case, there would not be one person in two distinct bodies, as much as one man is the same in two distinct clothings? Nor is it at all material to say that this same, and this distinct, consciousness, in the cases above mentioned, is owing to the same and distinct immaterial substances, bringing it with them to those bodies; which, whether true or no, alters not the case, since it is evident the personal identity would equally be determined by the consciousness, whether that consciousness were annexed to some individual immaterial substance or no. For, granting that the thinking substance in man must be necessarily supposed immaterial, it is evident that immaterial thinking thing may sometimes part with its past consciousness, and be restored to it again, as appears in the forgetfulness men often have of their past actions; and the mind many times recovers the memory of a past consciousness, which it had lost for twenty years together. Make these intervals of memory and forgetfulness to take their turns regularly by day and night, and you have two persons with the same immaterial spirit, as much as in the former instance two persons with the same body. So that self is not determined by identity or diversity of substance, which it cannot be sure of, but only by identity of consciousness.

(25) I agree, the more probable opinion is that this consciousness is annexed to, and the affection of, one individual immaterial substance.

But let men, according to their diverse hypotheses, resolve of that as they please. This every intelligent being, sensible of happiness or misery, must grant : that there is something that is *himself*, that he is concerned for, and would have happy; that this self has existed in a continued duration more than one instant, and therefore it is possible may exist, as it has done, months and years to come, without any certain bounds to be set to its duration; and may be the same self, by the same consciousness continued on for the future. And thus, by this consciousness he finds himself to be the same self which did such or such an action some years since, by which he comes to be happy or miserable now. In all which account of self, the same numerical *substance* is not considered as making the same self; but the same continued *consciousness,* in which several substances may have been united, and again separated from it, which, whilst they continued in a vital union with that wherein this consciousness then resided, made a part of that same self. Thus any part of our bodies, vitally united to that which is conscious in us, makes a part of ourselves; but upon separation from the vital union by which that consciousness is communicated, that which a moment since was part of ourselves is now no more so than a part of another man's self is a part of me; and it is not impossible but in a little time may become a real part of another person. And so we have the same numerical substance become a part of two different persons, and the same person preserved under the change of various substances. Could we suppose any spirit wholly stripped of all its memory or consciousness of past actions, as we find our minds always are of a great part of ours, and sometimes of them all, the union or separation of such a spiritual substance would make no variation of personal identity, any more than that of any particle of matter does. Any substance vitally united to the present thinking being is a part of that very same self which now is; anything united to it by a consciousness of former actions makes also a part of the same self, which is the same both then and now.

26. *Person a Forensic Term.* *Person,* as I take it, is the name for this self. Wherever a man finds what he calls himself, there, I think, another may say is the same person. It is a forensic term, appropriating actions and their merit, and so belongs only to intelligent agents, capable of a law, and happiness, and misery. This personality extends itself beyond present existence to what is past, only by consciousness, whereby it becomes concerned and accountable, owns and imputes to itself past actions, just upon the same ground and for the same reason as it does the present. All which is founded in a concern for happiness, the unavoidable concomitant of consciousness; that which is conscious of pleasure and pain desiring that that self that is conscious should be happy. And therefore whatever past actions it cannot reconcile or appropriate to that present self by consciousness, it can be no more concerned in than if they had never been done; and to receive pleasure or pain, i.e. reward or punishment, on the account of any such action, is all one as to be made happy or miserable in its first being, without any demerit at all. For, supposing a man punished now for what he had done in another life, whereof he could be made to have no consciousness at all, what difference is there between that punishment and being created miserable? And therefore, conformable to this, the apostle tells us that, at the great day, when everyone shall *receive according to his doings, the secrets of all hearts shall be laid open.* The sentence shall be justified by the consciousness all persons shall have that *they themselves,* in what bodies soever they appear, or what substances soever that consciousness adheres to, are the *same* that committed those actions, and deserve that punishment for them.

CHAPTER XXVIII

OF OTHER RELATIONS

1. *Proportional.* Besides the before-mentioned occasions of time, place, and causality of comparing or referring things one to another, there are, as I have said, infinite others, some whereof I shall mention.

First, the first I shall name is some one simple idea, which, being capable of parts or degrees, affords an occasion of comparing the subjects wherein it is to one another, in respect of that simple idea, v.g. *whiter, sweeter, bigger, equal, more,* &c. These relations, depending on the equality and excess of the same simple idea, in several subjects, may be called, if one will, *proportional*; and that these are only conversant about those simple ideas received from sensation or reflection is so evident that nothing need be said to evince it.

2. *Natural.* Secondly, another occasion of comparing things together, or considering one thing, so as to include in that consideration some other thing, is the circumstances of their origin or beginning; which, being not afterwards to be altered, make the relations depending thereon as lasting as the subjects to which they belong, v.g. *father* and *son, brothers, cousin-germans,* &c., which have their relations by one community of blood, wherein they partake in several degrees; *countrymen,* i.e. those who were born in the same country or tract of ground; and these I call *natural relations,* wherein we may observe that mankind have fitted their notions and words to the use of common life, and not to the truth and extent of things. For it is certain that, in reality, the relation is the same betwixt the begetter and the begotten, in the several races of other animals as well as men; but yet it is seldom said, this bull is the grandfather of such a calf, or that two pigeons are cousin-germans. It is very convenient that, by distinct names, these relations should be observed and

marked out in mankind, there being occasion, both in laws and other communications one with another, to mention and take notice of men under these relations; from whence also arise the obligations of several duties amongst men; whereas in brutes, men having very little or no cause to mind these relations, they have not thought fit to give them distinct and peculiar names.

3. *Instituted.* Thirdly, sometimes the foundation of considering things, with reference to one another, is some act whereby anyone comes by a moral right, power, or obligation to do something. Thus, a *general* is one that hath power to command an army; and an army under a general is a collection of armed men, obliged to obey one man. A *citizen,* or a *burgher,* is one who has a right to certain privileges in this or that place. All this sort depending upon men's wills, or agreement in society, I call *instituted,* or *voluntary*; and may be distinguished from the natural, in that they are most, if not all of them, some way or other alterable, and separable from the persons to whom they have sometimes belonged, though neither of the substances, so related, be destroyed.

4. *Moral.* Fourthly, there is another sort of relation, which is the conformity or disagreement men's *voluntary actions* have to a *rule* to which they are referred, and by which they are judged of; which, I think, may be called *moral relation,* as being that which denominates our moral actions, and deserves well to be examined.

5. *Moral Good and Evil.* Good and evil, as hath been shown (B. II. chap. xx. § 2, and chap. xxi. § 42), are nothing but pleasure or pain, or that which occasions or procures pleasure or pain to us. *Moral good and evil,* then, is only the conformity or disagreement of our voluntary actions to some law, whereby good or evil is drawn on us, from the will and power of the law-maker; which good and evil, pleasure or pain, attending our observance or breach of the law by the decree of the law-maker, is that we call *reward* and *punishment.*

6 *Moral Rules.* Of these moral rules or laws, to which men generally refer, and by which they judge of the rectitude or pravity of their actions, there seem to me to be *three sorts,*

with their three different enforcements, or rewards and punishments. For, since it would be utterly in vain to suppose a rule set to the free actions of men, without annexing to it some enforcement of good and evil to determine his will, we must, wherever we suppose a law, suppose also some reward or punishment annexed to that law. It would be in vain for one intelligent being to set a rule to the actions of another, if he had it not in his power to reward the compliance with, and punish deviation from, his rule, by some good and evil, that is not the natural product and consequence of the action itself. For that, being a natural convenience or inconvenience, would operate of itself, without a law. This, if I mistake not, is the true nature of all law, properly so called.

7. *Laws.* The laws that men generally refer their actions to, to judge of their rectitude or obliquity, seem to me to be these three : (1) The *divine* law. (2) The *civil* law. (3) The law of *opinion* or *reputation,* if I may so call it. By the relation they bear to the first of these, men judge whether their actions are sins or duties; by the second, whether they be criminal or innocent; and by the third, whether they be virtues or vices.

8. *Divine Law the Measure of Sin and Duty.* First, the *divine law,* whereby I mean that law which God has set to the actions of men, whether promulgated to them by the light of nature, or the voice of revelation. That God has given a rule whereby men should govern themselves, I think there is nobody so brutish as to deny. He has a right to do it; we are his creatures; he has goodness and wisdom to direct our actions to that which is best, and he has power to enforce it by rewards and punishments of infinite weight and duration in another life; for nobody can take us out of his hands. This is the only true touchstone of moral rectitude; and, by comparing them to this law, it is that men judge of the most considerable moral good or evil of their actions, that is, whether, as duties or sins, they are like to procure them happiness or misery from the hands of the ALMIGHTY.

9. *Civil Law the Measure of Crimes and Innocence.*

Secondly, the *civil law*—the rule set by the commonwealth to the actions of those who belong to it—is another rule to which men refer their actions; to judge whether they be criminal or no.

10. *Philosophical Law the Measure of Virtue and Vice.* Thirdly, the *law of opinion or reputation.* 'Virtue' and 'vice' are names pretended and supposed everywhere to stand for actions in their own nature right and wrong; and as far as they really are so applied, they so far are coincident with the divine law above mentioned. But yet, whatever is pretended, this is visible, that these names 'virtue' and 'vice', in the particular instances of their application, through the several nations and societies of men in the world, are constantly attributed only to such actions as in each country and society are in reputation or discredit. Nor is it to be thought strange that men everywhere should give the name of 'virtue' to those actions which amongst them are judged praiseworthy; and call that 'vice', which they account blamable; since otherwise they would condemn themselves, if they should think anything right, to which they allowed not commendation, anything wrong, which they let pass without blame. Thus the measure of what is everywhere called and esteemed virtue and vice is this approbation or dislike, praise or blame, which, by a secret and tacit consent, establishes itself in the several societies, tribes, and clubs of men in the world, whereby several actions come to find credit or disgrace amongst them, according to the judgment, maxims, or fashions of that place.

11. That this is the common measure of virtue and vice will appear to anyone who considers that, though that passes for vice in one country which is counted a virtue, or at least not vice, in another, yet everywhere virtue and praise, vice and blame, go together. Virtue is everywhere that which is thought praiseworthy; and nothing else but that which has the allowance of public esteem is called virtue.

12. *Its Enforcement is Commendation and Discredit.* If anyone shall imagine that I have forgot my own notion

of a law, when I make the law, whereby men judge of virtue and vice, to be nothing else but the consent of private men, who have not authority enough to make a law, especially wanting that which is so necessary and essential to a law, a power to enforce it; I think I may say that he who imagines commendation and disgrace not to be strong motives on men to accommodate themselves to the opinions and rules of those with whom they converse, seems little skilled in the nature or history of mankind; the greatest part whereof we shall find to govern themselves chiefly, if not solely, by this *law of fashion*; and, so they do that which keeps them in reputation with their company, little regard the laws of God, or the magistrate. The penalties that attend the breach of God's laws some, nay perhaps most men, seldom seriously reflect on; and amongst those that do, many, whilst they break the law, entertain thoughts of future reconciliation, and making their peace for such breaches. And as to the punishments due from the laws of the commonwealth, they frequently flatter themselves with the hopes of impunity. But no man escapes the punishment of their censure and dislike, who offends against the fashion and opinion of the company he keeps, and would recommend himself to.

14. *Morality is the Relation of Actions to these Rules.* Whether the rule to which, as to a touchstone, we bring our voluntary actions, to examine them by, and try their goodness, and accordingly to name them, which is, as it were, the mark of the value we set upon them; whether, I say, we take that rule from the fashion of the country, or the will of a law-maker, the mind is easily able to observe the relation any action hath to it, and to judge whether the action agrees or disagrees with the rule; and so hath a notion of moral goodness or evil, which is either conformity or not conformity of any action to that rule, and therefore is often called moral rectitude. This rule being nothing but a collection of several simple ideas, the conformity thereto is but so ordering the action that the simple ideas belonging to it may correspond to those which the law requires.

15. To conceive rightly of moral actions, we must take notice of them under this two-fold consideration. First, as they are in themselves, each made up of such a collection of simple ideas. Thus ' drunkenness ' or ' lying ' signify such or such a collection of simple ideas, which I call mixed modes; and in this sense they are as much *positive absolute* ideas, as the drinking of a horse, or speaking of a parrot. Secondly, our actions are considered as good, bad, or indifferent; and in this respect they are *relative,* it being their conformity to, or disagreement with, some rule that makes them to be regular or irregular, good or bad; and so, as far as they are compared with a rule, and thereupon denominated, they come under relation.

17. *Relations innumerable.* It would make a volume to go over all sorts of relations; it is not, therefore, to be expected that I should here mention them all. But before I quit this argument, from what has been said give me leave to observe:

18. *All Relations terminate in simple Ideas.* First, that it is evident that all relation terminates in, and is ultimately founded on, those simple ideas we have got from sensation or reflection: so that all we have in our thoughts ourselves (if we think of anything, or have any meaning), or would signify to others, when we use words standing for relations, is nothing but some simple ideas, or collections of simple ideas, compared one with another.

19. *We have ordinarily as clear (or clearer) a Notion of the Relation, as of its Foundation.* Secondly, that in relations we have for the most part, if not always, as clear a notion of *the relation* as we have of *those simple ideas wherein it is founded*; agreement or disagreement, whereon relation depends, being things whereof we have commonly as clear ideas as of any other whatsoever, it being but the distinguishing simple ideas, or their degrees one from another, without which we could have no distinct knowledge at all.

20. *The Notion of Relation is the same, whether the Rule any Action is compared to be true or false.* Thirdly, that in these I call *moral relations,* I have a true notion of relation, by comparing the action with the rule, whether the rule be true or

false. Though, measuring by a wrong rule, I shall thereby be brought to judge amiss of its moral rectitude, because I have tried it by that which is not the true rule, yet I am not mistaken in the relation which that action bears to that rule I compare it to, which is agreement or disagreement.

CHAPTER XXIX

OF CLEAR AND OBSCURE, DISTINCT AND CONFUSED IDEAS

1. *Ideas, some clear and distinct, others obscure and confused.* Having shown the original of our ideas, and taken a view of their several sorts; considered the difference between the simple and the complex; and observed how the complex ones are divided into those of modes, substances, and relations —all which, I think, is necessary to be done by anyone who would acquaint himself thoroughly with the progress of the mind, in its apprehension and knowledge of things—it will, perhaps, be thought I have dwelt long enough upon the examination of ideas. I must, nevertheless, crave leave to offer some few other considerations concerning them. The first is, that some are *clear* and others *obscure*; some *distinct* and others *confused*.

2. *Clear and obscure explained by Sight.* The perception of the mind being most aptly explained by words relating to the sight, we shall best understand what is meant by ' clear ' and ' obscure ' in our ideas by reflecting on what we call clear and obscure in the objects of sight. Light being that which discovers to us visible objects, we give the name of ' obscure ' to that which is not placed in a light sufficient to discover minutely to us the figure and colours which are observable in it, and which, in a better light, would be discernible. In like manner, our simple ideas are clear, when they are such as the objects themselves from whence they were taken did or might, in a well-ordered sensation or perception, present them.

Whilst the memory retains them thus, and can produce them to the mind whenever it has occasion to consider them, they are clear ideas. So far as they either want anything of that original exactness, or have lost any of their first freshness and are, as it were, faded or tarnished by time, so far are they obscure. Complex ideas, as they are made up of simple ones, so they are clear, when the ideas that go to their composition are clear, and the number and order of those simple ideas that are the ingredients of any complex one is determinate and certain.

3. *Causes of Obscurity.* The cause of obscurity, in simple ideas, seems to be either dull organs, or very slight and transient impressions made by the objects, or else a weakness in the memory, not able to retain them as received.

4. *Distinct and confused, what.* As a clear idea is that whereof the mind has such a full and evident perception as it does receive from an outward object operating duly on a well-disposed organ, so a *distinct* idea is that wherein the mind perceives a difference from all other; and a *confused* idea is such an one as is not sufficiently distinguishable from another, from which it ought to be different.

5. *Objection.* If no idea be confused but such as is not sufficiently distinguishable from another from which it should be different, it will be hard, may anyone say, to find anywhere a confused idea. For, let any idea be as it will, it can be no other but such as the mind perceives it to be; and that very perception sufficiently distinguishes it from all other ideas, which cannot be other, i.e. different, without being perceived to be so. No idea, therefore, can be indistinguishable from another from which it ought to be different, unless you would have it different from itself; for from all other it is evidently different.

6. *Confusion of Ideas is in Reference to their Names.* To remove this difficulty, and to help us to conceive aright what it is that makes the confusion ideas are at any time chargeable with, we must consider that things ranked under distinct names are supposed different enough to be distinguished, that so each sort by its peculiar name may be marked, and discoursed of apart upon any occasion; and

there is nothing more evident than that the greatest part of different names are supposed to stand for different things. Now every idea a man has, being visibly what it is, and distinct from all other ideas but itself, that which makes it confused is when it is such that it may as well be called by another name as that which it is expressed by; the difference which keeps the things (to be ranked under those two different names) distinct, and makes some of them belong rather to the one and some of them to the other of those names, being left out; and so the distinction, which was intended to be kept up by those different names, is quite lost.

7. *Defaults which make Confusion. First, complex Ideas made up of too few simple ones.* The defaults which usually occasion this confusion, I think, are chiefly these following: First, when any complex idea (for it is complex ideas that are most liable to confusion) is made up of too small a number of simple ideas, and such only as are common to other things, whereby the differences that make it deserve a different name are left out. Thus, he that has an idea made up of barely the simple ones of a beast with spots has but a confused idea of a leopard; it not being thereby sufficiently distinguished from a lynx, and several other sorts of beasts that are spotted. So that such an idea, though it hath the peculiar name 'leopard', is not distinguishable from those designed by the names 'lynx' or 'panther', and may as well come under the name 'lynx' as 'leopard'. How much the custom of defining of words by general terms contributes to make the ideas we would express by them confused and undetermined I leave others to consider. This is evident, that confused ideas are such as render the use of words uncertain, and take away the benefit of distinct names. When the ideas, for which we use different terms, have not a difference answerable to their distinct names, and so cannot be distinguished by them, there it is that they are truly confused.

8. *Secondly, Or its simple ones jumbled disorderly together.* Secondly, another default which makes our ideas confused is when, though the particulars that make up any idea are in

number enough, yet they are so jumbled together that it is not easily discernible whether it more belongs to the name that is given it than to any other.

9. *Thirdly, Or are mutable and undetermined.* Thirdly, a third defect that frequently gives the name of 'confused' to our ideas is when any one of them is uncertain and undetermined. Thus we may observe men who, not forbearing to use the ordinary words of their language till they have learned their precise signification, change the idea they make this or that term stand for almost as often as they use it. He that does this out of uncertainty of what he should leave out, or put into his idea of *church,* or *idolatry,* every time he thinks of either, and holds not steady to any one precise combination of ideas that makes it up, is said to have a confused idea of idolatry or the church; though this be still for the same reason as the former, viz. because a mutable idea (if we will allow it to be one idea) cannot belong to one name rather than another, and so loses the distinction that distinct names are designed for.

10. *Confusion without Reference to Names, hardly conceivable.* By what has been said, we may observe how much *names,* as supposed steady signs of things, and by their difference to stand for, and keep things distinct that in themselves are different, are the occasion of denominating ideas distinct or confused, by a secret and unobserved reference the mind makes of its ideas to such names.

12. *Causes of Confusion.* Some ideas are so complex, and made up of so many parts, that the memory does not easily retain the very same precise combination of simple ideas under one name; much less are we able constantly to divine for what precise complex idea such a name stands in another man's use of it. From the first of these follows confusion in a man's own reasonings and opinions within himself; from the latter frequent confusion in discoursing and arguing with others. But having more at large treated of words, their defects, and abuses, in the following Book, I shall here say no more of it.

13. *Complex Ideas may be distinct in one Part, and confused in another.* Our complex ideas, being made up of collections, and so variety of simple ones, may accordingly be very clear

and distinct in one part, and very obscure and confused in another.

14. *This, if not heeded, causes Confusion in our Arguings.* He that thinks he has a distinct idea of the figure of a *chiliahedron,* let him for trial's sake take another parcel of the same uniform matter, viz. gold or wax of an equal bulk, and make it into a figure of 999 sides. He will, I doubt not, be able to distinguish these two ideas one from another by the number of sides, and reason and argue distinctly about them, whilst he keeps his thoughts and reasoning to that part only of these ideas which is contained in their numbers; as that the sides of the one could be divided into two equal numbers, and of the other not, &c. But when he goes about to distinguish them by their figure, he will there be presently at a loss, and not be able, I think, to frame in his mind two ideas, one of them distinct from the other, by the bare figure of these two pieces of gold; as he could, if the same parcels of gold were made one into a cube, the other a figure of five sides.

15. *Instance in Eternity.* Having frequently in our mouths the name 'eternity', we are apt to think we have a positive comprehensive idea of it, which is as much as to say that there is no part of that duration which is not clearly contained in our idea. It is true that he that thinks so may have a clear idea of duration; he may also have a very clear idea of a very great length of duration; he may also have a clear idea of the comparison of that great one with still a greater : but it not being possible for him to include in his idea of any duration, let it be as great as it will, the whole extent together of a duration where he supposes no end, that part of his idea, which is still beyond the bounds of that large duration he represents to his own thoughts, is very obscure and undetermined. And hence it is that in disputes and reasonings concerning eternity, or any other infinite, we are apt to blunder, and involve ourselves in manifest absurdities.

16. *Divisibility of Matter.* In matter, we have no clear ideas of the smallness of parts much beyond the smallest that occur to any of our senses; and therefore, when we talk of the

divisibility of matter *in infinitum,* though we have clear ideas of division and divisibility, and have also clear ideas of parts made out of a whole by division; yet we have but very obscure and confused ideas of corpuscles, or minute bodies, so to be divided, when, by former divisions, they are reduced to a smallness much exceeding the perception of any of our senses; and so all that we have clear and distinct ideas of is of what division in general or abstractly is, and the relation of *totum* and *pars*: but of the bulk of the body, to be thus infinitely divided after certain progressions, I think, we have no clear nor distinct idea at all. Thus it is also in our idea of extension, when we increase it by addition, as well as when we diminish it by division, and would enlarge our thoughts to infinite space. After a few doublings of those ideas of extension, which are the largest we are accustomed to have, we lose the clear distinct idea of that space; it becomes a confusedly great one, with a surplus of still greater, about which, when we would argue or reason, we shall always find ourselves at a loss; confused ideas, in our arguings and deductions from that part of them which is confused, always leading us into confusion.

CHAPTER XXX

OF REAL AND FANTASTICAL IDEAS

1. *Real Ideas are Conformable to their Archetypes.* Besides what we have already mentioned concerning ideas, other considerations belong to them, in reference to things from whence they are taken, or which they may be supposed to represent; and thus, I think, they may come under a threefold distinction, and are:

First, either real or fantastical;

Secondly, adequate or inadequate;

Thirdly, true or false.

First, by *real ideas,* I mean such as have a foundation in

nature; such as have a conformity with the real being and existence of things, or with their archetypes. *Fantastical* or *chimerical* I call such as have no foundation in nature, nor have any conformity with that reality of being to which they are tacitly referred, as to their archetypes. If we examine the several sorts of ideas before mentioned, we shall find that,

2. *Simple ideas all Real.* First, our *simple ideas* are all real, all agree to the reality of things; not that they are all of them the images or representations of what does exist, the contrary whereof, in all but the primary qualities of bodies, hath been already shown. But, though whiteness and coldness are no more in snow than pain is, yet those ideas of whiteness and coldness, pain, &c., being in us the effects of powers in things without us, ordained by our Maker to produce in us such sensations, they are real ideas in us, whereby we distinguish the qualities that are really in things themselves. For, these several appearances being designed to be the marks whereby we are to know and distinguish things which we have to do with, our ideas do as well serve us to that purpose, and are as real distinguishing characters, whether they be only constant effects, or else exact resemblances of something in the things themselves, the reality lying in that steady correspondence they have with the distinct constitutions of real beings. But whether they answer to those constitutions, as to causes or patterns, it matters not; it suffices that they are constantly produced by them. And thus our simple ideas are all real and true, because they answer and agree to those powers of things which produce them in our minds, that being all that is requisite to make them real, and not fictions at pleasure. For in simple ideas (as has been shown) the mind is wholly confined to the operation of things upon it, and can make to itself no simple idea, more than what it has received.

3. *Complex Ideas are voluntary Combinations.* Though the mind be wholly passive in respect of its simple ideas, yet, I think, we may say it is not so in respect of its complex ideas. For those being combinations of simple ideas put together, and united under one general name, it is plain

that the mind of man uses some kind of liberty in forming those complex ideas; how else comes it to pass that one man's idea of gold or justice is different from another's, but because he has put in, or left out of his, some simple idea which the other has not? The question then is, which of these are real, and which barely imaginary combinations? What collections agree to the reality of things, and what not? And to this I say that,

4. *Mixed Modes made of consistent Ideas, are real.* Secondly, *mixed modes* and *relations,* having no other reality but what they have in the minds of men, there is nothing more required to this kind of ideas to make them real, but that they be so framed, that there be a possibility of existing conformable to them. These ideas, being themselves archetypes, cannot differ from their archetypes, and so cannot be chimerical, unless anyone will jumble together in them inconsistent ideas. Indeed, as any of them have the names of a known language assigned to them, by which he that has them in his mind would signify them to others, so bare possibility of existing is not enough; they must have a conformity to the ordinary signification of the name that is given them, that they may not be thought fantastical; as if a man would give the name of 'justice' to that idea which common use calls 'liberality'. But this fantasticalness relates more to propriety of speech than reality of ideas.

5. *Ideas of Substances are real, when they agree with the Existence of Things.* Thirdly, *our complex* ideas of *substances,* being made all of them in reference to things existing without us, and intended to be representations of substances as they really are, are no further real than as they are such combinations of simple ideas as are really united, and co-exist, in things without us. On the contrary, those are fantastical which are made up of such collections of simple ideas as were really never united, never were found together in any substance: v.g. a rational creature, consisting of a horse's head, joined to a body of human shape, or such as the *centaurs* are described; or, a body yellow, very malleable, fusible, and fixed, but lighter than common water; or an

uniform, unorganized body, consisting, as to sense, all of similar parts, with perception and voluntary motion joined to it. Whether such substances as these can possibly exist or no, it is probable we do not know; but be that as it will, these ideas of substances, being made conformable to no pattern existing that we know, and consisting of such collections of ideas as no substance ever showed us united together, they ought to pass with us for barely imaginary; but much more are those complex ideas so, which contain in them any inconsistency or contradiction of their parts.

CHAPTER XXXI

OF ADEQUATE AND INADEQUATE IDEAS

1. *Adequate Ideas are such as perfectly represent their Archetypes.* Of our real ideas, some are adequate, and some are inadequate. Those I call *adequate* which perfectly represent those archetypes which the mind supposes them taken from, which it intends them to stand for, and to which it refers them. *Inadequate ideas* are such which are but a partial or incomplete representation of those archetypes to which they are referred. Upon which account it is plain,

2. *Simple Ideas all adequate.* First, that *all our simple ideas are adequate.* Because, being nothing but the effects of certain powers in things, fitted and ordained by God to produce such sensations in us, they cannot but be correspondent and adequate to those powers; and we are sure they agree to the reality of things. For, if sugar produce in us the ideas which we call whiteness and sweetness, we are sure there is a power in sugar to produce those ideas in our minds, or else they could not have been produced by it. It is true, the things producing in us these simple ideas are but few of them denominated by us as if they were only the causes of them, but as if those ideas were real beings in them. For, though fire be called painful

to the touch, whereby is signified the power of producing in us
the idea of pain, yet it is denominated also light and hot; as if
light and heat were really something in the fire, more than a
power to excite these ideas in us, and therefore are called
qualities in or of the fire. But these being nothing, in truth, but
powers to excite such ideas in us, I must in that sense be
understood when I speak of secondary qualities as being
in things, or of their ideas as being in the objects that excite
them in us. Such ways of speaking, though accommodated
to the vulgar notions, without which one cannot be well
understood, yet truly signify nothing but those powers which
are in things to excite certain sensations or ideas in us.
Solidity and extension, and the termination of it, figure, with
motion and rest, whereof we have the ideas, would be really in
the world as they are, whether there were any sensible being to
perceive them or no; and therefore these we have reason to
look on as the real modifications of matter, and such as are
the exciting causes of all our various sensations from bodies.
But this being an inquiry not belonging to this place, I shall
enter no further into it, but proceed to show what complex
ideas are adequate, and what not.

3. *Modes are all adequate.*   Secondly, *our complex ideas of
modes,* being voluntary collections of simple ideas, which the
mind puts together, without reference to any real archetypes, or
standing patterns, existing anywhere, are and cannot but be
adequate ideas. Thus, by having the idea of a figure with three
sides meeting at three angles, I have a complete idea, wherein
I require nothing else to make it perfect. But in our *ideas of
substances* it is otherwise. For there, desiring to copy things as
they really do exist, and to represent to ourselves that constitution on which all their properties depend, we perceive our ideas
attain not that perfection we intend; we find they still want
something we should be glad were in them; and so are all inadequate. But *mixed modes* and *relations,* being archetypes without
patterns, and so having nothing to represent but themselves,
cannot but be adequate, everything being so to itself. He
that at first put together the idea of danger perceived, absence

of disorder from fear, sedate consideration of what was justly to be done, and executing of that without disturbance, or being deterred by the danger of it, had certainly in his mind that complex idea made up of that combination; and intending it to be nothing else but what is, nor to have in it any other simple ideas but what it hath, it could not also but be an adequate idea; and laying this up in his memory, with the name 'courage' annexed to it, to signify to others, and denominate from thence any action he should observe to agree with it, had thereby a standard to measure and denominate actions by, as they agreed to it. This idea, thus made and laid up for a pattern, must necessarily be adequate, being referred to nothing else but itself, nor made by any other original but the good liking and will of him that first made this combination.

4. *Modes, in reference to settled Names, may be inadequate.* Indeed another coming after, and in conversation learning from him the word ' courage ', may make an idea to which he gives the name ' courage ', different from what the first author applied it to, and has in his mind when he uses it. And in this case, if he designs that his idea in thinking should be conformable to the other's idea, as the name he uses in speaking is conformable in sound to his from whom he learned it, his idea may be very wrong and inadequate; because in this case, making the other man's idea the pattern of his idea in thinking, as the other man's word or sound is the pattern of his in speaking, his idea is so far defective and inadequate, as it is distant from the archetype and pattern he refers it to, and intends to express and signify by the name he uses for it; which name he would have to be a sign of the other man's idea, (to which, in its proper use, it is primarily annexed), and of his own, as agreeing to it; to which if his own does not exactly correspond, it is faulty and inadequate.

5. And on this account our ideas of mixed modes are the most liable to be faulty of any other; but this refers more to proper speaking than knowing right.

6. *Ideas of Substances, as referred to real Essences, not adequate. Thirdly,* what *ideas we have of substances* I have

above shown[1]. Now, those ideas have in the mind a double reference : 1. Sometimes they are referred to a supposed real essence of each species of things. 2. Sometimes they are only designed to be pictures and representations in the mind of things that do exist, by ideas of those qualities that are discoverable in them. In both which ways these copies of those originals and archetypes are imperfect and inadequate.

First, it is usual for men to make the names of substances stand for things as supposed to have certain real essences, whereby they are of this or that species; and names standing for nothing but the ideas that are in men's minds, they must constantly refer their ideas to such real essences, as to their archetypes. That men (especially such as have been bred up in the learning taught in this part of the world) do suppose certain specific essences of substances, which each individual in its several kinds is made conformable to and partakes of, is so far from needing proof that it will be thought strange if anyone should do otherwise. And thus they ordinarily apply the specific names they rank particular substances under to things as distinguished by such specific real essences. Who is there almost, who would not take it amiss if it should be doubted whether he called himself a man with any other meaning than as having the real essence of a man? And yet if you demand what those real essences are, it is plain men are ignorant and know them not. From whence it follows that the ideas they have in their minds, being referred to real essences, as to archetypes which are unknown, must be so far from being adequate that they cannot be supposed to be any representation of them at all. The complex ideas we have of substances are, as it has been shown, certain collections of simple ideas that have been observed or supposed constantly to exist together. But such a complex idea cannot be the real essence of any substance; for then the properties we discover in that body would depend on that complex idea, and be deducible from it, and their necessary connexion with it be known; as all properties of a triangle depend on, and, as far as they are discoverable, are deducible from the complex

[1] II xxiii

idea of three lines including a space. But it is plain that in our complex ideas of substances are not contained such ideas, on which all the other qualities that are to be found in them do depend. The common idea men have of iron is a body of a certain colour, weight, and hardness; and a property that they look on as belonging to it is malleableness. But yet this property has no necessary connexion with that complex idea, or any part of it; and there is no more reason to think that malleableness depends on that colour, weight, and hardness, than that that colour or that weight depends on its malleableness. And yet, though we know nothing of these real essences, there is nothing more ordinary than that men should attribute the sorts of things to such essences. The particular parcel of matter which makes the ring I have on my finger is forwardly by most men supposed to have a real essence, whereby it is gold; and from whence those qualities flow which I find in it, viz. its peculiar colour, weight, hardness, fusibility, fixedness, and change of colour upon a slight touch of mercury, &c. If anyone will say that the real essence and internal constitution, on which these properties depend, is not the figure, size, and arrangement or connexion of its solid parts, but something else, called its particular *form*, I am further from having any idea of its real essence than I was before. For I have an idea of figure, size, and situation of solid parts in general, though I have none of the particular figure, size, or putting together of parts whereby the qualities above mentioned are produced; which qualities I find in that particular parcel of matter that is on my finger, and not in another parcel of matter, with which I cut the pen I write with. But, when I am told that something besides the figure, size, and posture of the solid parts of that body is its essence, something called *substantial form,* of that I confess I have no idea at all, but only of the sound 'form'; which is far enough from an idea of its real essence or constitution.

7. Now then, when men apply to this particular parcel of matter on my finger a general name already in use, and denominate it ' gold ', do they not ordinarily, or are they not understood to give it that name, as belonging to a particular

species of bodies, having a real internal essence, by having of which essence this particular substance comes to be of that species, and to be called by that name? If it be so, as it is plain it is, the name by which things are marked as having that essence must be referred primarily to that essence; and consequently the idea to which that name is given must be referred also to that essence, and be intended to represent it. Which essence, since they who so use the names know not, their ideas of substances must be all inadequate in that respect, as not containing in them that real essence which the mind intends they should.

8. *Ideas of Substances, as Collections of their Qualities, are all inadequate.* Secondly, those who, neglecting that useless supposition of unknown real essences whereby they are distinguished, endeavour to copy the substances that exist in the world by putting together the ideas of those sensible qualities which are found co-existing in them, though they come much nearer a likeness of them than those who imagine they know not what real specific essences; yet they arrive not at perfectly adequate ideas of those substances they would thus copy into their minds, nor do those copies exactly and fully contain all that is to be found in their archetypes. Because those qualities and powers of substances, whereof we make their complex ideas, are so many and various that no man's complex idea contains them all. The simple ideas whereof we make our complex ones of substances are all of them (bating only the figure and bulk of some sorts) powers; which being relations to other substances, we can never be sure that we know all the powers that are in any one body, till we have tried what changes it is fitted to give to or receive from other substances in their several ways of application; which being impossible to be tried upon any one body, much less upon all, it is impossible we should have adequate ideas of any substance made up of a collection of all its properties.

11. *Ideas of substances as collections of their qualities are all inadequate.* So that all our complex ideas of substances are imperfect and inadequate. Which would be so also in mathematical figures, if we were to have our complex ideas of them

only by collecting their properties in reference to other figures. How uncertain and imperfect would our ideas be of an ellipsis, if we had no other idea of it but some few of its properties? Whereas, having in our plain idea the whole essence of that figure, we from thence discover those properties, and demonstratively see how they flow, and are inseparable from it.

12. *Simple ideas,* ἔκτυπα, *and adequate.* Thus the mind has three sorts of abstract ideas or nominal essences :

First, *simple* ideas, which are ἔκτυπα or *copies,* but yet certainly *adequate.* Because, being intended to express nothing but the power in things to produce in the mind such a sensation, that sensation, when it is produced, cannot but be the effect of that power. So the paper I write on, having the power in the light (I speak according to the common notion of light) to produce in me the sensation which I call white, it cannot but be the effect of such a power in something without the mind, since the mind has not the power to produce any such idea in itself; and being meant for nothing else but the effect of such a power, that simple idea is real and adequate; the sensation of white, in my mind, being the effect of that power which is in the paper to produce it, is perfectly adequate to that power; or else that power would produce a different idea.

13. *Ideas of substances are* ἔκτυπα, *inadequate.* Secondly, the *complex* ideas of *substances* are *ectypes, copies* too; but not perfect ones, not *adequate;* which is very evident to the mind, in that it plainly perceives that whatever collection of simple ideas it makes of any substance that exists, it cannot be sure that it exactly answers all that are in that substance. Since, not having tried all the operations of all other substances upon it, and found all the alterations it would receive from, or cause in, other substances, it cannot have an exact adequate collection of all its active and passive capacities, and so not have an adequate complex idea of the powers of any substance existing, and its relations; which is that sort of complex idea of substances we have. And, after all, if we would have, and actually had, in our complex idea, an exact collection of all the secondary qualities or powers of any substance, we should not

yet thereby have an idea of the essence of that thing. For, since the powers or qualities that are observable by us are not the real essence of that substance, but depend on it and flow from it, any collection whatsoever of these qualities cannot be the real essence of that thing. Whereby it is plain that our ideas of substances are not adequate, are not what the mind intends them to be. Besides, a man has no idea of substance in general, nor knows what substance is in itself.

14. *Ideas of Modes and Relations are Archetypes, and cannot but be adequate.* Thirdly, *complex* ideas of *modes and relations* are originals, and *archetypes;* are not copies, nor made after the pattern of any real existence, to which the mind intends them to be conformable and exactly to answer. These being such collections of simple ideas that the mind itself puts together, and such collections that each of them contains in it precisely all that the mind intends it should, they are archetypes and essences of modes that may exist; and so are designed only for, and belong only to such modes as, when they do exist, have an exact conformity with those complex ideas. The ideas, therefore, of modes and relations cannot but be adequate.

CHAPTER XXXII

OF TRUE AND FALSE IDEAS

1. *Truth and Falsehood properly belong to Propositions.* Though truth and falsehood belong, in propriety of speech, only to *propositions,* yet ideas are oftentimes termed *true* or *false* (as what words are there that are not used with great latitude, and with some deviation from their strict and proper significations?). Though I think that when ideas themselves are termed true or false, there is still some secret or tacit proposition, which is the foundation of that denomination; as we shall see, if we examine the particular occasions wherein they come to be called true or false. In all which

we shall find some kind of affirmation or negation, which is the reason of that denomination. For our ideas, being nothing but bare appearances or perceptions in our minds, cannot properly and simply in themselves be said to be true or false, no more than a single name of anything can be said to be true or false.

4. *Ideas referred to anything may be true or false.* Whenever the mind refers any of its ideas to anything extraneous to them, they are then capable to be called true or false. Because the mind, in such a reference, makes a tacit supposition of their conformity to that thing; which supposition as it happens to be true or false, so the ideas themselves come to be denominated. The most usual cases wherein this happens, are these following:

5. *Other Men's Ideas, real Existence and supposed real Essences, are what Men usually refer their Ideas to.* First, when the mind supposes any idea it has *conformable* to that in *other men's minds*, called by the same common name; v.g. when the mind intends or judges its ideas of *justice, temperance, religion* to be the same with what other men give those names to.

Secondly, when the mind supposes any idea it has in itself to be *conformable* to some *real existence.* Thus the two ideas of a *man* and a *centaur,* supposed to be the ideas of real substances, are the one true and the other false, the one having a conformity to what has really existed, the other not.

Thirdly, when the mind *refers* any of its ideas to that *real* constitution and *essence* of anything, whereon all its properties depend; and thus the greatest part, if not all our ideas of substances, are false.

6. *The cause of such References.* These suppositions the mind is very apt tacitly to make concerning its own ideas. But yet, if we will examine it, we shall find it is chiefly, if not only, concerning its abstract complex ideas. For the natural tendency of the mind being towards knowledge, and finding that, if it should proceed by and dwell upon only particular things, its progress would be very slow, and its work endless; therefore, to shorten its way to knowledge, and make each

perception the more comprehensive, the first thing it does, as the foundation of the easier enlarging its knowledge, either by contemplation of the things themselves that it would know, or conference with others about them, is to bind them into bundles, and rank them so into sorts, that what knowledge it gets of any of them it may thereby with assurance extend to all of that sort; and so advance by larger steps in that which is its great business, knowledge. This, as I have elsewhere shown[1], is the reason why we collect things under comprehensive ideas, with names annexed to them, into genera and species, i.e. into kinds and sorts.

8. *The cause of such references.* But this abstract idea, being something in the mind between the thing that exists and the name that is given to it, it is in our ideas that both the rightness of our knowledge, and the propriety or intelligibleness of our speaking, consists. And hence it is that men are so forward to suppose that the abstract ideas they have in their minds are such as agree to the things existing without them, to which they are referred; and are the same also to which the names they give them do by the use and propriety of that language belong. For without this double conformity of their ideas, they find they should both think amiss of things in themselves, and talk of them unintelligibly to others.

9. *Simple Ideas may be false, in reference to others of the same Name, but are least liable to be so.* First, then, I say that when the truth of our ideas is judged of by the conformity they have to the ideas which other men have, and commonly signify by the same name, they may be any of them false. But yet simple ideas are least of all liable to be so mistaken. Because a man, by his senses and every day's observation, may easily satisfy himself what the simple ideas are which their several names that are in common use stand for, they being but few in number, and such as, if he doubts or mistakes in, he may easily rectify by the objects they are to be found in.

10. *Ideas of mixed Modes most liable to be false in this Sense.* Complex ideas are much more liable to be false in this respect; and the complex ideas of mixed modes, much

[1] III iii

more than those of substances, because in substances (especially those which the common and unborrowed names of any language are applied to) some remarkable sensible qualities, serving ordinarily to distinguish one sort from another, easily preserve those who take any care in the use of their words, from applying them to sorts of substances to which they do not at all belong. But in mixed modes we are much more uncertain, it being not so easy to determine of several actions whether they are to be called *justice* or *cruelty*, *liberality* or *prodigality*.

11. *Or at least to be thought false.*   When a man is thought to have a false idea of *justice*, or *gratitude*, or *glory*, it is for no other reason but that his agrees not with the ideas which each of those names are the signs of in other men.

12. *And why.*   The reason whereof seems to me to be this : that the abstract ideas of mixed modes, being men's voluntary combinations of such a precise collection of simple ideas, and so the essence of each species being made by men alone, whereof we have no other sensible standard existing anywhere but the name itself, or the definition of that name; we having nothing else to refer these our ideas of mixed modes to as a standard to which we would conform them, but the ideas of those who are thought to use those names in their most proper significations; and so, as our ideas conform or differ from them, they pass for true or false. And thus much concerning the truth and falsehood of our ideas in reference to their names.

13. *As referred to Real Existences, none of our Ideas can be false but those of Substances.*   Secondly, as to the truth and falsehood of our ideas in reference to the real existence of things. When that is made the standard of their truth, none of them can be termed false but only our complex ideas of substances.

14. *First, simple Ideas in this Sense not false, and why.* First, our simple ideas, being barely such perceptions as God has fitted us to receive, and given power to external objects to produce in us by established laws and ways, suitable to his wisdom and goodness, though incomprehensible to us, their truth consists in nothing else but in such appearances

as are produced in us, and must be suitable to those powers he has placed in external objects or else they could not be produced in us; and thus answering those powers, they are what they should be, true ideas.

15. *Though one Man's Idea of Blue should be different from another's.* Neither would it carry any imputation of falsehood to our simple ideas, if by the different structure of our organs it were so ordered that *the same object should produce in several men's minds different ideas* at the same time; v.g. if the idea that a violet produced in one man's mind by his eyes were the same that a marigold produced in another man's, and *vice versa*. For, since this could never be known, because one man's mind could not pass into another man's body, to perceive what appearances were produced by those organs, neither the ideas hereby, nor the names, would be at all confounded, or any falsehood be in either. For all things that had the texture of a violet producing constantly the idea which he called blue, and those which had the texture of a marigold producing constantly the idea which he as constantly called yellow, whatever those appearances were in his mind, he would be able as regularly to distinguish things for his use by those appearances, and understand and signify those distinctions marked by the names 'blue' and 'yellow', as if the appearances or ideas in his mind received from those two flowers were exactly the same with the ideas in other men's minds.

16. *First Simple Ideas in this Sense not false, and why.* From what has been said concerning our simple ideas I think it evident that our simple ideas can none of them be false in respect of things existing without us. For the truth of these appearances or perceptions in our minds consisting, as has been said, only in their being answerable to the powers in external objects to produce by our senses such appearances in us, and each of them being in the mind such as it is, suitable to the power that produced it, and which alone it represents, it cannot upon that account, or as referred to such a pattern, be false. Blue or yellow, bitter or sweet, can never be false ideas; these perceptions in the mind are just such as they are

there, answering the powers appointed by God to produce
them, and so are truly what they are, and are intended to be.
Indeed the names may be misapplied, but that in this respect
makes no falsehood in the ideas; as if a man ignorant in the
English tongue should call purple scarlet.

17. *Secondly, Modes not false.* Secondly, neither can our
complex ideas of modes, in reference to the essence of anything
really existing, be false, because whatever complex idea I have
of any mode, it hath no reference to any pattern existing, and
made by nature; it is not supposed to contain in it any other
ideas than what it hath, nor to represent anything but such a
complication of ideas as it does. Thus, when I have the idea of
such an action of a man who forbears to afford himself such
meat, drink, and clothing, and other conveniences of life as his
riches and estate will be sufficient to supply and his station
requires, I have no false idea; but such an one as represents
an action, either as I find or imagine it, and so is capable
of neither truth nor falsehood. But when I give the name
' frugality ' or ' virtue ' to this action, then it may be called a
false idea, if thereby it be supposed to agree with that idea to
which, in propriety of speech, the name of ' frugality ' doth
belong, or to be conformable to that law which is the
standard of virtue and vice.

18. *Thirdly, Ideas of Substances when false.* Thirdly, our
complex ideas of substances, being all referred to patterns in
things themselves, may be false. That they are all false, when
looked upon as the representations of the unknown essences of
things, is so evident that there needs nothing to be said of it.
I shall therefore pass over that chimerical supposition, and
consider them as collections of simple ideas in the mind, taken
from combinations of simple ideas existing together constantly
in things, of which patterns they are the supposed copies; and
in this reference of them to the existence of things, they are
false ideas : (1) When they put together simple ideas, which
in the real existence of things have no union : as when to the
shape and size that exist together in a horse is joined in the
same complex idea the power of barking like a dog; which
three ideas, however, put together into one in the mind, were

never united in nature; and this, therefore, may be called a false idea of a horse. (2) Ideas of substances are, in this respect, also false, when, from any collection of simple ideas that do always exist together, there is separated, by a direct negation any other simple idea which is constantly joined with them. Thus, if to extension, solidity, fusibility, the peculiar weightiness, and yellow colour of gold anyone join in his thoughts the negation of a greater degree of fixedness than is in lead or copper, he may be said to have a false complex idea, as well as when he joins to those other simple ones the idea of perfect absolute fixedness. For either way, the complex idea of gold, being made up of such simple ones as have no union in nature, may be termed false. But, if he leave out of this his complex idea that of fixedness quite, without either actually joining to or separating of it from the rest in his mind, it is, I think, to be looked on as an inadequate and imperfect idea, rather than a false one; since, though it contains not all the simple ideas that are united in nature, yet it puts none together but what do really exist together.

19. *Truth or Falsehood always supposes Affirmation or Negation.* Though in compliance with the ordinary way of speaking, I have shown in what sense and upon what ground our ideas may be sometimes called true or false; yet if we will look a little nearer into the matter, in all cases where any idea is called true or false, it is from some *judgment* that the mind makes, or is supposed to make, that is true or false. For truth or falsehood, being never without some affirmation or negation, express or tacit, it is not to be found but where signs are joined or separated, according to the agreement or disagreement of the things they stand for. The signs we chiefly use are either ideas or words, wherewith we make either mental or verbal propositions. Truth lies in so joining or separating these representatives as the things they stand for do in themselves agree or disagree; and falsehood in the contrary, as shall be more fully shown hereafter[1].

25. *Ideas when false.* To conclude, a man having no notion of anything without him but by the idea he has of it in

---

[1] IV v-viii

his mind (which idea he has a power to call by what name he pleases), he may indeed make an idea neither answering the reality of things, nor agreeing to the idea commonly signified by other people's words, but cannot make a wrong or false idea of a thing which is not otherwise known to him but by the idea he has of it; v.g. when I frame an idea of the legs, arms, and body of a man, and join to this a horse's head and neck, I do not make a false idea of anything, because it represents nothing without me. But when I call it a *man* or *Tartar*, and imagine it either to represent some real being without me, or to be the same idea that others call by the same name, in either of these cases I may err. And upon this account it is that it comes to be termed a false idea; though indeed the falsehood lies not in the idea, but in that tacit mental proposition wherein a conformity and resemblance is attributed to it which it has not. But yet, if, having framed such an idea in my mind, without thinking either that existence, or the name ' man ' or ' Tartar ', belongs to it, I will call it man or Tartar, I may be justly thought fantastical in the naming, but not erroneous in my judgment, nor the idea any way false.

26. *More properly to be called Right or Wrong.* Upon the whole matter I think that our ideas, as they are considered by the mind—either in reference to the proper signification of their names, or in reference to the reality of things—may very fitly be called *right* or *wrong* ideas, according as they agree or disagree to those patterns to which they are referred. But if anyone had rather call them true or false, it is fit he use a liberty, which everyone has, to call things by those names he thinks best; though, in propriety of speech, *truth* or *falsehood* will, I think, scarce agree to them, but as they, some way or other, virtually contain in them some mental proposition.

CHAPTER XXXIII

OF THE ASSOCIATION OF IDEAS

1. *Something unreasonable in most Men.* There is scarce anyone that does not observe something that seems odd to him, and is in itself really extravagant, in the opinions, reasonings, and actions of other men. The least flaw of this kind, if at all different from his own, everyone is quick-sighted enough to espy in another, and will by the authority of reason forwardly condemn; though he be guilty of much greater unreasonableness in his own tenets and conduct, which he never perceives, and will very hardly, if at all, be convinced of.

2. *Not wholly from Self-love.* This proceeds not wholly from self-love, though that has often a great hand in it. Men of fair minds, and not given up to the overweening of self-flattery, are frequently guilty of it; and in many cases one with amazement hears the arguings, and is astonished at the obstinacy, of a worthy man who yields not to the evidence of reason, though laid before him as clear as daylight.

3. *Nor from Education.* This sort of unreasonableness is usually imputed to education and prejudice, and for the most part truly enough, though that reaches not the bottom of the disease nor shows distinctly enough whence it rises, or wherein it lies.

4. *A Degree of Madness.* And if this be a weakness to which all men are so liable, if this be a taint which so universally infects mankind, the greater care should be taken to lay it open under its due name, thereby to excite the greater care in its prevention and cure.

5. *From a wrong Connexion of Ideas.* Some of our ideas have a *natural* correspondence and connexion one with another; it is the office and excellency of our reason to trace these, and hold them together in that union and correspondence which is founded in their peculiar beings. Besides this, there is another

connexion of ideas wholly owing to *chance* or *custom*. Ideas that in themselves are not at all of kin come to be so united in some men's minds that it is very hard to separate them; they always keep in company, and the one no sooner at any time comes into the understanding but its associate appears with it; and if they are more than two which are thus united, the whole gang, always inseparable, show themselves together.

6. *This Connexion how made.* This strong combination of ideas, not allied by nature, the mind makes in itself either voluntarily or by chance; and hence it comes in different men to be very different, according to their different inclinations, educations, interests, &c. Custom settles habits of thinking in the understanding, as well as of determining in the will, and of motions in the body; all which seems to be but trains of motions in the animal spirits, which, once set a-going, continue in the same steps they have been used to, which, by often treading, are worn into a smooth path, and the motion in it becomes easy, and as it were natural. As far as we can comprehend thinking, thus ideas seem to be produced in our minds; or, if they are not, this may serve to explain their following one another in an habitual train when once they are put into their track, as well as it does to explain such motions of the body. A musician used to any tune will find that, let it but once begin in his head, the ideas of the several notes of it will follow one another orderly in his understanding, without any care or attention, as regularly as his fingers move orderly over the keys of the organ to play out the tune he has begun, though his inattentive thoughts be elsewhere a-wandering. Whether the natural cause of these ideas, as well as of that regular dancing of his fingers be the motion of his animal spirits, I will not determine, how probable soever, by this instance, it appears to be so; but this may help us a little to conceive of intellectual habits, and of the tying together of ideas.

7. *Some Antipathies an Effect of it.* That there are such associations of them made by custom in the minds of most men, I think nobody will question who has well considered himself or others; and to this, perhaps, might be justly attributed most of the sympathies and antipathies observable in men, which

work as strongly, and produce as regular effects, as if they were natural; and are therefore called so, though they at first had no other original but the accidental connexion of two ideas, which either the strength of the first impression or future indulgence so united, that they always afterwards kept company together in that man's mind, as if they were but one idea. I say most of the antipathies, I do not say all; for some of them are truly natural, depend upon our original constitution, and are born with us; but a great part of those which are counted natural would have been known to be from unheeded, though perhaps early, impressions, or wanton fancies at first, which would have been acknowledged the original of them, if they had been warily observed. A grown person surfeiting with honey no sooner hears the name of it, but his fancy immediately carries sickness and qualms to his stomach, and he cannot bear the very idea of it; other ideas of dislike, and sickness, and vomiting, presently accompany it, and he is disturbed; but he knows from whence to date this weakness, and can tell how he got this indisposition. Had this happened to him by an over-dose of honey when a child, all the same effects would have followed; but the cause would have been mistaken, and the antipathy counted natural.

9. *A Great Cause of Errors.*   This wrong connexion in our minds of ideas in themselves loose and independent one of another has such an influence, and is of so great force to set us awry in our actions, as well moral as natural, passions, reasonings, and notions themselves, that perhaps there is not any one thing that deserves more to be looked after.

10. *Instances.*   The ideas of goblins and sprites have really no more to do with darkness than light; yet let but a foolish maid inculcate these often on the mind of a child, and raise them there together, possibly he shall never be able to separate them again so long as he lives, but darkness shall ever afterwards bring with it those frightful ideas, and they shall be so joined that he can no more bear the one than the other.

11. A man receives a sensible injury from another, thinks on the man and that action over and over, and by ruminating on them strongly, or much, in his mind, so cements those two

ideas together that he makes them almost one; never thinks on the man, but the pain and displeasure he suffered comes into his mind with it, so that he scarce distinguishes them, but has as much an aversion for the one as the other. Thus hatreds are often begotten from slight and almost innocent occasions, and quarrels propagated and continued in the world.

12. A man has suffered pain or sickness in any place; he saw his friend die in such a room : though these have in nature nothing to do one with another, yet when the idea of the place occurs to his mind, it brings (the impression being once made) that of the pain and displeasure with it; he confounds them in his mind, and can as little bear the one as the other.

13. *Why Time cures some Disorders in the Mind, which Reason cannot.* When this combination is settled, and whilst it lasts, it is not in the power of reason to help us, and relieve us from the effects of it. Ideas in our minds, when they are there, will operate according to their natures and circumstances. And here we see the cause why time cures certain affections, which reason, though in the right, and allowed to be so, has not power over, nor is able against them to prevail with those who are apt to hearken to it in other cases. The death of a child that was the daily delight of his mother's eyes and joy of her soul, rends from her heart the whole comfort of her life, and gives her all the torment imaginable; use the consolations of reason in this case, and you were as good preach ease to one on the rack, and hope to allay by rational discourses the pain of his joints tearing asunder. Till time has by disuse separated the sense of that enjoyment and its loss from the idea of the child returning to her memory, all representations, though never so reasonable, are in vain; and therefore some in whom the union between these ideas is never dissolved spend their lives in mourning, and carry an incurable sorrow to their graves.

14. *Further instances of the Effect of the Association of Ideas.* A friend of mine knew one perfectly cured of madness by a very harsh and offensive operation. The gentleman who was thus recovered with great sense of gratitude and acknowledgment owned the cure all his life after as the greatest

obligation he could have received; but, whatever gratitude and reason suggested to him, he could never bear the sight of the operator; that image brought back with it the idea of that agony which he suffered from his hands, which was too mighty and intolerable for him to endure.

15. Many children, imputing the pain they endured at school to their books they were corrected for, so join those ideas together that a book becomes their aversion, and they are never reconciled to the study and use of them all their lives after; and thus reading becomes a torment to them, which otherwise possibly they might have made the great pleasure of their lives.

18. *Observable in different Sects.*   Some such wrong and unnatural combinations of ideas will be found to establish the irreconcilable opposition between different sects of philosophy and religion; for we cannot imagine every one of their followers to impose wilfully on himself, and knowingly refuse truth offered by plain reason. Interest, though it does a great deal in the case, yet cannot be thought to work whole societies of men to so universal a perverseness as that every one of them to a man should knowingly maintain falsehood. Some at least must be allowed to do what all pretend to, i.e. to pursue truth sincerely; and therefore there must be something that blinds their understandings, and makes them not see the falsehood of what they embrace for real truth. That which thus captivates their reasons, and leads men of sincerity blindfold from common sense, will, when examined, be found to be what we are speaking of; some independent ideas, of no alliance to one another, are, by education, custom, and the constant din of their party so coupled in their minds that they always appear there together; and they can no more separate them in their thoughts than if they were but one idea, and they operate as if they were so. This gives sense to jargon, demonstration to absurdities, and consistency to nonsense, and is the foundation of the greatest, I had almost said of all the errors in the world; or, if it does not reach so far, it is at least the most dangerous one, since, so far as it obtains, it hinders men from seeing and examining.

19. *Conclusion.* Having thus given an account of the original, sorts, and extent of our *ideas,* with several other considerations about these (I know not whether I may say) instruments, or materials of our knowledge, the method I at first proposed to myself would now require that I should immediately proceed to show what use the understanding makes of them, and what *knowledge* we have by them. This was that which, in the first general view I had of this subject, was all that I thought I should have to do; but, upon a nearer approach, I find that there is so close a connexion between ideas and *words,* and our abstract ideas and general words have so constant a relation one to another, that it is impossible to speak clearly and distinctly of our knowledge, which all consists in propositions, without considering first the nature, use and signification of Language; which, therefore, must be the business of the next Book.

BOOK THREE

OF WORDS

CHAPTER I

OF WORDS OR LANGUAGE IN GENERAL

1. *Man fitted to form articulate Sounds.* God, having designed man for a sociable creature, made him not only with an inclination and under a necessity to have fellowship with those of his own kind, but furnished him also with language, which was to be the great instrument and common tie of society. Man, therefore, had by nature his organs so fashioned as to be fit to frame articulate sounds, which we call words. But this was not enough to produce language; for parrots, and several other birds, will be taught to make articulate sounds distinct enough, which yet by no means are capable of language.

2. *To make them Signs of Ideas.* Besides articulate sounds, therefore, it was further necessary that he should be able to use these sounds as signs of internal conceptions, and to make them stand as marks for the ideas within his own mind, whereby they might be made known to others, and the thoughts of men's minds be conveyed from one to another.

3. *To make general Signs.* But neither was this sufficient to make words so useful as they ought to be. It is not enough for the perfection of language that sounds can be made signs of ideas, unless those signs can be so made use of as to comprehend several particular things; for the multiplication of words would have perplexed their use, had every particular thing need of a distinct name to be signified by. To remedy this inconvenience, language had yet a further improvement in the use of *general terms,* whereby one word was made to mark

a multitude of particular existences; which advantageous use of sounds was obtained only by the difference of the ideas they were made signs of, those names becoming general, which are made to stand for *general ideas*, and those remaining particular, where the *ideas* they are used for are *particular*.

4. Besides these names which stand for ideas, there be other words which men make use of, not to signify any idea, but the want or absence of some ideas, simple or complex, or all ideas together; such as are *nihil* in Latin, and in English *ignorance* and *barrenness*. All which negative or privative words cannot be said properly to belong to or signify no ideas; for then they would be perfectly insignificant sounds; but they relate to positive ideas, and signify their absence.

5. *Words ultimately derived from such as signify sensible Ideas.* It may also lead us a little towards the original of all our notions and knowledge, if we remark how great a dependence our words have on common sensible ideas; and how those which are made use of to stand for actions and notions quite removed from sense have their rise from thence, and from obvious sensible ideas are transferred to more abstruse significations, and made to stand for ideas that come not under the cognizance of our senses; v.g. to 'imagine', 'apprehend', 'comprehend', 'adhere', 'conceive', 'instil', 'disgust', 'disturbance', 'tranquillity', &c., are all words taken from the operations of sensible things, and applied to certain modes of thinking. 'Spirit', in its primary signification, is breath; 'angel', a messenger; and I doubt not but, if we could trace them to their sources, we should find, in all languages, the names which stand for things that fall not under our senses to have had their first rise from sensible ideas. By which we may give some kind of guess what kind of notions they were, and whence derived, which filled their minds who were the first beginners of languages, and how nature, even in the naming of things, unawares suggested to men the originals and principles of all their knowledge; whilst, to give names that might make known to others any operations they felt in themselves, or any other ideas that came not under their

senses, they were fain to borrow words from ordinary known ideas of sensation, by that means to make others the more easily to conceive those operations they experimented in themselves, which made no outward sensible appearances; and then, when they had got known and agreed names to signify those internal operations of their own minds, they were sufficiently furnished to make known by words all their other ideas; since they could consist of nothing but either of outward sensible perceptions, or of the inward operations of their minds about them.

6. *Distribution.* But to understand better the use and force of language, as subservient to instruction and knowledge, it will be convenient to consider :

First, *to what it is that names, in the use of language, are immediately applied.*

Secondly, since all (except proper) names are general, and so stand not particularly for this or that single thing, but for sorts and ranks of things, it will be necessary to consider, in the next place, what the sorts and kinds, or, if you rather like the Latin names, *what the Species and Genera of things are, wherein they consist, and how they come to be made.* These being (as they ought) well looked into, we shall the better come to find the right use of words, the natural advantages and defects of language, and the remedies that ought to be used, to avoid the inconveniences of obscurity or uncertainty in the signification of words; without which it is impossible to discourse with any clearness or order concerning knowledge; which, being conversant about propositions, and those most commonly universal ones, has greater connexion with words than perhaps is suspected.

These considerations, therefore, shall be the matter of the following chapters.

CHAPTER II

OF THE SIGNIFICATION OF WORDS

1. *Words are sensible Signs, necessary for Communication.* Man, though he have great variety of thoughts, and such from which others as well as himself might receive profit and delight; yet they are all within his own breast, invisible and hidden from others, nor can of themselves be made appear. The comfort and advantage of society not being to be had without communication of thoughts, it was necessary that man should find out some external sensible signs, whereof those invisible ideas, which his thoughts are made up of, might be made known to others. For this purpose nothing was so fit, either for plenty or quickness, as those articulate sounds, which with so much ease and variety he found himself able to make. Thus we may conceive how *words,* which were by nature so well adapted to that purpose, come to be made use of by men as the signs of their ideas; not by any natural connexion that there is between particular articulate sounds and certain ideas, for then there would be but one language amongst all men; but by a voluntary imposition, whereby such a word is made arbitrarily the mark of such an idea. The use, then, of words, is to be sensible marks of ideas; and the ideas they stand for are their proper and immediate signification.

2. *Words are the sensible Signs of his Ideas who uses them.* Words, in their primary or immediate signification, stand for nothing but *the ideas in the mind of him that uses them,* how imperfectly soever or carelessly those ideas are collected from the things which they are supposed to represent. When a man speaks to another, it is that he may be understood; and the end of speech is that those sounds, as marks, may make known his ideas to the hearer. That then which words are the marks of are the ideas of the speaker; nor can anyone

apply them as marks, immediately, to anything else but the ideas that he himself hath; for this would be to make them signs of his own conceptions, and yet apply them to other ideas; which would be to make them signs and not signs of his ideas at the same time, and so in effect to have no signification at all. Words being voluntary signs, they cannot be voluntary signs imposed by him on things he knows not. That would be to make them signs of nothing, sounds without signification. A man cannot make his words the signs either of qualities in things, or of conceptions in the mind of another, whereof he has none in his own. Till he has some ideas of his own, he cannot suppose them to correspond with the conceptions of another man; nor can he use any signs for them; for thus they would be the signs of he knows not what, which is in truth to be the signs of nothing. But when he represents to himself other men's ideas by some of his own, if he consent to give them the same names that other men do, it is still to his own ideas; to ideas that he has, and not to ideas that he has not.

3. A child having taken notice of nothing in the metal he hears called *gold* but the bright shining yellow colour, he applies the world ‘ gold ’ only to his own idea of that colour, and nothing else, and therefore calls the same colour in a peacock's tail gold. Another that hath better observed adds to shining yellow great weight; and then the sound ‘ gold ’, when he uses it, stands for a complex idea of a shining yellow and very weighty substance. Another adds to those qualities fusibility; and then the word ‘ gold ’ signifies to him a body, bright, yellow, fusible, and very heavy. Another adds malleability. Each of these uses equally the word ‘ gold ’, when they have occasion to express the idea which they have applied it to; but it is evident that each can apply it only to his own idea; nor can he make it stand as a sign of such a complex idea as he has not.

4. *Words often secretly referred, First to the Ideas in other Men's Minds.* But though words, as they are used by men, can properly and immediately signify nothing but the ideas that are in the mind of the speaker, yet they in their thoughts give them a secret reference to two other things.

First, *they suppose their words to be marks of the ideas in the minds also of other men, with whom they communicate*; for else they should talk in vain, and could not be understood, if the sounds they applied to one idea were such as by the hearer were applied to another, which is to speak two languages.

5. *Secondly, to the Reality of Things.* Secondly, because men would not be thought to talk barely of their own imaginations, but of things as really they are, therefore they often suppose the *words to stand also for the reality of things.* But this relating more particularly to substances and their names, as perhaps the former does to simple ideas and modes, we shall speak of these two different ways of applying words more at large, when we come to treat of the names of mixed modes and substances in particular[1]; though give me leave here to say that it is a perverting the use of words, and brings unavoidable obscurity and confusion into their signification, whenever we make them stand for anything but those ideas we have in our own minds.

6. *Words by Use readily excite Ideas.* Concerning words, also, it is further to be considered :

First, that there comes, by constant use, to be such a connexion between certain sounds and the ideas they stand for that the names heard almost as readily excite certain ideas as if the objects themselves, which are apt to produce them, did actually affect the senses. Which is manifestly so in all obvious sensible qualities, and in all substances that frequently and familiarly occur to us.

7. *Words often used without Signification.* Secondly, that though the proper and immediate signification of words are ideas in the mind of the speaker, yet, because by familiar use from our cradles we come to learn certain articulate sounds very perfectly, and have them readily on our tongues, and always at hand in our memories, but yet are not always careful to examine or settle their significations perfectly; it often happens that men, even when they would apply themselves to an attentive consideration, do set their thoughts more on words than things.

[1] III v-vi

Therefore some, not only children but men, speak several words no otherwise than parrots do, only because they have learned them, and have been accustomed to those sounds. But so far as words are of use and signification, so far is there a constant connexion between the sound and the idea, and a designation that the one stand for the other; without which application of them, they are nothing but so much insignificant noise.

8. *Their Signification perfectly arbitrary.* Words, by long and familiar use, as has been said, come to excite in men certain ideas so constantly and readily, that they are apt to suppose a natural connexion between them. But that they signify only men's peculiar ideas, and that *by a perfect arbitrary imposition,* is evident, in that they often fail to excite in others (even that use the same language) the same ideas we take them to be the signs of; and every man has so inviolable a liberty to make words stand for what ideas he pleases, that no one hath the power to make others have the same ideas in their minds that he has, when they use the same words that he does. It is true, common use, by a tacit consent, appropriates certain sounds to certain ideas in all languages, which so far limits the signification of that sound that, unless a man applies it to the same idea, he does not speak properly; and let me add that, unless a man's words excite the same ideas in the hearer which he makes them stand for in speaking, he does not speak intelligibly. But whatever be the consequence of any man's using of words differently, either from their general meaning, or the particular sense of the person to whom he addresses them, this is certain, their signification, in his use of them, is limited to his ideas, and they can be signs of nothing else.

CHAPTER III

OF GENERAL TERMS

1. *The greatest Part of Words general.* All things that exist being particulars, it may perhaps be thought reasonable that words, which ought to be conformed to things, should be so too—I mean in their signification; but yet we find the quite contrary. The far greatest part of words that make all languages are general terms; which has not been the effect of neglect or chance, but of reason and necessity.

2. *For every particular Thing to have a Name is impossible.* First, it is impossible that every particular thing should have a distinct peculiar name. For, the signification and use of words depending on that connexion which the mind makes between its ideas and the sounds it uses as signs of them, it is necessary, in the application of names to things, that the mind should have distinct ideas of the things, and retain also the particular name that belongs to every one, with its peculiar appropriation to that idea. But it is beyond the power of human capacity to frame and retain distinct ideas of all the particular things we meet with : every bird and beast men saw; every tree and plant that affected the senses, could not find a place in the most capacious understanding.

3. *And useless.* Secondly, if it were possible, it would yet be useless, because it would not serve to the chief end of language. Men would in vain heap up names of particular things that would not serve them to communicate their thoughts. Men learn names, and use them in talk with others, only that they may be understood; which is then only done when, by use or consent, the sound I make by the organs of speech excites in another man's mind who hears it the idea I apply it to in mine when I speak it. This cannot be done by names applied to particular things; whereof I alone having the ideas in my mind, the names of them could not be significant or

intelligible to another, who was not acquainted with all those very particular things which had fallen under my notice.

4. Thirdly, but yet, granting this also feasible (which I think is not), yet a distinct name for every particular thing would not be of any great use for the improvement of knowledge, which, though founded in particular things, enlarges itself by general views; to which things reduced into sorts, under general names, are properly subservient. These, with the names belonging to them, come within some compass, and do not multiply every moment beyond what either the mind can contain, or use requires. And therefore, in these men have for the most part stopped, but yet not so as to hinder themselves from distinguishing particular things by appropriated names where convenience demands it. And therefore in their own species, which they have most to do with, and wherein they have often occasion to mention particular persons, they make use of proper names; and there distinct individuals have distinct denominations.

5. *What things have proper Names.* Besides persons, countries also, cities, rivers, mountains, and other the like distinctions of place have usually found peculiar names, and that for the same reason; they being such as men have often an occasion to mark particularly, and, as it were, set before others in their discourses with them.

6. *How general Words are made.* The next thing to be considered is how general words come to be made. For, since all things that exist are only particulars, how come we by general terms, or where find we those general natures they are supposed to stand for? Words become general by being made the signs of general ideas; and ideas become general by separating from them the circumstances of time and place, and any other ideas that may determine them to this or that particular existence. By this way of abstraction they are made capable of representing more individuals than one; each of which, having in it a conformity to that abstract idea, is (as we call it) of that sort.

7. But to deduce this a little more distinctly, it will not perhaps be amiss to trace our notions and names from their

beginning, and observe by what degrees we proceed, and by what steps we enlarge our ideas from our first infancy. There is nothing more evident than that the ideas of the persons children converse with (to instance in them alone) are, like the persons themselves, only particular. The ideas of the nurse and the mother are well framed in their minds; and, like pictures of them there, represent only those individuals. The names they first gave to them are confined to these individuals; and the names of ' nurse ' and ' mamma ', the child uses, determine themselves to those persons. Afterwards, when time and a larger acquaintance have made them observe that there are a great many other things in the world, that in some common agreements of shape, and several other qualities, resemble their father and mother, and those persons they have been used to, they frame an idea, which they find those many particulars do partake in; and to that they give, with others, the name ' man ', for example. And thus they come to have a general name, and a general idea. Wherein they make nothing new, but only leave out of the complex idea they had of Peter and James, Mary and Jane, that which is peculiar to each, and retain only what is common to them all.

8. By the same way that they come by the general name and idea of *man*, they easily advance to more general names and notions. For, observing that several things that differ from their idea of man, and cannot therefore be comprehended under that name, have yet certain qualities wherein they agree with man, by retaining only those qualities, and uniting them into one idea, they have again another and more general idea; to which having given a name they make a term of a more comprehensive extension; which new idea is made, not by any new addition, but only as before, by leaving out the shape, and some other properties signified by the name ' man ', and retaining only a body, with life, sense, and spontaneous motion, comprehended under the name ' animal '.

9. *General natures are nothing but abstract Ideas.* He that thinks *general natures* or *notions* are anything else but such abstract and partial ideas of more complex ones, taken at first from particular existences, will, I fear, be at a loss where to

find them. For let anyone reflect, and then tell me wherein does his idea of *man* differ from that of *Peter* and *Paul,* or his idea of *horse* from that of *Bucephalus* but in the leaving out something that is peculiar to each individual, and retaining so much of those particular complex ideas of several particular existences as they are found to agree in? Of the complex ideas signified by the names 'man' and 'horse', leaving out but those particulars wherein they differ, and retaining only those wherein they agree, and of those making a new distinct complex idea, and giving the name 'animal' to it, one has a more general term that comprehends with man several other creatures. Leave out of the idea of *animal* sense and spontaneous motion, and the remaining complex idea, made up of the remaining simple ones of body, life, and nourishment, becomes a more general one, under the more comprehensive term, *vivens.* And, not to dwell longer upon this particular, so evident in itself, by the same way the mind proceeds to *body, substance,* and at last to *being, thing,* and such universal terms, which stand for any of our ideas whatsoever. To conclude: this whole mystery of genera and species, which make such a noise in the schools, and are with justice so little regarded out of them, is nothing else but *abstract ideas,* more or less comprehensive, with names annexed to them. In all which this is constant and invariable, that every more general term stands for such an idea, as is but a part of any of those contained under it

10. *Why the Genus is ordinarily made Use of in Definitions.* This may show us the reason why, in the defining of words, which is nothing but declaring their signification, we make use of the *genus,* or next general word that comprehends it. Which is not out of necessity, but only to save the labour of enumerating the several simple ideas which the next general word or *genus* stands for; or, perhaps, sometimes the shame of not being able to do it. But though defining by *genus* and *differentia* be the shortest way, yet I think it may be doubted whether it be the best. This I am sure, it is not the only, and so not absolutely necessary. For, definition being nothing but making another understand by words what idea the term

defined stands for, a definition is best made by enumerating those simple ideas that are combined in the signification of the term defined; and if, instead of such an enumeration, men have accustomed themselves to use the next general term, it has not been out of necessity, or for greater clearness, but for quickness and dispatch sake. For I think that, to one who desired to know what idea the word ' man ' stood for, if it should be said that man was a solid extended substance, having life, sense, spontaneous motion, and the faculty of reasoning, I doubt not but the meaning of the term ' man ' would be as well understood, and the idea it stands for be at least as clearly made known, as when it is defined to be a rational animal; which, by the several definitions of *animal, vivens,* and *corpus,* resolves itself into those enumerated ideas. I have, in explaining the term ' man ', followed here the ordinary definition of the schools; which, though perhaps not the most exact, yet serves well enough to my present purpose. And one may, in this instance, see what gave occasion to the rule that a definition must consist of *genus* and *differentia*; and it suffices to show us the little necessity there is of such a rule, or advantage in the strict observing of it. For, definitions, as has been said, being only the explaining of one word by several others, so that the meaning or idea it stands for may be certainly known, languages are not always so made according to the rules of logic, that every term can have its signification exactly and clearly expressed by two others.

11. *General and Universal are Creatures of the Understanding.* To return to general words : it is plain, by what has been said, that *general* and *universal* belong not to the real existence of things, but are the inventions and creatures of the understanding, made by it for its own use, and concern only signs, whether words or ideas. Words are general, as has been said, when used for signs of general ideas, and so are applicable indifferently to many particular things; and ideas are general when they are set up as the representatives of many particular things; but universality belongs not to things themselves, which are all of them particular in their existence, even those words and ideas which in their signifi-

cation are general. The signification they have is nothing but a relation that, by the mind of man, is added to them.

12. *Abstract Ideas are the Essences of the Genera and Species.* That then which general words signify is a *sort* of things, and each of them does that by being a sign of an abstract idea in the mind; to which idea, as things existing are found to agree, so they come to be ranked under that name, or, which is all one, be of that sort. Whereby it is evident that the *essences* of the sorts, or, if the Latin word pleases better, *species* of things, are nothing else but these abstract ideas. For the having the essence of any species being that which makes anything to be of that species, and the conformity to the idea to which the name is annexed being that which gives a right to that name, the having the essence, and the having that conformity must needs be the same thing, since to be of any species, and to have a right to the name of that species, is all one. As, for example, to be a man, or of the *species* man, and to have right to the name 'man' is the same thing. From whence it is easy to observe that the essences of the sorts of things, and, consequently, the sorting of things, is the workmanship of the understanding that abstracts and makes those general ideas.

13. *They are the Workmanship of the Understanding, but have their foundation in the similitude of Things.* I would not here be thought to forget, much less to deny, that Nature, in the production of things, makes several of them alike; there is nothing more obvious, especially in the races of animals, and all things propagated by seed. But yet I think we may say, *the sorting of them under names is the workmanship of the understanding, taking occasion from the similitude it observes amongst them to make abstract general ideas,* and set them up in the mind, with names annexed to them, as patterns or forms (for, in that sense, the word 'form' has a very proper signification), to which, as particular things existing are found to agree, so they come to be of that species, have that denomination, or are put into that *classis.* For when we say this is a man, that a horse; this justice, that cruelty; this a

watch, that a jack; what do we else but rank things under different specific names, as agreeing to those abstract ideas, of which we have made those names the signs? And what are the essences of those species set out and marked by names, but those abstract ideas in the mind, which are, as it were, the bonds between particular things that exist, and the names they are to be ranked under? And when general names have any connexion with particular beings, these abstract ideas are the medium that unites them, so that the essences of species, as distinguished and denominated by us, neither are nor can be anything but those precise abstract ideas we have in our minds. And therefore the supposed real essences of substances, if different from our abstract ideas, cannot be the essences of the species *we* rank things into. For two species may be one, as rationally as two different essences be the essence of one species; and I demand what are the alterations may or may not be made in a *horse* or *lead,* without making either of them to be of another species? In determining the species of things by *our* abstract ideas this is easy to resolve; but, if anyone will regulate himself herein by supposed *real* essences, he will, I suppose, be at a loss : and he will never be able to know when anything precisely ceases to be of the species of a *horse* or *lead.*

14. *Each distinct abstract Idea is a distinct Essence.* Nor will anyone wonder that I say these essences, or abstract ideas (which are the measures of name, and the boundaries of species) are the workmanship of the understanding, who considers that at least the complex ones are often, in several men, different collections of simple ideas; and therefore that is *covetousness* to one man which is not so to another. So that, in truth, every distinct abstract idea is a distinct essence; and the names that stand for such distinct ideas are the names of things essentially different. Thus a circle is as essentially different from an oval as a sheep from a goat; and rain is as essentially different from snow as water from earth, that abstract idea which is the essence of one being impossible to be communicated to the other. And thus any two abstract ideas,

that in any part vary one from another, with two distinct names annexed to them, constitute two distinct sorts, or, if you please, *species,* as essentially different as any two of the most remote or opposite in the world.

15. *Real and nominal Essence.*   But since the essences of things are thought by some (and not without reason) to be wholly unknown, it may not be amiss to consider the several significations of the word ' essence '.

First, essence may be taken for the being of anything, whereby it is what it is. And thus the real internal, but generally (in substances) unknown constitution of things, whereon their discoverable qualities depend, may be called their essence. This is the proper original signification of the word, as is evident from the formation of it, *essentia,* in its primary notation, signifying properly being. And in this sense it is still used, when we speak of the essence of *particular* things, without giving them any name.

Secondly, it being evident that things are ranked under names into sorts or species only as they agree to certain abstract ideas, to which we have annexed those names, the essence of each *genus,* or sort, comes to be nothing but that abstract idea which the general, or sortal (if I may have leave so to call it from *sort,* as I do *general* from *genus*) name stands for. And this we shall find to be that which the word *essence* imports in its most familiar use. These two sorts of essences, I suppose, may not unfitly be termed, the one the *real,* the other *nominal essence.*

16. *Constant Connexion between the Name and Nominal Essence.*   Between the *nominal essence* and the *name* there is so near a connexion that the name of any sort of things cannot be attributed to any particular being but what has this essence, whereby it answers that abstract idea whereof that name is the sign.

17. *Supposition, that Species are distinguished by their real Essences useless.*   Concerning the *real essences* of corporeal substances (to mention those only) there are, if I mistake not, two opinions. The one is of those who, using the word

'essence' for they know not what, suppose a certain number of those essences, according to which all natural things are made, and wherein they do exactly every one of them partake, and so become of this or that species. The other and more rational opinion is of those who look on all natural things to have a real, but unknown, constitution of their insensible parts, from which flow those sensible qualities which serve us to distinguish them one from another, according as we have occasion to rank them into sorts, under common denominations. The former of these opinions, which supposes these essences as a certain number of forms or moulds, wherein all natural things that exist are cast, and do equally partake, has, I imagine, very much perplexed the knowledge of natural things. The frequent productions of monsters, in all the species of animals, and of changelings, and other strange issues of human birth, carry with them difficulties, not possible to consist with this hypothesis, since it is as impossible that two things partaking exactly of the same real essence should have different properties, as that two figures partaking of the same real essence of a circle should have different properties.

18. *Real and nominal Essence the same in simple Ideas and Modes, different in Substances.* Essences being thus distinguished into nominal and real, we may further observe that, in the species of simple ideas and modes, they are always the same, but in substances always quite different. Thus, a figure including a space between three lines is the real as well as nominal essence of a triangle, it being not only the abstract idea to which the general name is annexed, but the very *essentia* or being of the thing itself: that foundation from which all its properties flow, and to which they are all inseparably annexed. But it is far otherwise concerning that parcel of matter which makes the ring on my finger, wherein these two essences are apparently different. For, it is the real constitution of its insensible parts, on which depend all those properties of colour, weight, fusibility, fixedness, &c., which makes it to be gold, or gives it a right to that name, which is therefore its nominal essence.

19. *Essences ingenerable and incorruptible.* That such abstract ideas, with names to them, as we have been speaking of are essences may further appear by what we are told concerning essences, viz. that they are all ingenerable and incorruptible. For, whatever becomes of *Alexander* and *Bucephalus,* the ideas to which 'man' and 'horse' are annexed are supposed nevertheless to remain in the same; and so the essences of those species are preserved whole and undestroyed, whatever changes happen to any or all of the individuals of those species. By this means the essence of a species rests safe and entire, without the existence of so much as one individual of that kind. For, were there now no circle existing anywhere in the world, (as perhaps that figure exists not anywhere exactly marked out), yet the idea annexed to that name would not cease to be what it is, nor cease to be as a pattern to determine which of the particular figures we meet with have or have not a right to the name 'circle', and so to show which of them, by having that essence, was of that species. And though there neither were nor had been in nature such a beast as an unicorn, or such a fish as a mermaid, yet, supposing those names to stand for complex abstract ideas that contained no inconsistency in them, the essence of a mermaid is as intelligible as that of a man, and the idea of an unicorn as certain, steady, and permanent as that of a horse. From what has been said it is evident that the doctrine of the immutability of essences proves them to be only abstract ideas, and is founded on the relation established between them and certain sounds as signs of them, and will always be true, as long as the same name can have the same signification.

CHAPTER IV

OF THE NAMES OF SIMPLE IDEAS

1. *Names of simple Ideas, Modes, and Substances, have each something peculiar.* Though all words, as I have shown, signify nothing immediately but the ideas in the mind of the speaker; yet, upon a nearer survey, we shall find that the names of *simple ideas, mixed modes* (under which I comprise *relations too*), and *natural substances,* have each of them something peculiar and different from the other. For example :

2. *First, Names of simple Ideas, and Substances intimate real Existence.* First, the names of *simple ideas* and *substances,* with the abstract ideas in the mind which they immediately signify, intimate also some real existence, from which was derived their original pattern. But the names of *mixed modes* terminate in the idea that is in the mind, and lead not the thoughts any further, as we shall see more at large in the following chapter.

3. *Secondly, Names of simple Ideas and Modes signify always both real and nominal Essence.* Secondly, the names of simple ideas and modes signify always the real as well as nominal essence of their species. But the names of natural substances signify rarely, if ever, anything but barely the nominal essences of those species, as we shall show in the chapter that treats of the names of substances in particular.

4. *Thirdly, Names of simple Ideas indefinable.* Thirdly, the names of simple ideas are not capable of any definitions; the names of all complex ideas are.

5. *If all were definable, it would be a Process in infinitum.* I will not here trouble myself to prove that all terms are not definable from that progress *in infinitum,* which it will visibly lead us into, if we should allow that all names could be defined. For, if the terms of one definition were still to be defined by another, where at last should we stop? But I

shall, from the nature of our ideas, and the signification of our words, show *why some names can, and others cannot be defined*; and *which they are*.

7. *Simple Ideas, why undefinable.* I say that the *names of simple ideas, and those only, are incapable of being defined*. The reason whereof is this, that the several terms of a definition signifying several ideas, they can all together by no means represent an idea which has no composition at all; and therefore a definition, which is properly nothing but the showing the meaning of one word by several others not signifying each the same thing, can in the names of simple ideas have no place.

8. *Instances: Motion.* The not observing this difference in our ideas, and their names, has produced that eminent trifling in the schools, which is so easy to be observed in the definitions they give us of some few of these simple ideas. For, as to the greatest part of them, even those masters of definitions were fain to leave them untouched, merely by the impossibility they found in it. What more exquisite jargon could the wit of man invent, than this definition: *the act of a being in power, as far forth as in power*; which would puzzle any rational man, to whom it was not already known by its famous absurdity, to guess what word it could ever be supposed to be the explication of.

9. Nor have the modern philosophers, who have endeavoured to throw off the jargon of the schools, and speak intelligibly, much better succeeded in defining simple ideas, whether by explaining their causes, or any otherwise. The atomists, who define motion to be *a passage from one place to another*, what do they more than put one synonymous word for another? For what is *passage* other than *motion*?

10. *Light.* Those who tell us that light is a great number of little globules, striking briskly on the bottom of the eye, speak more intelligibly than the Schools; but yet these words never so well understood would make the idea the word 'light' stands for no more known to a man that understands it not before, than if one should tell him that light was nothing but a company of little tennis-balls which fairies all day long

struck with rackets against some men's foreheads whilst they passed by others. For granting this explication of the thing to be true, yet the idea of the cause of light, if we had it never so exact, would no more give us the idea of light itself, as it is such a particular perception in us, than the idea of the figure and motion of a sharp piece of steel would give us the idea of that pain which it is able to cause in us. For the cause of any sensation, and the sensation itself, in all the simple ideas of one sense, are two ideas, and two ideas so different and distant one from another, that no two can be more so.

11. *Simple Ideas, why indefinable, further explained.* Simple ideas, as has been shown, are only to be got by those impressions objects themselves make on our minds, by the proper inlets appointed to each sort. If they are not received this way, all the words in the world, made use of to explain or define any of their names, will never be able to produce in us the idea it stands for. For, words being sounds can produce in us no other simple ideas than of those very sounds; nor excite any in us, but by that voluntary connexion which is known to be between them and those simple ideas which common use has made them signs of. He that thinks otherwise, let him try if any words can give him the taste of a pine apple, and make him have the true idea of the relish of that celebrated delicious fruit. So far as he is told it has a resemblance with any tastes whereof he has the ideas already in his memory, imprinted there by sensible objects, not strangers to his palate, so far may he approach that resemblance in his mind. But this is not giving us that idea by a definition, but exciting in us other simple ideas by their known names; which will be still very different from the true taste of that fruit itself. In light and colours, and all other simple ideas, it is the same thing : for the signification of sounds is not natural, but only imposed and arbitrary. And no definition of light or redness is more fitted or able to produce either of those ideas in us, than the sound 'light' or 'red', by itself. For to hope to produce an idea of light or colour by a sound, however formed, is to expect that sounds should be visible, or colours audible; and to make the ears do the office of all the

other senses. And therefore he that has not before received into his mind, by the proper inlet, the simple idea which any word stands for, can never come to know the signification of that word by any other words or sounds whatsoever, put together according to any rules of definition. The only way is by applying to his senses the proper object, and so producing that idea in him, for which he has learned the name already. A studious blind man, who had mightily beat his head about visible objects, and made use of the explication of his books and friends, to understand those names of light and colours which often came in his way, bragged one day that he now understood what ' scarlet ' signified. Upon which, his friend demanding what scarlet was, the blind man answered it was like the sound of a trumpet. Just such an understanding of the name of any other simple idea will he have, who hopes to get it only from a definition, or other words made use of to explain it.

12. *The contrary shown in complex Ideas, by instances of a Statue and Rainbow.* The case is quite otherwise in *complex ideas*; which consisting of several simple ones, it is in the power of words standing for the several ideas that make that composition to imprint complex ideas in the mind which were never there before, and so make their names be understood. In such collections of ideas, passing under one name, definition, or the teaching the signification of one word by several others, has place, and may make us understand the names of things which never came within the reach of our senses, and frame ideas suitable to those in other men's minds, when they use those names; provided that none of the terms of the definition stand for any such simple ideas which he to whom the explication is made has never yet had in his thought. Thus the word ' statue ' may be explained to a blind man by other words, when ' picture ' cannot, his senses having given him the idea of figure, but not of colours, which therefore words cannot excite in him.

15. *Names of simple Ideas least doubtful.* Fourthly, but though the names of simple ideas have not the help of definition to determine their signification, yet that hinders not

bu: that they are generally less doubtful and uncertain than those of mixed modes and substances; because they standing only for one simple perception, men for the most part easily and perfectly agree in their signification, and there is little room for mistake and wrangling about their meaning. He that knows once that ' whiteness ' is the name of that colour he has observed in snow or milk, will not be apt to misapply that word, as long as he retains that idea; which when he has quite lost, he is not apt to mistake the meaning of it, but perceives he understands it not. In simple ideas the whole signification of the name is known at once, and consists not of parts, whereof more or less being put in, the idea may be varied, and so the signification of its name be obscure or uncertain.

CHAPTER V

OF THE NAMES OF MIXED MODES AND RELATIONS

1. *They stand for abstract Ideas, as other general Names.* The names of *mixed modes* being general, they stand, as has been shewn, for sorts or species of things, each of which has its peculiar essence. The essences of these species also, as has been shewn, are nothing but the abstract ideas in the mind, to which the name is annexed. Thus far the names and essences of mixed modes have nothing but what is common to them with other ideas; but, if we take a little nearer survey of them, we shall find that they have something peculiar, which perhaps may deserve our attention.

2. *First, The Ideas they stand for are made by the Understanding.* The first particularity I shall observe in them is that the abstract ideas, or, if you please, the essences, of the several species of mixed modes are *made by the understanding*, wherein they differ from those of simple ideas; in which sort the mind has no power to make any one, but only receives such

as are presented to it by the real existence of things operating upon it.

3. *Secondly, made arbitrarily, and without Patterns.* In the next place, these essences of the species of mixed modes are not only made by the mind, but *made very arbitrarily, made without patterns, or reference to any real existence.* Wherein they differ from those of substances, which carry with them the supposition of some real being, from which they are taken, and to which they are conformable. But, in its complex ideas of mixed modes, the mind takes a liberty not to follow the existence of things exactly. It unites and retains certain collections as so many distinct specific ideas; whilst others, that as often occur in nature, and are as plainly suggested by outward things, pass neglected, without particular names or specifications. Nor does the mind, in these of mixed modes, as in the complex ideas of substances, examine them by the real existence of things, or verify them by patterns containing such peculiar compositions in nature.

4. *How this is done.* To understand this aright, we must consider wherein this making of these complex ideas consists; and that is not in the making any new idea, but putting together those which the mind had before. Wherein the mind does these three things: first, it chooses a certain number; secondly, it gives them connexion, and makes them into one idea; thirdly, it ties them together by a name. If we examine how the mind proceeds in these, and what liberty it takes in them, we shall easily observe how these essences of the species of mixed modes are the workmanship of the mind, and, consequently, that the species themselves are of men's making.

5. *Evidently arbitrary, that the Idea is often before the Existence.* Nobody can doubt but that these ideas of mixed modes are made by a voluntary collection of ideas, put together in the mind independent from any original patterns in nature, who will but reflect that this sort of complex ideas may be made, abstracted, and have names given them, and so a species be constituted, before any one individual of that species ever

existed. Who can doubt but the ideas of *sacrilege* or *adultery* might be framed in the minds of men, and have names given them, and so these species of mixed modes be constituted, before either of them was ever committed; and might be as well discoursed of and reasoned about, and as certain truths discovered of them, whilst yet they had no being but in the understanding, as well as now, that they have but too frequently a real existence?

7. *But still subservient to the End of Language.* But, though these complex ideas or essences of mixed modes depend on the mind, and are made by it with great liberty, yet they are not made at random, and jumbled together without any reason at all. They are always made for the convenience of communication, which is the chief end of language. The use of language is by short sounds to signify with ease and dispatch general conceptions, wherein not only abundance of particulars may be contained, but also a great variety of independent ideas collected into one complex one. In the making therefore of the species of mixed modes men have had regard only to such combinations as they had occasion to mention one to another. If they join to the idea of killing the idea of father or mother, and so make a distinct species from killing a man's son or neighbour, it is because of the different heinousness of the crime, and the distinct punishment is due to the murdering a man's father and mother, different from what ought to be inflicted on the murder of a son or neighbour; and therefore they find it necessary to mention it by a distinct name, which is the end of making that distinct combination.

8. *Whereof the untranslatable Words of divers Languages are a Proof.* A moderate skill in different languages will easily satisfy one of the truth of this, it being so obvious to observe great store of words in one language which have not any that answer them in another. Which plainly shows that those of one country, by their customs and manner of life, have found occasion to make several complex ideas, and give names to them, which others never collected into specific ideas. This could not have happened if these species were the steady

workmanship of nature, and not collections made and abstracted by the mind, in order to naming, and for the convenience of communication. Nay, if we will look a little more nearly into this matter, and exactly compare different languages, we shall find that, though they have words which in translations and dictionaries are supposed to answer one another, yet there is scarce one of ten amongst the names of complex ideas, especially of mixed modes, that stands for the same precise idea which the word does that in dictionaries it is rendered by. There are no ideas more common and less compounded than the measures of time, extension, and weight; and the Latin names, ' hora ', ' pes ', ' libra ' are without difficulty rendered by the English names, ' hour ', ' foot ', and ' pound '; but yet there is nothing more evident than that the ideas a Roman annexed to these Latin names were very far different from those which an Englishman expresses by those English ones.

9. *This shows Species to be made for Communication.* The reason why I take so particular notice of this is that we may not be mistaken about *genera* and *species,* and their *essences*, as if they were things regularly and constantly made by nature, and had a real existence in things; when they appear, upon a more wary survey, to be nothing else but an artifice of the understanding, for the easier signifying such collections of ideas as it should often have occasion to communicate by one general term, under which divers particulars, as far forth as they agreed to that abstract idea, might be comprehended.

10. *In mixed Modes it is the Name that ties the Combination together, and makes it a species.* The near relation that there is between *species, essences* and their *general name,* at least in mixed modes, will further appear when we consider that it is the name that seems to preserve those essences, and give them their lasting duration. For, the connexion between the loose parts of those complex ideas being made by the mind, this union, which has no particular foundation in nature, would cease again, were there not something that did, as it were, hold

it together, and keep the parts from scattering. Though therefore it be the mind that makes the collection, it is the name which is as it were the knot that ties them fast together. What a vast variety of different ideas does the word ' *triumphus* ' hold together, and deliver to us as one species! Had this name been never made, or quite lost, we might, no doubt, have had descriptions of what passed in that solemnity; but yet, I think, that which holds those different parts together in the unity of one complex idea is that very word annexed to it; without which the several parts of that would no more be thought to make one thing, than any other show, which having never been made but once, had never been united into one complex idea, under one denomination. How much, therefore, in mixed modes, the unity necessary to any essence depends on the mind, and how much the continuation and fixing of that unity depends on the name in common use annexed to it, I leave to be considered by those who look upon essences and species as real established things in nature.

12. *For the Originals of mixed Modes, we look no further than the Mind; which also shows them to be the Workmanship of Understanding.* Conformable also to what has been said concerning the essences of the species of mixed modes, that they are the creatures of the understanding rather than the works of nature; conformable, I say, to this, we find that their names lead our thoughts to the mind, and no further. When we speak of *justice,* or *gratitude,* we frame to ourselves no imagination of anything existing, which we would conceive, but our thoughts terminate in the abstract ideas of those virtues, and look not further; as they do when we speak of a *horse,* or *iron,* whose specific ideas we consider not as barely in the mind, but as in things themselves, which afford the original patterns of those ideas. But in mixed modes, at least the most considerable parts of them, which are moral beings, we consider the original patterns as being in the mind, and to those we refer for the distinguishing of particular beings under names. And hence I think it is that these essences of the species of mixed modes are by a more particular name called

notions; as, by a peculiar right, appertaining to the understanding.

14. *Names of mixed Modes stand always for their real Essences.*   Another thing we may observe from what has been said is that the names of mixed modes always signify (when they have any determined signification) the *real* essences of their species. For, these abstract ideas being the workmanship of the mind, and not referred to the real existence of things, there is no supposition of anything more signified by that name but barely that complex idea the mind itself has formed; which is all it would have expressed by it, and is that on which all the properties of the species depend, and from which alone they all flow : and so in these the real and nominal essence is the same, which, of what concernment it is to the certain knowledge of general truth, we shall see hereafter[1].

15. *Why their Names are usually got before their Ideas.* This also may show us the reason why for the most part the names of mixed modes are got before the ideas they stand for are perfectly known. Because there being no species of these ordinarily taken notice of but what have names, and those species, or rather their essences, being abstract complex ideas made arbitrarily by the mind, it is convenient, if not necessary, to know the names before one endeavour to frame these complex ideas; unless a man will fill his head with a company of abstract complex ideas, which, others having no names for, he has nothing to do with, but to lay by and forget again. I confess that, in the beginning of languages, it was necessary to have the idea before one gave it the name; and so it is still, where, making a new complex idea, one also, by giving it a new name, makes a new word. But this concerns not languages made, which have generally pretty well provided for ideas which men have frequent occasion to have and communicate; and in such, I ask whether it be not the ordinary method that children learn the names of mixed modes before they have their ideas? What one of a thousand ever frames the abstract ideas of *glory* and *ambition* before he

[1] IV iv 5-9; vi

has heard the names of them? In simple ideas and substances I grant it is otherwise; which, being such ideas as have a real existence and union in nature, the ideas and names are got one before the other, as it happens.

16. *Reason of my being so large on this Subject.* What has been said here of mixed modes is, with very little difference, applicable also to *relations*; which, since every man himself may observe, I may spare myself the pains to enlarge on, especially since what I have here said concerning words in this third Book will possibly be thought by some to be much more than what so slight a subject required.

CHAPTER VI

OF THE NAMES OF SUBSTANCES

1. *The common Names of Substances stand for Sorts.* The common names of substances, as well as other general terms, stand for *sorts*; which is nothing else but the being made signs of such complex ideas wherein several particular substances do or might agree, by virtue of which they are capable of being comprehended in one common conception, and be signified by one name. I say do or might agree; for though there be but one sun existing in the world, yet the idea of it being abstracted, so that more substances (if there were several) might each agree in it, it is as much a sort as if there were as many suns as there are stars.

2. *The Essence of each Sort is the abstract Idea.* The measure and boundary of each sort or species, whereby it is constituted that particular sort, and distinguished from others, is that we call its *essence*, which is nothing but that abstract idea to which the name is annexed, so that everything contained in that idea is essential to that sort. This, though it be all the essence of natural substances that we know, or by which we distinguish them into sorts, yet I call it by a peculiar name, the *nominal essence*, to distinguish it from that real constitution

of substances, upon which depends this nominal essence, and all the properties of that sort; which, therefore, as has been said, may be called the *real essence* : v.g. the nominal essence of gold is that complex idea the word ' gold ' stands for, let it be, for instance, a body yellow, of a certain weight, malleable, fusible, and fixed. But the real essence is the constitution of the insensible parts of that body, on which those qualities and all the other properties of gold depend. How far these two are different, though they are both called essence, is obvious at first sight to discover.

(3.) *The nominal and real Essence different.* For, though perhaps voluntary motion, with sense and reason, joined to a body of a certain shape, be the complex idea to which I and others annex the name ' man ' and so be the nominal essence of the species so called; yet nobody will say that that complex idea is the real essence and source of all those operations which are to be found in any individual of that sort. The foundation of all those qualities which are the ingredients of our complex idea is something quite different; and had we such a knowledge of that constitution of man, from which his faculties of moving, sensation, and reasoning, and other powers flow, and on which his so regular shape depends, as it is possible angels have, and it is certain his Maker has, we should have a quite other idea of his essence than what now is contained in our definition of that species, be it what it will; and our idea of any individual man would be as far different from what it now is, as is his who knows all the springs and wheels and other contrivances within of the famous clock at Strasbourg, from that which a gazing countryman has of it, who barely sees the motion of the hand, and hears the clock strike, and observes only some of the outward appearances.

(4.) *Nothing essential to Individuals.* That *essence,* in the ordinary use of the word, relates to sorts, and that it is considered in particular beings no further than as they are ranked into sorts, appears from hence : that, take but away the abstract ideas by which we sort individuals, and rank them under common names, and then the thought of anything essential to any of them instantly vanishes; we have no notion of the one without the other, which plainly shows their relation. It is necessary for me to be as I am—God and nature has made me so; but there is nothing I have is essential to me. An accident or disease may very much alter my colour or shape; a fever or fall may take away my reason or memory, or both; and an apoplexy leave neither sense, nor understanding, no, nor life. Other creatures of my shape may be made with more and better, or fewer and worse faculties than I have; and others may have reason and sense in a shape and body very different from mine. None of these are essential to the one or the other, or to any individual whatsoever, till the mind refers it to some sort or species of things; and then presently, according to the abstract idea of that sort, something is found essential. Let anyone examine his own thoughts, and he will find that as soon as he supposes or speaks of *essential*, the consideration of some species, or the complex idea signified by some general name, comes into his mind; and it is in reference to that that this or that quality is said to be essential. So that if it be asked whether it be essential to me or any other particular corporeal being to have reason, I say no; no more than it is essential to this white thing I write on to have words in it. But if that particular being be to be counted of the sort *man,* and to have the name 'man' given it, then reason is essential to it, supposing reason to be a part of the complex idea the name 'man' stands for; as it is essential to this thing I write on to contain words, if I will give it the name 'treatise', and rank it under that species. So that essential and not essential relate only to our abstract ideas, and the names annexed to them; which amounts to no more but this, that whatever particular thing has not in it those qualities which are contained in the abstract idea which any general term stands for, cannot be ranked under that species, nor be called by that name, since that abstract idea is the very essence of that species.

(5.) Thus, if the idea of *body* with some people be bare extension or space, then solidity is not essential to body; if others make the idea to which they give the name 'body' to be solidity and extension, then solidity is essential to body.

which makes a part of the complex idea the name of a sort stands for; without which no particular thing can be reckoned of that sort, nor be entitled to that name. Should there be found a parcel of matter that had all the other qualities that are in iron, but wanted obedience to the loadstone, and would neither be drawn by it nor receive direction from it, would anyone question whether it wanted anything essential? It would be absurd to ask whether a thing really existing wanted anything essential to it. Or could it be demanded whether this made an essential or specific difference or no, since we have no other measure of essential or specific but our abstract ideas? And to talk of specific differences in nature, without reference to general ideas in names, is to talk unintelligibly. For I would ask anyone what is sufficient to make an essential difference in nature between any two particular beings, without any regard had to some abstract idea which is looked upon as the essence and standard of a species? All such patterns and standards being quite laid aside, particular beings, considered barely in themselves, will be found to have all their qualities equally essential; and everything in each individual will be essential to it; or, which is more, nothing at all.

6. It is true, I have often mentioned a *real essence,* distinct in substances from those abstract ideas of them which I call their nominal essence. By this *real essence* I mean that real constitution of anything, which is the foundation of all those properties that are combined in, and are constantly found to co-exist with, the nominal essence : that particular constitution which everything has within itself, without any relation to anything without it. But essence, even in this sense, *relates to a sort, and supposes a species.* Indeed, as to the real essences of substances, we only suppose their being, without precisely knowing what they are; but that which annexes them still to the species is the nominal essence, of which they are the supposed foundation and cause.

7. *The nominal Essence bounds the Species.* The next thing to be considered is, by which of those essences it is that substances are determined into sorts or species; and that, it is evident, is by the nominal essence. For it is that alone that That therefore, and that alone, is considered as essential,

the name, which is the mark of the sort, signifies. It is impossible, therefore, that anything should determine the sorts of things, which we rank under general names, but that idea which that name is designed as a mark for; which is that, as has been shown, which we call the nominal essence.

8. And that the species of things to us are nothing but the ranking them under distinct names, according to the complex ideas in *us,* and not according to precise, distinct, real essences in *them,* is plain from hence: that we find many of the individuals that are ranked into one sort, called by one common name, and so received as being of one species, have yet qualities, depending on their real constitutions, as far different one from another as from others from which they are accounted to differ specifically.

9. *Not the real Essence, which we know not.* Nor indeed can we rank and sort things, and consequently (which is the end of sorting) denominate them, by their real essences; because we know them not. Our faculties carry us no further towards the knowledge and distinction of substances than a collection of those sensible ideas which we observe in them; which, however made with the greatest diligence and exactness we are capable of, yet is more remote from the true internal constitution from which those qualities flow, than, as I said, a countryman's idea is from the inward contrivance of that famous clock at Strasbourg, whereof he only sees the outward figure and motions. There is not so contemptible a plant or animal that does not confound the most enlarged understanding. Though the familiar use of things about us take off our wonder, yet it cures not our ignorance. When we come to examine the stones we tread on, or the iron we daily handle, we presently find we know not their make, and can give no reason of the different qualities we find in them. It is evident the internal constitution, whereon their properties depend, is unknown to us. Therefore we in vain pretend to range things into sorts, and dispose them into certain classes under names, by their real essences, that are so far from our discovery or comprehension.

10. *Not substantial forms which we know less.* Those, therefore, who have been taught that the several species of

substances had their distinct internal *substantial forms*, and that it was those *forms* which made the distinction of substances into their true species and genera, were led yet further out of the way by having their minds set upon fruitless inquiries after substantial forms, wholly unintelligible, and whereof we have scarce so much as any obscure or confused conception in general.

11. *That the Nominal Essence is that whereby we distinguish Species further evident from Spirits.* That our ranking and distinguishing natural substances into species consists in the nominal essences the mind makes, and not in the real essences to be found in the things themselves, is further evident from our ideas of spirits. For the mind getting only by reflecting on its own operations those simple ideas which it attributes to spirits, it hath or can have no other notion of spirit but by attributing all those operations it finds in itself to a sort of beings, without consideration of matter. And even the most advanced notion we have of God is but attributing the same simple ideas which we have got from reflection on what we find in ourselves, and which we conceive to have more perfection in them than would be in their absence; attributing, I say, those simple ideas to Him in an unlimited degree. Thus, having got from reflecting on ourselves the idea of existence, knowledge, power and pleasure —each of which we find it better to have than to want; and the more we have of each the better—joining all these together, with infinity to each of them, we have the complex idea of an eternal, omniscient, omnipotent, infinitely wise and happy being.

12. *Whereof there are probably numberless Species.* It is not impossible to conceive, nor repugnant to reason, that there may be many species of spirits, as much separated and diversified one from another by distinct properties whereof we have no ideas, as the species of sensible things are distinguished one from another by qualities which we know and observe in them. That there should be more species of intelligent creatures above us than there are of sensible and material below us is probable to me from hence: that in all

the visible corporeal world we see no chasms or gaps. All quite down from us the descent is by easy steps, and a continued series of things, that in each remove differ very little one from the other. The animal and vegetable kingdoms are so nearly joined that, if you will take the lowest of one and the highest of the other, there will scarce be perceived any great difference between them; and so on, till we come to the lowest and the most inorganical parts of matter, we shall find everywhere that the several species are linked together, and differ but in almost insensible degrees.

13. *The Nominal Essence that of the Species, proved from Water and Ice.* But to return to the species of corporeal substances. If I should ask anyone whether ice and water were two distinct species of things, I doubt not but I should be answered in the affirmative; and it cannot be denied but he that says they are two distinct species is in the right. But if an Englishman bred in Jamaica, who perhaps had never seen nor heard of ice, coming into England in the winter, find the water he put in his basin at night in a great part frozen in the morning, and, not knowing any peculiar name it had, should call it hardened water, I ask whether this would be a new species to him, different from water? And I think it would be answered here, it would not be to him a new species, no more than congealed jelly, when it is cold, is a distinct species from the same jelly fluid and warm; or than liquid gold in the furnace is a distinct species from hard gold in the hands of a workman. And if this be so, it is plain that *our distinct species* are *nothing but distinct complex ideas, with distinct names annexed to them.*

14. *Difficulties against a certain number of real Essences.* To distinguish substantial beings into species, according to the usual supposition that there are certain precise essences or forms of things, whereby all the individuals existing are by nature distinguished into species, these things are necessary:

15. First, to be assured that nature, in the production of things, always designs them to partake of certain regulated established essences, which are to be the models of all things

to be produced. This, in that crude sense it is usually proposed, would need some better explication, before it can fully be assented to.

16. Secondly, it would be necessary to know whether nature always attains that essence it designs in the production of things. The irregular and monstrous births, that in divers sorts of animals have been observed, will always give us reason to doubt of one or both of these.

17. Thirdly, it ought to be determined whether those we call monsters be really a distinct species, according to the scholastic notion of the word ' species '; since it is certain that everything that exists has its particular constitution. And yet we find that some of these monstrous productions have few or none of those qualities which are supposed to result from, and accompany, the essence of that species from whence they derive their originals, and to which, by their descent, they seem to belong.

18. *Our Nominal Essences of Substances not perfect collections of Properties.* Fourthly, the real essences of those things which we distinguish into species, and as so distinguished we name, ought to be known, i.e. we ought to have ideas of them. But since we are ignorant in these four points, the supposed real essences of things stand us not in stead for the distinguishing substances into species.

19. Fifthly, the only imaginable help in this case would be that, having framed perfect complex ideas of the properties of things flowing from their different real essences, we should thereby distinguish them into species. But neither can this be done. For, being ignorant of the real essence itself, it is impossible to know all those properties that flow from it, and are so annexed to it that, any one of them being away, we may certainly conclude that that essence is not there, and so the thing is not of that species.

21. *But such a Collection as our Name stands for.* But since, as has been remarked, we have need of general words, though we know not the real essences of things, all we can do is to collect such a number of simple ideas as, by examination, we find to be united together in things existing,

and thereof to make one complex idea. Which, though it be not the real essence of any substance that exists, is yet the specific essence to which our name belongs, and is convertible with it; by which we may at least try the truth of these nominal essences. The essence of anything in respect of us is the whole complex idea comprehended and marked by that name; and in substances, besides the several distinct simple ideas that make them up, the confused one of substance, or of an unknown support and cause of their union, is always a part; and therefore the essence of body is not bare extension, but an extended solid thing; and so to say an extended solid thing moves or impels another is all one, and as intelligible, as to say body moves or impels. Likewise, to say that a rational animal is capable of conversation is all one as to say a man; but none will say that rationality is capable of conversation, because it makes not the whole essence to which we give the name ' man '.

26. *Therefore very various and uncertain.* Since then it is evident that we sort and name substances by their nominal and not by their real essences, the next thing to be considered is how, and by whom, these essences come to be made. As to the latter, it is evident they are made by the mind, and not by nature; for were they Nature's workmanship, they could not be so various and different in several men as experience tells us they are. For if we will examine it, we shall not find the nominal essence of any one species of substances in all men the same : no, not of that which of all others we are the most intimately acquainted with.

28. *But not so arbitrary as Mixed Modes.* But though these nominal essences of substances are made by the mind, they are not yet made so arbitrarily as those of mixed modes. To the making of any nominal essence, it is necessary, first, that the ideas whereof it consists have such a union as to make but one idea, how compounded soever. Secondly, that the particular ideas so united be exactly the same, neither more nor less. For if two abstract complex ideas differ either in number or sorts of their component parts, they make two different, and not one and the same essence. In the first of these, the mind,

in making its complex ideas of substances, only follows nature, and puts none together which are not supposed to have a union in nature. Nobody joins the voice of a sheep with the shape of a horse, nor the colour of lead with the weight and fixedness of gold, to be the complex ideas of any real substances; unless he has a mind to fill his head with chimeras, and his discourse with unintelligible words. Men observing certain qualities always joined and existing together, therein copied nature, and of ideas so united made their complex ones of substances. For, though men may make what complex ideas they please, and give what names to them they will; yet, if they will be understood when they speak of things really existing, they must in some degree conform their ideas to the things they would speak of; or else men's language will be like that of Babel, and every man's words, being intelligible only to himself, would no longer serve to conversation and the ordinary affairs of life, if the ideas they stand for be not some way answering the common appearances and agreement of substances as they really exist.

29. *Though very imperfect.*   Secondly, though the mind of man, in making its complex ideas of substances, never puts any together that do not really, or are not supposed to, co-exist, and so it truly borrows that union from nature; yet the number it combines depends upon the various care, industry, or fancy of him that makes it. Men generally content themselves with some few sensible obvious qualities, and often, if not always, leave out others as material and as firmly united as those that they take   Of sensible substances there are two sorts: one of organized bodies, which are propagated by seed; and in these the *shape* is that which to us is the leading quality, and most characteristical part, that determines the species. And therefore in vegetables and animals an extended solid substance of such a certain figure usually serves the turn. As in vegetables and animals it is the shape, so in most other bodies, not propagated by seed, it is the *colour* we most fix on, and are most led by. Thus where we find the colour of gold, we are apt to imagine all the other qualities comprehended in our complex idea to be there also; and we commonly take these two obvious

qualities, viz. shape and colour, for so presumptive ideas of several species, that in a good picture we readily say, this is a lion, and that a rose, this is a gold, and that a silver goblet, only by the different figures and colours represented to the eye by the pencil.

(30) *Which yet serve for common converse.* But though this serves well enough for gross and confused conceptions, and inaccurate ways of talking and thinking, yet *men are far enough from having agreed on the precise number of simple ideas or qualities belonging to any sort of things, signified by its name.* Nor is it a wonder, since it requires much time, pains, and skill, strict inquiry, and long examination to find out what, and how many, those simple ideas are, which are constantly and inseparably united in nature, and are always to be found together in the same subject.

(32) *The more general our Ideas are, the more incomplete and partial they are.* If the number of simple ideas that make the nominal essence of the lowest species, or first sorting, of individuals depends on the mind of man, variously collecting them, it is much more evident that they do so in the more comprehensive *classis,* which, by the masters of logic, are called *genera.* These are complex ideas designedly imperfect; and it is visible at first sight that several of those qualities that are to be found in the things themselves are purposely left out of generical ideas. For, as the mind, to make general ideas comprehending several particulars, leaves out those of time and place, and such other that make them incommunicable to more than one individual, so to make other yet more general ideas, that may comprehend different sorts, it leaves out those qualities that distinguish them, and puts into its new collection only such ideas as are common to several sorts. So that in this whole business of genera and species, the genus, or more comprehensive, is but a partial conception of what is in the species, and the species but a partial idea of what is to be found in each individual. If therefore anyone will think that a man, and a horse, and an animal, and a plant, &c., are distinguished by real essences made by nature, he must think nature to be very liberal of these real essences, making one for

body, another for an animal, and another for a horse, and all these essences liberally bestowed upon Bucephalus. But if we would rightly consider what is done in all these genera and species, or sorts, we should find that there is no new thing made, but only more or less comprehensive signs, whereby we may be enabled to express in a few syllables great numbers of particular things, as they agree in more or less general conceptions, which we have framed to that purpose. In all which we may observe that the more general term is always the name of a less complex idea, and that each genus is but a partial conception of the species comprehended under it. So that if these abstract general ideas be thought to be complete, it can only be in respect of a certain established relation between them and certain names which are made use of to signify them; and not in respect of anything existing, as made by nature.

33. *This all accommodated to the end of Speech.* This is adjusted to the true end of speech, which is to be the easiest and shortest way of communicating our notions. For thus he that would make and discourse of things, as they agreed in the complex idea of extension and solidity, needed but use the word 'body' to denote all such. He that to these would join others, signified by the words 'life', 'sense', and 'spontaneous motion', needed but use the word 'animal' to signify all which partaked of those ideas; and he that had made a complex idea of a body, with life, sense, and motion, with the faculty of reasoning, and a certain shape joined to it, needed but use the short monosyllable 'man' to express all particulars that correspond to that complex idea. This is the proper business of genus and species; and this men do without any consideration of real essences, or substantial forms, which come not within the reach of our knowledge when we think of those things, nor within the signification of our words when we discourse with others.

36. *Nature makes the Similitude.* This, then, in short, is the case: nature makes many *particular things,* which do agree one with another in many sensible qualities, and probably too in their internal frame and constitution; but it is not this real

essence that distinguishes them into species; it is men who, taking occasion from the qualities they find united in them, and wherein they observe often several individuals to agree, range them into sorts, in order to their naming, for the convenience of comprehensive signs; under which individuals, according to their conformity to this or that abstract idea, come to be ranked as under ensigns : so that this is of the blue, that the red regiment, this is a man, that a drill; and in this, I think, consists the whole business of genus and species.

37. I do not deny but nature, in the constant production of particular beings, makes them not always new and various, but very much alike and of kin one to another; but I think it nevertheless true that the boundaries of the species, whereby men sort them, are made by men, since the essences of the species, distinguished by different names, are, as has been proved, of man's making, and seldom adequate to the internal nature of the things they are taken from. So that we may truly say such a manner of sorting of things is the workmanship of men.

40. *Species of artificial things less confused than natural.* From what has been before said we may see the reason why, in the species of artificial things, there is generally less confusion and uncertainty than in natural. Because an artificial thing being a production of man, which the artificer designed, and therefore well knows the idea of, the name of it is supposed to stand for no other idea, nor to import any other essence, than what is certainly to be known, and easy enough to be apprehended. For the idea or essence of the several sorts of artificial things consisting for the most part in nothing but the determinate figure of sensible parts, and sometimes motion depending thereon, which the artificer fashions in matter, such as he finds for his turn; it is not beyond the reach of our faculties to attain a certain idea thereof; and so settle the signification of the names whereby the species of artificial things are distinguished, with less doubt, obscurity, and equivocation than we can in things natural, whose differences and operations depend upon contrivances beyond the reach of our discoveries.

51. *Conclusion.*   To conclude : what liberty Adam had at first to make any complex ideas of *mixed modes* by no other pattern but by his own thoughts, the same have all men ever since had.   And the same necessity of conforming his ideas of *substances* to things without him, as to archetypes made by nature, that Adam was under, if he would not wilfully impose upon himself, the same are all men ever since under too.   The same liberty also that Adam had of affixing any new name to any idea, the same has anyone still (especially the beginners of languages, if we can imagine any such); but only with this difference, that in places where men in society have already established a language amongst them the significations of words are very warily and sparingly to be altered.   Because men being furnished already with names for their ideas, and common use having appropriated known names to certain ideas, an affected misapplication of them cannot but be very ridiculous.   He that hath new notions will perhaps venture sometimes on the coining new terms to express them; but men think it a boldness, and it is uncertain whether common use will ever make them pass for current.   But in communication with others it is necessary that we conform the ideas we make the vulgar words of any language stand for to their known proper significations (which I have explained at large already), or else to make known that new signification we apply them to.

[CHAPTER VII]

[OF PARTICLES]

CHAPTER VIII

OF ABSTRACT AND CONCRETE TERMS

(1.) *Abstract Terms not predicable one of another, and why.*
The ordinary words of language, and our common use
of them, would have given us light into the nature of our
ideas, if they had been but considered with attention. The
mind, as has been shown, has a power to abstract its ideas,
and so they become essences, general essences, whereby the
sorts of things are distinguished. Now each abstract idea
being distinct, so that of any two the one can never be the
other, the mind will, by its intuitive knowledge, perceive
their difference, and therefore in propositions no two whole
ideas can ever be affirmed one of another. This we see in
the common use of language, which permits not any two
abstract words, or names of abstract ideas, to be affirmed one
of another. For how near of kin soever they may seem to
be, and how certain soever it is that man is an animal, or
rational, or white, yet everyone at first hearing perceives the
falsehood of these propositions : *humanity is animality,* or
rationality, or whiteness; and this is as evident as any of
the most allowed maxims. All our affirmations then are only
in concrete, which is the affirming, not one abstract idea to
be another, but one abstract idea to be joined to another; which
abstract ideas, in substances, may be of any sort : in all the
rest are little else but of relations, and in substances the most
frequent are of powers : v.g. *a man is white* signifies that the
thing that has the essence of a man has also in it the essence
of whiteness, which is nothing but a power to produce the
idea of whiteness in one whose eyes can discover ordinary
objects. Or *a man is rational* signifies that the same thing
that hath the essence of a man hath also in it the essence of
rationality, i.e. a power of reasoning.

(2.) *They show the difference of our Ideas.* This distinction of names shows us also the difference of our ideas; for, if we observe them, we shall find that *our simple ideas have all abstract as well as concrete names,* the one whereof is (to speak the language of grammarians) a substantive, the other an adjective : as 'whiteness', 'white'; 'sweetness', 'sweet'. The like also holds in our ideas of modes and relations : as 'justice', 'just'; 'equality', 'equal'; only with this difference, that some of the concrete names of relations amongst men chiefly are substantives; as '*paternitas*', '*pater*', whereof it were easy to render a reason. But as to our ideas of substances, we have very few or no abstract names at all. For though the Schools have introduced '*animalitas*', '*human-itas*', '*corporietas*', and some others, yet they hold no proportion with that infinite number of names of substances, to which they never were ridiculous enough to attempt the coining of abstract ones; and those few that the Schools forged, and put into the mouths of their scholars, could never yet get admittance into common use, or obtain the licence of public approbation. Which seems to me at least to intimate the confession of all mankind, that they have no ideas of the real essences of substances, since they have not names for such ideas; which no doubt they would have had, had not their consciousness to themselves of their ignorance of them kept them from so idle an attempt. And therefore, though they had ideas enough to distinguish gold from a stone, and metal from wood; yet they but timorously ventured on such terms as '*aurietas*' and '*saxietas*', '*metallietas*' and '*lignietas*', or the like names, which should pretend to signify the real essences of those substances whereof they knew they had no ideas. And indeed it was only the doctrine of *substantial forms,* and the confidence of mistaken pretenders to a knowledge that they had not, which first coined and then introduced '*animalitas*' and '*humanitas*', and the like; which yet went very little further than their own Schools, and could never get to be current amongst understanding men.

CHAPTER IX

OF THE IMPERFECTION OF WORDS

1. Words are used for recording and communicating our Thoughts. From what has been said in the foregoing chapters it is easy to perceive what imperfection there is in language, and how the very nature of words makes it almost unavoidable for many of them to be doubtful and uncertain in their significations. To examine the perfection or imperfection of words, it is necessary first to consider their use and end, for as they are more or less fitted to attain that, so they are more or less perfect. We have, in the former part of this discourse often, upon occasion, mentioned a double use of words.

First, one for the recording of our own thoughts.

Secondly, the other for the communicating of our thoughts to others.

2. Any Words will serve for recording. As to the first of these, *for the recording our own thoughts for the help of our own memories,* whereby, as it were, we talk to ourselves, any words will serve the turn. For since sounds are voluntary and indifferent signs of any ideas, a man may use what words he pleases to signify his own ideas to himself; and there will be no imperfection in them, if he constantly use the same sign for the same idea; for then he cannot fail of having his meaning understood, wherein consists the right use and perfection of language.

3. Communication by Words Civil or Philosophical. Secondly, as to *communication of words,* that too has a double use.

I. *Civil.*

II. *Philosophical.*

First, by their *civil* use, I mean such a communication of thoughts and ideas by words as may serve for the upholding common conversation and commerce, about the ordinary affairs

300   *An Essay Concerning Human Understanding*

and conveniences of civil life, in the societies of men, one amongst another.

Secondly, by the *philosophical* use of words, I mean such a use of them as may serve to convey the precise notions of things, and to express in general propositions certain and undoubted truths, which the mind may rest upon and be satisfied with in its search after true knowledge. These two uses are very distinct; and a great deal less exactness will serve in the one than in the other, as we shall see in what follows.

4. *The Imperfections of Words is the Doubtfulness of their Signification.* The chief end of language in communication being to be understood, words serve not well for that end, neither in civil nor philosophical discourse, when any word does not excite in the hearer the same idea which it stands for in the mind of the speaker. Now, since sounds have no natural connexion with our ideas, but have all their signification from the arbitrary imposition of men, the doubtfulness and uncertainty of their signification, which is the imperfection we here are speaking of, has its cause more in the ideas they stand for than in any incapacity there is in one sound more than in another to signify any idea; for in that regard they are all equally perfect.

5. *Causes of their Imperfection.* Words having naturally no signification, the idea which each stands for must be learned and retained by those who would exchange thoughts and hold intelligible discourse with others, in any language. But this is hardest to be done where,

First, the ideas they stand for are very complex, and made up of a great number of ideas put together.

Secondly, where the ideas they stand for have no certain connexion in nature; and so no settled standard anywhere in nature existing, to rectify and adjust them by.

Thirdly, where the signification of the word is referred to a standard, which standard is not easy to be known.

Fourthly, where the signification of the word and the real essence of the thing are not exactly the same.

In all these cases we shall find an imperfection in words,

which I shall more at large explain in their particular application to our several sorts of ideas; for if we examine them, we shall find that the *names of Mixed Modes are most liable to doubtfulness and imperfection, for the two first of these reasons;* and the *names of Substances chiefly for the two latter.*

6. *The Names of Mixed Modes doubtful. First, Because the Ideas they stand for are so complex.* First, the names of *mixed modes* are, many of them, liable to great uncertainty and obscurity in their signification.

I. Because of that *great composition* these complex ideas are often made up of. To make words serviceable to the end of communication, it is necessary, as has been said, that they excite in the hearer exactly the same idea they stand for in the mind of the speaker. Without this, men fill one another's heads with noise and sounds, but convey not thereby their thoughts, and lay not before one another their ideas, which is the end of discourse and language. But when a word stands for a very complex idea that is compounded and decompounded, it is not easy for men to form and retain that idea so exactly as to make the name in common use stand for the same precise idea, without any the least variation. Hence it comes to pass that men's names of very compound ideas, such as for the most part are moral words, have seldom in two different men the same precise signification, since one man's complex idea seldom agrees with another's, and often differs from his own, from that which he had yesterday, or will have to-morrow.

7. *Secondly, because they have no Standards.* II. Because the names of mixed modes for the most part *want standards in nature,* whereby men may rectify and adjust their significations, therefore they are very various and doubtful. They are assemblages of ideas put together at the pleasure of the mind, pursuing its own ends of discourse, and suited to its own notions; whereby it designs not to copy anything really existing, but to denominate and rank things as they come to agree with those archetypes or forms it has made.

8. *Propriety not a sufficient Remedy.* It is true, common

use, that is the rule of propriety, may be supposed here to afford some aid, to settle the signification of language; and it cannot be denied but that in some measure it does. Common use regulates the meaning of words pretty well for common conversation; but nobody having an authority to establish the precise signification of words, nor determine to what ideas any one shall annex them, common use is not sufficient to adjust them to Philosophical Discourses. Besides, the rule and measure of propriety itself being nowhere established, it is often matter of dispute whether this or that way of using a word be propriety of speech or no.

(9) *The way of learning these Names contributes also to their Doubtfulness.* The way also wherein the names of mixed modes are ordinarily learned does not a little contribute to the doubtfulness of their signification. For if we will observe how children learn languages, we shall find that, to make them understand what the names of simple ideas or substances stand for, people ordinarily show them the thing whereof they would have them have the idea; and then repeat to them the name that stands for it, as 'white', 'sweet', 'milk', 'sugar', 'cat', 'dog'. But as for mixed modes, especially the most material of them, *moral words,* the sounds are usually learned first; and then, to know what complex ideas they stand for, they are either beholden to the explication of others, or (which happens for the most part) are left to their own observation and industry; which being little laid out in the search of the true and precise meaning of names, these moral words are in most men's mouths little more than bare sounds; or when they have any, it is for the most part but a very loose and undetermined, and, consequently, obscure and confused signification. And even those themselves who have with more attention settled their notions do yet hardly avoid the inconvenience to have them stand for complex ideas different from those which other, even intelligent and studious men, make them the signs of. Where shall one find any, either controversial debate, or familiar discourse, concerning honour, faith, grace, religion, church, &c., wherein it is not easy to observe the different

notions men have of them? Which is nothing but this, that
they are not agreed in the signification of those words, nor have
in their minds the same complex ideas which they make them
stand for, and so all the contests that follow thereupon are
only about the meaning of a sound.

11. If the signification of the names of mixed modes are
uncertain, because there be no real standards existing in nature
to which those ideas are referred, and by which they may be
adjusted, the names of substances are of a doubtful signification for a contrary reason, viz because the ideas they stand
for are supposed conformable to the reality of things, and are
referred to standards made by Nature. In our ideas of substances we have not the liberty, as in mixed modes, to
frame what combinations we think fit, to be the characteristical
notes to rank and denominate things by. In these we must
follow Nature, suit our complex ideas to real existences, and
regulate the signification of their names by the things themselves, if we will have our names to be the signs of them, and
stand for them. Here, it is true, we have patterns to follow, but
patterns that will make the signification of their names very
uncertain; for names must be of a very unsteady and various
meaning, if the ideas they stand for be referred to standards
without us, that either cannot be known at all, or can be known
but imperfectly and uncertainly.

12. *Names of Substances referred, First to real Essences that
cannot be known.* The names of substances have, as has been
shown[1], a double reference in their ordinary use.

First, sometimes they are made to stand for, and so their
signification is supposed to agree to, *the real constitution of
things,* from which all their properties flow, and in which
they all centre. But this real constitution, or (as it is apt to
be called) essence, being utterly unknown to us, any sound
that is put to stand for it must be very uncertain in its
application; and it will be impossible to know what things
are or ought to be called a *horse,* or *antimony,* when those
words are put for real essences that we have no ideas of at

[1] III vi

all. And therefore in this supposition, the names of substances being referred to standards that cannot be known, their significations can never be adjusted and established by those standards.

13. *Secondly, to co-existing Qualities, which are known but imperfectly.* Secondly, the simple ideas that are *found to co-exist in substances* being that which their names immediately signify, these, as united in the several sorts of things, are the proper standards to which their names are referred, and by which their significations may best be rectified. But neither will these archetypes so well serve to this purpose as to leave these names without very various and uncertain significations. Because these simple ideas that co-exist, and are united in the same subject, being very numerous, and having all an equal right to go into the complex specific idea which the specific name is to stand for, men, though they propose to themselves the very same subject to consider, yet frame very different ideas about it; and so the name they use for it unavoidably comes to have, in several men, very different significations. The simple qualities which make up the complex ideas, being most of them powers in relation to changes which they are apt to make in, or receive from, other bodies, are almost infinite. For the union in nature of these qualities being the true ground of their union in one complex idea, who can say one of them has more reason to be put in or left out than another? From whence it will always unavoidably follow that the complex ideas of substances in men using the same names for them will be very various, and so the significations of those names very uncertain.

15. *With this imperfection, they may serve for Civil, but not well for Philosophical Use.* It is true, as to *civil* and *common* conversation, the general names of substances, regulated in their ordinary signification by some obvious qualities (as by the shape and figure in things of known seminal propagation, and in other substances, for the most part by colour, joined with some other sensible qualities), do well enough to design the things men would be understood to speak of; and so they usually conceive well enough the substances meant by the word

'gold' or 'apple', to distinguish the one from the other. But in *philosophical* inquiries and debates, where general truths are to be established, and consequences drawn from positions laid down, there the precise signification of the names of substances will be found not only not to be well established, but also very hard to be so.

18. *The Names of simple Ideas the least doubtful.* From what has been said it is easy to observe what has been before remarked, viz. that the *names of simple ideas* are, of all others, the least liable to mistakes, and that for these reasons. First, because the ideas they stand for, being each but one single perception, are much easier got, and more clearly retained, than the more complex ones, and therefore are not liable to the uncertainty which usually attends those compounded ones of substances and mixed modes, in which the precise number of simple ideas that make them up are not easily agreed, and so readily kept in mind. And, secondly, because they are never referred to any other essence, but barely that perception they immediately signify; which reference is that which renders the signification of the names of substances naturally so perplexed, and gives occasion to so many disputes.

19. *And next to them, simple Modes.* By the same rule, the names of *simple modes* are, next to those of simple ideas, least liable to doubt and uncertainty; especially those of figure and number, of which men have so clear and distinct ideas. Whoever that had a mind to understand them mistook the ordinary meaning of 'seven', or 'a triangle'? And in general the least compounded ideas in every kind have the least dubious names.

20. *The most doubtful are the Names of very compounded mixed Modes and Substances.* Mixed modes, therefore, that are made up but of a few and obvious simple ideas, have usually names of no very uncertain signification. But the names of mixed modes which comprehend a great number of simple ideas are commonly of a very doubtful and undetermined meaning, as has been shown. The names of substances, being annexed to ideas that are neither the real essences, nor exact representations of the patterns they are referred to, are liable

yet to greater imperfection and uncertainty, especially when we come to a philosophical use of them.

21. *Why this imperfection charged upon words.* I am apt to imagine that, were the imperfections of language, as the instrument of knowledge, more thoroughly weighed, a great many of the controversies that make such a noise in the world, would of themselves cease; and the way to knowledge, and perhaps peace too, lie a great deal opener than it does.

CHAPTER X

OF THE ABUSE OF WORDS

1. *Abuse of Words.* Besides the imperfection that is naturally in language, and the obscurity and confusion that is so hard to be avoided in the use of words, there are several *wilful* faults and neglects which men are guilty of in this way of communication, whereby they render these signs less clear and distinct in their signification than naturally they need to be.

2. *First, Words without any, or without clear Ideas.* First, in this kind, the first and most palpable abuse is the using of words without clear and distinct ideas; or, which is worse, signs without anything signified. Of these there are two sorts :

I. One may observe, in all languages, certain words that, if they be examined, will be found in their first original, and their appropriated, use not to stand for any clear and distinct ideas. These, for the most part, the several sects of philosophy and religion have introduced. For their authors or promoters, either affecting something singular, and out of the way of common apprehensions, or to support some strange opinions, or cover some weakness of their hypothesis, seldom fail to coin new words, and such as, when they come to be examined, may justly be called *insignificant terms.*

3. II. Others there be who extend this abuse yet further, who take so little care to lay by words which in their primary notation have scarce any clear and distinct ideas which they are

annexed to, that, by an unpardonable negligence, they familiarly use words which the propriety of language has affixed to very important ideas, without any distinct meaning at all 'Wisdom', 'glory', 'grace', &c., are words frequent enough in every man's mouth; but if a great many of those who use them should be asked what they mean by them, they would be at a stand, and not know what to answer: a plain proof that, though they have learned those sounds, and have them ready at their tongues' ends, yet there are no determined ideas laid up in their minds, which are to be expressed to others by them.

5. *Secondly, Unsteady Application of them. Secondly,* another great abuse of words is *inconstancy* in the use of them. It is hard to find a discourse written on any subject, especially of controversy, whereon one shall not observe, if he read with attention, the same words (and those commonly the most material in the discourse, and upon which the argument turns) used sometimes for one collection of simple ideas, and sometimes for another; which is a perfect abuse of language. Words being intended for signs of my ideas, to make them known to others, not by any natural signification, but by a voluntary imposition, it is plain cheat and abuse when I make them stand sometimes for one thing and sometimes for another; the wilful doing whereof can be imputed to nothing but great folly, or greater dishonesty.

6. *Thirdly, Affected Obscurity by wrong Application. Thirdly,* another abuse of language is an *affected obscurity,* by either applying old words to new and unusual significations, or introducing new and ambiguous terms, without defining either, or else putting them so together as may confound their ordinary meaning. Though the Peripatetic philosophy has been most eminent in this way, yet other sects have not been wholly clear of it. There is scarce any of them that are not cumbered with some difficulties (such is the imperfection of human knowledge), which they have been fain to cover with obscurity of terms, and to confound the signification of words, which, like a mist before people's eyes, might hinder their weak parts from being discovered. That 'body' and 'extension' in

common use stand for distinct ideas, is plain to anyone that will but reflect a little. For were their signification precisely the same, it would be proper, and as intelligible to say *the body of an extension* as the *extension of a body*; and yet there are those who find it necessary to confound their signification.

14. *Fourthly, taking them for Things.* Fourthly, another great abuse of words is the *taking them for things*. This, though it in some degree concerns all names in general, yet more particularly affects those of substances. To this abuse those men are most subject who confine their thoughts to any one system, and give themselves up into a firm belief of the perfection of any received hypothesis; whereby they come to be persuaded that the terms of that sect are so suited to the nature of things, that they perfectly correspond with their real existence.

15. *Instance, in Matter.* How much names taken for things are apt to mislead the understanding, the attentive reading of philosophical writers would abundantly discover, and that perhaps in words little suspected of any such misuse. I shall instance in one only, and that a very familiar one. How many intricate disputes have there been about *matter,* as if there were some such thing really in nature, distinct from *body*, as it is evident the word 'matter' stands for an idea distinct from the idea of body? For, if the ideas these two terms stood for were precisely the same, they might indifferently in all places be put for one another. But we see that though it be proper to say, There is one matter of all bodies, one cannot say, There is one body of all matters; we familiarly say one body is bigger than another; but it sounds harsh (and I think is never used) to say one matter is bigger than another. Whence comes this, then? *Viz.* from hence: that, though matter and body be not really distinct, but wherever there is the one there is the other, yet 'matter' and 'body' stand for two different conceptions, whereof the one is incomplete, and but a part of the other. For 'body' stands for a solid extended figured substance, whereof 'matter' is but a partial

and more confused conception; it seeming to me to be used for the substance and solidity of body, without taking in its extension and figure; and therefore it is that, speaking of matter, we speak of it always as one, because in truth it expressly contains nothing but the idea of a solid substance which is everywhere the same, everywhere uniform. This being our idea of matter, we no more conceive or speak of different matters in the world than we do of different solidities; though we both conceive and speak of different bodies, because extension and figure are capable of variation. But, since solidity cannot exist without extension and figure, the taking 'matter' to be the name of something really existing under that precision has no doubt produced those obscure and unintelligible discourses and disputes which have filled the heads and books of philosophers concerning *materia prima*; which imperfection or abuse how far it may concern a great many other general terms I leave to be considered.

17. *Fifthly, setting them for what they cannot signify.* *Fifthly,* another abuse of words is *the setting them in the place of things which they do or can by no means signify.* We may observe that, in the general names of substances, whereof the *nominal* essences are only known to us, when we put them into propositions, and affirm or deny anything about them, we do most commonly tacitly suppose or intend they should stand for the *real* essence of a certain sort of substances. For, when a man says gold is malleable, he means and would insinuate something more than this, that *what I call gold is malleable*, (though truly it amounts to no more,) but would have this understood, viz. that *gold, i.e. what has the real essence of gold, is malleable;* which amounts to thus much, that malleableness depends on, and is inseparable from, the real essence of gold. But a man not knowing wherein that real essence consists, the connexion in his mind of malleableness is not truly with an essence he knows not, but only with the sound ' gold' he puts for it.

19. *Hence we think every Change of our Idea in Substances not to change the Species.* This shows us the reason why in *mixed modes,* any of the ideas that make the composition of

the complex one being left out or changed, it is allowed to be another thing, i.e. to be of another species, as is plain in *chance-medley, manslaughter, murder, parricide,* &c. The reason whereof is because the complex idea signified by that name is the real as well as nominal essence, and there is no secret reference of that name to any other essence but that. But in *substances,* it is not so.

20. *The Cause of the Abuse, a supposition of Nature's working always regularly.* That which I think very much disposes men to substitute their names for the real essences of species is the supposition before mentioned that nature works regularly in the production of things, and sets the boundaries to each of those species, by giving exactly the same real internal constitution to each individual which we rank under one general name. Whereas anyone who observes their different qualities can hardly doubt that many of the individuals, called by the same name, are, in their internal constitution, as different one from another as several of those which are ranked under different specific names.

22. *Sixthly, supposition that Words have a certain and evident Signification. Sixthly,* there remains yet another more general, though perhaps less observed, abuse of words; and that is that, men having by a long and familiar use annexed to them certain ideas, they are apt to imagine *so near and necessary a connexion between the names and the signification they use them in,* that they forwardly suppose one cannot but understand what their meaning is; and therefore one ought to acquiesce in the words delivered, as if it were past doubt that, in the use of those common received sounds, the speaker and hearer had necessarily the same precise ideas. This abuse of taking words upon trust has nowhere spread so far, nor with so ill effects, as amongst men of letters. The multiplication and obstinacy of disputes, which have so laid waste the intellectual world, is owing to nothing more than to this ill use of words. For, though it be generally believed that there is great diversity of opinions in the volumes and variety of controversies the world is distracted with, yet the most I can find that the contending learned men of different parties do, in

their arguings one with another, is, that they speak different languages. For I am apt to imagine that when any of them, quitting terms, think upon things, and know what they think, they think all the same; though perhaps what they would have be different.

31. He that hath names without ideas wants meaning in his words, and speaks only empty sounds. He that hath complex ideas without names for them wants liberty and dispatch in his expressions, and is necessitated to use periphrases. He that uses his words loosely and unsteadily will either be not minded or not understood. He that applies his names to ideas different from their common use wants propriety in his language, and speaks gibberish. And he that hath the ideas of substances disagreeing with the real existence of things so far wants the materials of true knowledge in his understanding, and hath instead thereof chimeras.

32. *How in Substances.* In our notions concerning substances we are liable to all the former inconveniences: v.g. he that uses the word ' *tarantula* ', without having any imagination or idea of what it stands for, pronounces a good word; but so long means nothing at all by it. 2. He that in a newly-discovered country shall see several sorts of animals and vegetables, unknown to him before, may have as true ideas of them, as of a horse or a stag; but can speak of them only by a description till he shall either take the names the natives call them by, or give them names himself. 3. He that uses the word ' body ' sometimes for pure extension, and sometimes for extension and solidity together, will talk very fallaciously. 4. He that gives the name ' horse ' to that idea which common usage calls ' mule ' talks improperly, and will not be understood. 5. He that thinks the name ' centaur ' stands for some real being imposes on himself, and mistakes words for things.

CHAPTER XI

OF THE REMEDIES OF THE FOREGOING IMPERFECTIONS AND ABUSES

8. *First, Remedy to use no Word without an Idea*. To remedy the defects of speech before mentioned to some degree, and to prevent the inconveniences that follow from them, I imagine the observation of these following rules may be of use, till somebody better able shall judge it worth his while to think more maturely on this matter, and oblige the world with his thoughts on it.

First, a man should take care to use no word without a signification, no name without an idea for which he makes it stand. This rule will not seem altogether needless to anyone who shall take the pains to recollect how often he has met with such words as 'instinct', 'sympathy', and 'antipathy', &c., in the discourse of others, so made use of as he might easily conclude that those that used them had no ideas in their minds to which they applied them, but spoke them only as sounds, which usually served instead of reasons on the like occasions.

9. *Secondly, To have distinct Ideas annexed to them in Modes*. Secondly, it is not enough a man uses his words as signs of some ideas; those he annexes them to, if they be simple, must be clear and distinct; if complex, must be determinate, i.e. the precise collection of simple ideas settled in the mind, with that sound annexed to it, as the sign of that precise determined collection, and no other. This is very necessary in names of modes, and especially moral words; which, having no settled objects in nature, from whence their ideas are taken, as from their original, are apt to be very confused. 'Justice' is a word in every man's mouth, but most commonly with a very undetermined, loose signification; which will always be so, unless a man has in his mind a distinct comprehension of the component parts that complex idea consists of; and if it be decompounded, must be able to resolve it still on, till he at last comes to the simple ideas that make it up; and unless this be done, a man makes an ill use of the word, let it be ' justice ', for example, or any other.

10. *And conformable in Substances.*   In the names of substances, for a right use of them, something more is required than barely *determined ideas.* In these the names must also be *conformable to things as they exist*; but of this I shall have occasion to speak more at large by and by[1]. This exactness is absolutely necessary in inquiries after philosophical knowledge, and in controversies about truth. And though it would be well, too, if it extended itself to common conversation and the ordinary affairs of life, yet I think that is scarce to be expected. Vulgar notions suit vulgar discourses; and both, though confused enough, yet serve pretty well the market and the wake. Merchants and lovers, cooks and tailors, have words wherewithal to dispatch their ordinary affairs; and so, I think, might philosophers and disputants too, if they had a mind to understand, and to be clearly understood.

11. *Thirdly, Propriety.*   Thirdly, it is not enough that men have ideas, determined ideas, for which they make these signs stand, but they must also take care to apply their words as near as may be to such ideas as common use has annexed them to. For words, especially of languages already framed, being no man's private possession, but the common measure of commerce and communication, it is not for anyone at pleasure to change the stamp they are current in, nor alter the ideas they are affixed to; or at least, when there is a necessity to do so, he is bound to give notice of it. Men's intentions in speaking are, or at least should be, to be understood; which cannot be without frequent explanations, demands, and other the like incommodious interruptions, where men do not follow common use.

12. *Fourthly, make known their meaning.*   Fourthly, it is sometimes necessary, for the ascertaining the signification of words, to *declare their meaning,* where either common use has left it uncertain and loose (as it has in most names of very

[1] §24; IV iv 11-14

complex ideas), or where the term, being very material in the discourse, and that upon which it chiefly turns, is liable to any doubtfulness or mistake.

13. *And that in three Ways.* As the ideas men's words stand for are of different sorts, so the way of making known the ideas they stand for, when there is occasion, is also different. For though defining be thought the proper way to make known the proper signification of words, yet there be some words that will not be defined, as there be others whose precise meaning cannot be made known but by definition : and perhaps a third, which partake somewhat of both the other, as we shall see in the names of simple ideas, modes, and substances.

14. *First, in Simple Ideas, by synonymous terms or showing.* First, when a man makes use of the name of any simple idea, which he perceives is not understood, or is in danger to be mistaken, he is obliged, by the laws of ingenuity and the end of speech, to declare his meaning, and make known what idea he makes it stand for. This, as has been shown, cannot be done by definition; and therefore, when a synonymous word fails to do it, there is but one of these ways left. First, sometimes the *naming* the subject wherein that simple idea is to be found will make its name to be understood by those who are acquainted with that subject, and know it by that name. So to make a countryman understand what ' *feuille-morte* ' colour signifies, it may suffice to tell him, it is the colour of withered leaves falling in autumn. Secondly, but the only sure way of making known the signification of the name of any simple idea is *by presenting to his senses that subject which may produce it in his mind,* and make him actually have the idea that word stands for.

15. *Secondly, in mixed Modes, by definition.* Secondly, mixed modes, especially those belonging to morality, being most of them such combinations of ideas as the mind puts together of its own choice, and whereof there are not always standing patterns to be found existing, the signification of their names cannot be made known, as those of simple ideas, by any showing : but, in recompense thereof, may be perfectly and exactly defined. For they being combinations of several

ideas that the mind of man has arbitrarily put together, without reference to any archetypes, men may, if they please, exactly know the ideas that go to each composition, and so both use these words in a certain and undoubted signification, and perfectly declare, when there is occasion, what they stand for.

16. *Morality capable of Demonstration.* Upon this ground it is that I am bold to think that morality is capable of demonstration, as well as mathematics; since the precise real essence of the things moral words stand for may be perfectly known, and so the congruity and incongruity of the things themselves be certainly discovered; in which consists perfect knowledge.

17. *Definitions can make moral Discourses clear.* A definition is the only way whereby the precise meaning of moral words can be known, and yet a way whereby their meaning may be known certainly, and without leaving any room for any contest about it. And therefore the negligence or perverseness of mankind cannot be excused, if their discourses in morality be not much more clear than those in natural philosophy; since they are about ideas in the mind, which are none of them false or disproportionate, they having no external beings for archetypes which they are referred to and must correspond with.

18. *And is the only way.* Another reason that makes the defining of mixed modes so necessary, especially of moral words, is what I mentioned a little before, viz. that it is the only way whereby the signification of the most of them can be known with certainty. For the ideas they stand for being for the most part such whose component parts nowhere exist together, but scattered and mingled with others, it is the mind alone that collects them, and gives them the union of one idea; and it is only by words enumerating the several simple ideas which the mind has united that we can make known to others what their names stand for; the assistance of the senses in this case not helping us, by the proposal of sensible objects, to show the ideas which our names of this kind stand for, as it does often in the names of sensible simple ideas, and also to some degree in those of substances.

19. *Thirdly, in Substances, by showing and defining.* Thirdly, for the explaining the signification of the names of substances, as they stand for the ideas we have of their distinct species, both the forementioned ways, viz. of showing and defining, are requisite, in many cases, to be made use of. For, there being ordinarily in each sort some leading qualities, to which we suppose the other ideas which make up our complex idea of that species annexed, we forwardly give the specific name to that thing wherein that characteristical mark is found, which we take to be the most distinguishing idea of that species.

21. *Ideas of the leading Qualities of Substances are best got by showing.* Now these leading qualities are best made known by showing, and can hardly be made known otherwise. For the shape of a horse or cassowary will be but rudely and imperfectly imprinted on the mind by words; the sight of the animals doth it a thousand times better. And the idea of the particular colour of gold is not to be got by any description of it, but only by the frequent exercise of the eyes about it; as is evident in those who are used to this metal, who will frequently distinguish true from counterfeit, pure from adulterate, by the sight, where others (who have as good eyes, but yet by use have not got the precise nice idea of that peculiar yellow) shall not perceive any difference.

22. *The Ideas of their Powers best by Definition.* But because many of the simple ideas that make up our specific ideas of substances are powers which lie not obvious to our senses in the things as they ordinarily appear, therefore, in the signification of our names of substances, some part of the signification will be better made known by enumerating those simple ideas, than in showing the substance itself. For, he that to the yellow shining colour of gold, got by sight, shall, from my enumerating them, have the ideas of great ductility, fusibility, fixedness and solubility in *aqua regia*, will have a perfecter idea of gold than he can have by seeing a piece of gold, and thereby imprinting in his mind only its obvious qualities. But if the formal constitution of this shining, heavy, ductile thing

(from whence all these its properties flow) lay open to our senses, as the formal constitution or essence of a triangle does, the signification of the word ' gold ' might as easily be ascertained as that of ' triangle '.

23. Hence we may take notice how much the foundation of all our knowledge of corporeal things lies in our senses. The whole extent of our knowledge or imagination reaches not beyond our own ideas limited to our ways of perception.

24. *Ideas also of Substances must be conformable to Things.* But, though definitions will serve to explain the names of substances as they stand for our ideas, yet they leave them not without great imperfection as they stand for things. For our names of substances being not put barely for our ideas, but being made use of ultimately to represent things, and so are put in their place, their signification must agree with the truth of things as well as with men's ideas. And therefore, in substances, we are not always to rest in the ordinary complex idea commonly received as the signification of that word, but must go a little further, and inquire into the nature and properties of the things themselves, and thereby perfect, as much as we can, our ideas of their distinct species; or else learn them from such as are used to that sort of things, and are experienced in them. This is the more necessary to be done by all those who search after knowledge and philosophical verity, in that children, being taught words, whilst they have but imperfect notions of things, apply them at random, and without much thinking, and seldom frame determined ideas to be signified by them. Which custom (it being easy, and serving well enough for the ordinary affairs of life and conversation) they are apt to continue when they are men; and so begin at the wrong end, learning words first and perfectly, but make the notions to which they apply those words afterwards very overtly. By this means it comes to pass that men speaking the proper language of their country, i.e. according to grammar rules of that language, do yet speak very improperly of things themselves; and, by their arguing one with another, make but small progress in the discoveries of useful truths, and the

knowledge of things, as they are to be found in themselves, and not in our imaginations; and it matters not much for the improvement of our knowledge how they are called.

25. *Not easy to be made so.* It were therefore to be wished that men versed in physical inquiries, and acquainted with the several sorts of natural bodies, would set down those simple ideas wherein they observe the individuals of each sort constantly to agree. This would remedy a great deal of that confusion which comes from several persons applying the same name to a collection of a smaller or greater number of sensible qualities, proportionably as they have been more or less acquainted with, or accurate in examining, the qualities of any sort of things which come under one denomination. But a dictionary of this sort, containing, as it were, a natural history, requires too many hands as well as too much time, cost, pains, and sagacity ever to be hoped for; and till that be done, we must content ourselves with such definitions of the names of substances as explain the sense men use them in. And it would be well, where there is occasion, if they would afford us so much. This yet is not usually done, but men talk to one another, and dispute in words, whose meaning is not agreed between them, out of a mistake that the significations of common words are certainly established, and the precise ideas they stand for perfectly known; and that it is a shame to be ignorant of them. Both which suppositions are false, no names of complex ideas having so settled determined significations that they are constantly used for the same precise ideas. Nor is it a shame for a man not to have a certain knowledge of anything but by the necessary ways of attaining it; and so it is no discredit not to know what precise idea any sound stands for in another man's mind, without he declare it to me by some other way than barely using that sound, there being no other way, without such a declaration, certainly to know it. Indeed the necessity of communication by language brings men to an agreement in the signification of common words within some tolerable latitude that may serve for ordinary conversation; and so a man cannot be supposed wholly ignorant of the ideas which are annexed

to words by common use in a language familiar to him. But common use being but a very uncertain rule, which reduces itself at last to the ideas of particular men, proves often but a very variable standard. But though such a dictionary as I have above mentioned will require too much time, cost, and pains to be hoped for in this age, yet methinks it is not unreasonable to propose that words standing for things which are known and distinguished by their outward shapes should be expressed by little draughts and prints made of them. A vocabulary made after this fashion would perhaps with more ease, and in less time, teach the true signification of many terms, especially in languages of remote countries or ages, and settle truer ideas in men's minds of several things, whereof we read the names in ancient authors, than all the large and laborious comments of learned critics. Naturalists, that treat of plants and animals, have found the benefit of this way; and he that has had occasion to consult them will have reason to confess that he has a clearer idea of *apium* or *ibex* from a little print of that herb or beast, than he could have from a long definition of the names of either of them. And so no doubt he would have of *strigil* and *sistrum,* if, instead of a ' currycomb' and ' cymbal' (which are the English names dictionaries render them by), he could see stamped in the margin small pictures of these instruments, as they were in use amongst the ancients.

26. *Fifthly, by Constancy in their signification.* Fifthly, if men will not be at the pains to declare the meaning of their words, and definitions of their terms are not to be had, yet this is the least can be expected, that, in all discourses wherein one man pretends to instruct or convince another, he should use the same word constantly in the same sense. If this were done (which nobody can refuse without great disingenuity), many of the books extant might be spared; many of the controversies in dispute would be at an end; several of those great volumes, swollen with ambiguous words, now used in one sense, and by and by in another, would shrink into a very narrow compass; and many of the philosophers' (to mention no other) as well as poets' works might be contained in a nutshell.

BOOK FOUR

OF KNOWLEDGE AND OPINION

CHAPTER I

OF KNOWLEDGE IN GENERAL

1. *Our Knowledge conversant about our Ideas.* Since the mind in all its thoughts and reasonings hath no other immediate object but its own ideas, which it alone does or can contemplate, it is evident that our knowledge is only conversant about them.

2. *Knowledge is the Perception of the Agreement or Disagreement of two Ideas.* Knowledge then seems to me to be nothing but *the perception of the connexion and agreement, or disagreement and repugnancy, of any of our ideas.* In this alone it consists. Where this perception is, there is knowledge, and where it is not, there, though we may fancy, guess, or believe, yet we always come short of knowledge. For when we know that white is not black, what do we else but perceive that these two ideas do not agree? When we possess ourselves with the utmost security of the demonstration that the three angles of a triangle are equal to two right ones, what do we more but perceive that equality to two right ones does necessarily agree to, and is inseparable from, the three angles of a triangle?

3. *This Agreement fourfold.* But to understand a little more distinctly wherein this agreement or disagreement consists, I think we may reduce it all to these four sorts:

1. *Identity,* or *diversity.*
2. *Relation.*
3. *Co-existence,* or *necessary connexion.*
4. *Real existence.*

4. *First, of Identity, or Diversity.* *First,* as to the first sort of agreement or disagreement, viz. *identity* or *diversity.* It is the first act of the mind, when it has any sentiments or ideas at all, to perceive its ideas; and so far as it perceives them, to know each what it is, and thereby also to perceive their difference, and that one is not another. This is so absolutely necessary that without it there could be no knowledge, no reasoning, no imagination, no distinct thoughts at all. By this the mind clearly and infallibly perceives each idea to agree with itself, and to be what it is, and all distinct ideas to disagree, i.e. the one not to be the other; and this it does without pains, labour, or deduction, but at first view, by its natural power of perception and distinction. And though men of art have reduced this into those general rules, *What is, is,* and *It is impossible for the same thing to be and not to be,* for ready application in all cases, wherein there may be occasion to reflect on it, yet it is certain that the first exercise of this faculty is about particular ideas. A man infallibly knows, as soon as ever he has them in his mind, that the ideas he calls *white* and *round* are the very ideas they are, and that they are not other ideas which he calls *red* or *square.* Nor can any maxim or proposition in the world make him know it clearer or surer than he did before, and without any such general rule. This then is the first agreement or disagreement which the mind perceives in its ideas, which it always perceives at first sight; and if there ever happen any doubt about it, it will always be found to be about the names, and not the ideas themselves, whose identity and diversity will always be perceived, as soon and as clearly as the ideas themselves are; nor can it possibly be otherwise.

5. *Secondly, Relative.* *Secondly,* the next sort of agreement or disagreement the mind perceives in any of its ideas may, I think, be called *relative,* and is nothing but the perception of the *relation* between any two ideas, of what kind soever, whether substances, modes, or any other. For, since all distinct ideas must eternally be known not to be the same, and so be universally and constantly denied one of another, there could be no room for any positive knowledge at all, if we could not

perceive any relation between our ideas, and find out the agreement or disagreement they have one with another, in several ways the mind takes of comparing them.

6. *Thirdly, of Co-existence. Thirdly,* the third sort of agreement or disagreement to be found in our ideas, which the perception of the mind is employed about, is *co-existence* or *non-co-existence* in the *same subject*; and this belongs particularly to substances. Thus when we pronounce concerning gold that it is fixed, our knowledge of this truth amounts to no more but this, that fixedness, or a power to remain in the fire unconsumed, is an idea that always accompanies and is joined with that particular sort of yellowness, weight, fusibility, malleableness, and solubility in *aqua regia,* which make our complex idea signified by the word ' gold '.

7. *Fourthly, of real Existence. Fourthly,* the fourth and last sort is that of *actual real existence* agreeing to any idea. Within these four sorts of agreement or disagreement is, I suppose, contained all the knowledge we have, or are capable of. For all the inquiries that we can make concerning any of our ideas, all that we know or can affirm concerning any of them, is that it is, or is not, the same with some other; that it does or does not always co-exist with some other idea in the same subject; that it has this or that relation to some other idea; or that it has a real existence without the mind. Thus, " Blue is not yellow " is of identity. " Two triangles upon equal bases between two parallels are equal " is of relation. " Iron is susceptible of magnetical impressions " is of co-existence. " God is " is of real existence. Though identity and co-existence are truly nothing but relations, yet they are so peculiar ways of agreement or disagreement of our ideas that they deserve well to be considered as distinct heads, and not under relation in general; since they are so different grounds of affirmation and negation, as will easily appear to anyone, who will but reflect on what is said in several places of this *Essay.* I should now proceed to examine the several degrees of our knowledge, but that it is necessary first to consider the different acceptations of the word ' knowledge '.

8. *Knowledge, actual or habitual.* There are several ways

wherein the mind is possessed of truth; each of which is called knowledge.

1. There is *actual knowledge,* which is the present view the mind has of the agreement or disagreement of any of its ideas, or of the relation they have one to another.

2. A man is said to know any proposition, which having been once laid before his thoughts, he evidently perceived the agreement or disagreement of the ideas whereof it consists; and so lodged it in his memory that, whenever that proposition comes again to be reflected on, he, without doubt or hesitation, embraces the right side, assents to, and is certain of the truth of it. This, I think, one may call *habitual knowledge.* And thus a man may be said to know all those truths which are lodged in his memory, by a foregoing clear and full perception, whereof the mind is assured past doubt as often as it has occasion to reflect on them. For our finite understandings being able to think clearly and distinctly but on one thing at once, if men had no knowledge of any more than what they actually thought on, they would all be very ignorant; and he that knew most would know but one truth, that being all he was able to think on at one time.

9. *Habitual Knowledge twofold.* Of habitual knowledge there are, also, vulgarly speaking, two degrees:

First, the one is of such truths laid up in the memory as, whenever they occur to the mind, it *actually perceives the relation* is between those ideas. And this is in all those truths whereof we have an intuitive knowledge; where the ideas themselves, by an immediate view, discover their agreement or disagreement one with another.

Secondly, the other is of such truths whereof the mind having been convinced, it *retains the memory of the conviction, without the proofs.* Thus, a man that remembers certainly that he once perceived the demonstration that the three angles of a triangle are equal to two right ones, is certain that he knows it, because he cannot doubt of the truth of it. In his adherence to a truth, where the demonstration by which it was at first known is forgot, though a man may be thought rather to believe his memory than really to know, and this way of entertaining a truth seemed formerly to me like something between opinion and knowledge, a sort of assurance which exceeds bare belief, for that relies on the testimony of another, yet upon a due examination I find it comes not short of perfect certainty, and is in effect true knowledge. That which is apt to mislead our first thoughts into a mistake in this matter is that the agreement or disagreement of the ideas in this case is not perceived, as it was at first, by an actual view of all the intermediate ideas whereby the agreement or disagreement of those in the proposition was at first perceived, but by other intermediate ideas, that show the agreement or disagreement of the ideas contained in the proposition whose certainty we remember. For example : in this proposition, that the three angles of a triangle are equal to two right ones, one who has seen and clearly perceived the demonstration of this truth knows it to be true, when that demonstration is gone out of his mind; so that at present it is not actually in view, and possibly cannot be recollected : but he knows it in a different way from what he did before. The agreement of the two ideas joined in that proposition is perceived, but it is by the intervention of other ideas than those which at first produced that perception. He remembers, i.e. he knows (for remembrance is but the reviving of some past knowledge) that he was once certain of the truth of this proposition, that the three angles of a triangle are equal to two right ones. The immutability of the same relations between the same immutable things is now the idea that shows him that, if the three angles of a triangle were once equal to two right ones, they will always be equal to two right ones. And hence he comes to be certain that what was once true in the case is always true; what ideas once agreed will always agree; and consequently what he once knew to be true he will always know to be true, as long as he can remember that he once knew it. Upon this ground it is that particular demonstrations in mathematics afford general knowledge. If then the perception that the same ideas will *eternally* have the same habitudes and relations be not a sufficient ground of knowledge, there could be no knowledge of general propositions in mathematics; for no mathematical demonstration would be any other than particular, and, when a man had demonstrated any proposition concerning one triangle or circle, his knowledge would not reach beyond that particular diagram. If he would extend it further, he must renew his demonstration in another instance, before he could know it to be true in another like triangle, and so on; by which means one could never come to the knowledge of any general propositions. But because the memory is not always so clear as actual perception, and does in all men more or less decay in length of time, this, amongst other differences, is one which shows that *demonstrative* knowledge is much more imperfect than *intuitive,* as we shall see in the following chapter.

CHAPTER II

OF THE DEGREES OF OUR KNOWLEDGE

(1) *Intuitive.* All our knowledge consisting, as I have said, in the view the mind has of its own ideas, which is the utmost light and greatest certainty we, with our faculties and in our way of knowledge, are capable of, it may not be amiss to consider a little the degrees of its evidence. The different clearness of our knowledge seems to me to lie in the different way of perception the mind has of the agreement or disagreement of any of its ideas. For if we will reflect on our own ways of thinking, we shall find that sometimes the mind perceives the agreement or disagreement of two ideas *immediately by themselves,* without the intervention of any other; and this I think we may call *intuitive knowledge.* For in this the mind is at no pains of proving or examining, but perceives the truth as the eye doth light, only by being directed toward it. Thus the mind perceives that white is not black, that a circle is not a triangle, that three are more than two and equal to one and two. Such kinds of truths the mind perceives at the

first sight of the ideas together by bare intuition, without the intervention of any other idea; and this kind of knowledge is the clearest and most certain that human frailty is capable of. It is on this intuition that depends all the certainty and evidence of all our knowledge; which certainty everyone finds to be so great that he cannot imagine, and therefore not require, a greater. He that demands a greater certainty than this demands he knows not what, and shows only that he has a mind to be a sceptic, without being able to be so.

2.) *Demonstrative.* The next degree of knowledge is where the mind perceives the agreement or disagreement of any ideas, but not immediately. Though, wherever the mind perceives the agreement or disagreement of any of its ideas, there be certain knowledge, yet it does not always happen that the mind sees that agreement or disagreement, which there is between them, even where it is discoverable; and in that case remains in ignorance, and at most gets no further than a probable conjecture. The reason why the mind cannot always perceive presently the agreement or disagreement of two ideas is because those ideas, concerning whose agreement or disagreement the inquiry is made, cannot by the mind be so put together as to show it. In this case then, when the mind cannot so bring its ideas together as by their immediate comparison, and as it were juxta-position or application one to another, to perceive their agreement or disagreement, it is fain, by the intervention of other ideas (one or more, as it happens) to discover the agreement or disagreement which it searches; and this is that which we call *reasoning.* Thus, the mind, being willing to know the agreement or disagreement in bigness between the three angles of a triangle and two right ones, cannot by an immediate view and comparing them do it; because the three angles of a triangle cannot be brought at once, and be compared with any one, or two, angles; and so of this the mind has no immediate, no intuitive, knowledge. In this case the mind is fain to find out some other angles, to which the three angles of a triangle have an equality; and, finding those equal to two right ones, comes to know their equality to two right ones.

3. *Depends on Proofs.* Those intervening ideas, which serve to show the agreement of any two others, are called *proofs*; and where the agreement and disagreement is by this means plainly and clearly perceived, it is called *demonstration*; it being *shown* to the understanding, and the mind made to see that it is so.

4. *But not so easy.* This knowledge by intervening proofs, though it be certain, yet the evidence of it is not altogether so clear and bright, nor the assent so ready, as in intuitive knowledge. For, though in demonstration the mind does at last perceive the agreement or disagreement of the ideas it considers, yet it is not without pains and attention; there must be more than one transient view to find it.

5. *Not without precedent Doubt.* Another difference between intuitive and demonstrative knowledge is that, though in the latter all doubt be removed when, by the intervention of the intermediate ideas, the agreement or disagreement is perceived, yet before the demonstration there was a doubt; which in intuitive knowledge cannot happen to the mind that has its faculty of perception left to a degree capable of distinct ideas, no more than it can be a doubt to the eye (that can distinctly see white and black) whether this ink and this paper be all of a colour.

6. *Not so clear.* It is true, the perception produced by demonstration is also very clear, yet it is often with a great abatement of that evident lustre and full assurance that always accompany that which I call intuitive; like a face reflected by several mirrors one to another, where, as long as it retains the similitude and agreement with the object, it produces a knowledge; but it is still, in every successive reflection, with a lessening of that perfect clearness and distinctness which is in the first; till at last, after many removes, it has a great mixture of dimness, and is not at first sight so knowable, especially to weak eyes. Thus it is with knowledge made out by a long train of proofs.

7. *Each Step must have Intuitive Evidence.* Now, in every step reason makes in demonstrative knowledge there is an intuitive knowledge of that agreement or disagreement it seeks

with the next intermediate idea which it uses as a proof; for, if it were not so, that yet would need a proof, since, without the perception of such agreement or disagreement, there is no knowledge produced. If it be perceived by itself, it is intuitive knowledge; if it cannot be perceived by itself, there is need of some intervening idea, as a common measure, to show their agreement or disagreement. By which it is plain that every step in reasoning that produces knowledge has intuitive certainty; which when the mind perceives, there is no more required but to remember it, to make the agreement or disagreement of the ideas concerning which we inquire visible and certain. This intuitive perception of the agreement or disagreement of the intermediate ideas, in each step and progression of the demonstration, must also be carried exactly in the mind, and a man must be sure that no part is left out; which because in long deductions, and the use of many proofs, the memory does not always so readily and exactly retain, therefore it comes to pass that this is more imperfect than intuitive knowledge, and men embrace often falsehood for demonstrations.

(8) *Hence the Mistake, ex præcognitis et præconcessis.* The necessity of this intuitive knowledge in each step of scientifical or demonstrative reasoning gave occasion, I imagine, to that mistaken axiom that all reasoning was *ex præcognitis et præconcessis* : which, how far it is mistaken, I shall have occasion to show more at large, when I come to consider propositions, and particularly those propositions which are called maxims, and to show that it is by a mistake that they are supposed to be the foundations of all our knowledge and reasonings.

(9) *Demonstration not limited to Quantity.* It has been generally taken for granted that mathematics alone are capable of demonstrative certainty; but to have such an agreement or disagreement as may intuitively be perceived being, as I imagine, not the privilege of the ideas of number, extension, and figure alone, it may possibly be the want of due method and application in us, and not of sufficient evidence in things, that demonstration has been thought to have so little to do in

other parts of knowledge, and been scarce so much as aimed at by any but mathematicians.

10. *Why it has been so thought.* The reason why it has been generally sought for, and supposed to be only in those, I imagine has been, not only the general usefulness of those sciences, but because, in comparing their equality or excess, the modes of numbers have every the least difference very clear and perceivable; and though in extension every the least excess is not so perceptible, yet the mind has found out ways to examine, and discover demonstratively, the just equality of two angles, or extensions, or figures; and both these, i.e. numbers and figures, can be set down by visible and lasting marks, wherein the ideas under consideration are perfectly determined; which for the most part they are not, where they are marked only by names and words.

11. But in other simple ideas, whose modes and differences are made and counted by degrees, and not quantity, we have not so nice and accurate a distinction of their differences as to perceive, or find ways to measure, their just equality, or the least differences. For those other simple ideas, being appearances or sensations produced in us by the size, figure, number, and motion of minute corpuscles singly insensible, their different degrees also depend upon the variation of some or all of those causes; which, since it cannot be observed by us, in particles of matter whereof each is too subtle to be perceived, it is impossible for us to have any exact measures of the different degrees of these simple ideas.

13. Not knowing, therefore, what number of particles, nor what motion of them, is fit to produce any precise degree of whiteness, we cannot demonstrate the certain equality of any two degrees of whiteness, because we have no certain standard to measure them by, nor means to distinguish every the least real difference, the only help we have being from our senses, which in this point fail us. But where the difference is so great as to produce in the mind clearly distinct ideas, whose differences can be perfectly retained, there these ideas of colours, as we see in different kinds, as blue and red, are as capable of demonstration as ideas of number and extension. What I have

here said of whiteness and colours I think holds true in all secondary qualities and their modes.

(14.) *Sensitive Knowledge of particular Existence.* These two, viz. intuition and demonstration, are the degrees of our *knowledge*; whatever comes short of one of these, with what assurance soever embraced, is but *faith* or *opinion,* but not knowledge, at least in all general truths. There is, indeed, another perception of the mind, employed about *the particular existence of finite beings without us,* which, going beyond bare probability, and yet not reaching perfectly to either of the foregoing degrees of certainty, passes under the name of *knowledge.* There can be nothing more certain than that the idea we receive from an external object is in our minds : this is intuitive knowledge. But whether there be anything more than barely that idea in our minds, whether we can thence certainly infer the existence of anything without us, which corresponds to that idea, is that whereof some men think there may be a question made; because men may have such ideas in their minds, when no such thing exists, no such object affects their senses. But yet here I think we are provided with an evidence that puts us past doubting. For I ask anyone whether he be not invincibly conscious to himself of a different perception when he looks on the sun by day, and thinks on it by night; when he actually tastes wormwood, or smells a rose, or only thinks on that savour or odour? We as plainly find the difference there is between any idea revived in our minds by our own memory and actually coming into our minds by our senses, as we do between any two distinct ideas. If anyone say a dream may do the same thing, and all these ideas may be produced in us without any external objects, he may please to dream that I make him this answer : 1. That it is no great matter whether I remove his scruple or no; where all is but dream, reasoning and arguments are of no use, truth and knowledge nothing. 2. That I believe he will allow a very manifest difference between dreaming of being in the fire and being actually in it. So that, I think, we may add to the two former sorts of knowledge this also, of the existence of particular external objects, by that perception and consciousness we have of the actual entrance of ideas from them, and allow these three degrees of knowledge, viz. *intuitive, demonstrative,* and *sensitive,* in each of which there are different degrees and ways of evidence and certainty.

15. *Knowledge not always clear, where the Ideas are so.* But since our knowledge is founded on and employed about our ideas only, will it not follow from thence that it is conformable to our ideas, and that where our ideas are clear and distinct, or obscure and confused, our knowledge will be so too? To which I answer, No; for, our knowledge consisting in the perception of the agreement or disagreement of any two ideas, its clearness or obscurity consists in the clearness or obscurity of that perception, and not in the clearness or obscurity of the ideas themselves: v.g. a man that has as clear ideas of the angles of a triangle, and of equality to two right ones, as any mathematician in the world, may yet have but a very obscure perception of their agreement, and so have but a very obscure knowledge of it. But ideas which, by reason of their obscurity or otherwise, are confused cannot produce any clear or distinct knowledge, because, as far as any ideas are confused, so far the mind cannot perceive clearly whether they agree or disagree. Or to express the same thing in a way less apt to be misunderstood : he that hath not determined ideas to the words he uses cannot make propositions of them of whose truth he can be certain.

CHAPTER III

OF THE EXTENT OF HUMAN KNOWLEDGE

1. *First, no further than we have Ideas.* Knowledge, as has been said, lying in the perception of the agreement or disagreement of any of our ideas, it follows from hence that,

First, we can have *knowledge* no further than we have *ideas.*

2. *Secondly, no further than we can perceive their Agree-*

ment or Disagreement. Secondly, that we can have no knowledge further than we can have *perception* of that agreement or disagreement. Which perception being : 1. Either by *intuition,* or the immediate comparing any two ideas; or, 2. By *reason,* examining the agreement or disagreement of two ideas, by the intervention of some others; or, 3. By *sensation,* perceiving the existence of particular things : hence it also follows :

3. *Thirdly, Intuitive Knowledge extends itself not to all the Relations of all our Ideas.*   Thirdly, that we cannot have an *intuitive knowledge* that shall extend itself to all our ideas, and all that we would know about them, because we cannot examine and perceive all the relations they have one to another, by juxta-position, or an immediate comparison one with another. Thus, having the ideas of an obtuse and an acute angled triangle, both drawn from equal bases, and between parallels, I can, by intuitive knowledge, perceive the one not to be the other, but cannot that way know whether they be equal or no, because their agreement or disagreement in equality can never be perceived by an immediate comparing them; the difference of figure makes their parts incapable of an exact immediate application, and therefore there is need of some intervening quantities to measure them by, which is demonstration, or rational knowledge.

4. *Fourthly, Nor Demonstrative Knowledge.*   Fourthly, it follows also from what is above observed that our *rational knowledge* cannot reach to the whole extent of our ideas, because between two different ideas we would examine we cannot always find such mediums as we can connect one to another with an intuitive knowledge in all the parts of the deduction; and wherever that fails, we come short of knowledge and demonstration.

5. *Fifthly, Sensitive Knowledge narrower than either.* Fifthly, *sensitive knowledge* reaching no further than the existence of things actually present to our senses is yet much narrower than either of the former.

6. *Sixthly, Our Knowledge, therefore, narrower than our Ideas.*   Sixthly, from all which it is evident that the *extent of*

our knowledge comes not only short of the reality of things, but even of the extent of our own ideas. Nevertheless, I do not question but that human knowledge, under the present circumstances of our beings and constitutions, may be carried much further than it hitherto has been, if men would sincerely, and with freedom of mind, employ all that industry and labour of thought in improving the means of discovering truth, which they do for the colouring or support of falsehood, to maintain a system, interest, or party they are once engaged in. We have the ideas of *matter* and *thinking*, but possibly shall never be able to know whether any mere material being thinks or no; it being impossible for us, by the contemplation of our own ideas, without revelation, to discover whether Omnipotency has not given to some systems of matter, fitly disposed, a power to perceive and think, or else joined and fixed to matter, so disposed, a thinking immaterial substance; it being, in respect of our notions, not much more remote from our comprehension to conceive that GOD can, if he pleases, superadd to matter a faculty of thinking, than that he should superadd to it another substance with a faculty of thinking; since we know not wherein thinking consists, nor to what sort of substances the Almighty has been pleased to give that power, which cannot be in any created being, but merely by the good pleasure and bounty of the Creator. I say not this, that I would any way lessen the belief of the soul's immateriality; I am not here speaking of probability, but knowledge; and I think not only that it becomes the modesty of philosophy not to pronounce magisterially, where we want that evidence that can produce knowledge, but also that it is of use to us to discern how far our knowledge does reach; for the state we are at present in not being that of vision, we must in many things content ourselves with faith and probability; and in the present question about the Immateriality of the Soul, if our faculties cannot arrive at demonstrative certainty, we need not think it strange. All the great ends of morality and religion are well enough secured without philosophical proofs of the soul's immateriality; since it is evident that he who made us at first begin to subsist here, sensible intelligent beings, and for several years continued us in such a state, can and will restore us to the like state of sensibility in another world, and make us capable there to receive the retribution he has designed to men, according to their doings in this life. He that considers how hardly sensation is, in our thoughts, reconcilable to extended matter, or existence to anything that has no extension at all, will confess that he is very far from certainly knowing what his soul is. It is a point which seems to me to be put out of the reach of our knowledge; and he who will give himself leave to consider freely, and look into the dark and intricate part of each hypothesis, will scarce find his reason able to determine him fixedly for or against the soul's materiality. Since, on which side soever he views it, either as an unextended substance, or as a thinking extended matter, the difficulty to conceive either will, whilst either alone is in his thoughts, still drive him to the contrary side. It is past controversy that we have in us something that thinks; our very doubts about what it is confirm the certainty of its being, though we must content ourselves in the ignorance of what kind of being it is; and it is in vain to go about to be sceptical in this, as it is unreasonable in most other cases to be positive against the being of anything, because we cannot comprehend its nature. For I would fain know what substance exists that has not something in it which manifestly baffles our understandings.

7. *How far our Knowledge reaches.* The affirmations or negations we make concerning the ideas we have, may, as I have before intimated in general, be reduced to these four sorts, viz. identity, co-existence, relation, and real existence. I shall examine how far our knowledge extends in each of these :

8. *Firstly, Our Knowledge of Identity and Diversity as far as our Ideas. First,* as to *identity* and *diversity.* In this way of the agreement or disagreement of our ideas our intuitive knowledge is as far extended as our ideas themselves; and there can be no idea in the mind, which it does not presently, by an intuitive knowledge, perceive to be what it is, and to be different from any other.

9. *Secondly, Of Co-existence a very little way. Secondly,*

as to *co-existence,* in this our knowledge is very short, though in this consists the greatest and most material part of our knowledge concerning substances. For our ideas of the species of substances being, as I have showed, nothing but certain collections of simple ideas united in one subject, and so co-existing together, when we would know anything further concerning these, or any other sort of substances, what do we inquire but what *other* qualities or powers these substances have or have not? Which is nothing else but to know what, *other* simple ideas do or do not co-exist with those that make up that complex idea?

10. *Because the Connexion between most simple Ideas is unknown.* This, how weighty and considerable a part soever of human science, is yet very narrow, and scarce any at all. The reason whereof is that the simple ideas whereof our complex ideas of substances are made up are, for the most part, such as carry with them, in their own nature, no visible necessary connexion or inconsistency with any other simple ideas, whose co-existence with them we would inform ourselves about.

11. *Especially of Secondary Qualities.* The ideas that our complex ones of substances are made up of, and about which our knowledge concerning substances is most employed, are those of their secondary qualities; which depending all (as has been shown) upon the primary qualities of their minute and insensible parts; or, if not upon them, upon something yet more remote from our comprehension; it is impossible we should know which have a <u>necessary union or inconsistency one with another</u>. For, not knowing the root they spring from, not knowing what size, figure, and texture of parts they are, on which depend, and from which result, those qualities which make our complex idea of gold, it is impossible we should know what other qualities result from, or are incompatible with, the same constitution of the insensible parts of gold; and so consequently must always co-exist with that complex idea we have of it, or else are inconsistent with it.

12. *Because all Connexion between any secondary and primary Qualities is undiscoverable.* Besides this ignorance of the primary qualities of the insensible parts of bodies, on

which depend all their secondary qualities, there is yet another and more incurable part of ignorance, which sets us more remote from a certain knowledge of the *co-existence* or *inco-existence* (if I may so say) of different ideas in the same subject; and that is, that there is no discoverable connexion between any secondary quality and those primary qualities that it depends on.

13) That the size, figure, and motion of one body should cause a change in the size, figure, and motion of another body, is not beyond our conception; the separation of the parts of one body upon the intrusion of another; and the change from rest to motion upon impulse; these and the like seem to us to have *some connexion* one with another. But our minds not being able to discover any connexion betwixt these primary qualities of bodies and the sensations that are produced in us by them, we can never be able to establish certain and undoubted rules of the *consequence* or *co-existence* of any secondary qualities, though we could discover the size, figure, or motion of those invisible parts which immediately produce them. We are so far from knowing what figure, size, or motion of parts produce a yellow colour, a sweet taste, or a sharp sound, that we can by no means conceive how any size, figure, or motion of any particles can possibly produce in us the idea of any colour, taste, or sound whatsoever : there is no conceivable connexion betwixt the one and the other.

14. So that, let our complex idea of any species of substances be what it will, we can hardly, from the simple ideas contained in it, certainly determine the necessary co-existence of any other quality whatsoever. Our knowledge in all these inquiries reaches very little further than our experience. Indeed some few of the primary qualities have a necessary dependence and visible connexion one with another, as figure necessarily supposes extension; receiving or communicating motion by impulse supposes solidity. But though these, and perhaps some others of our ideas have, yet there are so few of them that have a visible connexion one with another, that we can by intuition or demonstration discover the co-existence of very few of the qualities are to be found united in substances;

and we are left only to the assistance of our senses to make known to us what qualities they contain. For this co-existence can be no further known than it is perceived; and it cannot be perceived but either in particular subjects, by the observation of our senses, or, in general, by the necessary connexion of the ideas themselves.

(15.) *Of Repugnancy to co-exist, larger.* As to the incompatibility or repugnancy to co-existence, we may know that any subject can have of each sort of primary qualities but one particular at once : v.g. each particular extension, figure, number of parts, motion, excludes all other of each kind. The like also is certain of all sensible ideas peculiar to each sense; for whatever of each kind is present in any subject excludes all other of that sort : v.g. no one subject can have two smells or two colours at the same time. To this, perhaps will be said, has not an opal, or the infusion of *lignum nephriticum,* two colours at the same time? To which I answer. that these bodies, to eyes differently placed, may at the same time afford different colours; but I take liberty also to say that, to eyes differently placed, it is different parts of the object that reflect the particles of light; and therefore it is not the same part of the object, and so not the very same subject, which at the same time appears both yellow and azure. For, it is as impossible that the very same particle of any body should at the same time differently modify or reflect the rays of light, as that it should have two different figures and textures at the same time.

(16) *Of the Co-existence of Powers a very little Way.* But as to the powers of substances to change the sensible qualities of other bodies, which make a great part of our inquiries about them, and is no inconsiderable branch of our knowledge; I doubt as to these whether our knowledge reaches much further than our experience, or whether we can come to the discovery of most of these powers, and be certain that they are in any subject, by the connexion with any of those ideas which to us make its essence. Because the active and passive powers of bodies, and their ways of operating, consisting in a texture and motion of parts which we cannot by any means come to

discover, it is but in very few cases we can be able to perceive their dependence on, or repugnance to, any of those ideas which make our complex one of that sort of things.

17) *Spirits yet narrower.* If we are at a loss in respect of the powers and operations of bodies, I think it is easy to conclude we are much more in the dark in reference to spirits; whereof we naturally have no ideas but what we draw from that of our own, by reflecting on the operations of our own souls within us, as far as they can come within our observation.

18) *Thirdly, of other Relations it is not easy to say how far.* As to the third sort of our knowledge, viz. the agreement or disagreement of any of our ideas in any other relation : this, as it is the largest field of our knowledge, so it is hard to determine how far it may extend, because the advances that are made in this part of knowledge, depending on our sagacity in finding intermediate ideas, that may show the relations and habitudes of ideas whose co-existence is not considered, it is a hard matter to tell when we are at an end of such discoveries, and when reason has all the helps it is capable of, for the finding of proofs, or examining the agreement or disagreement of remote ideas. They that are ignorant of algebra cannot imagine the wonders in this kind are to be done by it, and what further improvements and helps advantageous to other parts of knowledge the sagacious mind of man may yet find out it is not easy to determine. This at least I believe, that the ideas of quantity are not those alone that are capable of demonstration and knowledge; and that other, and perhaps more useful, parts of contemplation would afford us certainty, if vices, passions, and domineering interest did not oppose or menace such endeavours.

Morality capable of Demonstration. The idea of a supreme Being, infinite in power, goodness, and wisdom, whose workmanship we are, and on whom we depend, and the idea of ourselves, as understanding, rational creatures, being such as are clear in us, would, I suppose, if duly considered and pursued, afford such foundations of our duty and rules of action as might place *morality* amongst the *sciences capable of demonstration*; wherein I doubt not but from self-evident propositions, by necessary consequences, as incontestible as those in mathematics, the measures of right and wrong might be made out, to anyone that will apply himself with the same indifferency and attention to the one as he does to the other of these sciences. The *relation* of other *modes* may certainly be perceived, as well as those of number and extension; and I cannot see why they should not also be capable of demonstration, if due methods were thought on to examine or pursue their agreement or disagreement. " Where there is no property there is no injustice " is a proposition as certain as any demonstration in Euclid; for the idea of property being a right to anything, and the idea to which the name ' Injustice ' is given being the invasion or violation of that right, it is evident that these ideas, being thus established, and these names annexed to them, I can as certainly know this proposition to be true as that a triangle has three angles equal to two right ones. Again : " No government allows absolute liberty ". The idea of government being the establishment of society upon certain rules or laws which require conformity to them, and the idea of absolute liberty being for anyone to do whatever he please, I am as capable of being certain of the truth of this proposition as of any in mathematics.

(19.) *Two things have made moral Ideas thought incapable of Demonstration. Their complexities and want of sensible Representation.* That which in this respect has given the advantage to the ideas of quantity, and made them thought more capable of certainty and demonstration, is,

First, that they can be set down and represented by sensible marks, which have a greater and nearer correspondence with them than any words or sounds whatsoever. Diagrams drawn on paper are copies of the ideas in the mind, and not liable to the uncertainty that words carry in their signification. An angle, circle, or square, drawn in lines, lies open to the view, and cannot be mistaken; it remains unchangeable, and may at leisure be considered and examined, and the demonstration be revised, and all the parts of it may be gone over more than once, without any danger of the least change in the ideas. This cannot be thus done in moral ideas :

we have no sensible marks that resemble them, whereby we can set them down; we have nothing but words to express them by; which, though when written they remain the same, yet the ideas they stand for may change in the same man; and it is very seldom that they are not different in different persons.

Secondly, another thing that makes the greater difficulty in ethics is that moral ideas are commonly more complex than those of the figures ordinarily considered in mathematics. From whence these two inconveniences follow: first, that their names are of more uncertain signification, the precise collection of simple ideas they stand for not being so easily agreed on; and so the sign that is used for them in communication always, and in thinking often, does not steadily carry with it the same idea. Secondly, that the mind cannot easily retain those precise combinations so exactly and perfectly as is necessary in the examination of the habitudes and correspondences, agreements or disagreements, of several of them one with another; especially where it is to be judged of by long deductions, and the intervention of several other complex ideas to show the agreement or disagreement of two remote ones.

20. *Remedies of these Difficulties.* One part of these disadvantages in moral ideas which has made them be thought not capable of demonstration may in a good measure be remedied by definitions, setting down that collection of simple ideas which every term shall stand for, and then using the terms steadily and constantly for that precise collection. And what methods algebra, or something of that kind, may hereafter suggest, to remove the other difficulties, is not easy to foretell. Confident I am that, if men would in the same method, and with the same indifferency, search after moral as they do mathematical truths, they would find them to have a stronger connexion one with another, and a more necessary consequence from our clear and distinct ideas, and to come nearer perfect demonstration than is commonly imagined.

21. *Fourthly, of real Existence we have an intuitive Knowledge of our own, demonstrative of God's, sensible of some few other Things.* As to the fourth sort of our knowledge, viz. of the *real actual existence of things,* we have an intuitive

knowledge of *our own existence*, and a demonstrative knowledge of the existence of a *God* : of the existence of *anything
else*, we have no other but a sensitive knowledge; which
extends not beyond the objects present to our senses.

22. *Our Ignorance great.* Our knowledge being so narrow,
as I have shown, it will perhaps give us some light into the
present state of our minds if we look a little into the dark side,
and consider the *causes of our ignorance*; which, from what
has been said, I suppose will be found to be chiefly these
three :—

First, want of ideas.

Secondly, want of a discoverable connexion between the
ideas we have.

Thirdly, want of tracing and examining our ideas.

23. *First, One cause of want of Ideas, either such as we have
no conception of, or such as particularly we have not.
First*, there are some things, and those not a few, that we are
ignorant of, for want of ideas.

First, all the simple ideas we have are confined (as I have
shown) to those we receive from corporeal objects by sensation,
and from the operations of our own minds as the objects of
reflection. But how much these few and narrow inlets are
disproportionate to the vast whole extent of all beings will
not be hard to persuade those who are not so foolish as to
think their span the measure of all things. What other simple
ideas it is possible the creatures in other parts of the universe
may have, by the assistance of senses and faculties more or
perfecter than we have, or different from ours, it is not for us
to determine. But to say or think there are no such, because
we conceive nothing of them, is no better an argument than
if a blind man should be positive in it, that there was no such
thing as sight and colours, because he had no manner of idea
of any such thing, nor could by any means frame to himself
any notions about seeing. And we may be convinced that the
ideas we can attain to by our faculties are very disproportionate
to things themselves, when a positive, clear, distinct one of
substance itself, which is the foundation of all the rest, is
concealed from us. But want of ideas of this kind, being a part

as well as cause of our ignorance, cannot be described. Only this I think I may confidently say of it, that the intellectual and sensible world are in this perfectly alike; that that part which we see of either of them holds no proportion with what we see not; and whatsoever we can reach with our eyes or our thoughts of either of them is but a point, almost nothing in comparison of the rest.

24. *Because of their remoteness, or,* Secondly, another great cause of ignorance is the want of ideas we are capable of. The want of ideas I now speak of keeps us in ignorance of things we conceive capable of being known to us. Bulk, figure, and motion we have ideas of. But though we are not without ideas of these primary qualities of bodies in general, yet not knowing what is the particular bulk, figure, and motion, of the greatest part of the bodies of the universe, we are ignorant of the several powers, efficacies, and ways of operation, whereby the effects which we daily see are produced. These are hid from us, in some things by being too remote, and in others by being too minute. When we consider the vast distance of the known and visible parts of the world, and the reasons we have to think that what lies within our ken is but a small part of the immense universe, we shall then discover a huge abyss of ignorance. If we narrow our contemplation, and confine our thoughts to this little canton, I mean this system of our sun, and the grosser masses of matter that visibly move about it, what several sorts of vegetables, animals, and intellectual corporeal beings, infinitely different from those of our little spot of earth, may there probably be in the other planets, to the knowledge of which, even of their outward figures and parts, we can no way attain whilst we are confined to this earth; there being no natural means, either by sensation or reflection, to convey their certain ideas into our minds? They are out of the reach of those inlets of all our knowledge; and what sorts of furniture and inhabitants those mansions contain in them we cannot so much as guess, much less have clear and distinct ideas of them.

25. *Because of their Minuteness.* If a great, nay, far the greatest part of the several ranks of bodies in the universe

escape our notice by their remoteness, there are others that are no less concealed from us by their minuteness. These insensible corpuscles being the active parts of matter, and the great instruments of nature, on which depend not only all their secondary qualities, but also most of their natural operations, our want of precise distinct ideas of their primary qualities keeps us in an incurable ignorance of what we desire to know about them. I doubt not but if we could discover the figure, size, texture, and motion of the minute constituent parts of any two bodies, we should know without trial several of their operations one upon another; as we do now the properties of a square or a triangle. But whilst we are destitute of senses acute enough to discover the minute particles of bodies, and to give us ideas of their mechanical affections, we must be content to be ignorant of their properties and ways of operation; nor can we be assured about them any further than some few trials we make are able to reach. But whether they will succeed again another time we cannot be certain. This hinders our certain knowledge of universal truths concerning natural bodies; and our reason carries us herein very little beyond particular matter of fact.

(26.) *Hence no Science of Bodies.* And therefore I am apt to doubt that, how far soever human industry may advance useful and experimental philosophy in *physical* things, *scientifical* will still be out of our reach, because we want perfect and adequate ideas of those very bodies which are nearest to us, and most under our command. Those which we have ranked into classes under names, and we think ourselves best acquainted with, we have but very imperfect and incomplete ideas of. Distinct ideas of the several sorts of bodies that fall under the examination of our senses perhaps we may have; but adequate ideas, I suspect, we have not of any one amongst them. And though the former of these will serve us for common use and discourse, yet whilst we want the latter, we are not capable of scientifical knowledge; nor shall ever be able to discover general, instructive, unquestionable truths concerning them. *Certainty* and *demonstration* are things we must not, in these matters, pretend to. By the colour, figure, taste, and smell, and other sensible qualities, we have as clear and distinct ideas of sage and hemlock, as we have of a circle and a triangle; but having no ideas of the particular primary qualities of the minute parts of either of these plants, nor of other bodies which we would apply them to, we cannot tell what effects they will produce; nor when we see those effects can we so much as guess, much less know, their manner of production.

27. *Much less Spirits.* To which if we add the consideration of that infinite number of spirits that may be, and probably are, which are yet more remote from our knowledge, whereof we have no cognizance, nor can frame to ourselves any distinct ideas of their several ranks and sorts, we shall find this cause of ignorance conceal from us in an impenetrable obscurity almost the whole intellectual world; a greater certainly, and more beautiful world than the material. That there are minds and thinking beings in other men as well as himself every man has a reason, from their words and actions, to be satisfied; and the knowledge of his own mind cannot suffer a man that considers to be ignorant that there is a God. But that there are degrees of spiritual beings between us and the great God, who is there, that, by his own search and ability, can come to know? Much less have we distinct ideas of their different natures, conditions, states, powers, and several constitutions wherein they agree or differ from one another and from us. And, therefore, in what concerns their different species and properties we are under an absolute ignorance.

28. *Secondly, want of a discoverable Connexion between Ideas we have.* Secondly, another cause of ignorance, of no less moment, is a want of a discoverable connexion between those ideas which we have. For wherever we want that, we are utterly incapable of universal and certain knowledge; and are, in the former case, left only to observation and experiment; which, how narrow and confined it is, how far from general knowledge, we need not be told. I shall give some few instances of this cause of our ignorance, and so leave it. It is evident that the bulk, figure, and motion of several bodies about us produce in us several sensations, as of colours, sounds,

tastes, smells, pleasure, and pain, &c. These mechanical affections of bodies having no affinity at all with those ideas they produce in us (there being no conceivable connexion between any impulse of any sort of body and any perception of a colour or smell which we find in our minds), we can have no distinct knowledge of such operations beyond our experience; and can reason no otherwise about them than as effects produced by the appointment of an infinitely wise Agent, which perfectly surpass our comprehensions. As the ideas of sensible secondary qualities which we have in our minds can by us be no way deduced from bodily causes, nor any correspondence or connexion be found between them and those primary qualities which (experience shows us) produce them in us; so, on the other side, the operation of our minds upon our bodies is as inconceivable. How any thought should produce a motion in body is as remote from the nature of our ideas, as how any body should produce any thought in the mind. That it is so, if experience did not convince us, the consideration of the things themselves would never be able in the least to discover to us. These, and the like, though they have a constant and regular connexion in the ordinary course of things; yet that connexion being not discoverable in the ideas themselves, which appearing to have no necessary dependence one on another, we can attribute their connexion to nothing else but the arbitrary determination of that all-wise Agent who has made them to be, and to operate as they do, in a way wholly above our weak understandings to conceive.

(29.) *Instances.* In some of our ideas there are certain relations, habitudes, and connexions, so visibly included in the nature of the ideas themselves, that we cannot conceive them separable from them by any power whatsoever. And in these only we are capable of certain and universal knowledge. Thus the idea of a right-lined triangle necessarily carries with it an equality of its angles to two right ones. Nor can we conceive this relation, this connexion of these two ideas, to be possibly mutable, or to depend on any arbitrary power, which of choice made it thus, or could make it otherwise. But the coherence and continuity of the parts of matter; the production of sensation in us of colours and sounds, &c., by impulse and motion; nay, the original rules and communication of motion being such, wherein we can discover no natural connexion with any ideas we have, we cannot but ascribe them to the arbitrary will and good pleasure of the Wise Architect. I need not, I think, here mention the resurrection of the dead, the future state of this globe of earth, and such other things, which are by everyone acknowledged to depend wholly on the determination of a free agent. The things that, as far as our observation reaches, we constantly find to proceed regularly, we may conclude do act by a law set them; but yet by a law that we know not; whereby, though causes work steadily, and effects constantly flow from them, yet their connexions and dependencies being not discoverable in our ideas, we can have but an experimental knowledge of them. But as to a *perfect science* of natural bodies, (not to mention spiritual beings,) we are, I think, so far from being capable of any such thing, that I conclude it lost labour to seek after it.

30. *Thirdly, want of tracing our Ideas.* Thirdly, where we have adequate ideas, and where there is a certain and discoverable connexion between them, yet we are often ignorant, for want of tracing those ideas which we have or may have; and for want of finding out those intermediate ideas, which may show us what habitude of agreement or disagreement they have one with another. And thus many are ignorant of mathematical truths, not out of any imperfection of their faculties, or uncertainty in the things themselves, but for want of application in acquiring, examining, and by due ways comparing those ideas. That which has most contributed to hinder the due tracing of our ideas, and finding out their relations, and agreements or disagreements, one with another, has been, I suppose, the ill use of words. But having spoken sufficiently of words, and the ill or careless use that is commonly made of them, I shall not say anything more of it here.

31. *Extent in respect of Universality.* Hitherto we have examined the extent of our knowledge, in respect of the several sorts of beings that are. There is another extent of it, in respect of *universality,* which will also deserve to be

considered; and in this regard our knowledge follows the nature of our ideas. If the ideas are abstract, whose agreement or disagreement we perceive, our knowledge is universal. For what is known of such general ideas will be true of every particular thing in whom that essence, i.e. that abstract idea, is to be found; and what is once known of such ideas will be perpetually and for ever true. So that as to all general knowledge we must search and find it only in our own minds; and it is only the examining of our own ideas that furnisheth us with that. Truths belonging to essences of things (that is, to abstract ideas) are eternal; and are to be found out by the contemplation only of those essences; as the existence of things is to be known only from experience. But having more to say of this in the chapters where I shall speak of general and real knowledge,[1] this may here suffice as to the universality of our knowledge in general.

CHAPTER IV

OF THE REALITY OF KNOWLEDGE

1. *Objection, Knowledge placed in Ideas may be all bare vision.* I doubt not but my reader, by this time, may be apt to think that I have been all this while only building a castle in the air; and be ready to say to me: "To what purpose all this stir? Knowledge, say you, is only the perception of the agreement or disagreement of our own ideas: but who knows what those ideas may be? If it be true, the visions of an enthusiast and the reasonings of a sober man will be equally certain. It is no matter how things are; so a man observe but the agreement of his own imaginations, and talk conformably, it is all truth, all certainty. Such castles in the air will be as strongholds of truth as the demonstrations of Euclid. That an harpy is not a centaur is by this way as certain knowledge, and as much a truth, as that a square is not a circle.

[1] IV v-viii

But of what use is all this fine knowledge of men's own imaginations to a man that inquires after the reality of things? It matters not what men's fancies are, it is the knowledge of things that is only to be prized; it is this alone gives a value to our reasonings, and preference to one man's knowledge over another's, that it is of things as they really are, and not of dreams and fancies."

(2.) *Answer. Not so, where Ideas agree with Things.* To which I answer, that if our knowledge of our ideas terminate in them, and reach no further, where there is something further intended, our most serious thoughts will be of little more use than the reveries of a crazy brain; and the truths built thereon of no more weight than the discourses of a man who sees things clearly in a dream, and with great assurance utters them. But I hope, before I have done, to make it evident that this way of certainty, by the knowledge of our own ideas, goes a little further than bare imagination; and I believe it will appear that all the certainty of general truths a man has lies in nothing else.

(3.) It is evident the mind knows not things immediately, but only by the intervention of the ideas it has of them. Our knowledge, therefore, is real only so far as there is a conformity between our ideas and the reality of things. But what shall be here the criterion? How shall the mind, when it perceives nothing but its own ideas, know that they agree with things themselves? This, though it seems not to want difficulty, yet, I think, there be two sorts of ideas that we may be assured agree with things.

(4.) *As, First, All Simple Ideas do. First,* the first are simple ideas, which since the mind, as has been showed, can by no means make to itself, must necessarily be the product of things operating on the mind, in a natural way, and producing therein those perceptions which by the wisdom and will of our Maker they are ordained and adapted to. From whence it follows that simple ideas are not fictions of our fancies, but the natural and regular productions of things without us, really operating upon us; and so carry with them all the conformity which is intended, or which our state requires; for they represent to us things under those appearances which they are fitted to produce in us, whereby we are enabled to distinguish the sorts of particular substances, to discern the states they are in, and so to take them for our necessities, and apply them to our uses. Thus the idea of whiteness, or bitterness, as it is in the mind exactly answering that power which is in any body to produce it there, has all the real conformity it can or ought to have, with things without us. And this conformity between our simple ideas and the existence of things is sufficient for real knowledge.

5. *Secondly, All Complex Ideas except of Substances.* Secondly, all our complex ideas, *except those of substances,* being archetypes of the mind's own making, not intended to be the copies of anything, nor referred to the existence of anything, as to their originals, cannot want any conformity necessary to real knowledge. For that which is not designed to represent anything but itself can never be capable of a wrong representation, nor mislead us from the true apprehension of anything, by its dislikeness to it; and such, excepting those of substances, are all our complex ideas. So that we cannot but be infallibly certain that all the knowledge we attain concerning these ideas is real, and reaches things themselves. Because in all our thoughts, reasonings, and discourses of this kind, we intend things no further than as they are conformable to our ideas. So that in these we cannot miss of a certain and undoubted reality.

6. *Hence the reality of Mathematical Knowledge.* I doubt not but it will be easily granted that the knowledge we have of mathematical truths is not only certain, but real knowledge, and not the bare empty vision of vain, insignificant chimeras of the brain; and yet, if we will consider, we shall find that it is only of our own ideas. The mathematician considers the truth and properties belonging to a rectangle or circle only as they are in idea in his own mind. For it is possible he never found either of them existing mathematically, i.e. precisely true, in his life. But yet the knowledge he has of any truths or properties belonging to a circle, or any other mathematical figure, are nevertheless true and certain, even of real things existing;

because real things are no further concerned, nor intended to be meant by any such propositions, than as things really agree to those archetypes in his mind. Is it true of the *idea* of a triangle that its three angles are equal to two right ones? It is true also of a triangle, wherever it *really exists*. Whatever other figure exists, that is not exactly answerable to that idea of a triangle in his mind, is not at all concerned in that proposition. And therefore he is certain all his knowledge concerning such ideas is real knowledge.

7. *And of Moral.* And hence it follows that moral knowledge is as capable of real certainty as mathematics. For certainty being but the perception of the agreement or disagreement of our ideas, and demonstration nothing but the perception of such agreement, by the intervention of other ideas or mediums; our moral ideas, as well as mathematical, being archetypes themselves, and so adequate and complete ideas; all the agreement or disagreement which we shall find in them will produce real knowledge, as well as in mathematical figures.

8. *Existence not required to make it real.* Nor let it be wondered that I place the certainty of our knowledge in the consideration of our ideas, with so little care and regard (as it may seem) to the real existence of things. All the discourses of the mathematicians about the squaring of a circle, conic sections, or any other part of mathematics, concern not the existence of any of those figures; but their demonstrations, which depend on their ideas, are the same, whether there be any square or circle existing in the world or no. In the same manner, the truth and certainty of moral discourses abstracts from the lives of men, and the existence of those virtues in the world whereof they treat; nor are Tully's *Offices* less true, because there is nobody in the world that exactly practises his rules, and lives up to that pattern of a virtuous man which he has given us, and which existed nowhere when he writ but in idea. If it be true in speculation, i.e. in idea, that murder deserves death, it will also be true in reality of any action that exists conformable to that idea of murder.

9. *Nor will it be less true or certain, because Moral Ideas are*

of our own making and naming. But it will here be said that, if moral knowledge be placed in the contemplation of our own moral ideas, and those, as other modes, be of our own making, what strange notions will there be of justice and temperance? What confusion of virtues and vices, if everyone may make what ideas of them he pleases? No confusion nor disorder in the things themselves, nor the reasonings about them; no more than (in mathematics) there would be a disturbance in the demonstration, or a change in the properties of figures, and their relations one to another, if a man should change the names of the figures, and call that by one name which mathematicians call ordinarily by another. Just the same is it in moral knowledge : let a man have the idea of taking from others, without their consent, what their honest industry has possessed them of, and call this *justice* if he please. He that takes the name here without the idea put to it will be mistaken, by joining another idea of his own to that name; but strip the idea of that name, or take it such as it is in the speaker's mind, and the same things will agree to it as if you called it *injustice.* But yet for all this, the miscalling of any of those ideas, contrary to the usual signification of the words of that language, hinders not but that we may have certain and demonstrative knowledge of their several agreements and disagreements, if we will carefully, as in mathematics, keep to the same precise ideas, and trace them in their several relations one to another, without being led away by their names. If we but separate the idea under consideration from the sign that stands for it, our knowledge goes equally on in the discovery of real truth and certainty, whatever sounds we make use of.

(11. *Ideas of Substances have their Archetypes without us.* Thirdly, there is another sort of complex ideas, which, being referred to archetypes without us, may differ from them, and so our knowledge about them may come short of being real. Such are our ideas of substances, which, consisting of a collection of simple ideas, supposed taken from the works of nature, may yet vary from them by having more or different ideas united in them than are to be found united in the things themselves. From whence it comes to

pass, that they may, and often do, fail of being exactly conformable to things themselves.

12. *So far as they agree with those so far our Knowledge concerning them is real.* The reason whereof is because we knowing not what real constitution it is of substances whereon our simple ideas depend, and which really is the cause of the strict union of some of them one with another, and the exclusion of others, there are very few of them that we can be sure are or are not inconsistent in nature, any further than experience and sensible observation reaches. Herein, therefore, is founded the reality of our knowledge concerning substances : that all our complex ideas of them must be such, and such only, as are made up of such simple ones as have been discovered to co-exist in nature. And our ideas being thus true, though not perhaps very exact copies, are yet the subjects of real (as far as we have any) knowledge of them. Which (as has been already shown) will not be found to reach very far; but so far as it does, it will still be real knowledge.

13. *In our inquiries about Substances, we must consider Ideas, and not confine our Thoughts to Names, or Species supposed set out by Names.* This if we rightly consider, and confine not our thoughts and abstract ideas to names, as if there were, or could be no other *sorts* of things than what known names had already determined, and, as it were, set out, we should think of things with greater freedom and less confusion than perhaps we do. It would possibly be thought a bold paradox, if not a very dangerous falsehood, if I should say that some *changelings,* who have lived forty years together, without any appearance of reason, are something between a man and a beast; which prejudice is founded upon nothing else but a false supposition, that these two names, ' man ' and ' beast ', stand for distinct species so set out by real essences, that there can come no other species between them; whereas if we will abstract from those names, and the supposition of such specific essences made by nature, wherein all things of the same denominations did exactly and equally partake; if we would not fancy that there were a certain number of these essences, wherein all things, as in moulds, were cast and

formed; we should find that the idea of the shape, motion, and life of a man without reason is as much a distinct idea, and makes as much a distinct sort of things from man and beast, as the idea of the shape of an ass with reason would be different from either that of man or beast, and be a species of an animal between, or distinct from both.

(14) *Objection against a Changeling being something between a Man and Beast, answered.* Here everybody will be ready to ask, If changelings may be supposed something between man and beast, pray what are they? I answer, *changelings*; which is as good a word to signify something different from the signification of 'man' or 'beast', as the names 'man' and 'beast' are to have significations different one from the other. This, well considered, would resolve this matter, and show my meaning without any more ado.

(17) *Words and Species.* I have mentioned this here, because I think we cannot be too cautious that words and species, in the ordinary notions which we have been used to of them, impose not on us. For, I am apt to think, therein lies one great obstacle to our clear and distinct knowledge, especially in reference to substances; and from thence has rose a great part of the difficulties about truth and certainty. Would we accustom ourselves to separate our contemplations and reasonings from words, we might in a great measure remedy this inconvenience within our own thoughts; but yet it would still disturb us in our discourse with others, as long as we retained the opinion that species and their essences were anything else but our abstract ideas (such as they are) with names annexed to them, to be the signs of them.

— STOP —

CHAPTER V

OF TRUTH IN GENERAL

1. *What Truth is.* What is truth was an inquiry many ages since; and it being that which all mankind either do, or pretend to, search after, it cannot but be worth our while carefully to examine wherein it consists, and so acquaint ourselves with the nature of it, as to observe how the mind distinguishes it from falsehood.

2. *A right joining or separating of Signs, i.e. Ideas or Words.* Truth, then, seems to me, in the proper import of the word, to signify nothing but *the joining or separating of Signs, as the Things signified by them do agree or disagree one with another.* The joining or separating of signs here meant is what by another name we call *proposition.* So that truth properly belongs only to propositions; whereof there are two sorts, viz. mental and verbal, as there are two sorts of signs commonly made use of, viz. ideas and words.

3. *Which make mental or verbal Propositions.* To form a clear notion of truth, it is very necessary to consider truth of thought, and truth of words, distinctly one from another; but yet it is very difficult to treat of them asunder. Because it is unavoidable, in treating of mental propositions, to make use of words; and then the instances given of mental propositions cease immediately to be barely mental, and become verbal. For a mental proposition being nothing but a bare consideration of the ideas as they are in our minds, stripped of names, they lose the nature of purely mental propositions as soon as they are put into words.

4. *Mental Propositions are very hard to be treated of.* And that which makes it yet harder to treat of mental and verbal propositions separately is that most men, if not all, in their thinking and reasonings within themselves make use of words instead of ideas, at least when the subject of

their meditation contains in it complex ideas. For when we make any propositions within our own thoughts about *white* or *black, sweet* or *bitter,* a *triangle* or a *circle,* we can and often do frame in our minds the ideas themselves, without reflecting on the names. But when we would consider, or make propositions about the more complex ideas, as of a *man, vitriol, fortitude, glory,* we usually put the name for the idea; because the ideas these names stand for being for the most part imperfect, confused, and undetermined, we reflect on the names themselves, because they are more clear, certain, and distinct, and readier occur to our thoughts than the pure ideas; and so we make use of these words instead of the ideas themselves, even when we would meditate and reason within ourselves, and make tacit mental propositions. In substances, as has been already noted, this is occasioned by the imperfections of our ideas; we making the name stand for the real essence, of which we have no idea at all. In modes, it is occasioned by the great number of simple ideas that go to the making them up. For many of them being compounded, the name occurs much easier than the complex idea itself, and is utterly impossible to be done by those who, though they have ready in their memory the greatest part of the common words of their language, yet perhaps never troubled themselves in all their lives to consider what precise ideas the most of them stood for.

5. *Being nothing but the joining or separating Ideas without Words.* · But to return to the consideration of truth : we must, I say, observe two sorts of propositions that we are capable of making :—

First, *mental,* wherein the ideas in our understandings are without the use of words put together, or separated, by the mind perceiving or judging of their agreement or disagreement.

Secondly, *verbal* propositions, which are words, the signs of our ideas, put together or separated in affirmative or negative sentences. By which way of affirming or denying, these signs made by sounds are, as it were, put together or separated one from another. So that proposition consists in joining or separating signs; and truth consists in the putting together or separating these signs, according as the things which they stand for agree or disagree.

6. *When Mental Propositions contain real Truth, and when verbal.* Everyone's experience will satisfy him that the mind, either by perceiving, or supposing, the agreement or disagreement of any of its ideas, does tacitly within itself put them into a kind of proposition affirmative or negative; which I have endeavoured to express by the terms ' putting together ' and ' separating '. But this action of the mind, which is so familiar to every thinking and reasoning man, is easier to be conceived by reflecting on what passes in us when we affirm or deny than to be explained by words. When ideas are so put together, or separated in the mind, as they or the things they stand for do agree or not, that is, as I may call it, *mental truth.* But *truth of words* is something more; and that is the affirming or denying of words one of another, as the ideas they stand for agree or disagree; and this again is two-fold : either purely verbal and trifling, which I shall speak of, (chap. viii.,) or real and instructive; which is the object of that real knowledge which we have spoken of already.

7. *Objection against verbal Truth, that thus it may all be chimerical.* But here again will be apt to occur the same doubt about truth, that did about knowledge; and it will be objected that, if truth be nothing but the joining or separating of words in propositions, as the ideas they stand for agree or disagree in men's minds, the knowledge of truth is not so valuable a thing as it is taken to be, nor worth the pains and time men employ in the search of it; since by this account it amounts to no more than the conformity of words to the chimeras of men's brains. Who knows not what odd notions many men's heads are filled with, and what strange ideas all men's brains are capable of? But if we rest here, we know the truth of nothing by this rule, but of the visionary world in our own imaginations; nor have other truth but what as much concerns harpies and centaurs, as men and horses.

8. *Answered, real Truth is about Ideas agreeing to things.* Yet it may not be amiss here again to consider that, though our words signify nothing but our ideas, yet being designed

by them to signify things, the truth they contain when put into propositions will be only verbal, when they stand for ideas in the mind that have not an agreement with the reality of things. And therefore truth as well as knowledge may well come under the distinction of verbal and real; that being only *verbal truth,* wherein terms are joined according to the agreement or disagreement of the ideas they stand for, without regarding whether our ideas are such as really have, or are capable of having, an existence in nature. But then it is they contain *real truth,* when these signs are joined as our ideas agree; and when our ideas are such as we know are capable of having an existence in nature; which in substances we cannot know but by knowing that such have existed.

9. *Falsehood is the joining of names otherwise than their Ideas agree.* Truth is the marking down in words the agreement or disagreement of ideas as it is. Falsehood is the marking down in words the agreement or disagreement of ideas otherwise than it is. And so far as these ideas, thus marked by sounds, agree to their archetypes, so far only is the truth real. The knowledge of this truth consists in knowing what ideas the words stand for, and the perception of the agreement or disagreement of those ideas, according as it is marked by those words.

10. *General Propositions to be treated of more at large.* But because words are looked on as the great conduits of truth and knowledge, and that in conveying and receiving of truth, and commonly in reasoning about it, we make use of words and propositions, I shall more at large inquire wherein the certainty of real truths contained in propositions consists, and where it is to be had; and endeavour to show in what sort of universal propositions we are capable of being certain of their real truth or falsehood.

I shall begin with general propositions, as those which most employ our thoughts, and exercise our contemplation. General truths are most looked after by the mind as those that most enlarge our knowledge; and, by their comprehensiveness satisfying us at once of many particulars, enlarge our view, and shorten our way to knowledge.

CHAPTER VI

OF UNIVERSAL PROPOSITIONS,
THEIR TRUTH AND CERTAINTY

2. *General Truths hardly to be understood, but in verbal Propositions.* All the knowledge we have being only of particular or general truths, is it evident that whatever may be done in the former of these, the latter, which is that which with reason is most sought after, can never be well made known, and is very seldom apprehended, but as conceived and expressed in words. It is not, therefore, out of our way, in the examination of our knowledge, to inquire into the truth and certainty of universal propositions.

3. *Certainty twofold—of Truth and of Knowledge.* But that we may not be misled in this case by that which is the danger everywhere, I mean by the doubtfulness of terms, it is fit to observe that certainty is twofold : *certainty of truth* and *certainty of knowledge.* Certainty of truth is when words are so put together in propositions as exactly to express the agreement or disagreement of the ideas they stand for, as really it is. Certainty of knowledge is to perceive the agreement or disagreement of ideas, as expressed in any proposition. This we usually call knowing, or being certain of the truth of any proposition.

4. *No Proposition can be known to be true, where the Essence of each Species mentioned is not known.* Now, because we cannot be certain of the truth of any general proposition, unless we know the precise bounds and extent of the species its terms stand for, it is necessary we should know the essence of each species, which is that which constitutes and bounds it. This, in all simple ideas and modes, is not hard to do. For in these the real and nominal essence being the same, or, which is all one, the abstract idea which the general term stands for being the sole essence and boundary that is or

can be supposed of the species, there can be no doubt how far the species extends, or what things are comprehended under each term; which, it is evident, are all that have an exact conformity with the idea it stands for, and no other. But in substances, wherein a real essence, distinct from the nominal, is supposed to constitute, determine, and bound the species, the extent of the general word is very uncertain; because, not knowing this real essence, we cannot know what is, or what is not of that species; and, consequently, what may or may not with certainty be affirmed of it. For 'man' or 'gold', taken in this sense, and used for species of things constituted by real essences, different from the complex idea in the mind of the speaker, stand for we know not what; and the extent of these species, with such boundaries, are so unknown and undetermined, that it is impossible with any certainty to affirm that all men are rational, or that all gold is yellow. But where the nominal essence is kept to as the boundary of each species, and men extend the application of any general term no further than to the particular things in which the complex idea it stands for is to be found, there they are in no danger to mistake the bounds of each species, nor can be in doubt, on this account, whether any proposition be true or no.

5. *This more particularly concerns Substances.* The names of substances, then, whenever made to stand for species which are supposed to be constituted by real essences which we know not, are not capable to convey certainty to the understanding. Of the truth of general propositions made up of such terms we cannot be sure. The reason whereof is plain; for how can we be sure that this or that quality is in gold, when we know not what is or is not gold?

6. *The Truth of few universal Propositions concerning Substances is to be known.* On the other side, the names of substances, when made use of as they should be, for the ideas men have in their minds, though they carry a clear and determinate signification with them, will not yet serve us to make many universal propositions of whose truth we can be certain. Not because in this use of them we are uncertain what things are signified by them, but because the complex

ideas they stand for are such combinations of simple ones as carry not with them any discoverable connexion or repugnancy, but with a very few other ideas.

7. *Because Co-existence of Ideas in few Cases to be known.* The complex ideas that our names of the species of substances properly stand for are collections of such qualities as have been observed to co-exist in an unknown substratum, which we call substance; but what other qualities necessarily co-exist with such combinations we cannot certainly know, unless we can discover their natural dependence; which, in their primary qualities, we can go but a very little way in; and in all their secondary qualities we can discover no connexion at all: for the reasons mentioned, chap. iii.

8. *Instance in Gold.* " All gold is fixed " is a proposition whose truth we cannot be certain of, how universally soever it be believed. For if, according to the useless imagination of the Schools, anyone supposes the term ' gold ' to stand for a species of things set out by nature, by a real essence belonging to it, it is evident he knows not what particular substances are of that species; and so cannot with certainty affirm anything universally of gold. But if he makes ' gold ' stand for a species determined by its nominal essence, let the nominal essence, for example, be the complex idea of a body of a certain yellow colour, malleable, fusible, and heavier than any other known: in this proper use of the word ' gold ', there is no difficulty to know what is or is not gold. But yet no other quality can with certainty be universally affirmed or denied of gold, but what hath a discoverable connexion or inconsistency with that nominal essence. Fixedness, for example, having no necessary connexion that we can discover with the colour, weight, or any other simple idea of our complex one, or with the whole combination together, it is impossible that we should certainly know the truth of this proposition, that all gold is fixed.

9. As there is no discoverable connexion between fixedness and the colour, weight, and other simple ideas of that nominal essence of gold; so, if we make our complex idea of gold a body yellow, fusible, ductile, weighty, and fixed, we shall

be at the same uncertainty concerning solubility in *aqua regia,* and for the same reason. I would gladly meet with one general affirmation concerning any quality of gold, that anyone can certainly know is true. It will, no doubt, be presently objected, Is not this a universal certain proposition, " All gold is malleable "? To which I answer, It is a very certain proposition, if malleableness be a part of the complex idea the word ' gold ' stands for. But then here is nothing affirmed of gold, but that that sound stands for an idea in which malleableness is contained : and such a sort of truth and certainty as this it is to say a centaur is four-footed. But if malleableness makes not a part of the specific essence the name of ' gold ' stands for, it is plain " all gold is malleable " is not a certain proposition. Because, let the complex idea of gold be made up of whichsoever of its other qualities you please, malleableness will not appear to depend on that complex idea, nor follow from any simple one contained in it; the connexion that malleableness has (if it has any) with those other qualities being only by the intervention of the real constitution of its insensible parts; which, since we know not, it is impossible we should perceive that connexion, unless we could discover that which ties them together.

10. *As far as any such Co-existence can be known, so far Universal Propositions may be certain. But this will go but a little way.* The more, indeed, of these co-existing qualities we unite into one complex idea, under one name, the more precise and determinate we make the signification of that word; but yet never make it thereby more capable of universal certainty, in respect of other qualities not contained in our complex idea; since we perceive not their connexion or dependence one on another, being ignorant both of that real constitution in which they are all founded, and also how they flow from it. No one, I think, by the colour that is in any body, can certainly know what smell, taste, sound, or tangible qualities it has, nor what alterations it is capable to make or receive on or from other bodies. The same may be said of the sound or taste, &c. Our specific names of substances standing for any collections of such ideas, it is not to be wondered

that we can with them make very few general propositions of undoubted real certainty. But yet so far as any complex idea of any sort of substances contains in it any simple idea, whose necessary co-existence with any other may be discovered, so far universal propositions may with certainty be made concerning it; v.g. could anyone discover a necessary connexion between malleableness and the colour or weight of gold, or any other part of the complex idea signified by that name, he might make a certain universal proposition concerning gold in this respect; and the real truth of this proposition, that *all gold is malleable,* would be as certain as of this, *the three angles of all right-lined triangles are equal to two right ones.*

11. *The Qualities which make our complex Ideas of Substances depend mostly on external, remote, and unperceived Causes.* We are wont to consider the substances we meet with, each of them, as an entire thing by itself, having all its qualities in itself, and independent of other things; over-looking, for the most part, the operations of those invisible fluids they are encompassed with, and upon whose motions and operations depend the greatest part of those qualities which are taken notice of in them, and are made by us the inherent marks of distinction whereby we know and denominate them. Take the air but a minute from the greatest part of living creatures, and they presently lose sense, life, and motion. This the necessity of breathing has forced into our know-ledge. But how many other extrinsical and possibly very remote bodies do the springs of these admirable machines depend on, which are not vulgarly observed, or so much as thought on; and how many are there which the severest inquiry can never discover? We see and perceive some of the motions and grosser operations of things here about us; but whence the streams come that keep all these curious machines in motion and repair, how conveyed and modified, is beyond our notice and apprehension; and the great parts and wheels, as I may so say, of this stupendous structure of the universe, may, for aught we know, have such a connexion and depend-ence in their influences and operations one upon another, that perhaps things in this our mansion would put on quite

another face, and cease to be what they are, if some one of the stars or great bodies incomprehensibly remote from us should cease to be or move as it does. This is certain : things, however absolute and entire they seem in themselves, are but retainers to other parts of nature, for that which they are most taken notice of by us. Their observable qualities, actions, and powers are owing to something without them; and there is not so complete and perfect a part that we know of nature, which does not owe the being it has, and the excellences of it, to his neighbours; and we must not confine our thoughts within the surface of any body, but look a great deal further, to comprehend perfectly those qualities that are in it.

13. *Judgment may reach further* : *but that is not Knowledge.* We are not therefore to wonder, if certainty be to be found in very few general propositions made concerning substances; our knowledge of their qualities and properties goes very seldom further than our senses reach and inform us. Possibly inquisitive and observing men may, by strength of judgment, penetrate further, and, on probabilities taken from wary observation, and hints well laid together, often guess right at what experience has not yet discovered to them. But this is but guessing still; it amounts only to opinion, and has not that certainty which is requisite to knowledge.

14. *What is requisite for our Knowledge of Substances.* Before we can have any tolerable knowledge of this kind, we must first know what changes the primary qualities of one body do regularly produce in the primary qualities of another, and how. Secondly, we must know what primary qualities of any body produce certain sensations or ideas in us. This is in truth no less than to know all the effects of matter, under its divers modifications of bulk, figure, cohesion of parts, motion and rest. Which I think everybody will allow is utterly impossible to be known by us without revelation.

15. *Whilst our Ideas of Substances contain not their real Constitutions, we can make but few general certain Propositions concerning them.* This is evident, the abstract complex ideas of substances, for which their general names

stand, not comprehending their real constitutions, can afford us but very little universal certainty, and therefore we cannot with certainty affirm : that all men sleep by intervals; that no man can be nourished by wood or stones; that all men will be poisoned by hemlock; because these ideas have no connexion nor repugnancy with this our nominal essence of man, with this abstract idea that name stands for. We must, in these and the like, appeal to trial in particular subjects, which can reach but a little way. We must content ourselves with probability in the rest. There are animals that safely eat hemlock, and others that are nourished by wood and stones; but as long as we want ideas of those real constitutions of different sorts of animals whereon these and the like qualities and powers depend, we must not hope to reach certainty in universal propositions concerning them.

16. *Wherein lies the general Certainty of Propositions.* To conclude : general propositions, of what kind soever, are then only capable of certainty, when the terms used in them stand for such ideas, whose agreement or disagreement, as there expressed, is capable to be discovered by us. And we are then certain of their truth or falsehood, when we perceive the ideas the terms stand for to agree or not agree, according as they are affirmed or denied one of another. Whence we may take notice that general certainty is never to be found but in our ideas. Whenever we go to seek it elsewhere, in experiment or observations without us, our knowledge goes not beyond particulars. It is the contemplation of our own abstract ideas that alone is able to afford us general knowledge.

CHAPTER VII

OF MAXIMS

1. *They are self-evident.* There are a sort of propositions which, under the name of *maxims* and *axioms*, have passed for principles of science; and because they are *self-evident*, have been supposed innate, without that anybody (that I know) ever went about to show the reason and foundation of their clearness or cogency. It may, however, be worth while to inquire into the reason of their evidence, and see whether it be peculiar to them alone; and also examine how far they influence and govern our other knowledge.

2. *Wherein that Self-evidence consists.* Knowledge, as has been shown, consists in the perception of the agreement or disagreement of ideas. Now, where that agreement or disagreement is perceived immediately by itself, without the intervention or help of any other, there our knowledge is self-evident. This will appear to be so to any who will but consider any of those propositions which, without any proof, he assents to at first sight; for in all of them he will find that the reason of his assent is from that agreement or disagreement which the mind, by an immediate comparing them, finds in those ideas answering the affirmation or negation in the proposition.

3. *Self-evidence not peculiar to received Axioms.* This being so, in the next place let us consider whether this self-evidence be peculiar only to those propositions which commonly pass under the name of maxims, and have the dignity of axioms allowed them. And here it is plain that several other truths, not allowed to be axioms, partake equally with them in this self-evidence. This we shall see, if we go over these several sorts of agreement or disagreement of ideas which I have above mentioned, viz. identity, relation, co-existence, and real existence; which will discover to us that

not only those few propositions which have had the credit of maxims are self-evident, but a great many, even almost an infinite number of, other propositions are such.

4. *First, as to Identity and Diversity, all Propositions are equally self-evident.* For, *first,* the immediate perception of the agreement or disagreement of *identity* being founded in the mind's having distinct ideas, this affords us as many self-evident propositions as we have distinct ideas. Everyone that has any knowledge at all, has, as the foundation of it, various and distinct ideas; and it is the first act of the mind (without which it can never be capable of any knowledge) to know every one of its ideas by itself, and distinguish it from others. Everyone finds in himself that he knows the ideas he has; that he knows also when any one is in his understanding, and what it is; and that when more than one are there, he knows them distinctly and unconfusedly one from another; which always being so (it being impossible but that he should perceive what he perceives), he can never be in doubt, when any idea is in his mind, that it is there, and is that idea it is; and that two distinct ideas, when they are in his mind, are there, and are not one and the same idea. So that all such affirmations and negations are made without any possibility of doubt, uncertainty, or hesitation, and must necessarily be assented to as soon as understood; that is, as soon as we have in our minds determined ideas, which the terms in the proposition stand for. It is not, therefore, alone to these two general propositions, " Whatsoever is, is ", and " It is impossible for the same thing to be and not to be ", and this self-evidence belongs by any peculiar right. The perception of being, or not being, belongs no more to these vague ideas, signified by the terms ' whatsoever ' and ' thing ', than it does to any other ideas. These two general maxims, amounting to no more, in short, but this, that *the same is the same,* and *the same is not different,* are truths known in more particular instances, as well as in these general maxims; and known also in particular instances, before these general maxims are ever thought on; and draw all their force from the discernment of the mind employed about particular ideas. So that,

in respect of identity, our intuitive knowledge reaches as far as our ideas. And we are capable of making as many self-evident propositions, as we have names for distinct ideas. And I appeal to everyone's own mind, whether this proposition, " A circle is a circle ", be not as self-evident a proposition as that consisting of more general terms, " Whatsoever is, is "; and again, whether this proposition, " Blue is not red ", be not a proposition that the mind can no more doubt of, as soon as it understands the words, than it does of that axiom, " It is impossible for the same thing to be and not to be "? And so of all the like.

5. *Secondly, in Co-existence we have few self-evident Propositions.* Secondly, as to *co-existence,* or such necessary connexion between two ideas that, in the subject where one of them is supposed, there the other must necessarily be also : of such agreement or disagreement as this, the mind has an immediate perception but in very few of them. And therefore in this sort we have but very little intuitive knowledge; nor are there to be found very many propositions that are self-evident, though some there are : v.g. the idea of filling a place equal to the contents of its superficies being annexed to our idea of body, I think it is a self-evident proposition, that two bodies cannot be in the same place.

6. *Thirdly, in other Relations we may have.* Thirdly, as to the *relations of modes,* mathematicians have framed many axioms concerning that one relation of equality. As " Equals taken from equals, the remainder will be equal "; which, with the rest of that kind, however they are received for maxims by the mathematicians, and are unquestionable truths, yet, I think, that anyone who considers them will not find that they have a clearer self-evidence than these, that " One and one are equal to two "; that " If you take from the five fingers of one hand two, and from the five fingers of the other hand two, the remaining numbers will be equal ". These and a thousand other such propositions may be found in numbers, which, at the very first hearing, force the assent, and carry with them an equal, if not greater, clearness than those mathematical axioms.

7. *Fourthly, concerning real Existence, we have none.*

Fourthly, as to *real existence,* since that has no connexion with any other of our ideas but that of ourselves, and of a First Being, we have in that, concerning the real existence of all other beings, not so much as demonstrative, much less a self-evident knowledge; and, therefore, concerning those there are no maxims.

8. *These Axioms do not much influence our other Knowledge.* In the next place let us consider what influence these received maxims have upon the other parts of our knowledge. The rules established in the schools, that all reasonings are *ex præcognitis et præconcessis,* seem to lay the foundation of all other knowledge in these maxims, and to suppose them to be *præcognita.* Whereby, I think, is meant these two things : first, that these axioms are those truths that are first known to the mind; and, secondly, that upon them the other parts of our knowledge depend.

9. *Because they are not the Truths we first knew. First,* that they are not the truths first known to the mind is evident to experience, as we have shown in another place, Book I. chap. ii. Whereof the reason is very plain; for that which makes the mind assent to such propositions being nothing else but the perception it has of the agreement or disagreement of its ideas, according as it finds them affirmed or denied one of another in words it understands; and every idea being known to be what it is, and every two distinct ideas being known not to be the same, it must necessarily follow that such self-evident truths must be first known which consist of ideas that are first in the mind. And the ideas first in the mind, it is evident, are those of particular things, from whence, by slow degrees, the understanding proceeds to some few general ones; which being taken from the ordinary and familiar objects of sense, are settled in the mind, with general names to them. Thus *particular ideas* are first received and distinguished, and so knowledge got about them; and next to them, the less general or specific, which are next to particular. For abstract ideas are not so obvious or easy to children, or the yet unexercised mind, as particular ones. If they seem so to grown men, it is only because by constant and familiar use

they are made so. For, when we nicely reflect upon them, we shall find that *general ideas* are fictions and contrivances of the mind, that carry difficulty with them, and do not so easily offer themselves as we are apt to imagine. For example, does it not require some pains and skill to form the general idea of a triangle (which is yet none of the most abstract, comprehensive, and difficult), for it must be neither oblique nor rectangle, neither equilateral, equicrural, nor scalenon; but all and none of these at once. In effect, it is something imperfect, that cannot exist; an idea wherein some parts of several different and inconsistent ideas are put together.

10. *Because on them the other Parts of our Knowledge do not depend*. *Secondly*, from what has been said it plainly follows that these magnified maxims are not the principles and foundations of all our other knowledge. For if there be a great many other truths, which have as much self-evidence as they, and a great many that we know before them, it is impossible they should be the principles from which we deduce all other truths. And indeed, I think, I may ask these men, who will needs have all knowledge, besides those general principles themselves, to depend on general, innate, and self-evident principles, what principle is requisite to prove that one and one are two, that two and two are four, that three times two are six? Which, being known without any proof, do evince that either all knowledge does not depend on certain *præcognita* or general maxims, called principles; or else that these are principles; and if these are to be counted principles, a great part of numeration will be so. To which if we add all the self-evident propositions which may be made about all our distinct ideas, principles will be almost infinite, at least innumerable, which men arrive to the knowledge of, at different ages; and a great many of these innate principles they never come to know all their lives.

11. *What use these general Maxims have*. What shall we then say? Are these general maxims of no use? By no means, though perhaps their use is not that which it is commonly taken to be. But, since doubting in the least of what hath been by some men ascribed to these maxims may

be apt to be cried out against, as overturning the foundations of all the sciences, it may be worth while to consider them with respect to other parts of our knowledge, and examine more particularly to what purposes they serve, and to what not.

(1) It is evident, from what has been already said, that they are of no use to prove or confirm less general self-evident propositions.

(2) It is as plain that they are not, nor have been, the foundations whereon any science hath been built. There is, I know, a great deal of talk, propagated from scholastic men, of sciences and the maxims on which they are built; but it has been my ill-luck never to meet with any such sciences, much less any one built upon these two maxims, " What is, is ", and " It is impossible for the same to be and not to be ". And I would be glad to be shown where any such science, erected upon these or any other general axioms is to be found; and should be obliged to anyone who would lay before me the frame and system of any science so built on these or any such like maxims, that could not be shown to stand as firm without any consideration of them.

(3) They are not of use to help men forwards in the advancement of sciences, or new discoveries of yet unknown truths. Mr. Newton, in his never enough to be admired book, has demonstrated several propositions, which are so many new truths, before unknown to the world, and are further advances in mathematical knowledge : but, for the discovery of these, it was not the general maxims " What is, is ", or " The whole is bigger than a part ", or the like, that helped him. Would those who have this traditional admiration of these propositions, that they think no step can be made in knowledge without the support of an axiom, no stone laid in the building of the sciences without a general maxim, but distinguish between the method of acquiring knowledge, and of communicating, between the method of raising any science, and that of teaching it to others, as far as it is advanced, they would see that those general maxims were not the foundations on which the first discoverers raised their admirable structures, nor the keys that unlocked and opened those secrets of knowledge.

Though afterwards, when schools were erected, and sciences had their professors to teach what others had found out, they often made use of maxims, i.e. laid down certain propositions which were self-evident, or to be received for true; which being settled in the minds of their scholars as unquestionable verities, they on occasion made use of, to convince them of truths in particular instances, that were not so familiar to their minds as those general axioms which had before been inculcated to them, and carefully settled in their minds. Though these particular instances, when well reflected on, are no less self-evident to the understanding than the general maxims brought to confirm them; and it was in those particular instances that the first discoverer found the truth, without the help of the general maxims; and so may anyone else do, who with attention considers them.

To come, therefore, to the use that is made of maxims.

(1) They are of use, as has been observed, in the ordinary methods of teaching sciences as far as they are advanced; but of little or none in advancing them further.

(2) They are of use in disputes, for the silencing of obstinate wranglers, and bringing those contests to some conclusion. Whether a need of them to that end came not in in the manner following, I crave leave to inquire. The Schools, having made disputation the touchstone of men's abilities, and the criterion of knowledge, adjudged victory to him that kept the field; and he that had the last word was concluded to have the better of the argument, if not of the cause. But because by this means there was like to be no decision between skilful combatants, certain general propositions, most of them, indeed, self-evident, were introduced into the Schools; which, being such as all men allowed and agreed in, were looked on as general measures of truth, and served instead of principles (where the disputants had not laid down any other between them) beyond which there was no going, and which must not be receded from by either side. And thus these maxims, getting the name of principles, beyond which men in dispute could not retreat, were by mistake taken to be the originals and sources from whence all knowledge began, and the foundations whereon the

sciences were built. Because when in their disputes they came to any of these, they stopped there, and went no further; the matter was determined. But how much this is a mistake, hath been already shown.

12. *Maxims, if Care be not taken in the Use of Words, may prove Contradictions.* One thing further, I think, it may not be amiss to observe concerning these general maxims, that they are so far from improving or establishing our minds in true knowledge, that if our notions be wrong, loose, or unsteady, and we resign up our thoughts to the sound of words, rather than fix them on settled, determined ideas of things; I say these general maxims will serve to confirm us in mistakes; and in such a way of use of words, which is most common, will serve to prove contradictions.

19. *Little use of these Maxims in Proofs where we have clear and distinct Ideas.* So that, if rightly considered, I think we may say that where our ideas are determined in our minds, and have annexed to them by us known and steady names under those settled determinations, there is little need, or no use at all, of these maxims, to prove the agreement or disagreement of any of them. He that cannot discern the truth or falsehood of such propositions without the help of these and the like maxims, will not be helped by these maxims to do it, since he cannot be supposed to know the truth of these maxims themselves without proof, if he cannot know the truth of others without proof, which are as self-evident as these. Upon this ground it is that intuitive knowledge neither requires nor admits any proof, one part of it more than another. He that will suppose it does, takes away the foundation of all knowledge and certainty; and he that needs any proof to make him certain, and give his assent to this proposition, that two are equal to two, will also have need of a proof to make him admit that what is, is. He that needs a probation to convince him that two are not three, that white is not black, that a triangle is not a circle, &c., or any other two determined distinct ideas are not one and the same, will need also a demonstration to convince him that it is impossible for the same thing to be and not to be.

CHAPTER VIII

OF TRIFLING PROPOSITIONS

1. *Some Propositions bring no Increase to our Knowledge.* Whether the maxims treated of in the foregoing chapter be of that use to real knowledge as is generally supposed, I leave to be considered. This, I think, may confidently be affirmed, that there are universal propositions, that, though they be certainly true, yet they add no light to our understanding, bring no increase to our knowledge. Such are,

2. *As, First, Identical Propositions. First,* all purely *identical propositions.* These obviously and at first blush appear to contain no instruction in them; for when we affirm the said term of itself, whether it be barely verbal, or whether it contains any clear and real idea, it shows us nothing but what we must certainly know before, whether such a proposition be either made by, or proposed to us. Indeed, that most general one, "What is, is", may serve sometimes to show a man the absurdity he is guilty of, when, by circumlocution or equivocal terms, he would in particular instances deny the same thing of itself; because nobody will so openly bid defiance to common sense as to affirm visible and direct contradictions in plain words; or, if he does, a man is excused if he breaks off any further discourse with him.

3. But how that vindicates the making use of identical propositions, for the improvement of knowledge, from the imputation of trifling, I do not see. Let anyone repeat, as often as he pleases, that "The will is the will", or lay what stress on it he thinks fit; of what use is this, and an infinite the like propositions, for the enlarging our knowledge? Let a man abound, as much as the plenty of words which he has will permit him, in such propositions as these: "A law is a law", and "Obligation is obligation"; "Right is right", and "Wrong is wrong"; will these and the like ever help him to

an acquaintance with ethics, or instruct him or others in the knowledge of morality? Those who know not, nor perhaps ever will know, what is right and what is wrong, nor the measures of them, can with as much assurance make, and infallibly know, the truth of these and all such propositions, as he that is best instructed in morality can do. But what advance do such propositions give in the knowledge of anything necessary or useful for their conduct?

Instruction lies in something very different; and he that would enlarge his own or another's mind to truths he does not yet know, must find out intermediate ideas, and then lay them in such order one by another, that the understanding may see the agreement or disagreement of those in question. Propositions that do this are instructive; but they are far from such as affirm the same term of itself; which is no way to advance one's self or others in any sort of knowledge.

4. *Secondly, when a complex Idea is predicated of the whole.* Secondly, another sort of trifling propositions is *when a part of the complex idea is predicated of the name of the whole;* a part of the definition of the word defined. Such are all propositions wherein the genus is predicated of the species, or more comprehensive of less comprehensive terms. For what information, what knowledge, carries this proposition in it, viz. "Lead is a metal", to a man who knows the complex idea the name 'lead' stands for? All the simple ideas that go to the complex one signified by the term 'metal' being nothing but what he before comprehended and signified by the name 'lead'. Indeed, to a man that knows the signification of the word 'metal', and not of the word 'lead', it is a shorter way to explain the signification of the word 'lead' by saying it is a metal, which at once expresses several of its simple ideas, than to enumerate them one by one, telling him it is a body very heavy, fusible, and malleable.

5. *As part of the Definition of the Defined.* A like trifling it is to predicate any other part of the definition of the term defined, or to affirm any one of the simple ideas of a complex one of the name of the whole complex idea; as "All gold is

fusible ". For fusibility being one of the simple ideas that goes to the making up the complex one the sound ' gold ' stands for, what can it be but playing with sounds, to affirm that of the name ' gold ' which is comprehended in its received signification? It would be thought little better than ridiculous to affirm gravely, as a truth of moment, that gold is yellow; and I see not how it is any jot more material to say it is fusible, unless that quality be left out of the complex idea, of which the sound ' gold ' is the mark in ordinary speech.

6. *Instance, Man and Palfrey.* " Every man is an animal, or living body " is as certain a proposition as can be; but no more conducing to the knowledge of things than to say a palfrey is an ambling horse, or a neighing, ambling animal, both being only about the signification of words, and make me know but this, that body, sense, and motion, or power of sensation and moving, are three of those ideas that I always comprehend and signify by the word ' man '; and where they are not to be found together, the name ' man ' belongs not to that thing; and so of the other, that body, sense, and a certain way of going, with a certain kind of voice, are some of those ideas which I always comprehend and signify by the word ' palfrey '; and when they are not to be found together, the name ' palfrey ' belongs not to that thing. But he that shall tell me that in whatever thing sense, motion, reason, and laughter, were united, that thing had actually a notion of God, or would be cast into a sleep by opium, made indeed an instructive proposition; because neither having the notion of God, nor being cast into sleep by opium, being contained in the idea signified by the word ' man ', we are by such propositions taught something more than barely what the word ' man ' stands for; and therefore the knowledge contained in it is more than verbal.

7. *For this teaches but the Signification of Words.* Before a man makes any proposition, he is supposed to understand the terms he uses in it, or else he talks like a parrot, only making a noise by imitation, and framing certain sounds, which he has learnt of others; but not as a rational creature, using them for

signs of ideas which he has in his mind. The hearer also is supposed to understand the terms as the speaker uses them, or else he talks jargon, and makes an unintelligible noise. And therefore he trifles with words who makes such a proposition, which, when it is made, contains no more than one of the terms does, and which a man was supposed to know before: v.g. "A triangle hath three sides", or "Saffron is yellow". And this is no further tolerable than where a man goes to explain his terms to one who is supposed or declares himself not to understand him; and then it teaches only the signification of that word, and the use of that sign.

8. *But no real Knowledge.*   We can know then the truth of two sorts of propositions with perfect certainty. The one is of those trifling propositions which have a certainty in them, but it is but a verbal certainty, but not instructive. And, secondly, we can know the truth, and so may be certain in propositions, which affirm something of another, which is a necessary consequence of its precise complex idea, but not contained in it: as that the external angle of all triangles is bigger than either of the opposite internal angles. Which relation of the outward angle to either of the opposite internal angles, making no part of the complex idea signified by the name 'triangle', this is a real truth, and conveys with it instructive real knowledge.

12. *Marks of verbal Propositions. First, Predication in Abstract.*   To conclude. Barely verbal propositions may be known by these following marks:

First, all propositions wherein two abstract terms are affirmed one of another are barely about the signification of sounds. For since no abstract idea can be the same with any other but itself, when its abstract name is affirmed of any other term, it can signify no more but this, that it may, or ought to be called by that name; or that these two names signify the same idea. Thus, should anyone say that parsimony is frugality, that gratitude is justice, that this or that action is or is not temperance; however specious these and the like propositions may at first sight seem, yet when we come to press them, and examine nicely what they contain, we shall find that it all amounts to nothing but the signification of those terms.

13. *Secondly, A part of the Definition predicated of any Term.* Secondly, all propositions wherein a part of the complex idea which any term stands for is predicated of that term, are only verbal; v.g. to say that gold is a metal, or heavy. And thus all propositions wherein more comprehensive words, called genera, are affirmed of subordinate or less comprehensive, called species, or individuals, are barely verbal.

When by these two rules we have examined the propositions that make up the discourses we ordinarily meet with, both in and out of books, we shall perhaps find that a greater part of them than is usually suspected are purely about the signification of words, and contain nothing in them but the use and application of these signs.

This I think I may lay down for an infallible rule, that, wherever the distinct idea any word stands for is not known and considered, and something not contained in the idea is not affirmed or denied of it, there our thoughts stick wholly in sounds, and are able to attain no real truth or falsehood. This, perhaps, if well heeded, might save us a great deal of useless amusement and dispute; and very much shorten our trouble and wandering in the search of real and true knowledge.

CHAPTER IX

OF OUR KNOWLEDGE OF EXISTENCE

1. *General Propositions concern not Existence.* Hitherto we have only considered the essences of things; which being only abstract ideas, and thereby removed in our thoughts from particular existence (that being the proper operation of the mind, in abstraction, to consider an idea under no other existence but what it has in the understanding), gives us no knowledge of real existence at all. Where, by the way, we

may take notice that universal propositions of whose truth or falsehood we can have certain knowledge concern not existence : and further, that all particular affirmations or negations that would not be certain if they were made general, are only concerning existence; they declaring only the accidental union or separation of ideas in things existing, which, in their abstract natures, have no known necessary union or repugnancy.

2. *A threefold Knowledge of Existence.* But, leaving the nature of propositions, and different ways of predication to be considered more at large in another place, let us proceed now to inquire concerning our knowledge of the *existence of things,* and how we come by it. I say, then, that we have the knowledge of *our own existence* by intuition; of the *existence of God* by demonstration; and of *other things* by sensation.

3. *Our Knowledge of our own Existence is Intuitive.* As for *our own existence,* we perceive it so plainly and so certainly that it neither needs nor is capable of any proof. For nothing can be more evident to us than our own existence. I think, I reason, I feel pleasure and pain : can any of these be more evident to me than my own existence? If I doubt of all other things, that very doubt makes me perceive my own existence, and will not suffer me to doubt of that. For if I know I feel pain, it is evident I have as certain perception of my own existence as of the existence of the pain I feel; or if I know I doubt, I have as certain perception of the existence of the thing doubting as of that thought which I call *doubt.* Experience then convinces us that we have an *intuitive knowledge* of our own existence, and an internal infallible perception that we are. In every act of sensation, reasoning, or thinking, we are conscious to ourselves of our own being; and, in this matter, come not short of the highest degree of certainty.

CHAPTER X

OF OUR KNOWLEDGE OF THE
EXISTENCE OF A GOD

1. *We are capable of knowing certainly that there is a God.* Though God has given us no innate ideas of himself, though he has stamped no original characters on our minds, wherein we may read his being, yet having furnished us with those faculties our minds are endowed with, he hath not left himself without witness; since we have sense, perception, and reason, and cannot want a clear proof of him, as long as we carry ourselves about us. Nor can we justly complain of our ignorance in this great point, since he has so plentifully provided us with the means to discover and know him, so far as is necessary to the end of our being, and the great concernment of our happiness. But, though this be the most obvious truth that reason discovers, and though its evidence be (if I mistake not) equal to mathematical certainty, yet it requires thought and attention; and the mind must apply itself to a regular deduction of it from some part of our intuitive knowledge, or else we shall be as uncertain and ignorant of this as of other propositions, which are in themselves capable of clear demonstration. To show, therefore, that we are capable of *knowing,* i.e. *being certain* that there is a God, and how we may come by this certainty, I think we need go no further than ourselves, and that undoubted knowledge we have of our own existence.

3. *He knows also that Nothing cannot produce a Being; therefore Something eternal.* In the next place, man knows, by an intuitive certainty, that bare *nothing can no more produce any real being, than it can be equal to two right angles.* If a man knows not that nonentity, or the absence of all being, cannot be equal to two right angles, it is impossible he should know any demonstration in Euclid. If, therefore, we know

there is some real being, and that nonentity cannot produce any real being, it is an evident demonstration, that from eternity there has been something; since what was not from eternity had a beginning; and what had a beginning must be produced by something else.

4. *That eternal Being must be most powerful.* Next, it is evident that what had its being and beginning from another must also have all that which is in and belongs to its being from another too. All the powers it has must be owing to and received from the same source. This eternal source, then, of all being must also be the source and original of all power; and so *this eternal Being must be also the most powerful.*

5. *And most knowing.* Again, a man finds in himself perception and knowledge. We have then got one step further; and we are certain now that there is not only some being, but some knowing, intelligent being in the world.

There was a time, then, when there was no knowing being, and when knowledge began to be; or else there has been also a *knowing being from eternity.* If it be said, there was a time when no being had any knowledge, when that eternal being was void of all understanding, I reply that then it was impossible there should ever have been any knowledge; it being as impossible that things wholly void of knowledge, and operating blindly, and without any perception, should produce a knowing being, as it is impossible that a triangle should make itself three angles bigger than two right ones. For it is as repugnant to the idea of senseless matter that it should put into itself sense, perception, and knowledge, as it is repugnant to the idea of a triangle that it should put into itself greater angles than two right ones.

6. *And therefore God.* Thus, from the consideration of ourselves, and what we infallibly find in our own constitutions, our reason leads us to the knowledge of this certain and evident truth, *That there is an eternal, most powerful, and most knowing Being;* which whether anyone will please to call God, it matters not. The thing is evident; and from this idea duly considered, will easily be deduced all those other attributes, which we ought to ascribe to this eternal Being.

If, nevertheless, anyone should be found so senselessly arrogant, as to suppose man alone knowing and wise, but yet the product of mere ignorance and chance, and that all the rest of the universe acted only by that blind haphazard, I shall leave with him that very rational and emphatical rebuke of Tully (I. ii. *De Leg.*), to be considered at his leisure : " What can be more sillily arrogant and misbecoming than for a man to think that he has a mind and understanding in him, but yet in all the universe beside there is no such thing? Or that those things, which with the utmost stretch of his reason he can scarce comprehend, should be moved and managed without any reason at all?"

7. *Our idea of a most perfect Being, not the sole Proof of a God.* How far the *idea* of a most perfect being, which a man may frame in his mind, does or does not prove the *existence* of a God, I will not here examine. For in the different make of men's tempers and application of their thoughts, some arguments prevail more on one, and some on another, for the confirmation of the same truth. But yet, I think, this I may say, that it is an ill way of establishing this truth, and silencing atheists, to lay the whole stress of so important a point as this upon that sole foundation; and take some men's having that idea of God in their minds (for it is evident some men have none, and some worse than none, and the most very different), for the only proof of the Deity.

8. *Something from Eternity.* There is no truth more evident than that *something* must be *from eternity*. I never yet heard of anyone so unreasonable, or that could suppose so manifest a contradiction, as a time wherein there was perfectly nothing. This being of all absurdities the greatest, to imagine that pure nothing, the perfect negation and absence of all beings, should ever produce any real existence.

9. *Two Sorts of Beings, Cogitative and Incogitative.* There are but two sorts of beings in the world that man knows or conceives.

First, such as are purely material, without sense, perception, or thought, as the clippings of our beards, and parings of our nails.

Secondly, sensible, thinking, perceiving beings, such as we find ourselves to be. Which, if you please, we will hereafter call *cogitative* and *incogitative* beings; which to our present purpose, if for nothing else, are perhaps better terms than material and immaterial.

10. *Incogitative Being cannot produce a Cogitative.* If, then, there must be something eternal, let us see what sort of being it must be. And to that it is very obvious to reason that it must necessarily be a cogitative being. For it is as impossible to conceive that ever bare incogitative matter should produce a thinking intelligent being, as that nothing should of itself produce matter. Let us suppose any parcel of matter eternal, great or small, we shall find it, in itself, able to produce nothing. For example: let us suppose the matter of the next pebble we meet with eternal, closely united, and the parts firmly at rest together; if there were no other being in the world, must it not eternally remain so, a dead inactive lump? Is it possible to conceive it can add motion to itself, being purely matter, or produce anything? Matter, then, by its own strength, cannot produce in itself so much as motion; the motion it has must also be from eternity, or else be produced, and added to matter by some other being more powerful than matter; matter, as is evident, having not power to produce motion in itself. But let us suppose motion eternal too: yet matter, *incogitative* matter and motion, whatever changes it might produce of figure and bulk, could never produce thought; knowledge will still be as far beyond the power of motion and matter to produce, as matter is beyond the power of nothing or nonentity to produce. And I appeal to everyone's own thoughts, whether he cannot as easily conceive matter produced by *nothing,* as thought to be produced by pure matter, when, before, there was no such thing as thought or an intelligent being existing? It is impossible to conceive that matter, either with or without motion, could have, originally, in and from itself, sense, perception, and knowledge; as is evident from hence, that then sense, perception, and knowledge must be a property eternally inseparable from matter and every particle of it. Since, therefore, whatsoever is

the first eternal being must necessarily be cogitative; and whatsoever is first of all things must necessarily contain in it, and actually have, at least, all the perfections that can ever after exist; nor can it ever give to another any perfection that it hath not either actually in itself, or, at least, in a higher degree; it necessarily follows, that the first eternal being cannot be matter.

11. *Therefore, there has been an Eternal Wisdom.* If, therefore, it be evident that something necessarily must exist from eternity, it is also as evident that that something must necessarily be a cogitative being; for it is as impossible that incogitative matter should produce a cogitative being, as that nothing, or the negation of all being, should produce a positive being or matter.

12. Though this discovery of the *necessary existence of an eternal Mind* does sufficiently lead us into the knowledge of God; since it will hence follow, that all other knowing beings that have a beginning must depend on him, and have no other ways of knowledge or extent of power than what he gives them; and therefore, if he made those, he made also the less excellent pieces of this universe, all inanimate beings, whereby his omniscience, power, and providence will be established, and all his other attributes necessarily follow; yet, to clear up this a little further, we will see what doubts can be raised against it.

13. *Whether material or no.* First, perhaps it will be said that, though it be as clear as demonstration can make it, that there must be an eternal Being, and that Being must also be knowing; yet it does not follow but that thinking Being may also be material. Let it be so, it equally still follows that there is a God. For if there be an eternal, omniscient, omnipotent Being, it is certain that there is a God, whether you imagine that Being to be material or no. But herein, I suppose, lies the danger and deceit of that supposition; there being no way to avoid the demonstration that there is an eternal knowing Being, men, devoted to matter, would willingly have it granted that this knowing Being is material; and then, letting slide out of their minds, or the discourse, the demonstration whereby an eternal

knowing Being was proved necessarily to exist, would argue all to be matter, and so deny a God, that is, an eternal cogitative Being; whereby they are so far from establishing, that they destroy their own hypothesis. For, if there can be, in their opinion, eternal matter, without any eternal cogitative Being, they manifestly separate matter and thinking, and suppose no necessary connexion of the one with the other, and so establish the necessity of an eternal Spirit, but not of matter; since it has been proved already that an eternal cogitative Being is unavoidably to be granted. Now, if thinking and matter may be separated, the eternal existence of matter will not follow from the eternal existence of a cogitative Being, and they suppose it to no purpose.

14. *Not material : First, because each Particle of Matter is not cogitative.* But now let us see how they can satisfy themselves, or others, that this eternal thinking Being is material.

First, I would ask them, whether they imagine that all matter, *every particle of matter,* thinks? This, I suppose, they will scarce say, since then there would be as many eternal thinking beings as there are particles of matter, and so an infinity of gods. And yet, if they will not allow matter as matter, that is, every particle of matter, to be as well cogitative as extended, they will have as hard a task to make out to their own reasons a cogitative being out of incogitative particles, as an extended being out of unextended parts, if I may so speak.

15. *Secondly, one Particle alone of Matter cannot be cogitative.* Secondly, if all matter does not think, I next ask, whether it be *only one atom* that does so? This has as many absurdities as the other, for then this atom of matter must be alone eternal or not. If this alone be eternal, then this alone, by its powerful thought or will, made all the rest of matter. And so we have the creation of matter by a powerful thought, which is that the materialists stick at; for, if they suppose one single thinking atom to have produced all the rest of matter, they cannot ascribe that pre-eminency to

it upon any other account than that of its thinking, the only supposed difference.

16. *Thirdly, a System of incogitative Matter cannot be cogitative.* Thirdly, if then neither one peculiar atom alone can be this eternal thinking being, nor all matter, as matter, i.e. every particle of matter, can be it, it only remains that it is some certain *system* of matter, duly put together, that is this thinking eternal Being. This is that which, I imagine, is that notion which men are aptest to have of God; who would have him a material being, as most readily suggested to them by the ordinary conceit they have of themselves and other men, which they take to be material thinking beings. But this imagination, however more natural, is no less absurd than the other; for to suppose the eternal thinking Being to be nothing else but a composition of particles of matter, each whereof is incogitative, is to ascribe all the wisdom and knowledge of that eternal Being only to the juxta-position of parts; than which nothing can be more absurd. For unthinking particles of matter, however put together, can have nothing thereby added to them but a new relation of position, which it is impossible should give thought and knowledge to them.

17. *Whether in Motion or at Rest.* But further, this corporeal system either has all its parts at rest, or it is a certain motion of the parts wherein its thinking consists. If it be perfectly at rest, it is but one lump, and so can have no privileges above one atom.

If it be the motion of its parts on which its thinking depends, all the thoughts there must be unavoidably accidental and limited; since all the particles that by motion cause thought, being each of them in itself without any thought, cannot regulate its own motions, much less be regulated by the thought of the whole; since that thought is not the cause of motion (for then it must be antecedent to it, and so without it), but the consequence of it; whereby freedom, power, choice, and all rational and wise thinking or acting, will be quite taken away; so that such a thinking being will be no better nor wiser than pure blind matter; since to resolve all into the accidental unguided motions of blind matter, or into thought depending on unguided motions of blind matter, is the same thing; not to mention the narrowness of such thoughts and knowledge that must depend on the motion of such parts.

18. *Matter not co-eternal with an Eternal Mind.* Others would have *Matter* to be *eternal,* notwithstanding that they allow an eternal, cogitative, immaterial Being. This, though it take not away the being of a God, yet, since it denies one and the first great piece of his workmanship, the creation, let us consider it a little. Matter must be allowed eternal. Why? Because you cannot conceive how it can be made out of nothing. Why do you not also think yourself eternal? You will answer, perhaps, because, about twenty or forty years since, you began to be. But if I ask you, what that *you* is which began then to be, you can scarce tell me. The matter whereof you are made began not then to be; for if it did, then it is not eternal; but it began to be put together in such a fashion and frame as makes up your body; but yet that frame of particles is not you, it makes not that thinking thing you are; (for I have now to do with one who allows an eternal, immaterial, thinking Being, but would have unthinking Matter eternal too;) therefore, when did that thinking thing begin to be? If it did never begin to be, then have you always been a thinking thing from eternity; the absurdity whereof I need not confute, till I meet with one who is so void of understanding as to own it. If, therefore, you can allow a thinking thing to be made out of nothing (as all things that are not eternal must be), why also can you not allow it possible for a material being to be made out of nothing by an equal power, but that you have the experience of the one in view, and not of the other? Though, when well considered, creation of a spirit will be found to require no less power than the creation of matter. Nay, possibly, if we would emancipate ourselves from vulgar notions, and raise our thoughts, as far as they would reach, to a closer contemplation of things, we might be able to aim at some dim and seeming conception how matter might at first be made, and begin to exist, by the power of that eternal first Being; but to give beginning and being to

a spirit would be found a more inconceivable effect of omnipotent power.

19. But you will say, is it not impossible to admit of the making anything out of nothing, since we cannot possibly conceive it? I answer, No. Because it is not reasonable to deny the power of an infinite being, because we cannot comprehend its operations. We do not deny other effects upon this ground, because we cannot possibly conceive the manner of their production. We cannot conceive how anything but impulse of body can move body; and yet that is not a reason sufficient to make us deny it possible, against the constant experience we have of it in ourselves, in all our voluntary motions; which are produced in us only by the free action or thought of our own minds, and are not, nor can be, the effects of the impulse or determination of the motion of blind matter in or upon our bodies; for then it could not be in our power or choice to alter it. For example : my right hand writes, whilst my left hand is still. What causes rest in one, and motion in the other? Nothing but my will, a thought of my mind; my thought only changing, the right hand rests, and the left hand moves. This is matter of fact, which cannot be denied; explain this and make it intelligible, and then the next step will be to understand creation.

CHAPTER XI

OF OUR KNOWLEDGE OF THE EXISTENCE OF OTHER THINGS

1. *It is to be had only by Sensation.* The knowledge of our own being we have by intuition. The existence of a God reason clearly makes known to us, as has been shown.

The knowledge of the existence of any other thing we can have only by *sensation*; for, there being no necessary connexion of real existence with any *idea* a man hath in his memory, nor of any other existence but that of God with the existence of any particular man, no particular man can know the existence of any other being, but only when, by actual operating upon him, it makes itself perceived by him. For, the having the idea of anything in our mind no more proves the existence of that thing, than the picture of a man evidences his being in the world, or the visions of a dream make thereby a true history.

2. *Instance* : *Whiteness of this Paper*. It is therefore the actual receiving of ideas from without that gives us notice of the existence of other things, and makes us know that something doth exist at that time without us, which causes that idea in us, though perhaps we neither know nor consider how it does it. For it takes not from the certainty of our senses, and the ideas we receive by them, that we know not the manner wherein they are produced : v.g. whilst I write this, I have, by the paper affecting my eyes, that idea produced in my mind, which, whatever object causes, I call *white* ; by which I know that that quality or accident (i.e. whose appearance before my eyes always causes that idea) doth really exist, and hath a being without me. And of this the greatest assurance I can possibly have, and to which my faculties can attain, is the testimony of my eyes, which are the proper and sole judges of this thing; whose testimony I have reason to rely on as so certain, that I can no more doubt, whilst I write this, that I see white and black, and that something really exists that causes that sensation in me, than that I write or move my hand; which is a certainty as great as human nature is capable of, concerning the existence of anything but a man's self alone, and of God.

3. *This though not so certain as Demonstration, yet may be called Knowledge, and proves the Existence of Things without us.* The notice we have by our senses of the existing of things without us, though it be not altogether so certain as our intuitive knowledge, or the deductions of our reason employed about the clear abstract ideas of our own minds; yet it is an assurance that deserves the name of *knowledge*. If we persuade ourselves that our faculties act and inform us right concerning the existence of those objects that affect

them, it cannot pass for an ill-grounded confidence; for I think nobody can, in earnest, be so sceptical as to be uncertain of the existence of those things which he sees and feels. At least, he that can doubt so far (whatever he may have with his own thoughts), will never have any controversy with me, since he can never be sure I say anything contrary to his opinion. As to myself, I think God has given me assurance enough of the existence of things without me; since, by their different application, I can produce in myself both pleasure and pain, which is one great concernment of my present state. This is certain : the confidence that our faculties do not herein deceive us is the greatest assurance we are capable of concerning the existence of material beings. For we cannot act anything but by our faculties; nor talk of knowledge itself, but by the help of those faculties which are fitted to apprehend even what knowledge is. But besides the assurance we have from our senses themselves, that they do not err in the information they give us of the existence of things without us, when they are affected by them, we are further confirmed in this assurance by other concurrent reasons.

4. *First, Because we cannot have them but by the Inlet of the Senses.* First, it is plain those perceptions are produced in us by exterior causes affecting our senses; because those that want the *organs* of any sense never can have the ideas belonging to that sense produced in their minds. This is too evident to be doubted; and therefore we cannot but be assured that they come in by the organs of that sense, and no other way. The organs themselves, it is plain, do not produce them; for then the eyes of a man in the dark would produce colours, and his nose smell roses in the winter; but we see nobody gets the relish of a pineapple, till he goes to the Indies, where it is, and tastes it.

5. *Because an Idea from actual Sensation, and another from Memory, are very distinct Perceptions.* Secondly, because sometimes I find that *I cannot avoid the having those ideas produced in my mind.* For though, when my eyes are shut, or windows fast, I can at pleasure recall to my mind the ideas of light, or the sun, which former sensations had lodged in my

memory; so I can at pleasure lay by that idea, and take into my view that of the smell of a rose, or taste of sugar. But, if I turn my eyes at noon towards the sun, I cannot avoid the ideas which the light or sun then produces in me. So that there is a manifest difference between the ideas laid up in my memory (over which, if they were there only, I should have constantly the same power to dispose of them, and lay them by at pleasure), and those which force themselves upon me, and I cannot avoid having. And therefore it must needs be some exterior cause, and the brisk acting of some objects without me, whose efficacy I cannot resist, that produces those ideas in my mind, whether I will or no. Besides, there is nobody who doth not perceive the difference in himself between contemplating the sun, as he hath the idea of it in his memory, and actually looking upon it; of which two, his perception is so distinct that few of his ideas are more distinguishable one from another. And therefore he hath certain knowledge that they are not both memory, or the actions of his mind, and fancies only within him; but that actual seeing hath a cause without.

6. *Thirdly, Pleasure or Pain, which accompanies actual Sensation, accompanies not the returning of those Ideas without the external Objects.*   Thirdly, add to this, that many of those ideas are *produced in us with pain,* which afterwards we remember without the least offence. Thus, the pain of heat or cold, when the idea of it is revived in our minds, gives us no disturbance; which, when felt, was very troublesome; and is again, when actually repeated, which is occasioned by the disorder the external object causes in our bodies when applied to them; and we remember the pains of hunger, thirst, or the headache, without any pain at all; which would either never disturb us, or else constantly do it, as often as we thought of it, were there nothing more but ideas floating in our minds, and appearances entertaining our fancies, without the real existence of things affecting us from abroad. The same may be said of *pleasure,* accompanying several actual sensations.

7. *Fourthly, our Senses assist one another's Testimony of the Existence of outward Things.*   Fourthly, our *senses* in many

cases bear witness to the truth of each other's report, concerning the existence of sensible things without us. He that *sees* a fire, may, if he doubt whether it be anything more than a bare fancy, *feel* it too; and be convinced by putting his hand in it. Which certainly could never be put into such exquisite pain by a bare idea or phantom, unless that the pain be a fancy too; which yet he cannot, when the burn is well, by raising the idea of it, bring upon himself again.

Thus I see, whilst I write this, I can change the appearance of the paper; and by designing the letters, tell beforehand what new idea it shall exhibit the very next moment, barely by drawing my pen over it. To which if we will add, that the sight of those shall, from another man, draw such sounds as I beforehand design they shall stand for, there will be little reason left to doubt that those words I write do really exist without me, when they cause a long series of regular sounds to affect my ears, which could not be the effect of my imagination, nor could my memory retain them in that order.

8. *This Certainty is as great as our Condition needs.* But yet, if after all this anyone will be so sceptical as to distrust his senses, and to affirm that all we see and hear, feel and taste, think and do, during our whole being, is but the series and deluding appearances of a long dream, whereof there is no reality; and therefore will question the existence of all things, or our knowledge of anything; I must desire him to consider that, if all be a dream, then he doth but dream that he makes the question, and so it is not much matter that a waking man should answer him. But yet, if he pleases, he may dream that I make him this answer, That the certainty of things existing in *rerum natura* when we have the testimony of our senses for it is not only as great as our frame can attain to, but as our condition needs. For, our faculties being suited not to the full extent of being, nor to a perfect, clear, comprehensive knowledge of things free from all doubt and scruple, but to the preservation of us, in whom they are, and accommodated to the use of life, they serve to our purpose well enough, if they will but give us certain notice of those things, which are convenient or inconvenient to us. For he that sees a candle

burning, and hath experimented the force of its flame by putting his finger in it, will little doubt that this is something existing without him, which does him harm, and puts him to great pain; which is assurance enough, when no man requires greater certainty to govern his actions by than what is as certain as his actions themselves. And if our dreamer pleases to try whether the glowing heat of a glass furnace be barely a wandering imagination in a drowsy man's fancy, by putting his hand into it, he may perhaps be wakened into a certainty greater than he could wish that it is something more than bare imagination.

9. *But reaches no further than actual Sensation.* But this knowledge extends as far as the present testimony of our senses, employed about particular objects that do then affect them, and no further. For if I saw such a collection of simple ideas as is wont to be called *man,* existing together one minute since, and am now alone, I cannot be certain that the same man exists now, since there is no necessary connexion of his existence a minute since with his existence now; by a thousand ways he may cease to be, since I had the testimony of my senses for his existence. And if I cannot be certain that the man I saw last to-day is now in being, I can less be certain that he is so who hath been longer removed from my senses, and I have not seen since yesterday, or since the last year; and much less can I be certain of the existence of men that I never saw. And, therefore, though it be highly probable that millions of men do now exist, yet, whilst I am alone, writing this, I have not that certainty of it which we strictly call knowledge; though the great likelihood of it puts me past doubt, and it be reasonable for me to do several things upon the confidence that there are men (and men also of my acquaintance, with whom I have to do) now in the world; but this is but probability, not knowledge.

10. *Folly to expect Demonstration in everything.* Whereby yet we may observe how foolish and vain a thing it is for a man of a narrow knowledge, who having reason given him to judge of the different evidence and probability of things, and

to be swayed accordingly, to expect demonstration and certainty in things not capable of it; and refuse assent to very rational propositions, and act contrary to very plain and clear truths, because they cannot be made out so evident, as to surmount every the least (I will not say reason, but) pretence of doubting. He that, in the ordinary affairs of life, would admit of nothing but direct plain demonstration, would be sure of nothing in this world, but of perishing quickly. The wholesomeness of his meat or drink would not give him reason to venture on it; and I would fain know what it is he could do upon such grounds as are capable of no doubt, no objection.

11. *Past Existence is known by Memory.* As *when our senses are actually employed about any object,* we do know that it does exist; so *by our memory* we may be assured that heretofore things that affected our senses have existed. And thus we have knowledge of the past existence of several things, whereof our senses having informed us, our memories still retain the ideas; and of this we are past all doubt, so long as we remember well. But this knowledge also reaches no further than our senses have formerly assured us. Thus, seeing water at this instant, it is an unquestionable truth to me that water doth exist; and remembering that I saw it yesterday, it will also be always true, and as long as my memory retains it always an undoubted proposition to me, that water did exist the 10th of July, 1688.

12. *The Existence of Spirits not knowable.* What ideas we have of spirits, and how we come by them, I have already shown[1]. But though we have those ideas in our minds, and know we have them there, the having the ideas of spirits does not make us know that any such things do exist without us, or that there are any finite spirits, or any other spiritual beings, but the Eternal God. We have ground from revelation, and several other reasons, to believe with assurance that there are such creatures; but our senses not being able to discover them, we want the means of knowing their particular existences. For we can no more know that there are finite spirits really existing, by the idea we have of such beings in our minds,

[1] II xxiii 5, 15; IV iii 27

than by the ideas any one has of fairies or centaurs he can come to know that things answering those ideas do really exist.

And therefore concerning the existence of finite spirits, as well as several other things, we must content ourselves with the evidence of faith; but universal, certain propositions concerning this matter are beyond our reach. For however true it may be, v.g., that all the intelligent spirits that God ever created do still exist, yet it can never make a part of our certain knowledge. These and the like propositions we may assent to, as highly probable, but are not, I fear, in this state capable of knowing. We are not, then, to put others upon demonstrating, nor ourselves upon search of universal certainty in all those matters; wherein we are not capable of any other knowledge, but what our senses give us in this or that particular.

13. *Particular Propositions concerning Existence are knowable.* By which it appears that there are two sorts of propositions : (1) There is one sort of propositions concerning the *existence* of anything answerable to such an idea : as having the idea of an elephant, phoenix, motion, or an angel, in my mind, the first and natural inquiry is whether such a thing does anywhere exist? And this knowledge is only of particulars. No existence of anything without us, but only of God, can certainly be known further than our senses inform us. (2) There is another sort of propositions, wherein is expressed the agreement or disagreement of *our abstract ideas,* and their dependence one on another. Such propositions may be universal and certain. So, having the idea of God and myself, of fear and obedience, I cannot but be sure that God is to be feared and obeyed by me; and this proposition will be certain, concerning man in general, if I have made an abstract idea of such a species, whereof I am one particular. But yet this proposition, how certain soever, that *men ought to fear and obey God* proves not to me the existence of men in the world; but will be true of all such creatures, whenever they do exist; which certainty of such general propositions depends on the agreement or disagreement is to be discovered in those abstract ideas.

14. *And general Propositions concerning abstract Ideas.*   In the former case, our knowledge is the consequence of the existence of things, producing ideas in our minds by our senses; in the latter, knowledge is the consequence of the ideas (be they what they will) that are in our minds, producing there general certain propositions. Many of these are called *aeternae veritates,* and all of them indeed are so; not from being written, all or any of them, in the minds of all men; or that they were any of them propositions in anyone's mind, till he, having got the abstract ideas, joined or separated them by affirmation or negation. Such propositions are therefore called *eternal truths,* not because they are eternal propositions actually formed, and antecedent to the understanding that at any time makes them; nor because they are imprinted on the mind from any patterns that are anywhere of them out of the mind, and existed before; but because, being once made about abstract ideas, so as to be true, they will, whenever they can be supposed to be made again at any time, past or to come, by a mind having those ideas, always actually be true.

CHAPTER XII

OF THE IMPROVEMENT OF OUR
KNOWLEDGE

1. *Knowledge is not from Maxims.* It having been the common received opinion amongst men of letters that *maxims* were the foundation of all knowledge; and that the sciences were each of them built upon certain *præcognita,* from whence the understanding was to take its rise, and by which it was to conduct itself in its inquiries into the matters belonging to that science, the beaten road of the Schools has been to lay down in the beginning one or more *general propositions,* as foundations whereon to build the knowledge that was to be had of that subject. These doctrines, thus laid down for foundations of any science, were called *principles,* as the beginnings from

which we must set out, and look no further backwards in our inquiries, as we have already observed.

2. (*The Occasion of that Opinion.*) One thing which might probably give an occasion to this way of proceeding in other sciences was (as I suppose) the good success it seemed to have in *mathematics,* wherein, men being observed to attain a great certainty of knowledge, these sciences came by pre-eminence to be called Μαθήματα, and Μάθησις, learning, or things learned, thoroughly learned, as having of all others the greatest certainty, clearness, and evidence in them.

3. *But from the comparing clear and distinct Ideas.* But if anyone will consider, he will (I guess) find that the great advancement and certainty of real knowledge which men arrived to in these sciences was not owing to the influence of these principles, nor derived from any peculiar advantage they received from two or three general maxims, laid down in the beginning; but from the clear, distinct, complete ideas their thoughts were employed about, and the relation of equality and excess so clear between some of them, that they had an intuitive knowledge, and by that a way to discover it in others; and this without the help of those maxims. For I ask, is it not possible for a young lad to know that his whole body is bigger than his little finger, but by virtue of this axiom, that *the whole is bigger than a part*; nor be assured of it, till he has learned that maxim?

4. *Dangerous to build upon precarious Principles.* But be it in the mathematics as it will, that which I have here to do is to inquire whether, if it be the readiest way to knowledge to begin with general maxims, and build upon them, it be yet a safe way to take the *principles* which are laid down in any other science as unquestionable truths; and so receive them without examination, and adhere to them, without suffering them to be doubted of, because mathematicians have been so happy, or so fair, to use none but self-evident and undeniable. If this be so, I know not what may not pass for truth in morality, what may not be introduced and proved in natural philosophy.

5. *This is no certain Way to Truth.* If, therefore, those

that pass for *principles* are *not certain* (which we must have some way to know, that we may be able to distinguish them from those that are doubtful), but are only made so to us by our blind assent, we are liable to be misled by them; and instead of being guided into truth, we shall, by principles, be only confirmed in mistake and error.

6. *But to compare clear, complete Ideas under steady Names.* But since the knowledge of the certainty of principles, as well as of all other truths, depends only upon the perception we have of the agreement or disagreement of our ideas, the way to improve our knowledge is not, I am sure, blindly, and with an implicit faith, to receive and swallow principles; but is, I think, to get and fix in our minds clear, distinct, and complete ideas, as far as they are to be had, and annex to them proper and constant names. And thus, perhaps, without any other principles, but barely considering those ideas, and by *comparing them one with another,* finding their agreement and disagreement, and their several relations and habitudes; we shall get more true and clear knowledge by the conduct of this one rule, than by taking up principles, and thereby putting our minds into the disposal of others.

7. *The true Method of advancing Knowledge is by considering our abstract Ideas.* We must, therefore, if we will proceed as reason advises, adapt our methods of inquiry to *the nature of the ideas we examine,* and the truth we search after. General and certain truths are only founded in the habitudes and relations of *abstract ideas.* A sagacious and methodical application of our thoughts, for the finding out these relations, is the only way to discover all that can be put with truth and certainty concerning them into general propositions. By what steps we are to proceed in these is to be learned in the schools of the mathematicians, who, from very plain and easy beginnings, by gentle degrees, and a continued chain of reasonings, proceed to the discovery and demonstration of truths that appear at first sight beyond human capacity. The art of finding proofs, and the admirable methods they have invented for the singling out and laying in order those intermediate ideas that demonstratively show the equality or inequality of inapplicable

quantities, is that which has carried them so far, and produced such wonderful and unexpected discoveries; but whether something like this, in respect of other ideas, as well as those of magnitude, may not in time be found out, I will not determine. This, I think, I may say, that if other ideas that are the real as well as nominal essences of their species were pursued in the way familiar to mathematicians, they would carry our thoughts further, and with greater evidence and clearness than possibly we are apt to imagine.

8. *By which Morality also may be made clearer.*   This gave me the confidence to advance that conjecture, which I suggest, (chap. iii.) viz. that *morality* is capable of demonstration as well as mathematics. For the ideas that ethics are conversant about being all real essences, and such as I imagine have a discoverable connexion and agreement one with another, so far as we can find their habitudes and relations, so far we shall be possessed of certain, real, and general truths; and I doubt not but, if a right method were taken, a great part of morality might be made out with that clearness, that could leave, to a considering man, no more reason to doubt, than he could have to doubt of the truth of propositions in mathematics, which have been demonstrated to him.

9. *But Knowledge of Bodies is to be improved, only by Experience.*   In our search after the knowledge of *substances,* our want of ideas that are suitable to such a way of proceeding obliges us to a quite different method. We advance not here, as in the other (where our abstract ideas are real as well as nominal essences), by contemplating our ideas, and considering their relations and correspondences; that helps us very little, for the reasons that in another place we have at large set down[1]. By which I think it is evident that substances afford matter of very little general knowledge, and the bare contemplation of their abstract ideas will carry us but a very little way in the search of truth and certainty. What, then, are we to do for the improvement of our knowledge in substantial beings? Here we are to take a quite contrary course: the want of ideas of their real essences sends us from our own

----

[1] II xxiii; III vi

thoughts to the things themselves as they exist. *Experience here must teach me what reason cannot* : and it is by trying alone, that I can certainly know what other qualities co-exist with those of my complex idea. Here, again, for assurance I must apply myself to experience; as far as that reaches, I may have certain knowledge, but no further.

10. *This may procure us Convenience, not Science.* I deny not but a man, accustomed to rational and regular experiments, shall be able to see further into the nature of bodies, and guess righter at their yet unknown properties, than one that is a stranger to them: but yet, as I have said, this is but judgment and opinion, not knowledge and certainty. Experiments and historical observations we may have, from which we may draw advantages of ease and health, and thereby increase our stock of conveniences for this life; but beyond this I fear our talents reach not, nor are our faculties, as I guess, able to advance.

11. *We are fitted for moral Knowledge and natural Improvements.* From whence it is obvious to conclude that, since our faculties are not fitted to penetrate into the internal fabric and real essences of bodies, but yet plainly discover to us the being of a God, and the knowledge of ourselves, enough to lead us into a full and clear discovery of our duty and great concernment; it will become us, as rational creatures, to employ those faculties we have about what they are most adapted to, and follow the direction of nature, where it seems to point us out the way. For it is rational to conclude that our proper employment lies in those inquiries, and in that sort of knowledge which is most suited to our natural capacities, and carries in it our greatest interest, i.e. the condition of our eternal estate. Hence I think I may conclude that *morality* is *the proper science and business of mankind in general* (who are both concerned and fitted to search out their *summum bonum*); as several arts, conversant about several parts of nature, are the lot and private talent of particular men, for the common use of human life, and their own particular subsistence in this world.

12. *But must beware of Hypotheses and wrong Principles.*

I would not, therefore, be thought to disesteem or dissuade the study of *nature*. He that first invented printing, discovered the use of the compass, or made public the virtue and right use of *kin kina,* did more for the propagation of knowledge, for the supply and increase of useful commodities, and saved more from the grave than those who built colleges, workhouses, and hospitals. All that I would say is that we should not be too forwardly possessed with the opinion or expectation of knowledge, where it is not to be had, or by ways that will not attain it; that we should not take doubtful systems for complete sciences, nor unintelligible notions for scientifical demonstrations. In the knowledge of bodies we must be content to glean what we can from particular experiments; since we cannot, from a discovery of their real essences, grasp at a time whole sheaves, and in bundles comprehend the nature and properties of whole species together.

13. *The true Use of Hypotheses.* Not that we may not, to explain any phenomena of nature, make use of any probable hypothesis whatsoever; hypotheses, if they are well made, are at least great helps to the memory, and often direct us to new discoveries. But my meaning is that we should not take up any one too hastily (which the mind, that would always penetrate into the causes of things, and have principles to rest on, is very apt to do), till we have very well examined particulars, and made several experiments, in that thing which we would explain by our hypothesis, and see whether it will agree to them all; whether our principles will carry us quite through, and not be as inconsistent with one phenomenon of nature, as they seem to accommodate and explain another. And at least that we take care that the name of *principles* deceive us not, nor impose on us, by making us receive that for an unquestionable truth, which is really at best but a very doubtful conjecture; such as are most (I had almost said all) of the hypotheses in natural philosophy.

14. *Clear and distinct Ideas with settled Names, and the finding of those which show their Agreement or Disagreement, are the Ways to enlarge our Knowledge.* But whether natural philosophy be capable of certainty or no, the ways to enlarge

our knowledge, as far as we are capable, seem to me, in short, to be these two :

First, the first is to get and settle in our minds determined ideas of those things whereof we have general or specific names; at least, of so many of them as we would consider and improve our knowledge in, or reason about. And if they be specific ideas of substances, we should endeavour also to make them as complete as we can, whereby I mean that we should put together as many simple ideas as, being constantly observed to co-exist, may perfectly determine the species; and each of those simple ideas which are the ingredients of our complex ones should be clear and distinct in our minds. For it being evident that our knowledge cannot exceed our ideas, as far as they are either imperfect, confused, or obscure, we cannot expect to have certain, perfect, or clear knowledge.

Secondly, the other is the art of finding out those intermediate ideas, which may show us the agreement or repugnancy of other ideas, which cannot be immediately compared.

15. *Mathematics an instance of it.* That these two (and not the relying on maxims, and drawing consequences from some general propositions) are the right methods of improving our knowledge in the ideas of other modes besides those of quantity, the consideration of mathematical knowledge will easily inform us. Where first we shall find that he that has not a perfect and clear idea of those angles or figures of which he desires to know anything, is utterly thereby incapable of any knowledge about them. Suppose but a man not to have a perfect exact idea of a right angle, a scalenum, or trapezium, and there is nothing more certain than that he will in vain seek any demonstration about them. Further, it is evident that it was not the influence of those maxims which are taken for principles in mathematics that hath led the masters of that science into those wonderful discoveries they have made. They have been discovered by the thoughts otherwise applied; the mind had other objects, other views before it, far different from those maxims, when it first got the knowledge of such kind of truths in mathematics, which men, well enough acquainted with those received axioms, but ignorant of their

method who first made these demonstrations, can never sufficiently admire. And who knows what methods to enlarge our knowledge in other parts of science may hereafter be invented, answering that of algebra in mathematics, which so readily finds out ideas of quantities to measure others by; whose equality or proportion we could otherwise very hardly, or, perhaps, never come to know?

[CHAPTER XIII]

[SOME FURTHER CONSIDERATIONS CONCERNING OUR KNOWLEDGE]

CHAPTER XIV

OF JUDGMENT

1. *Our Knowledge being short, we want something else.* The understanding faculties being given to man, not barely for speculation, but also for the conduct of his life, man would be at a great loss if he had nothing to direct him but what has the certainty of true *knowledge*. For that being very short and scanty, as we have seen, he would be often utterly in the dark, and in most of the actions of his life, perfectly at a stand, had he nothing to guide him in the absence of clear and certain knowledge. He that will not eat till he has demonstration that it will nourish him, he that will not stir till he infallibly knows the business he goes about will succeed, will have little else to do but sit still and perish.

3. *Judgment supplies the want of Knowledge.* The faculty which God has given man to supply the want of clear and certain knowledge, in cases where that cannot be had, is *judgment* : whereby the mind takes its ideas to agree or disagree; or, which is the same, any proposition to be true

or false, without perceiving a demonstrative evidence in the proofs. The mind sometimes exercises this judgment out of necessity, where demonstrative proofs and certain knowledge are not to be had; and sometimes out of laziness, unskilfulness, or haste, even where demonstrative and certain proofs are to be had. This faculty of the mind, when it is exercised immediately about things, is called *judgment*; when about truths delivered in words, is most commonly called *assent* or *dissent*; which being the most usual way, wherein the mind has occasion to employ this faculty, I shall, under these terms, treat of it, as least liable in our language to equivocation.

4. *Judgment is the presuming Things to be so, without perceiving it.* Thus the mind has two faculties conversant about truth and falsehood :—

First, *Knowledge,* whereby it certainly perceives, and is undoubtedly satisfied of the agreement or disagreement of any ideas.

Secondly, *Judgment,* which is the putting ideas together, or separating them from one another in the mind, when their certain agreement or disagreement is not perceived, but *presumed* to be so; which is, as the word imports, taken to be so before it certainly appears. And if it so unites or separates them as in reality things are, it is right judgment.

CHAPTER XV

OF PROBABILITY

1. *Probability is the appearance of Agreement upon fallible Proofs.* As demonstration is the showing the agreement or disagreement of two ideas, by the intervention of one or more proofs, which have a constant, immutable, and visible connexion one with another; so probability is nothing but the appearance of such an agreement or disagreement, by the intervention of proofs, whose connexion is not constant and immutable, or at least is not perceived to be so, but is, or

404	An Essay Concerning Human Understanding

appears for the most part to be so, and is enough to induce the mind to judge the proposition to be true or false, rather than the contrary. For example : in the demonstration of it a man perceives the certain, immutable connexion there is of equality between the three angles of a triangle and those intermediate ones which are made use of to show their equality to two right ones; and so, by an intuitive knowledge of the agreement or disagreement of the intermediate ideas in each step of the progress, the whole series is continued with an evidence, which clearly shows the agreement or disagreement of those three angles in equality to two right ones; and thus he has certain knowledge that it is so. But another·man, who never took the pains to observe the demonstration, hearing a mathematician, a man of credit, affirm the three angles of a triangle to be equal to two right ones, assents to it, i.e. receives it for true; in which case the foundation of his assent is the probability of the thing, the proof being such as for the most part carries truth with it; the man on whose testimony he receives it not being wont to affirm anything contrary to or besides his knowledge, especially in matters of this kind : so that that which causes his assent to this proposition, that the three angles of a triangle are equal to two right ones, that which makes him take these ideas to agree, without knowing them to do so, is the wonted veracity of the speaker in other cases, or his supposed veracity in this.

2. *It is to supply the Want of Knowledge.* Our knowledge, as has been shown, being very narrow, and we not happy enough to find certain truth in everything which we have occasion to consider, most of the propositions we think, reason, discourse, nay, act upon, are such as we cannot have undoubted knowledge of their truth; yet some of them border so near upon certainty that we make no doubt at all about them, but assent to them as firmly, and act, according to that assent, as resolutely as if they were infallibly demonstrated, and that our knowledge of them was perfect and certain. But there being degrees herein, from the very neighbourhood of certainty and demonstration, quite down to improbability and unlikeness, even to the confines of impossibility, and also degrees of assent from full assurance

and confidence, quite down to conjecture, doubt, and distrust; I shall come now (having, as I think, found out the bounds of human knowledge and certainty) in the next place to consider *the several degrees and grounds of probability, and assent or faith.*

3. *Being that which makes us presume Things to be true, before we know them to be so.* Probability is likeliness to be true, the very notation of the word signifying such a proposition, for which there be arguments or proofs to make it pass, or be received for true. The entertainment the mind gives this sort of propositions is called *belief, assent,* or *opinion,* which is the admitting or receiving any proposition for true, upon arguments or proofs that are found to persuade us to receive it as true, without certain knowledge that it is so. And herein lies the difference between *probability* and *certainty, faith* and *knowledge,* that in all the parts of knowledge there is intuition; each immediate idea, each step has its visible and certain connexion; in belief, not so. That which makes me believe is something extraneous to the thing I believe, something not evidently joined on both sides to, and so not manifestly showing the agreement or disagreement of, those ideas that are under consideration.

4. *The Grounds of Probability are two :* Conformity with *our own Experience, or the Testimony of others' experience.* Probability then, being to supply the defect of our knowledge, and to guide us where that fails, is always conversant about propositions whereof we have no certainty, but only some inducements to receive them for true. The grounds of it are, in short, these two following :

First, the conformity of anything with our own knowledge, observation, and experience.

Secondly, the testimony of others, vouching their observation and experience. In the testimony of others, is to be considered : 1. The number. 2. The integrity. 3. The skill of the witnesses. 4. The design of the author, where it is a testimony out of a book cited. 5. The consistency of the parts, and circumstances of the relation. 6. Contrary testimonies.

5. *In this, all the agreements pro and con ought to be*

examined, before we come to a Judgment. Probability wanting that intuitive evidence which infallibly determines the understanding and produces certain knowledge, the mind, if it *will proceed rationally,* ought to examine all the grounds of probability and see how they make more or less for or against any probable proposition, before it assents to or dissents from it; and, upon a due balancing the whole, reject or receive it, with a more or less firm assent, proportionably to the preponderancy of the greater grounds of probability on one side or the other. For example :

If I myself see a man walk on the ice, it is past probability; it is knowledge. But if another tells me he saw a man in England, in the midst of a sharp winter, walk upon water hardened with cold, this has so great conformity with what is usually observed to happen, that I am disposed by the nature of the thing itself to assent to it, unless some manifest suspicion attend the relation of that matter of fact. But if the same thing be told to one born between the tropics, who never saw nor heard of any such thing before, there the whole probability relies on testimony; and as the relators are more in number, and of more credit, and have no interest to speak contrary to the truth, so that matter of fact is like to find more or less belief. Though to a man whose experience has been always quite contrary, and who has never heard of anything like it, the most untainted credit of a witness will scarce be able to find belief. And as it happened to a Dutch ambassador, who entertaining the king of Siam with the particularities of Holland, which he was inquisitive after, amongst other things told him that the water in his country would sometimes, in cold weather, be so hard that men walked upon it, and that it would bear an elephant, if he were there. To which the king replied, *Hitherto I have believed the strange things you have told me, because I look upon you as a sober fair man, but now I am sure you lie.*

CHAPTER XVI

OF THE DEGREES OF ASSENT

1. *Our Assent ought to be regulated by the Grounds of Probability.* The grounds of probability we have laid down in the foregoing chapter; as they are the foundations on which our *assent* is built, so are they also the measure whereby its several degrees are, or ought to be, regulated; only we are to take notice that, whatever grounds of probability there may be, they yet operate no further on the mind which searches after truth, and endeavours to judge right, than they appear, at least, in the first judgment or search that the mind makes. I confess, in the opinions men have, and firmly stick to in the world, their assent is not always from an actual view of the reasons that at first prevailed with them; it being in many cases almost impossible, and in most, very hard, even for those who have very admirable memories, to retain all the proofs which, upon a due examination, made them embrace that side of the question. It suffices that they have once with care and fairness sifted the matter as far as they could, and that they have searched into all the particulars, that they could imagine to give any light to the question; and, with the best of their skill, cast up the account upon the whole evidence; and thus, having once found on which side the probability appeared to them, after as full and exact an inquiry as they can make, they lay up the conclusion in their memories, as a truth they have discovered; and for the future they remain satisfied with the testimony of their memories, that this is the opinion that, by the proofs they have once seen of it, deserves such a degree of their assent as they afford it.

2. *These cannot always be actually in View; and then we must content ourselves with the remembrance that we once saw ground for such a Degree of Assent.* It is unavoidable,

therefore, that the memory be relied on in the case, and that men be persuaded of several opinions, whereof the proofs are not actually in their thoughts, nay, which perhaps they are not able actually to recall. Without this, the greatest part of men must be either very sceptics, or change every moment, and yield themselves up to whoever, having lately studied the question, offers them arguments, which, for want of memory, they are not able presently to answer.

3. *The ill consequence of this, if our former Judgment were not rightly made.* I cannot but own that men's sticking to their past judgment, and adhering firmly to conclusions formerly made, is often the cause of great obstinacy in error and mistake. But the fault is not that they rely on their memories for what they have before well judged, but because they judged before they had well examined. What we once know, we are certain is so; and we may be secure that there are no latent proofs undiscovered, which may overturn our knowledge, or bring it in doubt. But, in matters of probability, it is not in every case we can be sure that we have all the particulars before us, that any way concern the question, and that there is no evidence behind, and yet unseen, which may cast the probability on the other side, and outweigh all that at present seems to preponderate with us.

4. *The right Use of it, mutual Charity and Forbearance.* Since, therefore, it is unavoidable to the greatest part of men, if not all, to have several *opinions,* without certain and indubitable proofs of their truths; and it carries too great an imputation of ignorance, lightness, or folly for men to quit and renounce their former tenets presently upon the offer of an argument which they cannot immediately answer, and show the insufficiency of; it would, methinks, become all men to maintain peace, and the common offices of humanity, and friendship, in the diversity of opinions; since we cannot reasonably expect that anyone should readily and obsequiously quit his own opinion, and embrace ours, with a blind resignation to an authority which the understanding of man acknowledges not. For where is the man that has incontestable

evidence of the truth of all that he holds, or of the falsehood of all he condemns, or can say that he has examined to the bottom all his own, or other men's opinions? The necessity of believing without knowledge, nay often upon very slight grounds, in this fleeting state of action and blindness we are in, should make us more busy and careful to inform ourselves than constrain others. At least, those who have not thoroughly examined to the bottom all their own tenets, must confess they are unfit to prescribe to others; and are unreasonable in imposing that as truth on other men's belief, which they themselves have not searched into, nor weighed the arguments of probability, on which they should receive or reject it.

5. *Probability is either of Matter of Fact, or speculation.* But to return to the grounds of assent, and the several degrees of it, we are to take notice that the propositions we receive upon inducements of *probability* are of *two sorts* : either concerning some particular existence, or, as it is usually termed, *matter of fact,* which, falling under observation, is capable of human testimony; or else concerning things, which, being beyond the discovery of our senses, are not capable of any such testimony.

6. *The concurrent Experience of* all *other Men with ours, produces Assurance approaching to Knowledge.* Concerning the *first* of these, viz. *particular matter of fact. First,* the first and *highest degree of probability* is, when the general consent of all men, in all ages, as far as it can be known, concurs with a man's constant and never-failing experience in like cases, to confirm the truth of any particular matter of fact attested by fair witnesses; such are all the stated constitutions and properties of bodies, and the regular proceedings of causes and effects in the ordinary course of nature. This we call an argument from the nature of things themselves. For what our own and other men's constant observation has found always to be after the same manner, that we with reason conclude to be the effects of steady and regular causes, though they. come not within the reach of our knowledge. These *probabilities* rise so near to *certainty,* that they govern our thoughts as absolutely, and influence all our actions

as fully, as the most evident demonstration; and in what concerns us we make little or no difference between them and certain knowledge. Our belief, thus grounded, rises to *assurance*.

7. *Unquestionable Testimony, and Experience for the most part, produce Confidence.* Secondly, the *next degree of probability is,* when I find by my own experience, and the agreement of all others that mention it, a thing to be for the most part so, and that the particular instance of it is attested by many and undoubted witnesses : v.g. history giving us such an account of men in all ages, and my own experience, as far as I had an opportunity to observe, confirming it, that most men prefer their private advantage to the public; if all historians that write of Tiberius say that Tiberius did so, it is extremely probable. And in this case, our assent has a sufficient foundation to raise itself to a degree which we may call *confidence*.

8. *Fair Testimony, and the Nature of the Thing indifferent, produces also confident Belief.* Thirdly, in things that happen indifferently, as that a bird should fly this or that way, that it should thunder on a man's right or left hand, &c., when any particular matter of fact is vouched by the concurrent testimony of unsuspected witnesses, there our assent is also unavoidable. Thus : that there is such a city in Italy as Rome : that about 1700 years ago there lived in it a man, called Julius Cæsar; that he was a general, and that he won a battle against another, called Pompey. This, though in the nature of the thing there be nothing for nor against it, yet being related by historians of credit, and contradicted by no one writer, a man cannot avoid believing it, and can as little doubt of it as he does of the being and actions of his own acquaintance, whereof he himself is a witness.

9. *Experiences and Testimonies clashing, infinitely vary the Degrees of Probability.* Thus far the matter goes easy enough. Probability upon such grounds carries so much evidence with it, that it naturally determines the judgment, and leaves us as little liberty to believe or disbelieve, as a demonstration does, whether we will know, or be ignorant. The difficulty is,

when testimonies contradict common experience, and the reports of history and witnesses clash with the ordinary course of nature, or with one another; there it is, where diligence, attention, and exactness is required, to form a right judgment, and to proportion the assent to the different evidence and probability of the thing; which rises and falls, according as those two foundations of credibility, viz. common observation in like cases, and particular testimonies in that particular instance, favour or contradict it. This only may be said in general, that as the arguments and proofs *pro* and *con,* upon due examination, nicely weighing every particular circumstance, shall to anyone appear, upon the whole matter, in a greater or less degree to preponderate on either side; so they are fitted to produce in the mind such different entertainments, as we call *belief, conjecture, guess, doubt, wavering, distrust, disbelief,* &c.

10. *Traditional Testimonies, the further removed the less their Proof.* This is what concerns assent in matters wherein testimony is made use of; concerning which, I think, it may not be amiss to take notice of a rule observed in the law of England; which is, that though the attested copy of a record be good proof, yet the copy of a copy, never so well attested, and by never so credible witnesses, will not be admitted as a proof in judicature. This is so generally approved as reasonable, and suited to the wisdom and caution to be used in our inquiry after material truths, that I never yet heard of any one that blamed it. This practice, if it be allowable in the decisions of right and wrong, carries this observation along with it, viz. that any testimony, the further off it is from the original truth, the less force and proof it has. The being and existence of the thing itself is what I call the original truth. A credible man vouching his knowledge of it is a good proof; but if another equally credible do witness it from his report, the testimony is weaker; and a third that attests the hearsay of an hearsay is yet less considerable. So that in traditional truths each remove weakens the force of the proof; and the more hands the tradition has successively passed through, the less strength and evidence does it receive

from them. This I thought necessary to be taken notice of, because I find amongst some men the quite contrary commonly practised, who look on opinions to gain force by growing older; and what a thousand years since would not, to a rational man contemporary with the first voucher, have appeared at all probable, is now urged as certain beyond all question, only because several have since, from him, said it one after another. Upon this ground propositions, evidently false or doubtful enough in their first beginning, come, by an inverted rule of probability, to pass for authentic truths; and those which found or deserved little credit from the mouths of their first authors, are thought to grow venerable by age, and are urged as undeniable.

11. *Yet History is of great Use.* I would not be thought here to lessen the credit and use of *history*; it is all the light we have in many cases, and we receive from it a great part of the useful truths we have, with a convincing evidence. I think nothing more valuable than the records of antiquity; I wish we had more of them, and more uncorrupted. But this truth itself forces me to say, that no probability can rise higher than its first original.

12 *In Things which Sense cannot discover, Analogy is the great Rule of Probability.* The probabilities we have hitherto mentioned are only such as concern matter of fact, and such things as are capable of observation and testimony. There remains that other sort, concerning which men entertain opinions with variety of assent, though *the things be such, that falling not under the reach of our senses, they are not capable of testimony.* Such are, 1. The existence, nature and operations of finite immaterial beings without us; as spirits, angels, devils, &c. Or the existence of material beings which, either for their smallness in themselves or remoteness from us, our senses cannot take notice of, as whether there be any plants, animals, and intelligent inhabitants in the planets, and other mansions of the vast universe. 2. Concerning the manner of operation in most parts of the works of nature, wherein, though we see the sensible effects, yet their causes are unknown, and we perceive not the ways and

manner how they are produced. *Analogy* in these matters is the only help we have, and it is from that alone we draw all our grounds of probability. Thus, observing that the bare rubbing of two bodies violently one upon another, produces heat, and very often fire itself, we have reason to think that what we call *heat* and *fire* consists in a violent agitation of the imperceptible minute parts of the burning matter. Thus, finding in all parts of the creation, that fall under human observation, that there is a gradual connexion of one with another, without any great or discernible gaps between, in all that great variety of things we see in the world, which are so closely linked together, that, in the several ranks of beings, it is not easy to discover the bounds betwixt them; we have reason to be persuaded that, by such gentle steps, things ascend upwards in degrees of perfection. It is a hard matter to say where sensible and rational begin, and where insensible and irrational end; and who is there quick-sighted enough to determine precisely which is the lowest species of living things, and which the first of those which have no life? Things, as far as we can observe, lessen and augment, as the quantity does in a regular cone; where, though there be a manifest odds betwixt the bigness of the diameter at a remote distance, yet the difference between the upper and under, where they touch one another, is hardly discernible. The difference is exceeding great between some men and some animals; but if we will compare the understanding and abilities of some men and some brutes, we shall find so little difference, that it will be hard to say that that of the man is either clearer or larger. Observing, I say, such gradual and gentle descents downwards in those parts of the creation that are beneath man, the rule of analogy may make it probable that it is so also in things above us and our observation; and that there are several ranks of intelligent beings, excelling us in several degrees of perfection, ascending upwards towards the infinite perfection of the Creator, by gentle steps and differences, that are every one at no great distance from the next to it. This sort of probability, which is the best conduct of rational experiments, and the rise of hypothesis, has also its use and influence; and a wary reasoning from analogy leads us often into the discovery of truths and useful productions, which would otherwise lie concealed.

13. *One Case where contrary Experience lessens not the Testimony.*   Though the common experience and the ordinary course of things have justly a mighty influence on the minds of men, to make them give or refuse credit to anything proposed to their belief; yet there is one case, wherein the strangeness of the fact lessens not the assent to a fair testimony given of it. For where such supernatural events are suitable to ends aimed at by Him who has the power to change the course of nature, there, under such circumstances, they may be the fitter to procure belief, by how much the more they are beyond or contrary to ordinary observation. This is the proper case of *miracles,* which, well attested, do not only find credit themselves, but give it also to other truths, which need such confirmation.

14. *The bare Testimony of Revelation is the highest Certainty.*   Besides those we have hitherto mentioned, there is one sort of propositions that challenge the highest degree of our assent, upon bare testimony, whether the thing proposed agree or disagree with common experience, and the ordinary course of things, or no. The reason whereof is, because the testimony is of such an one as cannot deceive nor be deceived : and that is of God himself. This carries with it assurance beyond doubt, evidence beyond exception. This is called by a peculiar name, *revelation,* and our assent to it, *faith,* which as absolutely determines our minds, and as perfectly excludes all wavering, as our knowledge itself; and we may as well doubt of our own being, as we can whether any revelation from God be true. So that faith is a settled and sure principle of assent and assurance, and leaves no manner of room for doubt or hesitation. Only we must be sure that it be a divine revelation, and that we understand it right; else we shall expose ourselves to all the extravagancy of enthusiasm, and all the error of wrong principles, if we have faith and assurance in what is not divine revelation. And therefore, in those cases, our assent can be rationally no higher than the evidence of its being a revelation, and that this is the meaning of the expressions it is delivered in.

If the evidence of its being a revelation, or that this is its true sense, be only on probable proofs, our assent can reach no higher than an assurance or diffidence, arising from the more or less apparent probability of the proofs.

CHAPTER XVII

OF REASON

1. *Various Significations of the word Reason.* The word 'reason' in the English language has different significations: sometimes it is taken for true and clear principles; sometimes for clear and fair deductions from those principles; and sometimes for the cause, and particularly the final cause. But the consideration I shall have of it here is in a signification different from all these; and that is, as it stands for a faculty in man, that faculty whereby man is supposed to be distinguished from beasts, and wherein it is evident he much surpasses them.

2. *Wherein Reasoning consists.* If general knowledge, as has been shown, consists in a perception of the agreement or disagreement of our own ideas, and the knowledge of the existence of all things without us (except only of a God, whose existence every man may certainly know and demonstrate to himself from his own existence), be had only by our senses, what room then is there for the exercise of any other faculty, but outward sense and inward perception? What need is there of reason? Very much, both for the enlargement of our knowledge, and regulating our assent. For it hath to do both in knowledge and opinion, and is necessary and assisting to all our other intellectual faculties, and indeed contains two of them, viz. *sagacity* and *illation.* By the one, it finds out; and by the other, it so orders the intermediate ideas as to discover what connexion there is in each link of the chain, whereby the extremes are held together; and thereby, as it were, to draw into view the truth sought for, which is that we call *illation* or

inference, and consists in nothing but the perception of the connexion there is between the ideas, in each step of the deduction; whereby the mind comes to see either the certain agreement or disagreement of any two ideas, as in demonstration, in which it arrives at *knowledge*; or their probable connexion, on which it gives or withholds its assent, as in *opinion.* Sense and intuition reach but a very little way. The greatest part of our knowledge depends upon deductions and intermediate ideas; and in those cases where we are fain to substitute assent instead of knowledge, and take propositions for true, without being certain they are so, we have need to find out, examine, and compare the grounds of their probability. In both these cases, the faculty which finds out the means, and rightly applies them, to discover certainty in the one, and probability in the other, is that which we call *reason.* For, as reason perceives the necessary and indubitable connexion of all the ideas or proofs one to another, in each step of any demonstration that produces knowledge; so it likewise perceives the probable connexion of all the ideas or proofs one to another, in every step of a discourse, to which it will think assent due.

3. *Its four parts.* So that we may in *reason* consider these *four degrees*: the first and highest is the discovering and finding out of proofs; the second, the regular and methodical disposition of them, and laying them in a clear and fit order, to make their connexion and force be plainly and easily perceived; the third is the perceiving their connexion; and the fourth, a making a right conclusion. These several degrees may be observed in any mathematical demonstration; it being one thing to perceive the connexion of each part, as the demonstration is made by another; another to perceive the dependence of the conclusion on all the parts; a third, to make out a demonstration clearly and neatly one's self; and something different from all these, to have first found out those intermediate ideas or proofs by which it is made.

4. *Syllogism not the great Instrument of Reason.* There is one thing more which I shall desire to be considered concerning reason; and that is, whether *syllogism,* as is generally thought,

be the proper instrument of it, and the usefullest way of exercising this faculty. The causes I have to doubt are these :

First, because syllogism serves our reason but in one only of the forementioned parts of it; and that is, to show the connexion of the proofs in any one instance, and no more; but in this it is of no great use, since the mind can perceive such connexion, where it really is, as easily, nay, perhaps better, without it.

If we will observe the actings of our own minds, we shall find that we reason best and clearest, when we only observe the connexion of the proof, without reducing our thoughts to any rule of syllogism. And therefore we may take notice that there are many men that reason exceeding clear and rightly, who know not how to make a syllogism. He that will look into many parts of Asia and America, will find men reason there perhaps as acutely as himself, who yet never heard of a syllogism, nor can reduce any one argument to those forms. All who have so far considered *syllogism,* as to see the reason why in three propositions laid together in one form, the conclusion will be certainly right, but in another not certainly so, I grant are certain of the conclusion they draw from the premises in the allowed *modes* and *figures.* But they who have not so far looked into those forms, are not sure by virtue of syllogism, that the conclusion certainly follows from the premises; they only take it to be so by an implicit faith in their teachers and a confidence in those forms of argumentation; but this is still but believing, not being certain. Now, if, of all mankind those who can make syllogisms are extremely few in comparison of those who cannot; and if, of those few who have been taught logic, there is but a very small number who do any more than believe that syllogisms, in the allowed *modes* and *figures* do conclude right, without knowing certainly that they do so; if syllogisms must be taken for the only proper instrument of reason and means of knowledge, it will follow, that, before Aristotle, there was not one man that did or could know anything by reason; and that, since the invention of syllogisms, there is not one of ten thousand that doth.

But God has not been so sparing to men to make them barely two-legged creatures, and left it to Aristotle to make them rational, i.e. those few of them that he could get so to examine the grounds of syllogisms, as to see that, in above three score ways that three propositions may be laid together, there are but about fourteen wherein one may be sure that the conclusion is right; and upon what grounds it is that, in these few, the conclusion is certain, and in the other not. God has been more bountiful to mankind than so. He has given them a mind that can reason, without being instructed in methods of syllogizing; the understanding is not taught to reason by these rules; it has a native faculty to perceive the coherence or incoherence of its ideas, and can range them right, without any such perplexing repetitions. I say not this any way to lessen Aristotle, whom I look on as one of the greatest men amongst the ancients, whose large views, acuteness, and penetration of thought and strength of judgment few have equalled; and who, in this very invention of forms of argumentation, wherein the conclusion may be shown to be rightly inferred, did great service against those who were not ashamed to deny anything. And I readily own that all right reasoning may be reduced to his forms of syllogism. But yet I think, without any diminution to him, I may truly say that they are not the only nor the best way of reasoning, for the leading of those into truth who are willing to find it, and desire to make the best use they may of their reason, for the attainment of knowledge. And he himself, it is plain, found out some forms to be conclusive, and others not, not by the forms themselves, but by the original way of knowledge, i.e. by the visible agreement of ideas. Tell a country gentle-woman that the wind is south-west, and the weather lowering, and like to rain, and she will easily understand it is not safe for her to go abroad thin clad in such a day, after a fever; she clearly sees the probable connexion of all these, viz. south-west wind, and clouds, rain, wetting, taking cold, relapse, and danger of death, without tying them together in those artificial and cumbersome fetters of several syllogisms, that clog and hinder the mind which proceeds from one part to another quicker and clearer without them; and the probability which she easily perceives in things thus in their native state would be quite lost if this argument were managed learnedly, and proposed in *mode* and *figure*. For it very often confounds the connexion; and, I think, everyone will perceive in mathematical demonstrations that the knowledge gained thereby comes shortest and clearest without syllogism.

To infer is nothing but, by virtue of one proposition laid down as true, to draw in another as true, i.e. to see or suppose such a connexion of the two ideas of the inferred proposition. V.g. Let this be the proposition laid down, " Men shall be punished in another world ", and from thence be inferred this other, " Then men can determine themselves ". The question now is to know whether the mind has made this inference right or no; if it has made it by finding out the intermediate ideas, and taking a view of the connexion of them, placed in a due order, it has proceeded rationally, and made a right inference; if it has done it without such a view, it has not so much made an inference that will hold, or an inference of right reason, as shown a willingness to have it be, or be taken for such. But in neither case is it syllogism that discovered those ideas, or showed the connexion of them; for they must be both found out, and the connexion everywhere perceived, before they can rationally be made use of in syllogism. In the instance above mentioned, what is it shows the force of the inference, and consequently the reasonableness of it, but a view of the connexion of all the intermediate ideas that draw in the conclusion, or proposition inferred? V.g. " Men shall be punished "; " God the punisher "; " Just punishment "; " The punished guilty "; " Could have done otherwise "; " Freedom "; " Self-determination "; by which chain of ideas thus visibly linked together in train, i.e. each intermediate idea agreeing on each side with those two it is immediately placed between, the ideas of *men* and *self-determination* appear to be connected, i.e. this proposition " men can determine themselves " is drawn in or inferred from this, " that they shall be punished in the other world ". For here the mind, seeing the connexion there is between the *idea*

of men's punishment in the other world and the *idea of God
punishing*; between *God punishing* and *the justice of the
punishment*; between *justice of punishment* and *guilt*; between
guilt and a *power to do otherwise*; between a *power to do
otherwise* and *freedom*; and between *freedom* and *self-
determination,* sees the connexion between *men* and *self-
determination.*

Of what use, then, are syllogisms? I answer, their chief
and main use is in the Schools, where men are allowed without
shame to deny the agreement of ideas that do manifestly
agree; or out of the Schools, to those who from thence have
learned without shame to deny the connexion of ideas, which
even to themselves is visible. But to an ingenuous searcher
after truth, who has no other aim but to find it, there is
no need of any such form to force the allowing of the
inference; the truth and reasonableness of it is better seen
in ranging of the ideas in a simple and plain order; and
hence it is that men, in their own inquiries after truth, never
use syllogisms to convince themselves or in teaching others
to instruct willing learners. Because, before they can put them
into a syllogism, they must see the connexion that is between
the intermediate idea and the two other ideas it is set between
and applied to, to show their agreement; and when they see
that, they see whether the inference be good or no; and so
syllogism comes too late to settle it.

Secondly, another reason that makes me doubt whether
syllogism be the only proper instrument of reason, in the
discovery of truth, is, that of whatever use *mode* and *figure*
is pretended to be in the laying open of fallacy, those scholastic
forms of discourse are not less liable to fallacies than the
plainer ways of argumentation; and for this I appeal to
common observation, which has always found these artificial
methods of reasoning more adapted to catch and entangle the
mind, than to instruct and inform the understanding. And hence
it is that men, even when they are baffled and silenced in this
scholastic way, are seldom or never convinced, and so brought
over to the conquering side; they perhaps acknowledge their
adversary to be the more skilful disputant, but rest nevertheless

persuaded of the truth on their side, and go away, worsted as they are, with the same opinion they brought with them; which they could not do if this way of argumentation carried light and conviction with it, and made men see where the truth lay; and therefore syllogism has been thought more proper for the attaining victory in dispute, than for the discovery or confirmation of truth in fair inquiries. And if it be certain that fallacies can be couched in syllogism, as it cannot be denied, it must be something else, and not syllogism, that must discover them.

5. *Helps little in Demonstration, less in Probability.* But however it be in knowledge, I think I may truly say, it is *of far less, or no use at all in probabilities.* For the assent there being to be determined by the preponderancy, after due weighing of all the proofs, with all circumstances on both sides, nothing is so unfit to assist the mind in that as syllogism; which running away with one assumed probability, or one topical argument, pursues that till it has led the mind quite out of sight of the thing under consideration; and, forcing it upon some remote difficulty, holds it fast there; entangled perhaps, and, as it were, manacled, in the chain of syllogisms, without allowing it the liberty, much less affording it the helps, requisite to show on which side, all things considered, is the greater probability.

6. *Serves not to increase our Knowledge, but fence with it.* But let it help us (as perhaps may be said) in convincing men of their errors and mistakes : (and yet I would fain see the man that was forced out of his opinion by dint of syllogism), yet still it fails our reason in that part, which, if not its highest perfection, is yet certainly its hardest task, and that which we most need its help in, and that is *the finding out of proofs, and making new discoveries.* The rules of syllogism serve not to furnish the mind with those intermediate ideas that may show the connexion of remote ones. This way of reasoning discovers no new proofs, but is the art of marshalling and ranging the old ones we have already.

8. *We reason about Particulars.* Having here had an occasion to speak of syllogism in general, and the use of it in

reasoning, and the improvement of our knowledge, it is fit, before I leave this subject, to take notice of one manifest mistake in the rules of syllogism : viz. that no syllogistical reasoning can be right and conclusive, but what has at least one *general* proposition in it. As if we could not reason, and have knowledge about particulars; whereas, in truth, the matter rightly considered, the immediate object of all our reasonings and knowledge is nothing but particulars. Every man's reasoning and knowledge is only about the ideas existing in his own mind; which are truly, every one of them, particular existences : and our knowledge and reasoning about other things is only as they correspond with those our particular ideas. So that the perception of the agreement or disagreement of our particular ideas is the whole and utmost of all our knowledge. Universality is but accidental to it, and consists only in this, that the particular ideas about which it is are such as more than one particular thing can correspond with and be represented by. But the perception of the agreement or disagreement of any two ideas, and consequently our knowledge, is equally clear and certain, whether either, or both, or neither of those ideas, be capable of representing more real beings than one, or no.

14. *Our Highest Degree of Knowledge is intuitive, without Reasoning.* Some of the ideas that are in the mind are so there that they can be by themselves immediately compared one with another; and in these the mind is able to perceive that they agree or disagree as clearly as that it has them. In this consists the evidence of all those *maxims* which nobody has any doubt about, but every man (does not, as is said, only assent to, but) *knows* to be true, as soon as ever they are proposed to his understanding. In the discovery of and assent to these truths there is no use of the discursive faculty, *no need of reasoning,* but they are known by a superior and higher degree of evidence.

18. *Consequences of Words, and Consequences of Ideas.* Though the deducing one proposition from another, or making inferences in words, be a great part of reason, and that which it is usually employed about; yet the principal act

of ratiocination is the finding the agreement or disagreement of two ideas one with another, by the intervention of a third. As a man, by a yard, finds two houses to be of the same length, which could not be brought together to measure their equality by juxta-position. Words have their consequences, as the signs of such ideas; and things agree or disagree, as really they are; but we observe it only by our ideas.

19. *Four sorts of Arguments.* Before we quit this subject, it may be worth our while a little to reflect on *four sorts of arguments* that men, in their reasonings with others, do ordinarily make use of to prevail on their assent, or at least so to awe them as to silence their opposition.

2. *First, Ad verecundiam.* First, the first is, to allege the opinions of men, whose parts, learning, eminency, power, or some other cause has gained a name, and settled their reputation in the common esteem with some kind of authority. This I think may be called *argumentum ad verecundiam.*

20. *Secondly, Ad Ignorantiam.* Secondly, another way that men ordinarily use to drive others, and force them to submit their judgments, and receive the opinion in debate, is to require the adversary to admit what they allege as a proof, or to assign a better. And this I call *argumentum ad ignorantiam.*

21. *Thirdly, Ad hominem.* Thirdly, a third way is to press a man with consequences drawn from his own principles or concessions. This is already known under the name of *argumentum ad hominem.*

22. *Fourthly, Ad judicium.* The fourth is the using of proofs drawn from any of the foundations of knowledge or probability. This I call *argumentum ad judicium.* This alone, of all the four, brings true instruction with it, and advances us in our way to knowledge. For, 1. It argues not another man's opinion to be right, because I, out of respect, or any other consideration but that of conviction, will not contradict him. 2. It proves not another man to be in the right way, nor that I ought to take the same with him, because I know not a better. 3. Nor does it follow that another man is in the right way, because he has shown me that I am in the wrong.

CHAPTER XVIII

OF FAITH AND REASON, AND THEIR DISTINCT PROVINCES

2. *Faith and Reason, what, as contradistinguished.* Reason, as contradistinguished to *faith,* I take to be the discovery of the certainty or probability of such propositions or truths, which the mind arrives at by deduction made from such ideas, which it has got by the use of its natural faculties, viz. by sensation or reflection.

Faith, on the other side, is the assent to any proposition, not thus made out by the deductions of reason, but upon the credit of the proposer, as coming from God, in some extraordinary way of communication. This way of discovering truths to men we call *revelation.*

3. *No new simple idea can be conveyed by traditional Revelation. First,* then I say, that *no man inspired by God can by any revelation communicate to others any new simple ideas which they had not before from sensation or reflection.* For, whatsoever impressions he himself may have from the immediate hand of God, this revelation, if it be of new simple ideas, cannot be conveyed to another, either by words or any other signs. Because words, by their immediate operation on us, cause no other ideas but of their natural sounds; and it is by the custom of using them for signs that they excite and revive in our minds latent ideas, but yet only such ideas as were there before. For our simple ideas, then, which are the foundation, and sole matter of all our notions and knowledge, we must depend wholly on our reason, I mean our natural faculties; and can by no means receive them, or any of them, from traditional revelation. I say *traditional revelation,* in distinction to *original revelation.* By the one I mean that first impression which is made immediately by God on the mind of any man, to which we cannot set any bounds;

and by the other those impressions delivered over to others in words, and the ordinary ways of conveying our conceptions one to another.

4. *Traditional Revelation may make us know Propositions knowable also by Reason, but not with the same Certainty that Reason doth.* Secondly, I say that *the same truths may be discovered, and conveyed down from revelation, which are discoverable to us by reason, and by those ideas we naturally may have.* So God might, by revelation, discover the truth of any proposition in Euclid; as well as men, by the natural use of their faculties, come to make the discovery themselves. In all things of this kind there is little need or use of revelation, God having furnished us with natural and surer means to arrive at the knowledge of them. For whatsoever truth we come to the clear discovery of, from the knowledge and contemplation of our own ideas, will always be certainer to us than those which are conveyed to us by *traditional revelation.* For the knowledge we have that this revelation came at first from God can never be so sure as the knowledge we have from the clear and distinct perception of the agreement or disagreement of our own ideas. The like holds in matter of fact knowable by our senses; v.g. the history of the deluge is conveyed to us by writings, which had their original from revelation; and yet nobody, I think, will say he has as certain and clear a knowledge of the flood as Noah, that saw it, or that he himself would have had, had he then been alive and seen it. For he has no greater an assurance than that of his senses that it is writ in the book supposed writ by Moses inspired; but he has not so great an assurance that Moses wrote that book as if he had seen Moses write it. So that the assurance of its being a revelation is less still than the assurance of his senses.

5. *Revelation cannot be admitted against the clear Evidence of Reason.* In propositions, then, whose certainty is built upon the clear perception of the agreement or disagreement of our ideas, attained either by immediate intuition, as in self-evident propositions, or by evident deductions of reason in demonstrations we need not the assistance of revelation, as

necessary to gain our assent, and introduce them into our minds. Because the natural ways of knowledge could settle them there, or had done it already; which is the greatest assurance we can possibly have of anything, unless where God immediately reveals it to us; and there too our assurance can be no greater than our knowledge is that it is a revelation from God. But yet nothing, I think, can, under that title, shake or overrule plain knowledge, or rationally prevail with any man to admit it for true, in a direct contradiction to the clear evidence of his own understanding. And therefore *no proposition can be received for divine revelation, or obtain the assent due to all such, if it be contradictory to our clear intuitive knowledge.* In propositions therefore contrary to the clear perception of the agreement or disagreement of any of our ideas it will be in vain to urge them as matters of faith. They cannot move our assent under that or any other title whatsoever.

7. *Things above Reason.* But, *thirdly,* there being many things wherein we have very imperfect notions, or none at all, and other things, of whose past, present, or future existence, by the natural use of our faculties, we can have no knowledge at all; these, as being beyond the discovery of our natural faculties, and *above reason,* are, when revealed, *the proper matter of faith.* Thus, that part of the angels rebelled against God, and thereby lost their first happy state, and that the dead shall rise, and live again : these and the like, being beyond the discovery of reason, are purely matters of faith, with which reason has directly nothing to do.

8. *Or not contrary to Reason, if revealed, are Matter of Faith.* But since God, in giving us the light of reason, has not thereby tied up his own hands from affording us, when he thinks fit, the light of revelation in any of those matters wherein our natural faculties are able to give a probable determination; *revelation,* where God has been pleased to give it, *must carry it against the probable conjectures of reason.* Because the mind not being certain of the truth of that it does not evidently know, but only yielding to the probability that appears in it, is bound to give up its assent to such a

testimony which, it is satisfied, comes from one who cannot err, and will not deceive. But yet, it still belongs to reason to judge of the truth of its being a revelation, and of the signification of the words wherein it is delivered.

9. *Revelation in Matters where Reason cannot judge, or but probably, ought to be hearkened to.* First, whatever proposition is revealed, of whose truth our mind, by its natural faculties and notions, cannot judge, that is purely matter of faith, and above reason.

Secondly, all propositions whereof the mind, by the use of its natural faculties, can come to determine and judge, from naturally acquired ideas, are matter of reason; with this difference still, that in those concerning which it has but an uncertain evidence, and so is persuaded of their truth only upon probable grounds, which still admit a possibility of the contrary to be true, without doing violence to the certain evidence of its own knowledge, and overturning the principles of all reason; in such probable propositions, I say, an evident revelation ought to determine our assent, even against probability.

11. *If the Boundaries be not set between Faith and Reason, no Enthusiasm or Extravagancy in Religion can be contradicted.* If the provinces of faith and reason are not kept distinct by these boundaries, there will, in matter of religion, be no room for reason at all; and those extravagant opinions and ceremonies that are to be found in the several religions of the world will not deserve to be blamed. For, to this crying up of faith in opposition to reason, we may, I think, in good measure ascribe those absurdities that fill almost all the religions which possess and divide mankind. For men having been principled with an opinion, that they must not consult reason in the things of religion, however apparently contradictory to common sense and the very principles of all their knowledge, have let loose their fancies and natural superstition; and have been by them led into so strange opinions, and extravagant practices in religion, that a considerate man cannot but stand amazed at their follies, and judge them so far from being acceptable to the great and

wise God, that he cannot avoid thinking them ridiculous and offensive, to a sober good man. So that, in effect, religion, which should most distinguish us from beasts, and ought most peculiarly to elevate us, as rational creatures, above brutes, is that wherein men often appear most irrational, and more senseless than beasts themselves. *Credo, quia impossibile est* : I believe, because it is impossible, might, in a good man, pass for a sally of zeal; but would prove a very ill rule for men to choose their opinions or religion by.

CHAPTER XIX

OF ENTHUSIASM

1. *Love of Truth necessary.* He that would seriously set upon the search of truth ought in the first place to prepare his mind with a love of it. For he that loves it not will not take much pains to get it, nor be much concerned when he misses it. There is nobody in the commonwealth of learning who does not profess himself a lover of truth; and there is not a rational creature that would not take it amiss to be thought otherwise of. And yet, for all this, one may truly say that there are very few lovers of truth, for truth's sake, even amongst those who persuade themselves that they are so. How a man may know whether he be so in earnest, is worth inquiry; and I think there is one unerring mark of it, viz. the not entertaining any proposition with greater assurance than the proofs it is built upon will warrant. Whoever goes beyond this measure of assent, it is plain receives not truth in the love of it, loves not truth for truth's sake, but for some other bye-end. For the evidence that any proposition is true (except such as are self-evident) lying only in the proofs a man has of it, whatsoever degrees of assent he affords it beyond the degrees of that evidence, it is plain all that surplusage of assurance is owing to some other affection, and not to the love of truth; it being as impossible that the

love of truth should carry my assent above the evidence there is to me, that it is true, as that the love of truth should make me assent to any proposition for the sake of that evidence which it has not, that it is true; which is in effect to love it as a truth, because it is possible or probable that it may not be true. In any truth that gets not possession of our minds by the irresistible light of self-evidence, or by the force of demonstration, the arguments that gain it assent are the vouchers and gauge of its probability to us; and we can receive it for no other than such as they deliver it to our understandings. Whatsoever credit or authority we give to any proposition more than it receives from the principles and proofs it supports itself upon, is owing to our inclinations that way, and is so far a derogation from the love of truth as such; which, as it can receive no evidence from our passions or interests, so it should receive no tincture from them.

3. *Force of Enthusiasm*. Upon this occasion I shall take the liberty to consider a third ground of assent, which with some men has the same authority, and is as confidently relied on as either faith or reason, I mean *enthusiasm*; which, laying by reason, would set up revelation without it. Whereby in effect it takes away both reason and revelation, and substitutes in the room of them the ungrounded fancies of a man's own brain, and assumes them for a foundation both of opinion and conduct.

5. *Rise of Enthusiasm*. Immediate revelation being a much easier way for men to establish their opinions and regulate their conduct than the tedious and not always successful labour of strict reasoning, it is no wonder that some have been very apt to pretend to revelation, and to persuade themselves that they are under the peculiar guidance of heaven in their actions and opinions, especially in those of them which they cannot account for by the ordinary methods of knowledge and principles of reason.

6. *Enthusiasm*. Their minds being thus prepared, whatever groundless opinion comes to settle itself strongly upon their fancies is an illumination from the Spirit of God, and presently of divine authority; and whatsoever odd action they

find in themselves a strong inclination to do, that impulse is concluded to be a call or direction from heaven, and must be obeyed; it is a commission from above, and they cannot err in executing it.

7. This I take to be properly enthusiasm, which, though founded neither on reason nor divine revelation, but rising from the conceits of a warmed or overweening brain, works yet, where it once gets footing, more powerfully on the persuasions and actions of men than either of those two, or both together, men being most forwardly obedient to the impulses they receive from themselves; and the whole man is sure to act more vigorously where the whole man is carried by a natural motion. For strong conceit, like a new principle, carries all easily with it, when got above common sense, and freed from all restraint of reason and check of reflection, it is heightened into a divine authority, in concurrence with our own temper and inclination.

8. *Enthusiasm mistaken for Seeing and Feeling.* The love of something extraordinary, the ease and glory it is to be inspired, and be above the common and natural ways of knowledge, so flatters many men's laziness, ignorance, and vanity, that, when once they are got into this way of immediate revelation, of illumination without search, and of certainty without proof and without examination, it is a hard matter to get them out of it. Reason is lost upon them, they are above it; they see the light infused into their understandings, and cannot be mistaken; it is clear and visible there, like the light of bright sunshine; shows itself, and needs no other proof but its own evidence; they feel the hand of God moving them within, and the impulses of the Spirit, and cannot be mistaken in what they feel.

10. But to examine a little soberly this internal light, and this feeling on which they build so much. These men have, they say, clear light, and they see; they have awakened sense, and they feel; this cannot, they are sure, be disputed them. For when a man says he sees or he feels, nobody can deny him that he does so. But here let me ask: this seeing, is it the perception of the truth of the proposition,

or of this, that it is a revelation from God? The knowledge of any proposition coming into my mind, I know not how, is not a perception that it is from God. Much less is a strong persuasion that it is true a perception that it is from God, or so much as true. But however it be called light and seeing, I suppose it is at most but belief and assurance; and the proposition taken for a revelation is not such as they know to be true, but take to be true. The question then here is: how do I know that God is the revealer of this to me, that this impression is made upon my mind by his Holy Spirit, and that therefore I ought to obey it? If I know not this, how great soever the assurance is that I am possessed with, it is groundless, whatever light I pretend to, it is but *enthusiasm*. For, whether the proposition supposed to be revealed be in itself evidently true, or visibly probable, or, by the natural ways of knowledge, uncertain, the proposition that must be well grounded and manifested to be true is this, that God is the revealer of it, and that what I take to be a revelation is certainly put into my mind by Him, and is not an illusion dropped in by some other spirit, or raised by my own fancy. For, if I mistake not, these men receive it for true, because they presume God revealed it. Does it not, then, stand them upon to examine upon what grounds they presume it to be a revelation from God? or else all their confidence is mere presumption; and this light they are so dazzled with is nothing but an *ignis fatuus*, that leads them continually round in this circle; *It is a revelation, because they firmly believe it*; and *they believe it, because it is a revelation*.

11. *Enthusiasm fails of Evidence, that the Proposition is from God.* Men thus possessed boast of a light whereby they say they are enlightened, and brought into the knowledge of this or that truth. But if they know it to be a truth, they must know it to be so, either by its own self-evidence to natural reason, or by the rational proofs that make it out to be so. If they see and know it to be a truth either of these two ways, they in vain suppose it to be a revelation. For they know it to be true by the same way that any other man naturally may know that it is so, without the help of revelation. For thus,

all the truths, of what kind soever, that men uninspired are enlightened with, came into their minds, and are established there. If they say they know it to be true, because it is a revelation from God, the reason is good; but then it will be demanded how they know it to be a revelation from God. If they say, by the light it brings with it, which shines bright in their minds, and they cannot resist; I beseech them to consider whether this be any more than what we have taken notice of already, viz. that it is a revelation, because they strongly believe it to be true. For all the light they speak of is but a strong, though ungrounded, persuasion of their own minds that it is a truth.

12. *Firmness of Persuasion no Proof that any Proposition is from God.* This cannot be otherwise, whilst firmness of persuasion is made the cause of believing, and confidence of being in the right is made an argument of truth. St. Paul himself believed he did well, and that he had a call to it, when he persecuted the Christians, whom he confidently thought in the wrong; but yet it was he, and not they, who were mistaken. Good men are men still liable to mistakes, and are sometimes warmly engaged in errors, which they take for divine truths, shining in their minds with the clearest light.

14. *Revelation must be judged of by Reason.* He, therefore, that will not give himself up to all the extravagances of delusion and error must bring this guide of his *light within* to the trial. God when he makes the prophet does not unmake the man. He leaves all his faculties in their natural state, to enable him to judge of his inspirations, whether they be of divine original or no. When he illuminates the mind with supernatural light, he does not extinguish that which is natural. If he would have us assent to the truth of any proposition, he either evidences that truth by the usual methods of natural reason, or else makes it known to be a truth which he would have us assent to by his authority, and convinces us that it is from him, by some marks which reason cannot be mistaken in. *Reason must be our last judge and guide in everything.* I do not mean that we must consult reason, and examine whether a proposition revealed from God can be made out by

natural principles, and if it cannot, that then we may reject it; but consult it we must, and by it examine whether it be a revelation from God or no; and if reason finds it to be revealed from God, reason then declares for it as much as for any other truth, and makes it one of her dictates. Every conceit that thoroughly warms our fancies must pass for an inspiration, if there be nothing but the strength of our persuasions, whereby to judge of our persuasions; if reason must not examine their truth by something extrinsical to the persuasions themselves, inspirations and delusions, truth and falsehood, will have the same measure, and will not be possible to be distinguished.

15. *Belief no Proof of Revelation.* Thus we see the holy men of old, who had revelations from God, had something else besides that internal light of assurance in their own minds, to testify to them that it was from God. They were not left to their own persuasions alone, that those persuasions were from God, but had outward signs to convince them of the author of those revelations. And when they were to convince others, they had a power given them to justify the truth of their commission from heaven, and by visible signs to assert the divine authority of a message they were sent with.

16. In what I have said I am far from denying that God can, or doth sometimes enlighten men's minds in the apprehending of certain truths or excite them to good actions, by the immediate influence and assistance of the Holy Spirit, without any extraordinary signs accompanying it. But in such cases too we have reason and Scripture, unerring rules to know whether it be from God or no. It is not the strength of our private persuasion within ourselves, that can warrant it to be a light or motion from heaven; nothing can do that but the written word of God without us, or that standard of reason which is common to us with all men.

CHAPTER XX

OF WRONG ASSENT, OR ERROR

1. *Causes of Error.* Knowledge being to be had only of visible and certain truth, *error* is not a fault of our knowledge, but a mistake of our judgment giving assent to that which is not true.

But if assent be grounded on likelihood, if the proper object and motive of our assent be probability, and that probability consists in what is laid down in the foregoing chapters, it will be demanded how men come to give their assents contrary to probability. For there is nothing more common than contrariety of opinions, nothing more obvious than that one man wholly disbelieves what another only doubts of, and a third steadfastly believes and firmly adheres to. The reasons whereof, though they may be very various, yet, I suppose may all be reduced to these four:

1. *Want of proofs.*
2. *Want of ability to use them.*
3. *Want of will to see them.*
4. *Wrong measures of probability.*

2. *First, Want of Proofs.* First, by *want of proofs,* I do not mean only the want of those proofs which are nowhere extant, and so are nowhere to be had, but the want even of those proofs which are in being, or might be procured. And thus men want proofs, who have not the convenience or opportunity to make experiments and observations themselves, tending to the proof of any proposition, nor likewise the convenience to inquire into and collect the testimonies of others; and in this state are the greatest part of mankind, who are given up to labour, and enslaved to the necessity of their mean condition, whose lives are worn out only in the provisions for living. These men's opportunity of knowledge and inquiry are commonly as narrow as their fortunes; and their

understandings are but little instructed, when all their whole time and pains is laid out to still the croaking of their own bellies, or the cries of their children. It is not to be expected that a man who drudges on all his life in a laborious trade should be more knowing in the variety of things done in the world than a packhorse, who is driven constantly forwards and backwards in a narrow lane and dirty road, only to market, should be skilled in the geography of the country.

4. *People hindered from Inquiry*. Besides those whose improvements and informations are straitened by the narrowness of their fortunes, there are others whose largeness of fortune would plentifully enough supply books, and other requisites for clearing of doubts, and discovering of truth; but they are cooped in close by the laws of their countries, and the strict guards of those whose interest it is to keep them ignorant, lest, knowing more, they should believe the less in them. This is generally the case of all those who live in places where care is taken to propagate truth without knowledge; where men are forced, at a venture, to be of the religion of the country; and must therefore swallow down opinions, as silly people do empirics' pills, without knowing what they are made of, or how they will work, and having nothing to do but believe that they will do the cure; but in this are much more miserable than they, in that they are not at liberty to refuse swallowing what perhaps they had rather let alone, or to choose the physician, to whose conduct they would trust themselves.

5. *Secondly, Want of skill to use them*. Secondly, those who *want skill to use those evidences they have of probabilities*, who cannot carry a train of consequences in their heads, nor weigh exactly the preponderancy of contrary proofs and testimonies, making every circumstance its due allowance, may be easily misled to assent to positions that are not probable. There are some men of one, some but of two syllogisms, and no more; and others that can but advance one step further. These cannot always discern that side on which the strongest proofs lie, cannot constantly follow that which in itself is the more probable opinion. Now that there is such a

difference between men, in respect of their understandings, I think nobody, who has had any conversation with his neighbours, will question; one may, without doing injury to mankind, affirm that there is a greater distance between some men and others in this respect, than between some men and some beasts. But how this comes about is a speculation, though of great consequence, yet not necessary to our present purpose.

6. *Thirdly, Want of Will to use them.* *Thirdly,* there are another sort of people that want proofs, not because they are out of their reach, but *because they will not use them*; who, though they have riches and leisure enough, and want neither parts nor other helps, are yet never the better for them. Their hot pursuit of pleasure, or constant drudgery in business, engages some men's thoughts elsewhere; laziness and oscitancy in general, or a particular aversion for books, study, and meditation, keep others from any serious thoughts at all; and some out of fear that an impartial inquiry would not favour those opinions which best suit their prejudices, lives, and designs, content themselves, without examination, to take upon trust what they find convenient and in fashion. How men, whose plentiful fortunes allow them leisure to improve their understandings, can satisfy themselves with a lazy ignorance, I cannot tell; but methinks they have a low opinion of their souls, who lay out all their incomes in provisions for the body, and employ none of it to procure the means and helps of knowledge; who take great care to appear always in a neat and splendid outside, and would think themselves miserable in coarse clothes, or a patched coat, and yet contentedly suffer their minds to appear abroad in a piebald livery of coarse patches and borrowed shreds, such as it has pleased chance, or their country tailor (I mean the common opinion of those they have conversed with) to clothe them in.

7. *Fourthly, Wrong Measures of Probability, whereof.* *Fourthly,* there remains yet the last sort, who, even where the real probabilities appear, and are plainly laid before them, do not admit of the conviction, nor yield unto manifest reasons, but do either ἐπέχειν, suspend their assent, or give it to the

less probable opinion. And to this danger are those exposed who have taken up *wrong measures of probability,* which are :

1. *Propositions that are not in themselves certain and evident, but doubtful and false, taken up for principles.*
2. *Received hypotheses.*
3. *Predominant passions or inclinations.*
4. *Authority.*

8. *First, Doubtful Propositions taken for Principles.* First, the first and firmest ground of probability is the conformity anything has to our own knowledge, especially that part of our knowledge which we have embraced, and continue to look on as *principles.* This I readily grant, that one truth cannot contradict another; but withal I take leave also to say that everyone ought very carefully to beware what he admits for a principle, to examine it strictly, and see whether he certainly knows it to be true of itself, by its own evidence, or whether he does only with assurance believe it to be so, upon the authority of others. For he hath a strong bias put into his understanding, which will unavoidably misguide his assent, who hath imbibed *wrong principles,* and has blindly given himself up to the authority of any opinion in itself not evidently true.

9. There is nothing more ordinary than that children should receive into their minds propositions (especially about matters of religion) from their parents, nurses, or those about them; which being insinuated into their unwary as well as unbiassed understandings, and fastened by degrees, are at last (equally whether true or false) riveted there by long custom and education, beyond all possibility of being pulled out again.

10. The great obstinacy that is to be found in men firmly believing quite contrary opinions, though many times equally absurd, in the various religions of mankind, are as evident a proof as they are an unavoidable consequence of this way of reasoning from received traditional principles. So that men will disbelieve their own eyes, renounce the evidence of their senses, and give their own experience the lie, rather than admit of anything disagreeing with these sacred tenets. And what way will you take to convince a man of any improbable

opinion he holds, who, with some philosophers, hath laid down this as a foundation of reasoning, that he must believe his reason (for so men improperly call arguments drawn from their principles) against their senses? Let an enthusiast be principled that he or his teacher is inspired, and acted by an immediate communication of the Divine Spirit, and you in vain bring the evidence of clear reasons against his doctrine. Whoever, therefore, have imbibed wrong principles, are not, in things inconsistent with these principles, to be moved by the most apparent and convincing probabilities, till they are so candid and ingenuous to themselves, as to be persuaded to examine even those very principles, which many never suffer themselves to do.

11. *Secondly, Received Hypotheses.* Secondly, next to these are men whose understandings are cast into a mould, and fashioned just to the size of a *received hypothesis.* The difference between these and the former is that they will admit of matter of fact, and agree with dissenters in that, but differ only in assigning of reasons and explaining the manner of operation. These are not at that open defiance with their senses, as the former; they can endure to hearken to their information a little more patiently; but will by no means admit of their reports in the explanation of things; nor be prevailed on by probabilities, which would convince them that things are not brought about just after the same manner that they have decreed within themselves that they are. Would it not be an insufferable thing for a learned professor, and that which his scarlet would blush at, to have his authority of forty years standing, wrought out of hard rock, Greek and Latin, with no small expense of time and candle, and confirmed by general tradition and a reverend beard, in an instant overturned by an upstart novelist? Can anyone expect that he should be made to confess that what he taught his scholars thirty years ago was all error and mistake, and that he sold them hard words and ignorance at a very dear rate. What probabilities, I say, are sufficient to prevail in such a case? To this of wrong hypothesis may be reduced the errors that may be occasioned by a true hypothesis, or right principles,

but not rightly understood. There is nothing more familiar than this. The instances of men contending for different opinions, which they all derive from the infallible truth of the Scripture, are an undeniable proof of it. All that call themselves Christians, allow the text that says, μετανοεῖτε, to carry in it the obligation to a very weighty duty. But yet how very erroneous will one of their practices be, who, understanding nothing but the French, take this rule with one translation to be, *Repentez-vous,* repent; or with the other, *Faitez pénitence,* do penance.

12. *Thirdly, Predominant Passions.* Thirdly, probabilities which cross men's appetites and prevailing passions run the same fate. Let never so much probability hang on one side of a covetous man's reasoning, and money on the other, it is easy to foresee which will outweigh. Tell a man passionately in love that he is jilted; bring a score of witnesses of the falsehood of his mistress, it is ten to one but three kind words of hers shall invalidate all their testimonies. *Quod volumus, facile credimus.*

15. *What Probabilities determine the Assent.* But yet there is some end of it; and a man having carefully inquired into all the grounds of probability and unlikeliness, done his utmost to inform himself in all particulars fairly, and cast up the sum total on both sides, may, in most cases, come to acknowledge, upon the whole matter, on which side the probability rests; wherein some proofs in matter of reason, being suppositions upon universal experience, are so cogent and clear, and some testimonies in matter of fact so universal, that he cannot refuse his assent. So that I think we may conclude that, in propositions, where though the proofs in view are of most moment, yet there are sufficient grounds to suspect that there is either fallacy in words, or certain proofs as considerable to be produced on the contrary side, there assent, suspense, or dissent, are often voluntary actions. But where the proofs are such as make it highly probable, and there is not sufficient ground to suspect that there is either fallacy of words (which sober and serious consideration may discover) nor equally valid proofs yet undiscovered, latent on

the other side (which also the nature of the thing may, in some cases, make plain to a considerate man); there, I think, a man who has weighed them can scarce refuse his assent to the side on which the greater probability appears. In other less clear cases I think it is in a man's power to suspend his assent, and perhaps content himself with the proofs he has, if they favour the opinion that suits with his inclination or interest, and so stop from further search. But that a man should afford his assent to that side on which the less probability appears to him, seems to me utterly impracticable, and as impossible as it is to believe that same thing probable and improbable at the same time.

16. *Where it is in our Power to suspend it.* As knowledge is no more arbitrary than perception, so, I think, assent is no more in our power than knowledge. When the agreement of any two ideas appears to our minds, whether immediately or by the assistance of reason, I can no more refuse to perceive, no more avoid knowing it, than I can avoid seeing those objects which I turn my eyes to, and look on in daylight; and what upon full examination I find the most probable I cannot deny my assent to. But, though we cannot hinder our knowledge, where the agreement is once perceived, nor our assent, where the probability manifestly appears upon due consideration of all the measures of it; yet we can hinder both *knowledge* and *assent, by stopping our inquiry,* and not employing our faculties in the search of any truth. If it were not so, ignorance, error, or infidelity, could not in any case be a fault. In cases where the assent one way or other is of no importance to the interest of anyone, no action, no concernment of his following or depending thereon, there it is not strange that the mind should give itself up to the common opinion, or render itself to the first comer. But where the mind judges that the proposition has concernment in it, where the assent or not assenting is thought to draw consequences of moment after it, and good or evil to depend on choosing or refusing the right side, and the mind sets itself seriously to inquire and examine the probability; there I think it is not in our choice to take which side we please, if manifest odds appear on either.

The greater probability, I think, in that case will determine the assent; and a man can no more avoid assenting, or taking it to be true, where he perceives the greater probability, than he can avoid knowing it to be true, where he perceives the agreement or disagreement of any two ideas.

If this be so, the foundation of error will lie in wrong measures of probability; as the foundation of vice in wrong measures of good.

17. *Fourthly, Authority.* Fourthly, the fourth and last wrong measure of probability I shall take notice of, and which keeps in ignorance or error more people than all the other together, is that which I have mentioned in the foregoing chapter: I mean the giving up our assent to the common received opinions, either of our friends or party, neighbourhood or country. How many men have no other ground for their tenets than the supposed honesty, or learning, or number of those of the same profession? As if honest or bookish men could not err, or truth were to be established by the vote of the multitude; yet this with most men serves the turn. If we could but see the secret motives that influenced the men of name and learning in the world, and the leaders of parties, we should not always find that it was the embracing of truth for its own sake, that made them espouse the doctrines they owned and maintained.

18. *Men not in so many Errors as is imagined.* But, notwithstanding the great noise is made in the world about errors and opinions, I must do mankind that right as to say, *There are not so many men in errors and wrong opinions as is commonly supposed.* Not that I think they embrace the truth, but indeed, because concerning those doctrines they keep such a stir about, they have no thought, no opinion at all. They are resolved to stick to a party that education or interest has engaged them in, and there, like the common soldiers of an army, show their courage and warmth as their leaders direct, without ever examining, or so much as knowing, the cause they contend for. Thus men become professors of, and combatants for, those opinions they were never convinced of nor proselytes to, no, nor ever had so much as floating in their heads; and

though one cannot say there are fewer improbable or erroneous opinions in the world than there are, yet this is certain : there are fewer that actually assent to them, and mistake them for truths, than is imagined.

CHAPTER XXI

OF THE DIVISION OF THE SCIENCES

1. *Three sorts.* All that can fall within the compass of human understanding, being either, *First,* the nature of things, as they are in themselves, their relations, and their manner of operation; or, *Secondly,* that which man himself ought to do, as a rational and voluntary agent, for the attainment of any end, especially happiness : or, *Thirdly,* the ways and means whereby the knowledge of both the one and the other of these are attained and communicated; I think science may be divided properly into these three sorts :

2. *First, Physica.* First, the knowledge of things, as they are in their own proper beings, their constitutions, properties, and operations; whereby I mean not only matter and body, but spirits also, which have their proper natures, constitutions, and operations, as well as bodies. This, in a little more enlarged sense of the word, I call Φυσική, or *natural philosophy.* The end of this is bare speculative truth; and whatsoever can afford the mind of man any such, falls under this branch, whether it be God himself, angels, spirits, bodies; or any of their affections, as number, and figure, &c.

3. *Secondly, Practica.* Secondly, Πρακτική, the skill of right applying our own powers and actions, for the attainment of things good and useful. The most considerable under this head is *ethics,* which is the seeking out those rules and measures of human actions which lead to happiness, and the means to practise them. The end of this is not bare speculation and the knowledge of truth; but right, and a conduct suitable to it.

4. *Thirdly,* Σημειωτική. *Thirdly,* the third branch may be called Σημειωτική, or *the doctrine of signs*; the most usual whereof being words, it is aptly enough termed also Λογική, *logic*; the business whereof is to consider the nature of signs the mind makes use of for the understanding of things, or conveying its knowledge to others. For, since the things the mind contemplates are none of them, besides itself, present to the understanding, it is necessary that something else, as a sign or representation of the thing it considers, should be present to it: and these are *ideas.* And because the scene of ideas that makes one man's thoughts cannot be laid open to the immediate view of another, nor laid up anywhere but in the memory, a no very sure repository; therefore to communicate our thoughts to one another, as well as record them for our own use, signs of our ideas are also necessary; those which men have found most convenient, and therefore generally make use of, are *articulate sounds.* The consideration, then, of *ideas* and *words* as the great instruments of knowledge makes no despicable part of their contemplation who would take a view of human knowledge in the whole extent of it. And perhaps if they were distinctly weighed, and duly considered, they would afford us another sort of logic and critic, than what we have been hitherto acquainted with.

5. *This is the first Division of the Objects of Knowledge.* This seems to me the first and most general, as well as natural, division of the objects of our understanding. For a man can employ his thoughts about nothing, but either, the contemplation of *things* themselves, for the discovery of truth; or about the things in his own power, which are his own *actions,* for the attainment of his own ends; or the *signs* the mind makes use of both in the one and the other, and the right ordering of them, for its clearer information. All which three, viz. *things,* as they are in themselves knowable, *actions* as they depend on us, in order to happiness, and the right use of *signs* in order to knowledge, being *toto coelo* different, they seemed to me to be the three great provinces of the intellectual world, wholly separate and distinct one from another.

*Appeddix: the controversy
with stilling fleet*

Bibliography

Chronological Table

Index

APPENDIX

THE CONTROVERSY WITH STILLINGFLEET

With four exceptions, Locke did not reply in print to authors who had criticized the *Essay*. In the 2nd edition he added five paragraphs to the *Epistle to the Reader* (later transferred to a footnote at II xxviii 11), in answer to comments made on his supposed views on morality by James Lowde in his *Discourse Concerning the Nature of Man* (1694). In the first French edition of the *Essay* Locke replied in a footnote at II xv 9 to a criticism made by the Dutch professor, Jean Barbeyrac, that he was inconsistent in maintaining both that the idea of space is a simple idea and that space consists of parts. As neither of these criticisms concerns themes central to the *Essay*, Locke's replies have been omitted from this edition.

In 1696 Edward Stillingfleet, Bishop of Worcester, published his *Discourse in Vindication of the Doctrine of the Trinity*, in the final chapter of which he attacked some of the main doctrines of the *Essay*. Locke published a letter in reply, and the controversy between them continued until 1699. The full texts are to be found in Stillingfleet's *Works*, Vol. III (1710) and Locke's *Works*, Vol. I (4th ed. 1740)[1]. In the 5th edition of the *Essay* Locke incorporated in long footnotes portions of his side of the controversy, at the following points : I i 8; I iv 8; II xxiii 1, 2; II xxvii 29; III iii 11; IV i 2; IV iii 6. As some of these footnotes provide additional material for an understanding of the *Essay*, a selection from them is given below.

Ideas (I i 8). Stillingfleet having objected to " the new way of

[1] To his second letter Locke added as a postscript a few contemptuous remarks on a criticism of the *Essay*, written by Thomas Burnet and published anonymously as *Remarks upon an Essay Concerning Human Understanding* (1697).

ideas " which he accused Locke of introducing, the latter replied that, as he meant by ' idea ' whatever was present in a man's mind when he thought, Stillingfleet could hardly be objecting to ideas, but only to Locke's choice of the word ' idea ' to stand for them. He was willing to accept a different term if a better could be found, disliked the suggestion of ' notion ' (for the reason given in III v 12), and concluded :

" My lord, the new way of ideas, and the old way of speaking intelligibly, was always, and ever will be the same. And if I may take the liberty to declare my sense of it, herein it consists :

(1) That a man use no words but such as he makes the signs of certain determined objects of his mind in thinking, which he can make known to another. (2) Next that he use the same word steadily for the sign of the same immediate object of his mind in thinking. (3) That he join these words together in propositions, according to the grammatical rules of that language he speaks in. (4) That he unite those sentences in a coherent discourse. Thus, and thus only, I humbly conceive, anyone may preserve himself from the confines and suspicion of jargon, whether he pleases to call those immediate objects of his mind, which his words do or should stand for, ideas or no."

General Idea of Substance (II ii 2). Locke writes : " Against this—that the materials of all our knowledge are suggested and furnished to the mind only by sensation and reflection—the Bishop of Worcester makes use of the idea of substance in these words : ' if the idea of substance be grounded upon plain and evident reason, then we must allow an idea of substance which comes not in by sensation or reflection; so we may be certain of something which we have not by those ideas '."

To which our author answers : " these words of your lordship's contain nothing, that I see in them, against me : for I never said that the general idea of substance comes in by sensation and reflection; or, that it is a simple idea of sensation or reflection, though it be ultimately founded in them : for it is a complex idea, made up of the general idea of something, or being, with the relation of a support to accidents. For general ideas come not into the mind by sensation or reflection, but are the creatures or inventions of the understanding, as, I think, I have shown; and also, how the mind makes them from ideas, which it has got by sensation and reflection : and as to the ideas of relation, how the mind forms them, and how they are derived from, and ultimately terminate in, ideas of sensation and reflection, I have likewise shown."

Your lordship's argument, in the passage we are upon, stands thus : ' If the general idea of substance be grounded upon plain and evident reason, then we must allow an idea of substance, which comes not in by sensation or reflection :' This is a consequence which, with submission, I think will not hold, because it is founded upon a supposition which, I think, will not hold, viz. that reason and ideas are inconsistent; for if that supposition be not true, then the general idea of substance may be grounded on plain and evident reason : and yet it will not follow from thence, that it is not ultimately grounded on, and derived from, ideas which come in by sensation or reflection, and so cannot be said to come in by sensation or reflection.

To explain myself, and clear my meaning in this matter : all the ideas of all the sensible qualities of a cherry come into my mind by sensation; the ideas of perceiving, thinking, reasoning, knowing, &c. come into my mind by reflection : the ideas of these qualities and actions, or powers, are perceived by the mind to be by themselves inconsistent with existence; or, as your lordship well expresses it, " we find that we can have no true conception of any modes or accidents, but we must conceive a substratum or subject, wherein they are;" i.e. that they cannot exist or subsist of themselves. Hence the mind perceives their necessary connexion with inherence or being supported; which being a relative idea superadded to the red colour in a cherry, or to thinking in a man, the mind frames the correlative idea of a support. For I never denied that the mind could frame to itself ideas of relation, but have showed the quite contrary in my chapters about relation. But because a relation cannot be founded in nothing, or be the relation of nothing, and the thing here related as a supporter or support, is not represented to the mind by any clear and distinct idea; therefore the obscure, indistinct, vague idea of thing or something is all that is left to be the positive idea, which has the relation of a support or substratum to modes or accidents; and that general indetermined idea of something, is, by the abstraction of the mind, derived also from the simple ideas of sensation and reflection; and thus the mind, from the positive, simple ideas got by sensation or reflection comes to the general relative idea of substance; which, without these positive simple ideas, it would never have."

At II xxiii 1, Locke continues: "your lordship seems to charge me with two faults; one, that I make ' the general idea of substance to be framed, not by abstracting and enlarging simple ideas, but by a complication of many simple ideas together ': the other, as if I had said, the being of substance had no other foundation but the fancies of men.

As to the first of these, I beg leave to remind your lordship, that I say in more places than one, and particularly III iii 6 and I xi 9 where, *ex professo* I treat of abstraction and general ideas, that they are all made by abstracting; and therefore could not be understood to mean that that of substance was made any other way; however my pen might have slipped, or the negligence of expression, where I might have something else than the general idea of substance in view, might make me seem to say so.

That I was not speaking of the general idea of substance in the passage your lordship quotes, is manifest from the title of that chapter, which is " *Of the Complex Ideas of Substances.*"

In which words I do not observe any that deny the general idea of substance to be made by abstraction; nor any that say, " it is made by a complication of many simple ideas together ". But speaking in that place of the ideas of distinct substances, such as man, horse, gold, &c. I say they are made up of certain combinations of simple ideas; which combinations are looked upon, each of them, as one simple idea, though they

were many; and we call it by one name of substance, though
made up of modes, from the custom of supposing a substratum,
wherein that combination does subsist. So that in this
paragraph I only give an account of the idea of distinct
substances, such as oak, elephant, iron, &c. how, though they
are made up of distinct complications of modes, yet they are
looked on as one idea, called by one name, as making distinct
sorts of substances.

But that my notion of substance in general is quite different
from these, and has no such combination of simple ideas in it,
is evident from the immediately following words, where I say :
" the idea of pure substance in general is only a supposition
of we know not what support of such qualities as are capable
of producing simple ideas in us ", and these two I plainly
distinguish all along, particularly where I say, "whatever
therefore be the secret and abstract nature of substance in
general, all the ideas we have of particular distinct substances
are nothing but several combinations of simple ideas, co-
existing in such, though unknown, cause of their union, as
makes the whole subsist of itself ".

The other thing laid to my charge, is, as if I took the being
of substance to be doubtful, or rendered it so by the imperfect
and ill-grounded idea I have given of it. To which I beg leave
to say that I ground not the being, but the idea, of substance,
on our accustoming ourselves to suppose some substratum; for
it is of the idea alone I speak there, and not of the being of
substance. And having everywhere affirmed and built upon it,
that a man is a substance, I cannot be supposed to question or
doubt of the being of substance, till I can question or doubt
of my own being. Further I say, "sensation convinces us that
there are solid extended substances; and reflection, that there
are thinking ones ". So that I think the being of substance is
not shaken by what I have said : and if the idea of it should
be, yet (the being of things depending not on our ideas) the
being of substance would not be at all shaken by my saying
we had but an obscure imperfect idea of it, and that that idea
came from our accustoming ourselves to suppose some substratum; or indeed, if I should say we had no idea of substance

at all. For a great many things may be and are granted to have a being, and be in nature, of which we have no ideas. For example; it cannot be doubted that there are distinct species of separate spirits, of which yet we have no distinct ideas at all; it cannot be questioned but spirits have ways of communicating their thoughts, and yet we have no idea of it at all.

The being then of substance being safe and secure, notwithstanding anything I have said, let us see whether the idea of it be not so too. Your lordship asks, with concern, "and is this all indeed that is to be said for the being" (if your lordship please, let it be the idea) "of substance, that we accustom ourselves to suppose a substratum? Is that custom grounded upon true reason, or no?" I have said, that it is grounded upon this, "that we cannot conceive how simple ideas of sensible qualities should subsist alone, and therefore we suppose them to exist in, and to be supported by, some common subject, which support we denote by the same 'substance'." Which I think is a true reason, because it is the same your lordship grounds the supposition of a substratum on, in this very page; even on the "the repugnancy to our conceptions, that modes and accident should subsist by themselves". So that I have the good luck to agree here with your lordship; and consequently conclude, I have your approbation in this, that the substratum to modes or accidents, which is our idea of substance in general, is founded in this, "that we cannot conceive how modes or accidents can subsist by themselves".

Abstract Ideas (III iii 11). Stillingfleet objected to Locke's view that abstract ideas of the essences of things were the work of the mind, because he argued that there must be something common to all things of one kind, so as to make them all things of that kind : "and if the difference of kinds be real, that which makes them all of one kind must not be a *nominal* but *real* essence". Locke replied :

"This may be some objection to the name of 'nominal essence'; but is, as I humbly conceive, none to the thing designed by it. There is an internal constitution of things,

on which their properties depend. This your lordship and I
are agreed of, and this we call the real essence. There are also
certain complex ideas, or combinations of these properties in
men's minds, to which they commonly annex specific names, or
names of sorts or kinds of things. This, I believe, your
lordship does not deny. These complex ideas, for want of a
better name, I have called nominal essences; how properly, I
will not dispute. But if anyone will help me to a better name
for them, I am ready to receive it; till then I must, to express
myself, use this. Now, my lord, body, life, and the power of
reasoning being not the real essence of a man, as I believe
your lordship will agree : will your lordship say that they are
not enough to make the thing wherein they are found, of the
kind called ' man ', and not of the kind called ' baboon ',
because the difference of these kinds is real? If this be not real
enough to make the thing of one kind and not of another, I do
not see how *animal rationale* can be enough to distinguish a
man from an horse; for that is but the nominal, not real
essence of that kind, designed by the name ' man '. And yet,
I suppose, everyone thinks it real enough, to make a real
difference between that and other kinds. And if nothing will
serve the turn, to *make* things of one kind and not of another
(which, as I have showed, signifies no more but ranking of
them under different specific names) but their real, unknown
constitutions, which are the real essences we are speaking of,
I fear it would be a long while before we should have really
different kinds of substances, or distinct names for them,
unless we could distinguish them by these differences, of which
we have no distinct conceptions. For I think it would not
be readily answered me, if I should demand wherein lies the
real difference in the internal constitution of a stag from that
of a buck, which are each of them very well known to be
of one kind, and not of the other; and nobody questions but
that the kinds whereof each of them is, are really different.
Your lordship farther says,

" And this difference doth not depend upon the complex
ideas of substances, whereby men arbitrarily join modes
together in their minds."

I confess, my lord, I know not what to say to this, because I do not know what these complex ideas of substances are, whereby men arbitrarily join modes together in their minds. But I am apt to think there is a mistake in the matter, by the words that follow, which are these :

" For let them mistake in their complication of ideas, either in leaving out or putting in what doth not belong to them; and let their ideas be what they will, the real essence of a man, and an horse, and a tree, are just what they were."

The mistake I spoke of I humbly suppose is this, that things are here taken to be distinguished by their real essences; when by the very way of speaking of them, it is clear that they are already distinguished by their nominal essences, and are so taken to be. For what, I beseech your lordship, does your lordship mean, when you say, " the real essence of a man, and an horse, and a tree ", but that there are such kinds already set out by the signification of these names, 'man', 'horse', 'tree'? And what, I beseech your lordship, is the signification of each of the specific names, but the complex idea it stands for? And that complex idea is the nominal essence, and nothing else. So that taking 'man', as your lordship does here, to stand for a kind or sort of individuals, all which agree in that common, complex idea, which that specific name stands for, it is certain that the real essence of all the individuals, comprehended under the specific name 'man', in your use of it, would be just the same, let others leave out or put into their complex idea of man what they please; because the real essence on which that unaltered complex idea, i.e. those properties depend, must necessarily be concluded to be the same.

For I take it for granted, that in using the name 'man', in this place, your lordship uses it for that complex idea which is in your lordship's mind of that species. So that your lordship, by putting it for, or substituting it in, the place of that complex idea, where you say the real essence of it is just as it was, or the very same it was, does suppose the idea it stands for to be steadily the same. For if I change the signification of the word 'man', whereby it may not comprehend just the same individuals which in your lordship's sense it does, but shut out some of those that to your lordship are men in your signification of the word 'man', or take in others to which your lordship does not allow the name 'man': I do not think you will say, that the real essence of man, in both these senses, is the same; and yet your lordship seems to say so, when you say, "let men mistake in the complication of their ideas, either in leaving out or putting in what doth not belong to them; and let their ideas be what they please; the real essence of the individuals comprehended under the names annexed to these ideas, will be the same"; for so, I humbly conceive, it must be put, to make out what your lordship aims at. For as your lordship puts it by the name of 'man', or any other specific name, your lordship seems to me to suppose, that that name stands for, and not for, the same idea, at the same time.

For example, my lord, let your lordship's idea, to which you annex the sign 'man', be a rational animal; let another man's idea be a rational animal of such a shape; let a third man's idea be of an animal of such a size and shape, leaving out rationality; let a fourth's be an animal with a body of such a shape, and an immaterial substance, with a power of reasoning; let a fifth leave out of his idea an immaterial substance : it is plain every one of these will call his a man, as well as your lordship; and yet it is as plain that man, as standing for all these distinct, complex ideas, cannot be supposed to have the same internal constitution, i.e. the same real essence. The truth is, every distinct, abstract idea, with a name to it, makes a real, distinct kind, whatever the real essence (which we know not of any of them) be.

And therefore I grant it true, what your lordship says in the next words, " and let the nominal essence differ never so much, the real, common essence or nature of the several kinds, is not at all altered by them"; i.e. that our thoughts or ideas cannot alter the real constitutions that are in things that exist; there is nothing more certain. But yet it is true that the change of ideas to which we annex them can and does alter the signification of their names, and thereby alter the kinds, which by these names we rank and sort them into. Your lordship farther adds,

"And these real essences are unchangeable, i.e. the internal constitutions are unchangeable." Of what, I beseech your lordship, are the internal constitutions unchangeable? Not of anything that exists, but of God alone; for they may be changed all as easily by that hand that made them, as the internal frame of a watch. What then is it that is unchangeable? The internal constitution or real essence of a species: which, in plain English, is no more but this, whilst the same specific name, v.g. of man, horse, or tree, is annexed to, or made the sign of the same abstract, complex idea, under which I rank several individuals, it is impossible but the real constitution on which that unaltered complex idea, or nominal essence, depends, must be the same: i.e. in other words, where we find all the same properties, we have reason to conclude there is the same real, internal constitution, from which those properties flow.

But your lordship proves the real essences to be unchangeable, because God makes them, in these following words:

"For however there may happen some variety in individuals by particular accidents, yet the essences of men and horses, and trees, remain always the same; because they do not depend on the ideas of men, but on the will of the Creator, who hath made several sort of beings."

It is true, the real constitutions or essences of particular things existing do not depend on the ideas of men, but on the will of the Creator; but their being ranked into sorts, under such and such names, does depend, and wholly depend, on the ideas of men."

Definition of Knowledge (IV i 2). Stillingfleet objected to Locke's definition of knowledge that it introduced a new method of certainty, which would have dangerous consequences for Christian faith. Locke replied (a) that it was no refutation of a proposition to show (even if it could be shown) that it had dangerous consequences. As Hume later pointed out in a different context (*Enquiry Concerning Human Understanding*

§75), a philosophical doctrine can be refuted only by arguments showing that it is false, not by protests that its truth would be unpalatable. (b) that what, if anything, he was doing that was new was to give a new *description* of knowledge. He was not *inventing* anything that did not exist before.

" There are several actions of men's minds that they are conscious to themselves of performing, as willing, believing, knowing, &c. which they have so particular sense of, that they can distinguish them one from another; or else they could not say when they willed, when they believed, and when they knew anything. But though these actions were different enough from one another, not to be confounded by those who spoke of them; yet nobody, that I had met with, had, in their writings, particularly set down wherein the act of knowing precisely consisted.

To this reflection upon the actions of my own mind, the subject of my *Essay Concerning Human Understanding* naturally led me; wherein, if I have done anything new, it has been to describe to others more particularly than had been done before, what it is their minds do, when they perform that action which they call knowing : and if, upon examination, they observe I have given a true account of that action of their minds in all the parts of it, I suppose it will be in vain to dispute against what they find and feel in themselves. And if I have not told them right, and exactly what they find and feel in themselves, when their minds perform the act of knowing, what I have said will be all in vain; men will not be persuaded against their senses. Knowledge is an internal perception of their minds; and if, when they reflect on it, they find it is not what I have said it is, my groundless conceit will not be hearkened to, but be exploded by everybody, and die of itself; and nobody need to be at any pains to drive it out of the world. So impossible is it to find out, or start new methods of certainty, or to have them received, if anyone places it in anything but in that wherein it really consists : much less can anyone be in danger to be misled into error by any such new, and to everyone visibly senseless, project. Can it be supposed, that anyone could start a new method of seeing, and persuade men thereby that they do not see what they do see? Is it to be feared that anyone can cast such a mist over their eyes that they should not know when they see, and so be let out of their way by it?

Knowledge, I find in myself, and I conceive in others, consists in the perception of the agreement or disagreement of the immediate objects of the mind in thinking, which I call ideas: but whether it does so in others or no must be determined by their own experience, reflecting upon the action of their mind in knowing; for that I cannot alter, nor I think they themselves. But whether they will call those immediate objects of their mind in thinking ideas or no, is perfectly in their own choice. If they dislike that name, they may call them notions or conceptions, or how they please; it matters not, if they use them so as to avoid obscurity and confusion. If they are constantly used in the same and a known sense, everyone has the liberty to please himself in his terms; there lies neither truth nor error, nor science, in that; though those that take them for things, and not for what they are, bare arbitrary signs of our ideas, make a great deal of do often about them, as if some great matter lay in the use of this or that sound. All that I know or can imagine of difference about them is that those words are always best, whose significations are best known in the sense they are used; and so are least apt to breed confusion.

My lord, your lordship has been pleased to find fault with my use of the new term 'ideas', without telling me a better name for the immediate objects of the mind in thinking. Your lordship has also been pleased to find fault with my definition of knowledge, without doing me the favour to give me a better. For it is only about my definition of knowledge that all this stir concerning certainty is made. For with me, to know and be certain is the same thing; what I know, that I am certain of; and what I am certain of, that I know. What reaches to knowledge I think may be called certainty; and what comes short of certainty I think cannot be called knowledge; as your lordship could not but observe in §18. of ch. iv. of my fourth book, which you have quoted.

My definition of knowledge stands thus: "knowledge seems to me to be nothing but the perception of the connexion and agreement or disagreement and repugnancy of any of our ideas". This definition your lordship dislikes, and apprehends "it may be of dangerous consequence as to that article of christian faith which your lordship has endeavoured to defend". For this there is a very easy remedy: it is but for your lordship to set aside this definition of knowledge by giving us a better, and this danger is over."

Matter and Thought (IV III 6). Stillingfleet objected to Locke's assertion that we "possibly shall never be able to know whether any mere material being thinks", on the ground that, if that were true, we could not prove that we had a spiritual substance in us. Locke replied:

"Your lordship argues that upon my principles it "cannot be proved that there is a spiritual substance in us". To which give me leave, with submission, to say that I think it may be proved from my principles, and I think I have done it; and the proof in my book stands thus. First, we experiment in ourselves thinking. The idea of this action or mode of thinking is inconsistent with the idea of self-subsistence, and therefore has a necessary connexion with a support or subject of inhesion; the idea of that support is what we call substance; and so from thinking experimented in us we have a proof of a thinking substance in us, which in my sense is a spirit. Against this your lordship will argue that by what I have said of the possibility that God may, if he pleased, superadd to matter a faculty of thinking, it can never be proved that there is a spiritual substance in us, because upon that supposition it is possible it may be a material substance that thinks in us. I grant it; but add that the general idea of substance being the same everywhere, the modification of thinking, or the power of thinking joined to it, makes it a spirit, without considering what other modifications it has, as whether it has the modification of solidity or no. As on the other side, substance, that has the modification or solidity, is matter, whether it has the modification of thinking or no. And therefore, if your lordship means by a spiritual an immaterial substance, I grant I have not proved, nor upon my principles can it be proved, (your lordship meaning, as I think you do, demonstratively proved) that there is an immaterial substance in us that thinks. Though I presume, from what I have said about the supposition of a system of matter thinking (which there demonstrates that God is immaterial) will prove it in the highest degree probable that the thinking substance in us is immaterial. But your lordship thinks not probability enough; and by charging the want of demonstration upon my principles, that the thinking thing in us is immaterial, your lordship seems to conclude it demonstrable from principles of philosophy. That demonstration I should with joy receive from your lordship, or anyone. For though all the great ends of morality and religion are well enough secured without it, as I have shown, yet it would be a great advance of our knowledge in nature and philosophy.

But it is further urged that we cannot conceive how matter can think. I grant it; but to argue from thence that God therefore cannot give to matter a faculty of thinking is to say God's omnipotency is limited to a narrow compass, because man's understanding is so; and brings down God's infinite power to the size of our capacities. If God can give no power to any parts of matter, but what men can account for from the essence of matter in general; if all such qualities and properties must destroy the essence, or change the essential properties of matter, which are to our conceptions above it, and we cannot conceive to be the natural consequence of that essence : it is plain that the essence of matter is destroyed, and its essential properties changed in most of the sensible parts of this our system. For it is visible that all the planets have revolutions about certain remote centres, which I would have anyone explain, or make conceivable by the bare essence or natural powers depending on the essence of matter in general, without something added to that essence, which we cannot conceive; for the moving of matter in a crooked line, or the attraction of matter by matter, is all that can be said in the case; either of which it is above our reach to derive from the essence of matter, or body in general; though one of these two must unavoidably be allowed to be superadded in this instance to the essence of matter in general. The omnipotent Creator advised not with us in the making of the world, and his ways are not the less excellent, because they are past our finding out.

To keep within the present subject of the power of thinking and self-motion, bestowed by omnipotent power on some parts of matter: the objection to this is, I cannot conceive how matter should think. What is the consequence? *ergo,* God cannot give it a power to think. Let this stand for a good reason, and then proceed in other cases by the same. You cannot conceive how matter can attract matter at any distance, much less at the distance of 1,000,000 miles; *ergo,* God cannot give it such a power. You cannot conceive how matter should feel or move itself, or affect an immaterial being, or be moved by it; *ergo,* God cannot give it such powers: which is in effect to deny gravity and the revolution of the planets about the sun; to make brutes mere machines, without sense or spontaneous motion; and to allow man neither sense nor voluntary motion.

Let us apply this rule one degree farther. You cannot conceive how an extended solid substance should think; therefore God cannot make it think. Can you conceive how your own soul, or any substance, thinks? You find indeed that you do think, and so do I; but I want to be told how the action of thinking is performed: this, I confess, is beyond my conception; and I would be glad anyone, who conceives it, would explain it to me. God, I find, has given me this faculty; and since I cannot but be convinced of his power in this instance, which though I every moment experiment in myself, yet I cannot conceive the manner of; what would it be less than an insolent absurdity to deny his power in other like cases only for this reason, because I cannot conceive the manner how?

That omnipotency cannot make a substance to be solid and not solid at the same time, I think, with due reverence, we may say; but that a solid substance may not have qualities, perfections and powers, which have no natural or visibly necessary connexion with solidity and extension, is too much for us (who are but of yesterday, and know nothing) to be positive in. If God cannot join things together by connexions inconceivable to us, we must deny even the consistency and being of matter itself; since every particle of it having some bulk has its parts connected by ways inconceivable to us. So that all the difficulties that are raised against the thinking of matter from our ignorance or narrow conceptions, stand not at all in the way of the power of God, if he pleases to ordain it so; nor prove anything against his having actually endued some parcels of matter, so disposed as he thinks fit, with a faculty of thinking, till it can be shown that it contains a contradiction to suppose it.

Though to me sensation be comprehended under thinking in general, yet in the foregoing discourse I have spoken of sense in brutes, as distinct from thinking; because your lordship, as I remember, speaks of sense in brutes. But here I take liberty to observe that, if your lordship allows brutes to have sensation, it will follow, either that God can and doth give to some parcels of matter a power of perception and thinking; or that all animals have immaterial, and consequently, according to your lordship, immortal souls, as well as men : and to say that fleas and mites, &c. have immortal souls as well as men, will possibly be looked on as going a great way to serve an hypothesis."

BIBLIOGRAPHY

1. PRINCIPAL WORKS

Essays on the Law of Nature (1633) (Latin text, with translation, ed. W. von Leyden, Oxford, 1954)

A Letter Concerning Toleration (1689)

A Second Letter Concerning Toleration (1690)

Two Treatises of Government (1690) (Ed. P. Laslett, Cambridge, 1960)

An Essay Concerning Human Understanding (1690) (2nd ed. 1694; 3rd 1695; 4th 1700; 5th 1706) (Ed. J. W. Yolton, Dent, 1961)

A Third Letter for Toleration (1692)

Some Considerations of the Consequences of the Lowering of Interest and the Raising of the Value of Money (1692)

Some Thoughts Concerning Education (1693)

Short Observations on a Printed Paper intituled For Encouraging the *Coinage of Silver Money in England* (1695)

The Reasonableness of Christianity (1695)

A Vindication of the Reasonableness of Christianity (1695)

A Letter to the Right Rev. Edward Lord Bishop of Worcester, concerning some Passages relating to Mr. Locke's Essay of Human Understanding (1697). (Further letters in 1697 and 1699)

Paraphrases of the Epistles of St. Paul (1705-7)

Posthumous Works of Mr. John Locke (1706), including *An Examination of P. Malebranche's opinion of seeing all things in God.*

Works of John Locke (1714) (2nd ed. 1722; 3rd 1727; 4th 1740)

The Correspondence of John Locke and Edward Clarke (ed. Benjamin Rand, Oxford, 1927)

2. BIOGRAPHY AND CRITICISM

Aaron, R. I., *John Locke* (Oxford, 2nd ed. 1955)

Cranston, M., *John Locke* (Longmans, 1957)

Gibson, J., *Locke's Theory of Knowledge* (Cambridge, 1917)

James, D. G., *The Life of Reason, Hobbes, Locke and Bolingbroke* (Longmans, 1949)

Polin, R., *La Politique Morale de John Locke* (Presses Universitaires de France, 1960)

Webb, T. E., *The Intellectualism of Locke* (McGee, 1857)

Yolton, J. W., *John Locke and the Way of Ideas* (Oxford, 1956)

For a fuller bibliography see Aaron and Yolton, op. cit.

CHRONOLOGICAL TABLE

1632   John Locke born on 29 August
1658   M.A., Oxford
1660   Lecturer in Greek, Christ Church
1662   Lecturer in Rhetoric, Christ Church
1663   Met Robert Boyle
1663   Senior Censor, Christ Church
1665   Secretary to diplomatic mission to Elector of Brandenburg
1667   Moved to London as physician and political adviser to Lord
            Ashley (later Earl of Shaftesbury)
1668   Fellow of the Royal Society
1669   Drafted constitution for government of Carolina
1672   Secretary for the Presentation of Benefices
1673-5 Secretary to the Council of Trade and Plantations
1675-9 Ill health, moved to France
1679-82 Back in Oxford
1683   Fled to Holland
1685   Accused of helping Monmouth's rebellion
1689   Returned to England with Princess of Orange
1690   Publication of *Letter Concerning Toleration, Two Treatises
            of Civil Government, Essay on Human Understanding*
1691   Made permanent home with Sir Francis and Lady Masham
            at Oates
1692   *Lowering of Interest and the Raising of Value of Money*
1693   *Some Thoughts Concerning Education*
1694   *Essay*, 2nd edition
1695   *The Reasonableness of Christianity*
1696   Appointed Commissioner of Trade
1696-9 Controversy with Stillingfleet
1698   Refused further diplomatic employment
1700   Resigned from Board of Trade
1704   Died on 28 October

For dates of other publications see Bibliography

INDEX

A priori system, 11, 15, 21-2, 46

abstract ideas: general notions as, 265-6; and genera and species, 268-70, 272; workmanship of understanding, 268-9, 281; and nominal essence, 282-3, 286; and general propositions, 395; and advancing knowledge, 397-8; Stillingfleet and, 452-6

abstract terms, 297-8

abstraction, 12, 40-2, 129

acceptance, 20

accident, 139-41

action, 176-8; and mixed modes, 183-4

active power, 162-3, 177

actual knowledge, 323

addition, 153, 156

adequate ideas, 235-7, 241, 242

affirmation, truth and, 248

agreement and disagreement of ideas, 320-2, 331-2

alteration, 204

analogy, 49, 412-14

anger, 161

'animal', general idea of, 265, 266

animals: reasoning powers, 12; perception in, 122; memory in, 126; compare imperfectly, 128; compound little, 128; do not abstract, 129-30; identity of, 209-10, 214

annihilation, 141-2

antipathies, 251-2

arguments, four sorts of, 423

Aristotle, 417-18

articulate sounds, 257; as signs of ideas, 256-7, 259-60, 443

artificial things: as collective

ideas, 199; species of, 295

assent, 49-50, 405; general, 67-8; degrees of, 407-15; wrong, 434-42

association of ideas, and custom, 250-5

assurance, 48, 49, 409-10

attention, 124, 157, 158

authority, and error, 441

axioms, 365-72

Barbeyrac, Jean, 447

belief, 15, 405, 410; distinct from knowledge, 44-50

Berkeley, George, Bishop, 14, 25, 26, 35, 37, 49, 50; on ideas, 40-3

bodies: qualities in, 112-19; identity of, 207; no science of, 343-4, 346; knowledge of, 398-400

body: extension as essence of, 11; interaction with mind, 12; extension not same as, 138-9, 143; space distinct from, 139, 142; motions of, 165, 167; and soul compared, 194-6; cohesion of solid parts, 194-5; matter distinct from, 308-9

Boyle, Robert, 11, 12-13

Burnet, Thomas, 447n

capacities, 20, 135

Cartesianism, 10-11, 12, 15, 23, 44, 46-7, 214

causality, 11, 22, 23, 27

cause and effect, 203-4

causes, 184

certainty, 405; of universal propositions, 358, 364

changeling, 353

charity, 408

children : no innate notions, 68-9, 73, 120; use of reason in, 71; ideas not born with, 83-4; growth of ideas observable in, 91-2, 97; ideas in womb, 120; and numeration, 155

Christ Church, Oxford, 9

civil law, 223-4

civil use of words, 299-300, 304

'clear and distinct ideas', 59-60, 227-8

co-existence, 45, 46, 47; of ideas, 320, 322; knowledge of, 334-8; little self-evidence, 367

cogitative being, 381-3

collective ideas, 198-9

colours, 110-11

commendation, 224-5

communication : words in, 259, 299-300; species for, 280

comparing, 127-8

complex ideas, 132-4; of substances, 185-98, 234-5, 236, 237-42, 245, 247-8, 351-3; and confusion, 229, 230-1; voluntary combinations, 233-4; truth or falsity of, 244-5, 247-8; definable, 276; and trifling propositions, 374, 377

composition, 12, 128

compounding, 128

concepts, vagueness of, 43

concrete terms, 297-8

confidence, 49

confused ideas, 228-32

consciousness, and personal identity, 212-13, 214-16, 218-19

consent, universal, 18-19

contemplation, 157

correlative terms, 200-1

creation, 204

crime and innocence, civil law and, 223-4

Cudworth, Ralph, 17

dark room, understanding as, 131

darkness, 110-11

De Veritate (Herbert of Cherbury), 17

deductive system, 11

definition, 273-6; limitations of, 11; and trifling propositions, 374-5, 377

definitions : and concepts, 43; genus in, 266-7

delight, 108

demonstration, not in everything, 392-3

demonstrative knowledge, 46-7, 49, 326-30, 331; extent, 332; of God, 378, 379-87

Descartes, René, 10-11, 12, 16, 17, 19, 44-5, 46, 47

desire, 160; and will, 171-2; and happiness, 173-4; and free-will, 175-6

despair, 161

'determinate', use of, 60-1

'determined', use of, 60-1

differentia, in definitions, 266-7

discerning, 127

Discourse Concerning the Nature of Man (Lowde), 447

Discourse on Method (Descartes), 10

discredit, 224-5

disputation, 371-2

distance, 135

distinct ideas, 228-32

diversity : and identity, 206-20; knowledge of, 334; and self-evidence, 366-7

divine law, 223

divisibility of matter, 231-2

dreaming, 94-6, 157, 159

Dublin, 9, 14

duration, 144-53, 178; measures of, 148-52, 155-6

ecstasy, 157

effect, 184; and cause, 203-4

efficacy, 184

empiricism, 11, 12, 15, 21, 23, 47-8

enthusiasm, 428-33

envy, 161

equality, 367

error, 434-42

essence, 284-6; nominal, 22, 44, 270-1, 282-3, 286-7, 288-9; of material objects, 29; real, 237-42, 243, 270-2, 282, 284, 286, 289-90; abstract idea and, 268-70, 272; significations of, 270

eternal Being, 379-80

eternal truths, 395

eternity, 144, 151-3, 156; confused ideas of, 231; something from, 381, 383

ethics, 442

evil, 159-60; and pain, 174

existence, 108, 178; propositions of, 45, 47, 48; real, 320, 322; real, ideas conformable to, 243, 245; real, knowledge of, 340-1; real, no maxims on, 368; knowledge of, 377-8; of other things, 387-95

expansion, 155-6

experience, 22, 23, 398-9; source of all ideas, 24; concurrent, 409-11

explicit acceptance, 20

extension, 106, 135, 178; as essence of body, 11; body not the same, 138-9, 143; duration and, 144; relations of, 206

external denominations, 201

faculties, 165-6, 168-9

faith, 15, 17, 394, 405, 414; not general principle, 78-9; and reason, 424-8

fallacy, 420, 439

false ideas, 242-9

falsehood, 357

fantastical ideas, 233, 234

fear, 161

figure, 106, 135, 417, 419, 420

finite intelligences, identity of, 207

free-will, 175-6

freedom, 171

Gassendi, Pierre, 11-12

general assent, 67-8

general ideas, 369

general terms, 263-72

generation, 204

genus, in definition, 266-7

God: existence of, 24, 47; idea of not innate, 84-5; different ideas of, 85; idea of, 197; identity of, 207; knowledge of, 341, 378, 379-87; and revelation, 424-6, 431-3

gold, as example, 13, 190, 198, 239, 260, 309, 322, 360-1

good: and evil, 159-60, 222; and pleasure, 174

good, greatest: uneasiness and, 173; not always desired, 174

habitual knowledge, 323-5

happiness, 173-4

hardness, distinct from solidity, 104-5

hatred, 160

Heliogabalus, 210

Herbert of Cherbury, Lord, 17

history, 412

hope, 160

Hume, David, 11, 14, 35, 37, 45, 50, 456

hypotheses, 400; received, 438-9

'idea', definition of, 25-35, 66, 111-12, 447-8

ideas, 89-255, 443; 'twin sources' of, 12, 101-25; and words, 35-44, 423; not born with children, 83-4; in general, 89-98; original of all knowledge, 97-8; and perception, 93, 119-23; simple, 98, 99-119, 229-30, 233, 235-6, 241, 244, 245-7, 273-7, 274, 275-6, 335; of one sense, 101-2; from sensation, 101-25; of reflection, 101, 107-9; positive from privative causes, 110-11; complex, 132-4, 185-98; collective, 198-9; identity suited to, 210-11; clear and obscure, 227-8; distinct and confused, 228-32; real and fantastical 232-5; adequate and inadequate, 235-42; false, 242-9; true, 242-9; association of, 250-5; words as signs of, 256-8, 259-60; no words without, 312; agreement and disagreement, perception of, 320-2, 331-2; knowledge no further than, 331, 332-4; want of, 341-4; connexion between, ignorance of, 344-6; tracing of, 346; co-existence of, 360-2; Stillingfleet on, 447-8

identical propositions, 373-4

identity, 206-20; knowledge of, 45; of substances, 207-8, 210, 213-16; of animals, 209-10, 214; of vegetables, 209; of man, 210-11; personal, 211-16; of ideas, 320, 321; and self-evidence, 366-7

idiots, have no innate notions, 68-9

ignorance, causes of, 341-7

illation, 415-16

image, 40-3

imagination, 100

immensity, 135-6

implicit acceptance, 20

implicit knowledge, 75

impressions, 157

impulse, 105-6, 164, 193; and motion, 193, 195-6

inadequate ideas, 235, 237-42

incogitative being, 381-3

incorrigible propositions, 47

individuals, nothing essential to, 284-5

inductive system, 11

infinity, 155-6

innate principles, 83-8; attack on, 16-24; none in mind, 67-78; no practical ones, 78-88; corruptible, 81-2

insignificant terms, 306

instant, 147

instituted relations, 222

intention, 157

intuitive knowledge, 46-7, 325-6, 327, 330, 331; extent, 332; of existence, 378

invention, 182

involuntary action, 165, 167

joy, 160

judgement, 363, 402-3, 406, 408; ideas of sensation changed by, 121-2

justice, not general principle, 78-9

Kant, Immanuel, 46; and *a priori*, 21, 22, 23

knowing Being, most, 380-1

knowledge, 15, 320-443; mathematics as ideal of, 11; twin sources of, 24, 28; distinct from belief, 44-50; defined, 45, 48, 456-9; kinds of, 45-6; degrees of, 46, 325-31; reality of, 49, 347-53; not innate, 67-78; how attained, 67, 72-3; simple ideas materials of, 109; perception the inlet of, 122-3; in general, 320-5; extent of, 331-47; method of acquiring, distinct from that of communicating, 368; of existence, 377-8; improvement of, 395-402; Stillingfleet and Locke's definition, 456-9

language, and thought, 35-44. *See also* words

languages: change in, 182; unique words in, 182

laws, 223-5

Leibniz, 13

Letter Concerning Toleration, 9
liberty, 166-9
light, 110-11, 274-5
love, 160
Lowde, James, 447

madness, and unreasonableness, 250
making, 204
Malebranche, Nicolas, 27
man: identity of, 210-11; same, 210, 211, 215-16, 217-18; general name of, 265, 266
material objects, 12, 29
mathematical knowledge, 401-2; certainty of, 349-50
mathematics, 11, 46, 47, 48, 396; demonstrable, 70-1, 75, 328-9; self-evident truths, 367
matter: divisibility of, 231-2; distinct from body, 308-9; and eternal Mind, 384-7; and thought, Stillingfleet on, 459-62
matter of fact, 409
maxims, 328, 365-72; use of, 369-72; knowledge not from, 395
Meditations (Descartes), 10, 11
memory, 46, 47, 72, 95, 96, 123-4, 125-6; no innate ideas in, 86-7; defects in, 125-6; and past experience, 393
mental image, idea as, 29-30
mental propositions, 36
microscopical eyes, 192
Mind, eternal, 383-4, 386-7
mind: thought as essence of, 11; as 'white paper', 12, 89; interaction with body, 12; no innate principles in, 67-78; as empty cabinet, 72; steps to attainment of truths, 72-3; operation of, as source of ideas, 90-1, 97-8; operations of about other ideas, 107; ideas in, and qualities in bodies, 111-12;

discerning by, 126; comparing by, 127-8; compounding by, 128; abstraction by, 129-30; faculties and operations of, 127-31; as dark room, 131; and complex ideas, 132; and mixed modes, 179-80
minute particles, primary qualities of, 190-2
miracles, 414
mixed modes, 133-4, 179-85, 309-10; as real ideas, 234; adequate, 236-7, 242; truth or falsity of, 244-5, 247; names of, 276-83, 301-3
mobility, 178; spirits and, 193
modes, 11, 32, 417, 419, 420; defined, 133; simple, 133-4, 135-61; mixed, 133-4, 179-85, 234, 236-7, 242, 244-5, 247, 276-83, 301-3; identity of, 207-8
Molyneux, William, 10, 11
moon, and measure of time, 149-50
Moore, G. E., 47
moral good and evil, 222
moral ideas, 339-40
moral knowledge, certainty of, 350-1
moral principles: not given general assent, 78-82; whole nations reject, 80-1
moral relations, 222-7
moral rules, 222-6; proof needed, 79
moral words, 302
morality, 225-6; demonstrable, 11, 338-40, 398; proper science of mankind, 399
motion, 106, 146-7, 148; vacuum proved by, 142; beginning of, 164; and mixed modes, 183; impulse and thought in, 193, 195-6; definition of, 274
motivity, 178, 193

names: general, use of, 72; necessary to numbers, 154-5; explication of, 180, 183; correlative, 201; and confused ideas, 228-9, 230; impossible for every thing, 263-4; and nominal essence, 270; of simple ideas, 273-7; of mixed modes and relations, 276-83; of substances, 283-96
naming, 128-9
nations, moral rules rejected by, 80-1
natural philosophy, 442
natural relations, 221-2
necessary connexion, 45, 46, 320, 322
necessity, 166, 167
negation, falsehood and, 248
Nestor, 215-16
Newton, Sir Isaac, 370
nominal essence, 22, 44, 270-1; and abstract idea, 282-3, 286; and species, 286-7, 288-9
nonentity, 379-80
nonsense words, 36
nothing, cannot produce existence, 379-80, 381, 387
notions, 180, 282
number, 153-6, 178

oblivion, 125
obscure ideas, 227-8
obscurity, affected, 307
observation, 182
opinion, 405, 408; law of, 224
Origin of Forms and Qualities (Boyle), 13
Oxford, 9

pain, 108, 390; ideas fixed by, 124-5; modes of, 159-61; and evil, 174
particular ideas, 39, 40, 368, 421-2
passions, 184; and good and evil, 160-1; predominant, 439

passive power, 162-3, 177
Paul, St., 432
perception, 107, 119-23; and ideas, 93; three sorts of, 165
perceptivity, 178
person, 211-12; a forensic term, 220
personal identity, 211-16
philosophical law, 224
philosophical use of words, 299-300, 304-5
picture-original thesis, 25-9, 33
place, 135-8; relation of, 205, 206
pleasure, 108, 390; ideas fixed by, 124-5; modes of, 159-61; and good, 174
positive ideas, from privative causes, 110-11
power, 108, 162-79; active and passive, 162-3, 177; and relation, 163; and mixed modes, 183-4
powerful Being, most 380-1
powers, 117-19; and complex ideas of substances, 188-9, 190; co-existence of, 337-8
practical principles: no innate, 78-88; contrary, 80, 82
pre-existence, 215-16
primary qualities, 13, 189-90, 335-6, 363; defined, 112; how ideas produced by, 113; and resemblances, 114-16, 118-19
principium individuationis, 208
Principles (Descartes), 10
principles, 395, 396; innate, 16-24, 67-88; practical, 80, 82, 78-88; contrary, 82; how men come by, 82; must be examined, 83; ideas of, not born with children, 83-4; supposedly not to be questioned, 87; and doubtful hypotheses, 437-8
Principles of Human Knowledge (Berkeley), 14, 40

privations, positive ideas from, 110-11

probability, 47-8, 49, 403-6; degrees of, 407-15; and syllogism, 421; wrong measures of, 436-42

proofs, 327-8, 403; maxims and, 372; want of, 434-6

proper names, 36, 38, 264

proportional relations, 221

propositions : mental, 354-5, 356; verbal, 354, 355-7; general, 357, 358-64; self-evident, 365-72; trifling, 373-7; doubtful, 437-8

protrusion, 105-6

punishment, 216-17, 220, 222-3, 419-20

qualities, 23, 111-19; defined, 112; primary, 112-19; secondary, 112, 113-14, 116, 117; three sorts of, 117-18

quantity, demonstration and, 328

ready assent : proves truths not innate, 73-4; and false supposition of no precedent teaching, 75-6

real essence, 237-42, 243, 270-2; and names of mixed modes, 282; distinct from nominal 284, 286; difficulties against, 289-90

real ideas, 232-5

reason, 415-23; and innate principles, 69-72; use of, 71-73; and faith, 424-8; and revelation, 432-3

reasoning, 326, 327-8, 332

received hypotheses, 438-9

recollection, 157

recording, words for, 299

reflection : source of knowledge, 24-5, 28-9, 89-91, 97-8, 101, 107, 108-9; lateness of, 92-3; perception first simple idea of,

119; ideas of duration from, 144-5, 152

Regulae (Descartes), 10, 46

Reid, Thomas, 47

reification, 26, 48

relation, 45, 200-3; defined, 134; power and, 163; of cause and effect, 203-4; of time, 205; of place and extension, 206; of identity and diversity, 206-20; of ideas, 320, 321-2; other, 221-7

relations, names of, 277-83

religion, 427-8

remembrance, 157

repetition, 124

representationalism, 25-9, 33-4

reputation, law of, 224

resemblances, and primary qualities, 114-16, 118-19

resistance, 105-6

rest, 106

retention, 123-6

revelation, 17, 414, 424-6, 431-3

rêverie, 157

reward, 216-17, 220, 222-3

right ideas, 249

Royal Society, 12

sagacity, 415

scepticism, 65

Schools, 371, 395, 420

sciences : teaching of, 370-2, 395; division of, 442-3

secondary qualities, 13, 112, 113-14, 116, 117, 189-91, 335

sects : and unreasonableness, 254; obscurity of, 307

self, 211; consciousness makes, 218-19

self-evidence, 365-8

self-evident truths, 74-5

sensation, 157; source of knowledge, 24-5, 28, 89-90, 91, 97-8, 101-6, 108-9; ideas of, changed by judgment, 121-2; idea of duration from, 144-5,

152; and knowledge of other things, 387-92

sense, one, ideas of, 101-2

sense-data, 27-8, 47

sense perception, 24-9

sensible ideas, words as signs of, 257-8, 259-60

sensible qualities, 117

sensitive knowledge, 46, 47, 330-1; extent of, 332; of things, 378, 387-95

shadow, 111

shame, 161

sight, 227

signs: truth a right joining of, 354; doctrine of, 443

simple ideas, 98, 99-119; division of, 101-2; of divers senses, 106; and confusion, 229-30; all real, 233; all adequate, 235-6, 241; truth or falsity of, 244, 245-7; names of, 273-7; undefinable, 274, 275-6; unknown connexion, 335

simple modes, 133-4, 135-61; of space, 135-43; of duration, 144-53; of number, 154-6; of thinking, 156-9; of pain and pleasure, 159-61; names of, 273, 305

sin and duty, divine law and, 223

sleep, 157; thinking during, 94-6; dreaming, 158-9

slowness, 125

smell, 101, 102

Socrates, 216

solidity, 101, 103-6, 178; distinct from space, 143; and body, 285

sorrow, 160

sorts, 282; essence of, 282-3

soul: and ideas, 93-7; not always thinking, 93-5, 96; and body compared, 194-6

sound, meaning in, 36. *See also* words

space, 135-43; solidity and, 103-4, 143; body distinct from, 139, 142

species, 353; abstract ideas and, 268, 270; and real essences, 270-1, 358-9; for communication, 280; and nominal essence, 286-7, 288-9; man-made boundaries, 295

speculation, 409

speculative principles, 76-8, 83-8

spirit, 139, 187; and idea of active power, 163-4; immaterial, 192-6; primary ideas of, 193; and mobility, 193; idea of, compared with body, 196

spirits: species and, 288-9; knowledge of, 338; ignorance of, 344, 346; existence not knowable, 393-4

Stillingfleet, Edward, Bishop of Worcester, 13, 23, 31, 32, 33, 34, 447-62

Strasbourg clock, 284, 287

substance, 23, 29, 31, 139-40; idea of, not innate, 85-6; and accident, 140-1; general, 185-6; sorts of, 186-8; Stillingfleet on, 448-52

substances: co-existence of qualities of, 47; defined, 134; spiritual, 192-3; collective ideas of, 198-9; identity of, 207-8, 210, 213-16; change of, 213-16; names of, 272, 283-96, 301, 303-4, 305; essences of, 283-93; propositions concerning, 359-64

substances, complex ideas of, 185-98; powers a great part of, 188-9, 190; three sorts of ideas in, 189-90; reality of, 234-5; inadequate, 236, 237-42; truth or falsity of, 245, 247-8; knowledge of, 351-3

succession, 109, 144-8, 152

sun, and measure of time, 149-50

syllogism, 416-22

taste, 101, 102
terms: general, 263-72; abstract and concrete, 297-8
testimony, 409-12, 414
Thersites, 215-6
things: words in reality of, 261; words taken for, 308; knowledge of existence of, 387-95
thinking, 164; idea the object of, 89; modes of, 156-9; and mixed modes, 183; primary idea of spirit, 193
thought: as essence of mind, 11; material substances capable of, 12; and language, 35-44; and motion, 195-6
time, 144, 148-51, 153; relations of, 205; mental disorders cured by, 253
token-words, 39
touch, 101-2, 103-6
triangle, 41-2, 46, 326, 332, 376
Trinity College, Dublin, 9, 14
true ideas, 242-9
truth, 17, 354-7; universal assent and, 68-9; defined, 354-5; of universal propositions, 358-64; love of, 428-9; no certain way to, 396-7
truths: self-evident, 365-72; eternal, 395
Tully, 350
Two Treatises of Government, 9
type-words, 39

uncertain ideas, 230
uncompounded appearances, 99
understanding, defined, 107, 165
uneasiness, 103; and will, 172-3
unity, 108, 153

universal consent, nothing proved innate by, 67-8
universality, 346-7
unreasonableness, 250-5

vacuum, proof of, 141-2
vegetable, identity of, 209; distinction between and animals, 122
verbal propositions, 376-7
vice, 224
virtue, 224; approved as profitable, 79-80; rule of, not internal principle, 80
volition (willing), 107, 165; without liberty, 166-7, 170; and will, 171-2
voluntary action, 165, 167
voluntary relations, 222

water and ice, and, species, 289
will, 107, 165; without liberty, 168-9; determination of, 171; and desire, 171-2; and uneasiness, 172-3
words, 353, 443; as signs of ideas, 30, 35-44; 'articulate sounds', 30, 35-6; general, 38-44, 256-8; and growth of reason in use of, 72-3; untranslatable, 182, 279-80; signifying effect, not action, 184; distribution of, 258; signification of, 259-62, 310-11, 375-6; as general terms, 263-72; how made, 264-6; and communication, 299-300; imperfection of, 299-306, 312-19; abuse of, 306-11, 312-19; wrong signification, 309
Wrington, 9
wrong ideas, 249

Titles of Related Interest from MERIDIAN